TORAH ETHICS

and

EARLY CHRISTIAN IDENTITY

TORAH ETHICS
and
EARLY CHRISTIAN IDENTITY

edited by

Susan J. Wendel and David M. Miller

William B. Eerdmans Publishing Company
Grand Rapids, Michigan

Wm. B. Eerdmans Publishing Co.
2140 Oak Industrial Drive N.E., Grand Rapids, Michigan 49505

Published 2016
Printed in the United States of America

22 21 20 19 18 17 16   1 2 3 4 5 6 7

Library of Congress Cataloging-in-Publication Data

Names: Wendel, Susan J., editor.
Title: Torah ethics and early Christian identity / edited by Susan J. Wendel and David M. Miller.
Description: Grand Rapids: Eerdmans Publishing Company, 2016. | Includes bibliographical references.
Identifiers: LCCN 2016006916 | ISBN 9780802873194 (pbk.: alk. paper)
Subjects: LCSH: Ethics in the Bible. | Bible—Criticism, interpretation, etc. | Christianity and other religions—Judaism. | Judaism—Relations—Christianity. | Christian ethics. | Jewish ethics.
Classification: LCC BS680.E84 T67 2016 | DDC 241.09—dc23
LC record available at http://lccn.loc.gov/2016006916

www.eerdmans.com

Contents

Contributors

S. A. Cummins
Professor of Religious Studies
Trinity Western University

Terence L. Donaldson
Lord and Lady Coggan Professor of New Testament Studies
Wycliffe College

Beverly Roberts Gaventa
Distinguished Professor of New Testament
Baylor University

Richard B. Hays
George Washington Ivey Professor of New Testament
Duke University

John W. Martens
Professor, Department of Theology
University of St. Thomas

Scot McKnight
Julius R. Mantey Professor of New Testament
Northern Seminary

David M. Miller
Associate Professor of New Testament and Early Judaism
Briercrest College and Seminary

Contributors

Wesley G. Olmstead
Professor of New Testament
Briercrest College and Seminary

Adele Reinhartz
Professor, Department of Classics and Religious Studies
University of Ottawa

Anders Runesson
Professor of New Testament
University of Oslo

Susan J. Wendel
Associate Professor of New Testament
Briercrest College and Seminary

Stephen Westerholm
Professor, Department of Religious Studies
McMaster University

Peter Widdicombe
Associate Professor, Department of Religious Studies
McMaster University

Abbreviations

All abbreviations of non-biblical ancient sources follow the *SBL Handbook of Style* (1st ed.).

AB	Anchor Bible
AGJU	Arbeiten zur Geschichte des antiken Judentums und des Urchristentums
ANTC	Abingdon New Testament Commentaries
ASSB	Runesson, Anders, Donald D. Binder, and Birger Olsson. *The Ancient Synagogue from Its Origins to 200 C.E.: A Source Book*. Leiden: Brill, 2008.
BDAG	Bauer, W., F. W. Danker, W. F. Arndt, and F. W. Gingrich. *Greek-English Lexicon of the New Testament and Other Early Christian Literature*. 3rd ed. Chicago, 1999.
BDB	Brown, F., S. R. Driver, and C. A. Briggs. *A Hebrew and English Lexicon of the Old Testament*. Oxford, 1907.
BETL	Bibliotheca ephemeridum theologicarum lovaniensium
BHT	Beiträge zur historischen Theologie
BJS	Brown Judaic Studies
BMSEC	Baylor-Mohr Siebeck Studies in Early Christianity
BR	*Biblical Research*
BSac	*Bibliotheca Sacra*
BZNW	Beihefte zur Zeitschrift für die neutestamentliche Wissenschaft
CBQ	*Catholic Biblical Quarterly*
ConBNT	Coniectanea Biblica: New Testament Series
ConBOT	Coniectanea Biblica: Old Testament Series
CRINT	Compendia rerum iudaicarum ad Novum Testamentum
EKKNT	Evangelisch-katholischer Kommentar zum Neuen Testament
ESV	English Standard Version
EvQ	*Evangelical Quarterly*

FRLANT	Forschungen zur Religion und Literatur des Alten und Neuen Testaments
GCS	Die griechische christliche Schriftsteller der ersten [drei] Jahrhunderte
HCSB	Holman Christian Standard Bible
HDR	Harvard Dissertations in Religion
HNTC	Harper's New Testament Commentaries
HTR	*Harvard Theological Review*
HUT	Hermeneutische Untersuchungen zur Theologie
HvTSt	*Hervormde teologiese studies*
ICC	International Critical Commentary
Int	*Interpretation*
JBL	*Journal of Biblical Literature*
JECS	*Journal of Early Christian Studies*
JJS	*Journal of Jewish Studies*
JQR	*Jewish Quarterly Review*
JSJSup	Journal for the Study of Judaism: Supplement Series
JSNT	*Journal for the Study of the New Testament*
JSNTSup	Journal for the Study of the New Testament: Supplement Series
JSPSup	Journal for the Study of the Pseudepigrapha: Supplement Series
JTS	*Journal of Theological Studies*
L&N	*Greek-English Lexicon of the New Testament: Based on Semantic Domains*. Edited by J. P. Louw and E. A. Nida. 2nd ed. New York, 1989.
LCL	Loeb Classical Library
LNTS	Library of New Testament Studies
LXX	Septuagint
MeyerK	Meyer, H. A. W. Kritisch-exegetischer Kommentar über das Neue Testament
MT	Masoretic Text
Neot	*Neotestamentica*
Nestle-Aland	Nestle, E., and K. Aland, eds. *Novum Testamentum Graece*
NET	New English Translation
NICNT	New International Commentary on the New Testament
NICOT	New International Commentary on the Old Testament
NIDB	*The New Interpreter's Dictionary of the Bible*. Edited by Katharine Doob Sakenfeld. 5 vols. Nashville: Abingdon, 2006-9.
NIDOTTE	*New International Dictionary of Old Testament Theology and Exegesis*. Edited by W. A. VanGemeren. 5 vols. Grand Rapids, 1997.
NIGTC	New International Greek Testament Commentary
NIV	New International Version

NJB	New Jerusalem Bible
NovT	*Novum Testamentum*
NovTSup	Supplements to Novum Testamentum
NPNF	*Nicene and Post-Nicene Fathers*
NRSV	New Revised Standard Version
NSBT	New Studies in Biblical Theology
NTD	Das Neue Testament Deutsch
NTS	*New Testament Studies*
OECS	Oxford Early Christian Studies
OTL	Old Testament Library
PhA	Philosophia Antiqua
PNTC	Pillar New Testament Commentary
ResQ	*Restoration Quarterly*
RSV	Revised Standard Version
SBLDS	Society of Biblical Literature Dissertation Series
SBLMS	Society of Biblical Literature Monograph Series
SC	Sources chrétiennes. Paris: Cerf, 1943-.
ScEs	*Science et esprit*
SCJ	Studies in Christianity and Judaism
SEÅ	*Svensk exegetisk årsbok*
SNTSMS	Society for New Testament Studies Monograph Series
SP	Sacra pagina
SPAW	*Sitzungsberichte der preussischen Akademie der Wissenschaften*
SPhilo	*Studia philonica*
SR	*Studies in Religion*
ST	*Studia theologica*
STAC	Studien und Texte zu Antike und Christentum
STDJ	Studies on the Texts of the Desert of Judah
StPB	*Studia post-biblica*
TLG	*Thesaurus linguae graecae: Canon of Greek Authors and Works.* Edited by L. Berkowitz and K. A. Squitier. 3rd ed. Oxford, 1990.
TLZ	*Theologische Literaturzeitung*
TSAJ	Texte und Studien zum antiken Judentum
TynBul	*Tyndale Bulletin*
VC	*Vigiliae christianae*
VT	*Vetus Testamentum*
WBC	Word Biblical Commentary
WUNT	Wissenschaftliche Untersuchungen zum Neuen Testament
ZTK	*Zeitschrift für Theologie und Kirche*

Preface

It gives the editors great pleasure to offer this collection of essays to Stephen Westerholm in honor of, and gratitude for, his outstanding work as a scholar of early Christianity. For his colleagues and former students, this gratefulness also extends to the generous hospitality of Stephen and his wife Gunilla. Many of us warmly recall spending time with them in their home over lively conversation and the best Swedish meatballs in the country.

As two of Stephen's former students, the editors of this volume fondly recall his attentiveness as a supervisor and his inspiring example. David remembers sitting in one of Stephen's graduate seminars, listening to yet another erudite, lucid explanation delivered without notes and wondering, "How does he do it?" In due course, the question shifted from incredulity to inquiry as David began to wonder, "How *does* he do it, and how can I do it better myself?" — and resolved to take advantage of the opportunity to learn firsthand from an exemplary scholar how to write clearly and winsomely, to evaluate the views of others fairly, and to do it all with grace and humility. Susan also recalls Stephen's humility and his constant encouragement to be productive. Not long after Susan's dissertation was published, Stephen quietly encouraged her to focus on her next research project. For a fleeting moment, she wished he had just left her to bask in the glory of the moment. Thankfully, Stephen Westerholm is not that type of supervisor or scholar. Instead, he quietly presses for more — indeed, for the best work possible.

The best work possible is what Stephen has always demanded from himself. Scholars describe Stephen's scholarship as insightful and clear, precise, fair-minded and irenic. Beyond recognizing his scholarly acumen, reviewers comment on his subtle humor and wit, and creative flair. Over the past thirty-five years, Stephen has earned a well-deserved reputation as a careful reader of early Christian literature and its interpreters, who keeps his own readers in mind by writing books and essays that are both "essential reading" and a pleasure to read.

The editors of this volume wish to honor Stephen Westerholm by advancing the study of early Christian interpretation of Torah, the area of scholarship for which he is best known. We invited contributions from experts in this field, as well as close colleagues and former students. Unlike many festschrifts, the essays circle around a central question: in what ways did the Mosaic law continue to serve as a positive reference point for Christ-believers regardless of whether they thought Torah observance was essential? This thematic unity will make the volume a useful teaching tool. We also hope the contributions will serve as a springboard for pastoral discussion surrounding the contemporary relevance of Torah ethics.

Finally, we would like to thank Briercrest College and Seminary for the course relief we received to complete the project, and the editors at Eerdmans for their generous assistance in the publication of this volume.

Introduction

Susan J. Wendel and David M. Miller

The law of the LORD is perfect, reviving the soul;
the decrees of the LORD are sure, making wise the simple;
the precepts of the LORD are right, rejoicing the heart;
the commandment of the LORD is clear, enlightening the eyes;
the fear of the LORD is pure, enduring forever;
the ordinances of the LORD are true and righteous altogether.

(Ps. 19:7-9 NRSV)

Torah was God's gift to his covenant people and a manifestation of the divine will. Although changing historical circumstances led to various interpretations of Mosaic law, and different Jewish groups implemented Torah in distinct ways, the commandments of Moses continued to function as the ancestral law code of the Jewish people.[1] Beyond its constitutional role, since Torah represented the revelation of God's will, it promised divine blessing for those who followed its ancient precepts (Deuteronomy 28–30). As Psalm 19 explains, "the law of the LORD" expresses his perfect, pure, and righteous decrees. Torah thus served as an expression of God's character and as an ongoing source of divine guidance.[2]

1. See Stephen Westerholm, "Law in Early Judaism," *NIDB*, 3:587-89.

2. For discussion regarding Torah as a source of ethical wisdom, especially its interpretation in the Psalms, see Gordon J. Wenham, *Psalms as Torah: Reading Biblical Song Ethically* (Grand Rapids: Baker Academic, 2012), chaps. 5-8; cf. Brian S. Rosner, *Paul and the Law: Keeping the Commandments of God* (NSBT 31; Downers Grove: IVP Academic, 2013), 159-205.

If Torah stated the perfect will of God, how was it possible for early Christ-believers to conclude that they need not follow the entire law?[3] Like their Jewish contemporaries, Jesus and his first followers appear to have recognized the authority of Mosaic law, and their ethical teaching remained grounded in the Jewish scriptures. Yet the rapid shift to a predominately non-Jewish membership, in part, led to a reevaluation of the role of Torah in the life of Christ-believing groups. Many early Christ-believers claimed the Jewish scriptures as their own sacred texts, on the one hand, but denied the necessity of keeping the entire Torah, on the other. This raised an obvious concern about the status of Mosaic law: in what sense could Christ-believers regard Torah as the disclosure of God's plan for humans if its precepts were no longer regarded as binding? Perhaps more significantly, how might Christ-believers continue to affirm the enduring value of Torah in light of a new revelation of God's will in Christ?

To be sure, a single edited volume on Torah ethics cannot provide exhaustive answers to these questions. For this reason, our study focuses on a more specific line of inquiry: in what ways did the Mosaic law continue to serve as a positive reference point for Christ-believers regardless of whether they thought Torah observance was essential? Examining early Christian appropriation of the Torah from this perspective raises three additional questions: (1) How did the Mosaic law continue to influence early Christ-believers' understanding of the will of God? (2) To what extent did Torah provide the basis for guiding the ethical responsibilities of Christ-believing communities, and how were such ethical values integrated with the teachings and work of Jesus? (3) How might presentations of the Mosaic law in early Christian literature inform contemporary Christian ethical practices? While only a few of the essays in this collection address the last question directly, the volume as a whole may serve as a catalyst for discussion of contemporary issues.

Previous studies have examined the use of Mosaic law in the New Testament.[4] Among these, some specialized works explore how Torah inter-

3. Although "Torah" can mean "instruction," by the first century CE the term more typically referred to "the sum of commandments given to Israel through Moses on Mount Sinai," or to the portion of scripture that contains these commands (i.e., The Five Books of Moses) (Westerholm, "Law in Early Judaism," 587). Cf. Stephen Westerholm, "*Torah, Nomos,* and Law: A Question of 'Meaning,'" *SR* 15, no. 3 (1986): 327-36.

4. For example, Barnabas Lindars, ed., *Law and Religion: Essays on the Place of the Law in Israel and Early Christianity* (Cambridge: James Clarke, 1988); Michael Tait and Peter Oakes, eds., *The Torah in the New Testament: Papers Delivered at the Manchester-Lausanne Seminar of June 2008* (LNTS 401; London: T&T Clark, 2009).

pretation informs ethical practices in specific texts,[5] but few attempt to offer a more comprehensive evaluation of how Mosaic law provides a moral compass for early Christ-believers. Because Markus Bockmuehl examines halakic (Jewish legal) reasoning in the development of early Christian public ethics,[6] his work has significant points of overlap with the topics covered in this volume (e.g., Torah and natural law, Torah as wisdom, purity regulations in Christian interpretation of Torah, and intersections between Torah and the teachings of Jesus). Nevertheless, as Bockmuehl himself affirms, studies such as his do not provide a comprehensive treatment of the subject. By offering a set of essays that discuss Torah ethics from a broader range of scholarly perspectives, and that probe more deeply into specific passages and aspects of this theme, the present volume extends the conversation surrounding the use of Mosaic law for ethical guidance in early Jewish and Christian texts.

The different perspectives of the essays highlight the complexity of our subject matter. This should come as no surprise since New Testament texts, not to mention other early Jewish and Christian texts, offer different configurations of continuity and discontinuity with Judaism, occur in different genres, and arise out of varied socio-historical circumstances. Complexity also arises in this study because of the differing perspectives and approaches of the contributors. Rather than presenting a barrier, such diversity challenges readers to wrestle with complexity and difference, even as it also invites comparison and attention to similarity.

The volume opens with chapters on Torah observance in Jewish synagogues and in the Hellenistic writings of Philo and Josephus. While the first two chapters contribute in their own right to an understanding of early Jewish Torah ethics, they also provide a context for the volume's larger question about the role of Torah in forming the ethical practices of early Christ-believers. Essays in the book's central section examine specific New Testament texts, including the Gospels, Acts, James, and the Pauline epistles. The final three chapters, which consider subsequent Christian reflection on the ethical role of Torah, offer a basis for comparison with earlier New Testament texts, and also draw

5. For example, Brian S. Rosner, *Paul, Scripture and Ethics: A Study of 1 Corinthians 5–7* (AGJU 22; Leiden: Brill, 1994); Bruce W. Longenecker, *Remember the Poor: Paul, Poverty, and the Greco-Roman World* (Grand Rapids: Eerdmans, 2010); James W. Thompson, *Moral Formation According to Paul: The Context and Coherence of Pauline Ethics* (Grand Rapids: Baker Academic, 2011).

6. Markus Bockmuehl, *Jewish Law in Gentile Churches: Halakhah and the Beginning of Christian Public Ethics* (Edinburgh: T&T Clark, 2000).

attention to ways in which Torah has continued to inform the identity and practices of the Christian church. Because they pose a unified set of questions to a diverse range of texts, this collection of essays is more than the sum of its parts. Although readers with a particular interest in John or Acts or Clement of Alexandria may read individual essays with profit, there is much to be gained from a comparison of the different ancient and modern perspectives on Torah ethics and identity represented here.

Torah Ethics in Early Judaism

In his chapter on Torah observance in first-century Jewish synagogues, Anders Runesson observes that disagreement about Jewish identity has always amounted to a disagreement about the interpretation of Torah. After examining evidence for Torah interpretation and practice in ancient synagogues, Runesson concludes that — in contrast to contemporary Judaism — there was no majority tradition that determined what counted as Torah observance, and no centralized authority structure that could enforce a particular practice. As a result, first-century Jewish groups held differing views on what constituted Torah observance and Jewish identity. The diversity was not unlimited, however. According to Runesson, Jews in both local public synagogues and more restrictive Jewish associations read and interpreted the Torah each week, and sought to apply its purity regulations. Runesson suggests that Paul shared these first-century Jewish concerns because he claimed that moral purity — the result of Spirit-enabled Torah observance — is necessary if God is to dwell "in the midst of those Jews and non-Jews who affiliate themselves with the Messiah."

John W. Martens's chapter on Philo and Josephus also examines the intersection of Jewish identity and Torah-based ethical practices. According to Martens, Philo and Josephus identify the Torah as the national law of the Jewish people but also associate it with the Hellenistic concept of an unwritten "higher law." Because he identifies the law of Moses with "the law of nature," Philo argues not only that the law articulates lofty ethical ideals, but also that people should change their identity by abandoning their own ethnic laws and adopting those of Israel. In contrast to Philo, Josephus treats the law primarily as the constitution of the Jewish *ethnos* and grants that other nations remain obligated to their own laws. Nevertheless, Josephus still maintains that Mosaic law is superior to the law codes of other nations and that it in some way expresses God's will for all people.

Torah Ethics and the New Testament

Within the New Testament, the Torah is employed in different ways by different writers to negotiate continuity and discontinuity with the past, as early Christ-believers engage in the process of defining themselves in relation to other Jews.

In the opening chapter of this section, Wesley G. Olmstead argues that, according to Matthew, Torah comes to its eschatological fulfillment in the Messiah, who shows what faithfulness to Torah looks like in the new age. Where this fulfillment entails the relativization of specific requirements, it does so not in opposition to Torah, which remains binding, but as its eschatological goal and as informed by the character of Israel's God. When Jesus quotes Hosea 6:6 ("I desire mercy not sacrifice"), he is summoning his followers to true covenant faithfulness that imitates God. For Matthew, this eschatological Torah obedience can only be expressed by a positive response to the Messiah who perfectly mirrors God's own covenant faithfulness.

S. A. Cummins's essay, "Torah, Jesus, and the Kingdom of God in the Gospel of Mark," comes to similar conclusions. Cummins finds in Mark's Gospel a consistently positive view of Torah. Instead of revoking or replacing the law, the Markan Jesus expresses concern for the well-being of all Israel, and his message calls for more — not less — Torah observance. Cummins concludes that, for Mark, Torah is "affirmed, taken up, and transposed" by Jesus, and its demands and benefits are extended to Jesus' followers through his life, death, and resurrection. Torah, which constituted the life and mission of Israel, "continues to be constitutive of life together for the Spirit-empowered covenant people of God," both Jews and Gentiles.

Unlike Matthew and Mark, Luke had the luxury of a second volume to show how Jewish and non-Jewish Christ-believers relate to the law differently. According to David M. Miller, Luke distinguishes between Jewish Christians, who remain oriented to the law, and Gentile Christians, who are not subject to the law. Luke draws on the law's demands as well as its predictions to present Torah-observant Jewish Christians — in contrast to other Jews — as faithful Israel, and to demonstrate that salvation legitimately extends to Gentiles apart from the law or membership in Israel. Although Miller argues that Acts does not directly articulate a Torah ethic for Gentiles, he suggests that Luke probably assumed that Torah should guide Gentiles ethically in the same way that Luke applied the predictions and demands of biblical prophecy by analogy to audiences not directly addressed by the prophets.

If the Synoptic Gospels and Acts emphasize continuity between Christ-believers and the law, John's Gospel, according to Adele Reinhartz, stands at the opposite end of the spectrum, at least in connection with the Gospel's central character. Using John 11:1-44 as the focus of her study, Reinhartz offers a "resistant reading" of the Fourth Gospel in which she argues that the Johannine Jesus breaches the ethical demands of Torah — in the story of Lazarus and elsewhere — because he was not bound by ethical requirements that governed the behavior of humans. Jesus' violation of Torah-based ethical norms, Reinhartz argues, is consistent with the Christology of the Gospel of John: "Neither God nor God's Logos is bound by the laws of the Torah or by the norms that make human relationships both possible and satisfying." This conclusion does not mean that the Fourth Gospel rejects the Torah as an ethical guide for ordinary human behavior; "it does suggest" that the author did not intend "to prescribe an ethical system for the sake of the Gospel's audiences."

We turn from the Gospels and Acts to James because, if Scot McKnight is correct, the canonical location of James among the "general epistles" belies its connection to the Synoptic Gospels and the ethic of Jesus. According to McKnight, the distinct identity of early Christians as reflected in James is characterized by a positive attitude toward Torah that is indebted to the hermeneutic of Jesus, James's older brother. Like Jesus, James combines Leviticus 19:18 with the Shema to provide a particular grid for reading Torah: the entire Mosaic law can be summed up in two commands — loving God and loving neighbor. James also internalized the Torah interpretation of Jesus by reverently receiving his teachings as wisdom rather than as law, as *hokmah* rather than *halakah*. These two aspects of his argument lead McKnight to the following conclusion: "James's theory of the Torah . . . is mediated to him through Jesus as the sage who interpreted the Torah itself through the Shema revised."

Instead of stressing a positive role for the law as a reference point for ethics and as an identity marker for the people of God, Beverly Roberts Gaventa argues that, in the letter to the Romans, Paul undermines the law and presents Christ as its replacement. Gaventa suggests that debate surrounding the meaning of τέλος in Romans 10:4 has led to an exegetical impasse: does this verse present Christ as the termination or goal of the Mosaic law? To address this impasse, her study attends to Paul's account of the law in Romans 1–8, before turning to a closer analysis of Romans 9:30–10:13. Gaventa's review of Romans 1–8 shows the complexity of Paul's treatment of the law, but it also reveals a pattern that repeats in Romans 9–11: "Paul raises questions about the law, but he answers those questions in terms of Christ." Whatever we make of Romans 10:4, Paul's subsequent argument in Romans 10–11 "implies the end of the law," not merely its goal or fulfillment.

In his exploration of Paul's construction of the identity of Gentile believers as Abraham's seed, Terence L. Donaldson maintains that Paul construes the relationship between the law and this Gentile group "positively as well as negatively." Donaldson argues that, according to Paul, the role once played by the law as the "foundation and boundary marker for the community of the righteous" has been replaced by Christ. This substitution makes it possible for Gentiles to become Abraham's "seed" without undergoing circumcision or becoming proselytes. But it also leads to a transformation in the law's function: whereas the pre-Damascus Paul held that both Torah and natural law functioned only to condemn those outside the covenant, the post-Damascus Paul thinks natural law — whose ethical requirements overlap with the law of Moses — corresponds to the moral behavior of "*ethnē*-in-Christ," in whom the "righteous requirement of the law is fulfilled" (Rom. 8:4).

A previously published essay by Richard B. Hays, entitled "The Conversion of the Imagination: Scripture and Eschatology in 1 Corinthians,"[7] brings our discussion of Torah ethics in the New Testament to a conclusion. In this essay, Hays argues that Paul teaches the Corinthian church to identify itself with Israel by recognizing how God has made them participants in the eschatological fulfillment of the Jewish scriptures. According to Hays, Paul's rereading of Israel's scriptures involves a reconfiguration of these texts in light of the cross and resurrection, and this shift in hermeneutic leads his non-Jewish readers to identify themselves with Israel's story. Key passages from 1 Corinthians (1:18-31; 5:1-13; 10:1-22) illustrate how Paul edits the Corinthians into the story of Israel so that they are "taken up into Israel in such a way that they now share in Israel's covenant privileges and obligations." This discussion of 1 Corinthians also illustrates how Paul can draw on Torah in a variety of ways, depending on the circumstances he addresses.

Beyond the New Testament

The themes of natural law, identity, and ethics reappear in Susan J. Wendel's chapter, which examines the treatment of the Mosaic law by early Christian apologists, with a particular focus on the writings of Justin Martyr. According to Wendel, Justin seeks to demonstrate that the behavior of Christians

7. *NTS* 45, no. 3 (1999): 391-412; reprinted in Richard B. Hays, *The Conversion of the Imagination: Paul as Interpreter of Israel's Scripture* (Grand Rapids: Eerdmans, 2005), 1-24. In this edition, the footnotes have been abbreviated and a new introduction has been added.

represents the most ancient and venerable form of virtuous living because it conforms to the ethical requirements of the Mosaic law, which "function as a type of universal, or natural, law code." Justin asserts this argument by differentiating between the ethical practices of Christ-believers and Jewish observance of the Mosaic law, on the one hand, and by depicting Christian understanding of Mosaic law as superior to the ethical teachings of Greek philosophers, on the other. For Justin, as for other early apologists, moreover, the identity of early Christians is defined by ethical practices, not merely belief.

Peter Widdicombe discusses the use of Torah in the Alexandrian tradition represented by Clement of Alexandria. Widdicombe argues that although Clement had a high view of the Mosaic law, and regarded this text as a guide for "right reason" and virtue, he ultimately gives preference to the Logos (i.e., Christ) as the ultimate source of revelation about God. According to Clement, Moses had a profound understanding of the nature of God, which qualified him to communicate the law, but the Logos had access to the indescribable depths of God. In Clement, then, we can identify points of continuity with earlier Christian writers treated in this volume, who also discuss the relationship between Christ and the law, and between the law of Moses and the laws of other nations. However, there is also a transition: as Widdicombe points out in his conclusion, subsequent theologians in the Alexandrian tradition increasingly favored the Logos, rather than the Mosaic law, as the guide for truth about God.

In a fitting conclusion to a volume that has presented such a variety of perspectives on Torah ethics, Stephen Westerholm considers the need for, and hazards of, a quest for a coherent scriptural position on the role of the law. Taking as his focus a comparison of what Luther, Calvin, and Paul have to say about Torah ethics, Westerholm finds that Luther imposes a Pauline perspective on the law onto all of scripture, while Calvin understands the law in scripture as "the all-encompassing designation for God's eternal plan," and imposes this perspective on Paul. According to Westerholm, attempts to establish the coherent message of scripture are not only commendable, but — within the community of faith — essential. Yet the survey serves as a reminder that distorted interpretations can follow from such attempts no less than from facile claims of scripture's diversity.

Torah Ethics in Early Judaism

Entering a Synagogue with Paul: First-Century Torah Observance

Anders Runesson

Who is a Jew? This deceptively simple question quickly opens up onto a hermeneutical quagmire, not only when put under the microscope in a scholarly lab but also when asked in an Israeli or British courtroom, as reports in recent years from the BBC and *The New York Times,* not to speak of debates between authorities within various Jewish denominations, have shown.[1]

A few years ago a Jewish publicly funded school in Britain turned down an applicant, who was a practicing Jew, on the basis that his mother had converted in a progressive synagogue and was therefore not regarded as Jewish according to the school's classification of "Jewish," which followed the orthodox definition of the chief rabbi Jonathan Sachs. The family sued, and the British Supreme Court eventually ruled that religious practice and faith must be the criteria for acceptance into any publicly funded "religious" school, not "ethnicity" — a thoroughly Christian perspective on "religion" to be sure. As Rabbi Yitzchak Schochet, the former chairman of the Rabbinical Council of

1. Sarah Lyall, "Who Is a Jew? Court Ruling in Britain Raises Question," *The New York Times,* November 8, 2009; Adam Mynott, "Row Rages Over Defining Who Is a Jew," *BBC News Middle East,* July 20, 2010. In the BBC report it is claimed that "[i]n Israel uncertainty has excluded more than a quarter of a million people, who think they are Jewish, from full membership." The quotes that follow below are from *The New York Times* article.

This essay is dedicated to my friend and colleague at McMaster University, Stephen Westerholm, on the occasion of his sixty-fifth birthday. Throughout the now more than a decade that I have had the honor and pleasure of working with Steve I have always been impressed by his erudition and sharp eye for detail in his work on Paul. I have greatly enjoyed, especially, our many discussions of the work of the apostle, as well as his later reception, Kierkegaard, and a myriad of other topics over a lunch sandwich in his office. Varma lyckönskningar på högtidsdagen, Steve!

the United Synagogue, commented, "having a ham sandwich on the afternoon of Yom Kippur doesn't make you less Jewish."

Still, however, the process of conversion itself, and its perceived validity or not by different denominations, show that the question "Who is a Jew?" quickly leads beyond ethnicity to the related questions of "What is Judaism?" and "Who gets to decide?" The answers to these questions redirect attention from what at the surface level seem to be straightforward assessments about ethnicity to issues about how to define Torah observance. Interpretation of Torah cannot be divorced from the question of ethnicity; definitions of Jewish ethnicity and identity ultimately depend on and revolve around issues of interpretive authority related to Torah.

This is further emphasized by a comment made by Rabbi Danny Rich, the chief executive of Liberal Judaism in Britain, that "[t]he Orthodox definition of 'Jewish' excludes 40 percent of the Jewish community in [Britain]." The question "Who is a Jew?" may thus function as an entry point to the larger issue of how Torah observance is to be defined. In this regard, it is of some interest to note that these modern disagreements build on an understanding of Judaism that is Rabbinic. Despite the heated arguments and irreconcilable differences, the diversity described exists within a single more broadly defined view of what Judaism is and how halakic arguments should be construed.

This form of Judaism, Rabbinic Judaism, originated after 70 CE, but did not become mainstream Judaism until the fourth or fifth century at the earliest.[2] It did not exist when Paul formulated his view on what Torah observance should or should not be, or who should be regarded as included in the people of God and on what basis. In Paul's day there was no single majority tradition within which Jews could agree or disagree. The closest thing to a majority Judaism at the time was what E. P. Sanders has called "Common Judaism," which revolved around the Jerusalem temple rather than being engaged in construing identity through interpretation of Talmudic texts that did not yet exist.[3] As for Jewish

2. For an even later estimation of this development, see Seth Schwartz, *Imperialism and Jewish Society, 200 B.C.E. to 640 C.E.* (Princeton: Princeton University Press, 2001).

3. E. P. Sanders suggested the concept of Common Judaism in his *Judaism: Practice and Belief: 63 BCE–66 CE* (Philadelphia: Trinity Press International, 1992). See also E. P. Sanders, "Common Judaism Explored," in *Common Judaism: Explorations in Second-Temple Judaism* (ed. Wayne O. McCready and Adele Reinhartz; Minneapolis: Fortress, 2008), 11-23. For further discussion of Common Judaism in relation to more specific interpretations of Jewish life, see Anders Runesson, "Rethinking Early Jewish-Christian Relations: Matthean Community History as Pharisaic Intragroup Conflict," *JBL* 127, no. 1 (2008): 95-132; note especially the table on p. 105.

identity and the issue of conversion, there was a range of more or less defined options in synagogue settings, based on different understandings of ethnicity and Torah.[4] There is a *qal va-homer* argument of sorts embedded here: if the modern situation, which builds on a broadly defined common understanding of Judaism as Rabbinic Judaism, reveals to us deep-seated diversity even in terms of core issues such as who is to be identified as a Jew, how much more so for the pre-70 CE period when we lack evidence of a majority form of Judaism based on specific understandings of Torah?

While the lack of a direct relationship between later Rabbinic (and modern) understandings of Torah observance, on the one hand, and pre-70 CE views of what constituted fidelity to the commandments, on the other, is chronologically and socio-institutionally unambiguous enough, such discontinuity often goes unnoticed in scholarship devoted to this time period. As Philip Alexander noted already in 1988, it is quite common among both Jewish and Christian scholars who discuss whether Jesus kept the law or not to take for granted that we know what keeping the law in the first century meant.[5] Almost thirty years later, the same basic assumptions still cause trouble in the field of Pauline studies. Alexander's point is worth quoting in full:

> [T]he nature and content of the law of Moses in the time of Jesus is far from clear: it certainly cannot be identified *simpliciter* with the Pentateuch. It is hard to determine what non-biblical traditions it contained. And while the centrality of the Torah of Moses to Judaism cannot in principle be questioned, the meaning of that centrality is not self-evident. It was not necessarily the centrality of a coherent body of doctrine universally believed. It was more the centrality of a national symbol, which was acknowledged by all, but which meant different things to different groups. Individual understandings of the significance of the symbol may have varied considerably. It is hard to say what would, or would not, have been an "acceptable" attitude towards the Torah of Moses. The upshot of

4. See Donald D. Binder, "The Synagogue and the Gentiles," in *Attitudes to Gentiles in Ancient Judaism and Early Christianity* (ed. David C. Sim and James S. McLaren; LNTS 499; London: Bloomsbury T&T Clark, 2013), 109-25. For source material and analysis of interaction between Jews and non-Jews more widely, see Terence L. Donaldson, *Judaism and the Gentiles: Jewish Patterns of Universalism (to 135 CE)* (Waco: Baylor University Press, 2007).

5. Philip S. Alexander, "Jewish Law in the Time of Jesus: Towards a Clarification of the Problem," in *Law and Religion: Essays on the Place of the Law in Israel and Early Christianity* (ed. Barnabas Lindars; Cambridge: James Clarke, 1988), 44-58.

> the analysis is that it is difficult, if not impossible, to lay down a base-line from which to measure Jesus' deviation from, or conformity to, the law. It is arguable that the whole problem of Jesus and the law, at least as traditionally stated, is misconceived.[6]

Now, if we apply this to Paul, a number of questions emerge. If Rabbinic Judaism, the mother of all forms of mainstream Judaism today, did not exist when Paul was around, within which context do we measure and understand Paul's interpretation of what Torah observance signifies, of what it means to "keep the law"?[7] In which way was he different from other Jews, and, if he was different, from what kind of Judaism was he different? Will this difference, in whichever way it is defined, make him "un-Jewish," or should Paul rather be understood more along the lines of the modern diversity described above, as an expression of diversity within Judaism? Who would decide this and on what basis? When dealing with similar issues in relation to Jesus, Alexander focuses on two key questions, revolving around the existence or not of Jewish courts and their possible jurisdiction, as well as the problem of what law such courts would have been administering.[8] As recent synagogue research has shown, court proceedings occurred within synagogue settings, the same setting in which all sources dating to this time claim that reading and teaching of Torah took place.[9] Investigating Torah instruction and practice in the context of the ancient synagogue may thus prove helpful as we consider the nature of Paul's teaching.

In this essay, I discuss the nature of the first-century Jewish institutions that we call "synagogues." I then proceed to focus on what went on in them in order to set Paul's teaching in context. As we will see, although some of the practices in these institutions were continued within later Rabbinic Judaism, the evidence implies that Paul needs to be read beyond the paradigm suggested by Rabbinic writings.

6. Alexander, "Jewish Law," 46.

7. See Alexander, "Jewish Law," 56: "[T]here was no universally acknowledged body of laws at the heart of Judaism in the time of Jesus."

8. Alexander, "Jewish Law," 46. As Alexander notes, the law of Rome provided a framework within which all other law functioned.

9. See especially Lee I. Levine, *The Ancient Synagogue: The First Thousand Years* (New Haven: Yale University Press, 2005), 135-73.

Defining Torah Observance beyond Rabbis and Christians

As I have argued elsewhere, the many Greek, Latin, and Hebrew terms that designated what we translate with one word today as "synagogue" referred, in the first century, to two types of institution: the public municipal synagogue in the land, on the one hand, and Jewish associations, or association synagogues, which were for members only, on the other, the latter existing both in the land and in the Diaspora.[10] Whenever we read the New Testament, or any other first-century text speaking of synagogues, we need to clarify which of the two types is referred to in order to avoid anachronistic reconstructions that reflect Rabbinic or modern definitions of "synagogue."[11] In the following, I first discuss public synagogue institutions and then association synagogues with a view to isolating information that will shed light on Torah observance as well as the context in which such observance was formed.

Open to All: Torah in Local Public Synagogues in the Land

It is beyond doubt that Torah was of major importance for Jews in the first century, and that the public municipal institutions, which ran the daily business of towns and villages and which were designated by synagogue terms, were places where Torah was read on Sabbaths for all to hear, without exclusion of

10. For extensive treatment, see Anders Runesson, *The Origins of the Synagogue: A Socio-Historical Study* (ConBNT 37; Stockholm: Almqvist & Wiksell International, 2001).

11. Both types of "synagogues" were spoken of using the same terms, such as συναγωγή, προσευχή, ἱερόν, and ἐκκλησία. For example, Josephus and Ben Sira use ἐκκλησία for public institutions in the land, whereas Matthew uses the same term for the association he claims Jesus founded (Matt. 16:18; 18:17). Συναγωγή is also used for both municipal institutions (the Gospels) and private associations (Acts 6:9, the synagogue of the Freedmen; Philo, the synagogue of the Essenes). In a Diaspora context, Paul uses ἐκκλησία for assemblies of followers of Jesus, but Philo uses the same term for more open synagogues lacking specific denominational or sectarian identities. It is necessary, therefore, to look at the context when we determine which type of synagogue we are dealing with. Torah observance would have been conceived of differently in the different types of institution; indeed, the very existence of association synagogues is an indication of the fact that various Jewish groups construed and maintained their identities around specific understandings of what constituted Torah observance. For sources in which the diverse terms for "synagogue" were used, see the index in *ASSB*. For ἐκκλησία as a synagogue term, see the extensive treatment in Ralph Korner, "Before 'Church': Political, Ethno-Religious and Theological Implications of the Collective Designation of Pauline Christ-Followers as *Ekklēsiai*" (Ph.D. diss., McMaster University, 2014).

women, lepers, people of so-called *mamzer* status,[12] or children. Torah was a public concern in Jewish society. This, Josephus insists to his Roman readers, makes the Jewish people the most law-abiding people of all. Indeed, the Jews were, he claims, ideal citizens; synagogues were referred to as proof of this.[13] The practice of reading Torah every Sabbath seems to have been regarded, in and of itself, as a sign of Torah observance.[14] Beyond this, however, evidence of forms of Torah observance in public synagogues is rather meager. There are a few things, though, that may shed light on the matter.

First, archaeological remains of first-century synagogues may tell us something about how Torah was read and understood in some local towns and villages, and this may, in turn, inform us about how Torah observance was shaped in such settings. A synagogue building had stepped benches around all four walls, the focal point being the empty space at the center of the main hall; from there Torah was read.[15] The interior design of the building suggests strongly that, like its closest modern architectural parallel, the British Parliament, it was made for interaction and debate. Reading Torah in such a setting would imply that whatever was read was discussed and debated by those present.

Village scribes most likely had prominent roles in these institutions, but we do not have information that would point to the exclusion of anyone present from either reading text or voicing an opinion.[16] No specific group, such as

12. Contra Bruce Chilton, *Rabbi Jesus: An Intimate Biography* (New York: Image, 2000), 12-16, who anachronistically reads later (Rabbinic) definitions of *mamzer* back into the first century, and assumes without evidence that it has implications for synagogue attendance. There are no first-century sources indicating that the passage in Deuteronomy 23:2 was applied in any sense in any known public synagogue settings at the time. For other forms of exclusion mechanisms in specific, non-public (sectarian) communal settings, see Cecilia Wassen, "What Do Angels Have against the Blind and the Deaf? Rules of Exclusion in the Dead Sea Scrolls," in *Common Judaism: Explorations in Second-Temple Judaism* (ed. Wayne O. McCready and Adele Reinhartz; Minneapolis: Fortress, 2008), 115-29.

13. See, for example, Josephus, *A.J.* 16.42-43 (*ASSB*, no. 119); 19.300-305 (*ASSB*, no. 193). Cf. Philo, for example, *Flacc.* 41-53 (*ASSB*, no. 138); *Legat.* 152-53 (*ASSB*, no. 164); *Hypoth.* 7.11-14 (*ASSB*, no. 162).

14. See Acts 15:21.

15. For a concise discussion of synagogue space, including viewshed analysis, see James F. Strange, "Archaeology and Ancient Synagogues up to about 200 CE," in *The Ancient Synagogue from Its Origins until 200 C.E.* (ed. Birger Olsson and Magnus Zetterholm; ConBNT 39; Stockholm: Almqvist & Wiksell International, 2003), 37-62.

16. On scribes and scribal culture, see Chris Keith, *Jesus against the Scribal Elite: The Origins of the Conflict* (Grand Rapids: Baker Academic, 2014).

the Pharisees, was in charge.[17] Ideas about Torah observance shaped in such a context would be the result of interaction among the many rather than of the rulings of the few. Further, we have no evidence of centralized control from Jerusalem over these local institutions and their understanding and implementation of Torah.[18] The lack of such centralized authority opens up for local variation regarding how Torah was interpreted.[19]

Still, while these synagogues seem to have been relatively independent in terms of political influence from the capital and the temple authorities, we may infer from the art displayed in the buildings in which gatherings took place that, contrary to later centuries, first-century Jews interpreted strictly the command in Exodus not to make images of living beings.[20] Further, the *mikvaot*, or ritual baths, and stone vessels found all over the land are indications of a shared understanding of Torah with regard to the purity rules of Leviticus.[21] This matches well what we see in some first-century Jewish texts,

17. See Levine, *Ancient Synagogue,* 41: "[T]he truth of the matter is, the Pharisees had little or nothing to do with the early synagogue, and there is not one shred of evidence pointing to a connection between the two. No references associate the early Pharisees (the 'Pairs' and others) with the synagogue, nor is there anything in early synagogue liturgy that is particularly Pharisaic."

18. We have no evidence from the first century mirroring the situation portrayed in 2 Chronicles 17:7-9, where it is stated that King Jehoshaphat sent traveling priests and Levites from Jerusalem to the cities of Judah to teach the people the law, using the "book of the law."

19. On the issue of regional differences from a political perspective, see Alexander, "Jewish Law," 46-47. As Alexander notes, "by exercising self-discipline the Jews had the possibility of running a largely autonomous Jewish legal system within Roman Palestine." This, however, does not imply uniformity within the Jewish legal system: "It is possible that there was considerable variation in the detailed application of the law, owing to the force of local custom" (50).

20. See Exod. 20:4 (cf. Deut. 4:23; 5:8). Even the elaborate art on the so-called Magdala temple stone lacks representation of living creatures. For a discussion of the Magdala stone and its iconography, see Donald D. Binder, "The Mystery of the Magdala Stone," in *City Set on a Hill: Essays in Honor of James F. Strange* (ed. Daniel Warner and Donald D. Binder; Mountain Home, Ark.: BorderStone, 2014), 17-48. On Jewish art in antiquity, see Lee I. Levine, *Visual Judaism in Late Antiquity: Historical Contexts of Jewish Art* (New Haven: Yale University Press, 2012), especially 31-65. Cf. Tryggve N. D. Mettinger, *No Graven Image? Israelite Aniconism in Its Ancient Near Eastern Context* (ConBOT 42; Stockholm: Almqvist & Wiksell International, 1995).

21. On stone vessels, see Roland Deines, *Jüdische Steingefäße und pharisäische Frömmigkeit. Ein archäologisch-historischer Beitrag zum Verständnis von Johannes 2,6 und der jüdischen Reinheitshalacha zur Zeit Jesu* (WUNT II 52; Tübingen: Mohr Siebeck, 1993); Yitzhak Magen, *The Stone Vessel Industry in the Second Temple Period: Excavations at Hizma and the Jerusalem Temple Mount* (Jerusalem: Israel Exploration Society, 2002); Mark A. Chancey, *The Myth of a Gentile Galilee* (SNTSMS 118; Cambridge: Cambridge University Press, 2002), 67-68. While

such as the Dead Sea Scrolls, *Jubilees*, and the Gospel of Matthew, namely, that purity concerns were very real in the time of Jesus and Paul, and that observance of Torah would have been understood as requiring various forms of ritual washings, even beyond what is stated in Leviticus. In a sense, one could say that purity practices in the first century could be understood as "enacted rewritten bible"; Torah observance was not about following verbatim the rules in Leviticus, but the text served as a point of departure for interpretations that structured various everyday, real-life narratives.

Other forms of generally agreed-on Torah observance include the Sabbath commandment, although exactly how it was to be done, the definition of "work," was a matter of dispute. Jesus' healing/exorcism of a woman who was present at a synagogue meeting on a Sabbath, as described in Luke 13:10-17, resulted in rebuke from a synagogue leader (ἀρχισυνάγωγος), not because of the presence of a woman, or even the presence of a woman regarded as "bound by Satan" (Luke 13:16), in a synagogue assembly, but because this leader defined healing/exorcism as work.[22] Jesus disagrees with his definition (Luke 13:15-16), and the Jewish crowds agree with Jesus (Luke 13:17). The story shows that Exodus 20, possibly together with Genesis 1, might have been one of the passages that provided a textual hub around which communal Torah observance in public synagogue settings was defined.[23]

Deines's study is helpful, I agree with Chancey that his thesis that the presence of stone vessels indicates Pharisaic influence is problematic. Regarding *mikvaot*, see Boaz Zissu and David Amit, "Common Judaism, Common Purity, and the Second Temple Period Judean *Miqwa'ot* (Ritual Immersion Baths)," in *Common Judaism: Explorations in Second-Temple Judaism* (ed. Wayne O. McCready and Adele Reinhartz; Minneapolis: Fortress, 2008), 47-62, who conclude that "[t]he wide distribution of ritual baths reinforces Sanders's assertion that the purity laws were generally obeyed by the Jewish populations" (62). On various understandings of (ritual and moral) purity, see Jonathan Klawans, *Impurity and Sin in Ancient Judaism* (Oxford: Oxford University Press, 2000).

22. Note the difference between public synagogues and the sectarian community rules found among the Dead Sea Scrolls, as discussed by Wassen, "Rules of Exclusion." As Wassen argues, the exclusion mechanisms targeting individuals with various forms of disabilities seem to be based on the conviction that evil forces were the root cause behind the disabilities and that by excluding the people afflicted the community was kept undefiled as it prepared for the eschatological battle against evil. Thus, people were excluded based on the community's fear of demonic powers. Luke describes the public Galilean synagogue in a very different way. None of the individuals involved in the story find the presence of the woman in the midst of the community to be in any way inappropriate. All of them, including, implicitly, the synagogue leader, understand her liberation as appropriate. The problem is the halakic definition of "work" as it relates to the Sabbath.

23. Key passages dealing with the Sabbath commandment include, for example, Gen. 2:3;

Before we turn to the Diaspora, we should also note that the public synagogues, like earlier gatherings in the city gates of ancient Israel,[24] served a number of functions, in which specific interpretations of Torah observance would have been brought into play. I am thinking especially of court proceedings, which were located in such institutions.[25] Verdicts would have been based on specific understandings of Torah since, as Josephus notes, there was no distinction between religious and secular law.[26] While we lack details of the proceedings themselves, both the New Testament and the Mishnah describe one of the punishments that could be meted out in synagogues: flogging.[27] Flogging is mentioned as punishment in court settings only in Deuteronomy 25:1-3. It is possible, perhaps even likely, therefore, that the book of Deuteronomy played a role in how Torah observance was shaped in judicial settings in synagogues.[28]

Exod. 12:16; 16:23; 20:10. Such texts provided a point of departure for later interpretations of how more specifically the commandment should be fulfilled. We do not find in the first century an understanding of "true" observance of Torah as verbatim enactment of the letters of the law. Rather, fulfillment of Torah meant observance of what one regarded as the intent of the law, that is, the spirit of the law.

24. For the origins of the synagogue in the land of Israel, see Runesson, *Origins*, 237-400. Cf. Levine, *Ancient Synagogue*, 21-44.

25. For discussion, see Donald D. Binder, *Into the Temple Courts: The Place of the Synagogues in the Second Temple Period* (Atlanta: Society of Biblical Literature, 1999), 445-50, who includes Diaspora evidence too; Levine, *Ancient Synagogue*, 30-32 (the city gate), 41 (the transition of such proceedings to synagogue institutions). See also pp. 3, 395-96. The New Testament, too, includes several passages indicating the presence of courts in synagogues (e.g., Matt. 23:34; Acts 22:19). See also discussion in Alexander, "Jewish Law," which outlines how law was administered locally and nationally in the land.

26. See Josephus, *C. Ap.* 2.170-71. See Binder, *Temple Courts*, 213, who notes that "religious law *was* civil law," and points out that Josephus himself coined the very term "theocracy" (*C. Ap.* 2.165).

27. Matt. 23:34 (*ASSB*, no. 68; cf. nos. 65, 66); *m. Mak.* 3:12 (*ASSB*, no. 86).

28. This does not imply that Deuteronomy itself constituted a law code; it certainly did not since it contained what has later been called haggadah and thus represents a different genre. Law codes likely existed, though, and as such they would have built their rulings on passages from authoritative texts like Deuteronomy combined with local custom. The genre situation is similar to what I have argued elsewhere is found in a comparison between Matthew's Gospel and the *Didache*. While the former presents rulings on various matters, especially in chapter 18, this is done in narrative form. The *Didache*, however, refers to "the gospel" as it presents a community rule (Anders Runesson, "Building Matthean Communities: The Politics of Textualization," in *Mark and Matthew I: Comparative Readings: Understanding the Earliest Gospels in Their First Century Settings* [ed. Eve-Marie Becker and Anders Runesson; WUNT I 271; Tübingen: Mohr Siebeck, 2011], 379-408).

These are some of the meager results that can be reported with regard to Torah observance as it applies to the very context in which all sources claim Torah was read and taught to all Jews, that is, the synagogue. This was the context in which Jesus was socialized, and in which he himself later taught. An important implication of the fact that public synagogues were independent and that supralocal authority structures were lacking is that ideas about what constituted Torah observance were not stable, but most likely varied between towns and communities depending on local tradition. Still, concerns about purity seem to have been almost universal, pointing to the importance of Leviticus in settings where Torah was read and taught. Also, Sabbath observance in the context of the synagogue, as well as the lack of figural art in all Second Temple synagogue buildings that have been excavated so far, point to the widespread importance of Exodus in the formation of Jewish communal identities. With regard to judicial proceedings and administration of law in court settings (within synagogues), Deuteronomy may have had some influence with regard to forms of punishment.

Shifting our focus to Jewish associations and the Diaspora, and, consequently, to Paul's context, things look different, although there is some overlap in certain areas.

Members Only: Torah in Jewish Associations in the Land and in the Diaspora

One of the most important factors for reconstructing first-century Torah observance in institutional settings in the Diaspora is the existence of community rules in Greco-Roman and Jewish associations.[29] Such rules stipulated what was acceptable behavior, but people's roles in certain rituals could also be regulated. In a Jewish setting, as shown by the Dead Sea Scrolls, the hermeneutical foundation for establishing a community rule was a specific understanding of Torah; the rule was understood to be an expression of communal Torah observance.[30] I will return to this below, after considering the evidence more broadly.

29. John Kloppenborg has analyzed the ἀποσυνάγωγος passages in the Gospel of John in light of association rules ("Disaffiliation in Associations and the Ἀποσυνάγωγος of John," *HvTSt* 67, no. 1 [2011]: art. #962). In the case of John's Gospel, however, I am more inclined to agree with Jonathan Bernier, Aposynagōgos *and the Historical Jesus in John: Rethinking the Historicity of the Johannine Expulsion Passages* (Biblical Interpretation Series 122; Leiden: Brill, 2013), who understands these references to refer to public institutions in Jerusalem.

30. See Yonder Moynihan Gillihan, *Civic Ideology, Organization, and Law in the Rule Scrolls: A Comparative Study of the Covenanters' Sect and Contemporary Voluntary Associations in Political Context* (STDJ 97; Leiden: Brill, 2012).

Roman authorities understood Diaspora synagogues to be the same kind of institution as the Greco-Roman *collegia* (voluntary associations).[31] Important for our purposes here are the Roman decrees, reproduced by Josephus, which were issued in response to local anti-Jewish developments.[32] In these decrees, all of which confirm Jewish communal rights, we learn something about the kinds of activities that took place in Jewish associations, and thus about how communal Torah observance was understood in the Diaspora.

In all decrees, the rights listed are said to be based on Jewish law and custom. Generally agreed-on forms of Torah observance according to these documents included the following aspects:[33]

1. communal gatherings of Jewish men, women, and children, in a place of their own
2. performance of "native, sacred, and holy rituals"
3. communal meals
4. celebration of customary festivals (New Moons,[34] Sukkot, Yom Kippur, possibly Hanukkah, public fasts)[35]
5. Sabbath observance[36]
6. collection of money for communal meals, and for sending to Jerusalem[37]

31. On synagogues as associations in the Greco-Roman world, see especially Philip A. Harland, *Associations, Synagogues, and Congregations: Claiming a Place in Ancient Mediterranean Society* (Minneapolis: Fortress, 2003).

32. For Jewish rights according to these Roman decrees, see Runesson, *Origins,* 468 n. 226. The texts, all found in Josephus, *Antiquities,* are reproduced and discussed in *ASSB*: nos. 93 (Delos), 108 (Ephesus), 109 (Halicarnassus), 110 (Miletus), 113 (Sardis), 114 (Sardis), 120 (by Augustus; unspecified locations), and 180 (Rome). Although there has been some discussion about the authenticity of these decrees, they should be understood as presenting a basic historical outline of rights enjoyed by Jews.

33. Sanders, "Common Judaism Explored," 19-20, also relates these decrees to Common Judaism.

34. On the observance of New Moons, see *ASSB,* no. 131 (Berenice). Cf. Num. 28:11-15; Lev. 23:24. For discussion, see Binder, *Temple Courts,* 416-18.

35. See the "stated days" and "customary festivals" mentioned in the decrees of Halicarnassus (*ASSB,* no. 109) and Sardis (*ASSB,* no. 113). It may be noted that the Therapeutae, as a Jewish sect entertaining a specific understanding of Torah observance, gathered every fiftieth day for a communal feast (perhaps following the liturgical calendar of *Jubilees*?).

36. As we know from other sources in Philo and Josephus, Sabbath observance included communal gathering for the reading and teaching of Torah.

37. *ASSB,* no. 120; cf. no. 108 (Ephesus).

7. the resolving of legal suits among themselves[38]
8. the managing of first-fruits[39]
9. the offering of ancestral prayers and sacrifices (θυσίαι)[40]
10. the eating of special (kosher) food[41]

These activities, several of which are confirmed by archaeological remains, inscriptions, and other texts, developed from a common understanding of what it meant to live like a Jew in the first-century Diaspora. Notably, the right to assemble on the Sabbath coincides with evidence that Torah was read, expounded, and discussed in synagogues on this day.[42] This indicates a common understanding in this regard between Diaspora synagogues and public synagogues in the land.

One of the activities mentioned, though, points to a different understanding of Torah observance in the Diaspora: sacrifice. While the Josephan passage mentioned above has been interpreted in different ways, other texts and archaeological evidence suggest a rather complex picture.

Even though it has rarely had any effect on modern scholarship on Jewish identity and Torah observance, we have evidence of several Jewish temples in the Diaspora, the most famous being the Leontopolis and the Elephantine temples.[43] While the Elephantine temple was destroyed in the late fifth century BCE, the Leontopolis temple was still in use during Paul's lifetime.[44] In fact, there never was a period in the history of the Jewish people when the Jerusalem temple was the only Jewish temple. The existence of these other temples indicates that the cult centralization as described in the Hebrew Bible was not understood by all to exclude the existence of temples outside the land. We must assume that these other Jews saw their ritual practices in terms of obedience to Torah, just as much as the Qumran community saw

38. This implies that the Jewish law was the basis for judicial proceedings.

39. *ASSB,* no. 110 (Miletus).

40. *ASSB,* no. 113 (Sardis).

41. In the decree by the people and council of Sardis (*ASSB,* no. 113), which lists prayers and sacrifices as synagogue activities, it is also stated that the city's market officials were responsible for bringing in food suitable for Jews.

42. For example, Philo, *Somn.* 2.123-28.

43. For sources on Jewish temples outside Jerusalem, see *ASSB,* nos. T1–T12.

44. According to Josephus, the Leontopolis temple was meant to be the solution to a Jewish cult-centralization process in Egypt, implying the previous existence of numerous Jewish temples in the area. For discussion of the process in Egypt (and possibly elsewhere), in which Jewish temples were transformed into what we call synagogues, see Runesson, *Origins,* chap. 5, especially 436-59.

their rejection of the Jerusalem temple as following logically from radical Torah observance.

But we do not need to point only to these Jewish temples to prove diversity in this regard. Archaeological evidence, inscriptions, and papyri indicate that, just as Greco-Roman temples would have provided basins outside their entrances for the purpose of ritual washing before entering sacred space, many of the institutions we call synagogues also had water basins by their entrances for ritual purification. Indeed, papyri from Egypt speak of synagogues (προσευχαί) as holy space, and there is a famous example of a water bill that indicates that the local synagogue used more water than a neighboring bathhouse.[45] The distinction between temple and synagogue, both understood as sacred space, was not at all that clear in the first century.[46] Since we know from Philo and Josephus that reading and discussing Torah was the main activity in these institutions, the sacred nature of these buildings and the washing of hands before entering were likely seen as important aspects of Torah observance. This, in turn, indicates that ritual purity would have been a concern for Diaspora Jews when they gathered as Jews, in accordance with their "native laws and traditions."

These features and activities of Diaspora synagogues were widely agreed on. There were, however, more exclusive Jewish associations too, both in the land and in the Diaspora: the synagogue of the Essenes,[47] the synagogue of the Freedmen in Jerusalem,[48] the associations implied in the community rule of the *Didache,* Matthew's eighteenth chapter, and the letter of James, as well as the institutions of the Therapeutae.[49] The Pharisees should also be understood as forming an association.[50] These groups construed Jewish communal identity and Torah observance differently, appealing to divine law for support for their specific practices.

In such settings there would be procedures in place for the exclusion of

45. *ASSB,* no. 149.

46. See Levine, *Ancient Synagogue,* 86.

47. Philo, *Prob.* 80-83 (*ASSB,* no. 40). Note that Philo understands these synagogues to be "sacred spots."

48. Acts 6:9 (*ASSB,* no. 18).

49. On the Therapeutae, see Philo, *Contempl.* 30-33 (*ASSB,* no. 160).

50. The associations provide the closest analogy that can describe the organization of Jewish groups, including the Pharisees. Note the possible mention of a Pharisaic synagogue in Matthew 12:9 (discussion in Runesson, *Origins,* 355-57). Note also that Luke 14:1 speaks of a leader of the Pharisees, indicating the existence of a hierarchy, which in turn reveals institutional structures such as we may also find in other associations.

members who broke the rules of the community. We have such evidence in Matthew 18:15-18, for example, where reluctance to reconcile with other members would lead to exclusion. Paul is also clear about correct behavior in the associations he is writing to, and he appeals to Jewish law in order to outline acceptable as well as unacceptable conduct (e.g., Gal. 5:19-23). The Community Rule, which is dated to the early first century BCE, also marks the boundaries of a dissident Jewish community.[51]

As Cecilia Wassen has shown in a comparative study on the Dead Sea Scrolls and Paul,[52] such mechanisms of exclusion may be based on concerns about the (moral) purity of the community. I would argue the same for the Matthean community.[53] For Pauline and Matthean communities, impurity resulting from sin (moral impurity) would have threatened the status of "the elect," that is, the members of the associations in question. Such views make sense when understood within the wider context of a first-century Jewish communal worldview, in which Torah observance and related purity issues were a major concern.

Conclusion

Entering a synagogue with Paul — what should we expect to encounter? Two key conclusions stand out. First, the institutional climate in which Torah observance was formed was open and non-static, lacking supra-local authority structures and thus allowing for local variation with regard to what constituted Torah observance and which texts would be important for establishing this.

51. Cf. also 1QSa and 1QSb, as well as the Damascus Document with its complicated relationship to 1QS.

52. Cecilia Wassen, "Do You Have to Be Pure in a Metaphorical Temple? Sanctuary Metaphors and Construction of Sacred Space in the Dead Sea Scrolls and Paul's Letters," in *Purity, Holiness, and Identity in Judaism and Christianity: Essays in Memory of Susan Haber* (ed. Carl S. Ehrlich, Anders Runesson, and Eileen M. Schuller; WUNT I 305; Tübingen: Mohr Siebeck, 2013), 55-86. See also the discussion in Stephen Westerholm, "Is Nothing Sacred? Holiness in the Writings of Paul," in *Purity, Holiness, and Identity in Judaism and Christianity: Essays in Memory of Susan Haber* (ed. Carl S. Ehrlich, Anders Runesson, and Eileen M. Schuller; WUNT I 305; Tübingen: Mohr Siebeck, 2013), 87-99, which comes to slightly different conclusions in this regard.

53. Anders Runesson, "Purity, Holiness, and the Kingdom of Heaven in Matthew's Narrative World," in *Purity, Holiness, and Identity in Judaism and Christianity: Essays in Memory of Susan Haber* (ed. Carl S. Ehrlich, Anders Runesson, and Eileen M. Schuller; WUNT I 305; Tübingen: Mohr Siebeck, 2013), 144-80.

This is especially true for the municipal synagogue institutions in the land, but also for the more open among the Jewish associations in the Diaspora. The specific groups that assembled in separate, or more sectarian, associations maintained their own distinct understanding of ideal Torah observance. Any attempts at generalizing what Torah observance constituted in communal local-specific settings to apply to all or most Jewish communities are therefore inherently precarious and at risk of falling prey to what Donald Binder has called provincialism (cf. anatopism), a common methodological flaw across most historical disciplines.[54]

Second, while generalizations should be avoided, there are some elements that stand out as common to most Jewish communities. Purity concerns, for example, seem to have been universally understood as important, both in the land and in the Diaspora, both among those who belonged to specific groups and those who did not, that is, the majority. If there is something that characterizes Common Judaism, defined as beliefs and practices that the people and the priests agreed on, this is it. This understanding of Torah was shaped in institutions in which weekly reading, expounding, and discussion of Torah was a key activity.

Thus, contrary to Christian desires and educational programs, which tend to focus on prophetic texts as background material necessary for the understanding of the New Testament, various interpretations of the book of Leviticus seem to have been what influenced most people's lives. Interestingly, Paul seems to have shared such concerns as he perceived his *ekklēsiai*, including the bodies of its members, as holy space, an abode within which the Spirit of God was to dwell.[55] Since, for Paul, one has to be pure even in a metaphorical temple, the apostle emerges as firmly embedded within first-century Jewish sensitivities in his understanding of Torah observance as meant to bring about conditions on earth that are acceptable to the God of Israel.[56] The keeping of

54. Binder, *Temple Courts,* 89. The core problem lies in the temptation to generalize conclusions drawn based on local-specific evidence beyond the geographical or institutional range covered by that evidence.

55. See, for example, 1 Cor. 3:16-17; 6:17-20; 2 Cor. 6:16-18; cf. Rom. 15:16; 1 Cor. 1:2; 9:13-14; 2 Cor. 1:1; Phil. 1:1; 4:21. It should be noted that many Diaspora synagogues were regarded as sacred space. See, for example, Levine, *Ancient Synagogue,* 86; Binder, *Temple Courts,* 32. What Paul is doing when he speaks of the *ekklēsia* as holy space where God dwells is to give already existing notions of holiness related to Jewish synagogue institutions an additional level of theological meaning.

56. Note that Paul's focus is on moral, rather than ritual, purity. See Klawans, *Impurity,* who compares Jesus and Paul, noting that while Paul seems uninterested in ritual purity "we still see some degree of continuity in his lasting interest in the notion of moral defilement" (156).

the law, while for Paul subsumed under the category of Christ and enabled only through the active interference of the Holy Spirit (Rom. 5:5; 13:10; cf. 1 Cor. 7:19), will produce behavior that does not defile the person morally (Gal. 5:22) and so allows for God's presence in the midst of those Jews and non-Jews who affiliate themselves with the Messiah (1 Thess. 2:12; Rom. 14:17).[57] Entering a synagogue with Paul would have meant affirmation of one's fundamental understanding of the Jewish worldview, with the added announcement from the apostle that there was now a new way for Jews and non-Jews alike to be reached by God's mercy as the kingdom was fast approaching.[58]

We should perhaps also note, finally, the fact that the institutional setting that eventually gave rise to what is today known as Judaism and Christianity was not the public synagogues of the land in which Jesus proclaimed his message but the Jewish associations in which smaller groups decided what was to be defined as Torah observance. Paul would have had a leg in both institutional worlds, although debates about the eschatological processes he understood himself to be a part of soon became isolated in settings less conducive to open debate among people conversant in Jewish ways of understanding Torah. Reading Paul historically within his own institutional settings, we need to find ways of cutting across these later contexts in which the church fathers wrote and reach back into the conceptual and material world(s) of first-century synagogues. As we do so, we should expect to find, at times, opposing views on what Torah observance really means on a scale surpassing the diversity we find in modern forms of Rabbinic Judaism, as I noted at the beginning of this essay, even when it comes to such controversial issues as the identification of who belongs within the people of God.

57. Paul uses sacrificial language to emphasize the importance of his communities' members being acceptable to God (e.g., Rom. 12:1).

58. See Westerholm, "Is Nothing Sacred?" 97: "Certainly there is enough similarity [between Paul and the Dead Sea Scrolls] to remind ourselves that Paul is not un-Jewish when he gives language rooted in the Temple cult a radically different application. Here, as throughout this paper, we see that Paul, the apostle of Jesus Christ, retains a fundamental conviction that he held already as a zealous Pharisee: The holy God of Abraham, Isaac, and Jacob is committed to creating a people to share in his holiness and, thereby, a people in whose midst he may live."

The Meaning and Function of the Law in Philo and Josephus

John W. Martens

There is no questioning the importance of law for the Jews of antiquity[1] or the basic equivalence of the terms "law," νόμος, and תּוֹרָה.[2] But in the Hellenistic period, whenever Jewish thinkers began to consider the law of Moses, the ancestral law of the Jewish people, philosophical questions that emerged first among the Greeks and the Romans came to the fore. There is no way to avoid it: once one begins to think about law in the midst of Hellenism, issues related to the law's particularity and universality naturally emerge. Is this the only law? The best law? How is "this" law related to the laws of "others"? Is this law related in any particular manner to universal law, the law of God, the law of nature, or eternal law? It is in this context that I wish to consider the responses of Philo of Alexandria and Flavius Josephus to the meaning and function of the law of Moses. I look at how they understand the role of the Torah for Jews and the nations around them; I also consider the means by which the law was intended to create boundaries with other peoples and so remain the particular law of the Jews, or to break such barriers down and so function as a universal law for all people.

Both Philo and Josephus wrote about the law in the context of its national or ethnic significance for the Jewish people. It defines in many respects who the people are, especially in relation to the peoples and nations around them. For Philo and Josephus, the law understood in its national and ethnic implications forges the Jews as a continuing people and, in its ancient implications, a political entity. It also has, naturally, religious implications, defining the

1. Geza Vermes, "A Summary of the Law by Flavius Josephus," *NovT* 24, no. 4 (1982): 289.

2. Stephen Westerholm, "*Torah, Nomos,* and Law: A Question of 'Meaning,'" *SR* 15, no. 3 (1986): 327-36.

worship, practice, and beliefs of the Jewish people. The Hellenistic and universal tendencies of these two thinkers emerge in the consideration of "higher law" — that law which transcended written codes of law, such as the "law of nature" (νόμος φύσεως), "living law" (νόμος ἔμψυχος), and "unwritten law" (ἄγραφος νόμος).[3] Jewish law could be integrated with this type of Hellenistic legal and philosophical thought since Judaism proclaimed one God, whose law had been revealed in scripture, a religious and philosophical stance that was most amenable to linking written law to forms of "higher law." Philo has profound philosophical insights related to questions of the law, and while Josephus seems to absent himself from universalizing philosophical discussions, he still occasionally refers to the law of nature. As a result, both of them must be seen in the context of Judaism embedded in the matrix of Hellenism. Whatever the responses of these Jewish thinkers to the law of Moses, it is not just a Jewish response, but a Hellenistic response.

Philo on the Law

The law of Moses is the foundation of Philo's philosophy, yet even more the means by which he believes the vast majority of people should order their lives. The "vast majority of people" is not exclusive to the Jews, but inclusive of all humanity: Philo believes that the law of Moses is the law for human beings whatever their ethnicity, religion, or political affiliation. Since "the writings of Moses, properly interpreted, are simply for Philo the supreme and perfect statement of all religious and philosophical truth,"[4] the truth of the law reveals a claim that was not found regarding Greek or Roman written law: God, the true lawgiver, revealed the law to Moses, so all people should order their lives by it (*Sacr.* 131; *Mos.* 2.48). Since Moses' laws are given by the voice of God (*Mos.* 2.34; *Decal.* 15; *Legat.* 210), it is an immortal law (*Mos.* 2.13), designed to govern the whole world (*QE* 2.42).

3. On the relationship of these forms of law, see John W. Martens, *One God, One Law: Philo of Alexandria on the Mosaic and Greco-Roman Law* (Studies in Philo of Alexandria 2; Leiden: Brill, 2003); and Hindy Najman, *Seconding Sinai: The Development of Mosaic Discourse in Second Temple Judaism* (JSJSup 77; Leiden: Brill, 2003).

4. David M. Hay, "Philo of Alexandria," in *Justification and Variegated Nomism,* vol. 1, *The Complexities of Second Temple Judaism* (ed. D. A. Carson, Peter T. O'Brien, and Mark A. Seifrid; WUNT II 140; Tübingen: Mohr Siebeck, 2001), 361; André Myre, "Les caractéristiques de la loi mosaïque selon Philon d'Alexandrie," *ScEs* 27, no. 1 (1975): 37, 67; Adele Reinhartz, "The Meaning of *Nomos* in Philo's *Exposition of the Law,*" *SR* 15, no. 3 (1986): 340.

Hellenistic lawgivers might be divinely inspired, but these writers did not understand the law to be revealed by God. The Spartan lawgiver Lycurgus was inspired by the Oracle at Delphi (Plutarch, *Lycurgus* 5.3), but also by the laws of Crete (*Lycurgus* 4.1). Lycurgus only intended to create a polity for the Spartans, not that Sparta should impose its laws on other cities (*Lycurgus* 31.1-2). Cicero had higher hopes for Roman law, but he believed that the Roman "civil law is not necessarily also the universal law; but the universal law ought to be also the civil law. But we possess no substantial, life-like image of true Law and genuine Justice; a mere outline sketch is all that we enjoy" (*Off.* 3.69).[5] Cicero desired a written law that would govern all humanity according to the dictates of the "universal law," but believed that no written law, including Roman law, fit the bill.

This is where Philo is at once most Hellenistic and most Jewish. From Philo's perspective the Jews had a written law that was a copy of the law of nature (*Opif.* 3, 69, 71; *Abr.* 3; *Mos.* 2.11, 13, 48). It is a most outstanding claim: the law of nature, which Philo will equate with God's reason, or λόγος, and which was present at the creation of the cosmos, is fundamentally the law of Moses.[6] As a result, Philo believed that the Mosaic law should be observed, its precepts followed, by almost everyone, except those few heroes of the past and present-day sages who could follow the law of nature. And since Philo acknowledged that the status of the sage was unattainable for most, people needed the written law and had to follow its commandments. Philo's focus is often on the allegorical interpretation of law, but it is necessary to grasp that he does not reduce the written law to its philosophical meaning or general guidelines; Philo expects people to follow the whole of the law, doing the "deeds" (ἔργα) of the Torah (*Praem.* 82; *Spec.* 4.143).[7]

Philo's allegorical interpretation is not intended to diminish the unity of the Mosaic law: "[t]he legislation is in some sense a unified creature, which one should view from all sides in its entirety with open eyes and examine the intention of the entire writing exactly, truly and clearly, not cutting up its harmony or dividing its unity" (*QG* 3.3).[8] Neither is Philo's distinction between

5. Marcus Tullius Cicero, *De officiis* (trans. Walter Miller; LCL 30; Cambridge: Harvard University Press, 1913).

6. Markus Bockmuehl, *Jewish Law in Gentile Churches: Halakhah and the Beginning of Christian Public Ethics* (Edinburgh: T&T Clark, 2000), 108; and Martens, *One God, One Law,* 103-30. For a dissenting opinion, see Najman, *Seconding Sinai,* 80f.

7. Hay, "Philo," 375.

8. Unless otherwise noted, all citations are taken from *Philo* (trans. Francis Henry Colson, George Herbert Whitaker, and Ralph Marcus; 12 vols.; LCL; Cambridge: Harvard University

the letter of the law and the inner meaning of the law intended to weaken adherence to the commands (*Agr.* 157). The inner meaning of the law is clearly more important for Philo, but he still wants people to follow every law. Philo refuses to reduce the law to its symbolic or allegorical meaning. In *Migr.* 89, he rejects those who are "overpunctilious" regarding symbolic readings of the laws while treating the literal laws with "easy-going neglect." He continues in *Migr.* 92-93 to agree that circumcision, for instance, is symbolically about excising pleasure and pruning the passions, but says, "let us not on this account repeal the law laid down for circumcising" for "we must pay heed to the letter of the laws" (*Migr.* 93).

Philo also accounts for the laws of other nations, claiming that any law that is in accord with nature in the code of another city or state is already found in Moses' law (*Congr.* 120). Zeno (*Prob.* 57), Heraclitus (*QG* 4.152), and Socrates (*QG* 2.6; *Spec.* 4.61) all drew laws from the Mosaic code. Those laws that do not agree with the law of Moses Philo explains as "additions" to nature and inventions (*Ios.* 29-31).[9] This is why Moses' laws won fame (*Mos.* 1.1; 2.20), why he was the best of all lawgivers (*Mos.* 2.12), and why almost every other people honors and respects the Mosaic law (*Mos.* 2.17, 43). Yet in a moment of rare sentiment, Philo speaks of the Jewish ἔθνος as an orphan who never receives international aid because "the Jewish nation has none to take its part, as it lives under exceptional laws which are necessarily grave and severe, because they inculcate the highest standard of virtue" (*Spec.* 4.179). This does not sound like a philosopher who believes that all those around him accept the law of his polity.

Why then does Philo make such claims, practical and philosophical, about the superiority and fame of the law of Moses? He has no choice if "the world is in harmony with the Law, and the Law with the world, and that the man who observes the Law is constituted thereby a loyal citizen of the world (κοσμοπολίτης), regulating his doings by the purpose and will of Nature, in accordance with which the entire world itself also is administered" (*Opif.* 3). Philo's view of the Mosaic law as the true and reasonable copy of the law of nature is dependent on his view of a transcendent God and God's role as the Creator of nature and law. At a practical level, it leads Philo to stretch the truth about the acceptance of the Mosaic law by other nations or people. He might also intend to counter polemic directed against the Jews, which claims they are

Press, 1929-62) and *Josephus* (trans. H. St. J. Thackeray et al.; 10 vols.; LCL; Cambridge: Harvard University Press, 1926-65).

9. Alan Mendelson, *Philo's Jewish Identity* (Atlanta: Scholars, 1988), 27-28, points out that in practice Philo accepts other people's laws (see *Ebr.* 36-37, 80-81).

misanthropic (*Legat.* 353; *Contempl.* 24), or to defend the Jewish polity in general (*Legat.* 115-17; *Prob.* 75-87). Finally, he desires to convince Jews, especially those philosophically inclined and attracted to Hellenism, not to apostatize and to exchange the Mosaic law for that of the Romans or other nations, as his own nephew Tiberius Alexander did.

There is no reason to abandon the law of Moses, Philo says, since the laws that govern the Jewish polity govern the world polity itself. The laws of Moses are "most excellent and truly come from God" (*Mos.* 2.12). André Myre points to the tension of claiming equality between the written law and the eternal law, pointing out that "la caractère historique de la révélation s'oppose à sa préexistence."[10] How does one resolve this tension between the historic character of written law and the preexistence of the law of nature? Philo claims that the differences between the two laws rest more with the people who do the law than the forms of law. Philo makes two moves: first, he connects all forms of higher law to one another and then to the law of Moses; he then claims that certain people could follow "higher law" without benefit of a written code.[11] The unity, of course, is a result of Philo's use of all forms of higher law in Greek legal thought. He alters "unwritten law" to signify one who follows the law of nature and who becomes its embodiment. The "living law" comes to mean not only one who is the king, but the one who follows the law of nature. These forms of law find their content in the law of Moses.[12]

Who could follow law by nature? According to Philo, the patriarchs followed nature and became the archetypes for the written law (*Prob.* 62). The patriarchs followed the law guided only by reason and it seems that Philo believes they actually observed the laws of Moses.[13] In *Abr.* 4–5, Philo says that the "originals" of the particular laws are the men who "lived good and blameless lives" and are "living and reasonable" laws. Moses writes of them for two reasons: to show that the "enacted ordinances are not inconsistent

10. Myre, "Les caractéristiques," 67.

11. Hay, "Philo," 374-75, speaks of how Philo connects the Mosaic law to the law of nature, to the living law, and to the unwritten law, which leads to the "audacious claim" that the law of Moses is valid for all humanity. Those who follow Moses' law "are citizens of the world — and they only!" See also Martens, *One God, One Law,* especially 103-30 and 131-48.

12. Martens, *One God, One Law,* 103-30.

13. Erwin Ramsdell Goodenough, *By Light, Light: The Mystic Gospel of Hellenistic Judaism* (New Haven: Yale University Press, 1935), 74, rejects the view that the patriarchs were "bundles of commands which were written down by Moses...there is no thought of deducing the specific commands from the incidents of the lives of the Patriarchs," as does Najman, *Seconding Sinai,* 80-89.

with nature"; and to demonstrate that the written law is not difficult to follow because earlier generations followed the unwritten law (*Abr.* 5). The enacted laws, therefore, "are nothing else than memorials of the life of the ancients," "preserving to a later generation their actual words and deeds" (*Abr.* 5). The enacted ordinances are not only consistent with nature, they "preserve" the actual "deeds and words" of the patriarchs. Again, in *Abr.* 275-76, Philo follows Genesis 26:5 when he claims that Abraham was said to have done "the divine law and all the divine commands." Philo replaces the verb "guard" or "protect" from the LXX (φυλάσσω) with "do" (ποιέω) and says that Abraham "did" (ἐποίησεν) these laws, not that he "guarded" or "protected" them. This alteration is replicated in *Migr.* 130, where Philo takes up Genesis 26:5 once again and again replaces φυλάσσω with ποιέω. Philo says that Abraham "did (ἐποίησεν) all my [God's] law (πάντα τὸν νόμον μου)." Philo also describes Abraham's actions more explicitly:

> "Law" being evidently nothing else than the divine word enjoining what we ought to do and forbidding what we should not do, as Moses testifies by saying, "he received a law from His words" (Deut. 33:3-4). If, then, the law is a Divine word, and the man of true worth "does" (ποιεῖ) the law, he assuredly "does" (ποιεῖ) the word: so that, as I said, God's words are the wise man's doings (πράξεις). (*Migr.* 130)

That the patriarchs transcend the written law does not mean for Philo that they surpass the contents of the written code, as one does in Greek and Roman natural law. Rather, the patriarchs provide the models for the laws and demonstrate conformity with the law of Moses.

Did Philo think it still possible in his day for an individual to follow the law of nature without knowing of the law of Moses? Philo believes that just as "in the past there have been those . . . who took God for their sole guide and lived according to a law of nature's right reason," so "also in our own time there are still men formed as it were in the likeness of the original picture supplied by the high excellence of sages" (*Prob.* 62). Philo provides an example of Gentiles observing the law of nature in *Spec.* 2.42-48. In the midst of a discussion of the Sabbath and other festivals, Philo discusses the feast of "every day" (ἅπασα ἡμέρα), based on Numbers 28:1-7, and the instructions regarding the "continual" offerings. He understands these verses to mean that "every day" is a feast for the special few, those righteous people who follow nature and its ordinances (*Spec.* 2.42), some of whom are Greeks and Barbarians (*Spec.* 2.44). Philo says, "they are the closest observers of nature and all that it contains . . .

true cosmopolitans (κοσμοπολίτας) who have recognized the world to be a city having for its citizens the associates of wisdom, registered as such by virtue to whom is entrusted the headship of the universal commonwealth (τὸ κοινὸν πολίτευμα)" (*Spec.* 2.45). These Gentile "cosmopolitans" (as in *Mos.* 2.51 and *Opif.* 3) "make their whole life a feast. These are indeed but a small number left in their cities like an ember of wisdom to smoulder, that virtue may not be altogether lost to our race" (*Spec.* 2.46, 47). If everyone were as virtuous as this small number of Gentiles, every day in the world would indeed be a feast (*Spec.* 2.48). In *Spec.* 2.73, Philo grants that Gentiles are aliens to the Jewish polity "unless indeed by a transcendency of virtues he converts even it into a tie of kinship, since it is a general truth that common citizenship rests on virtues and laws which propound the morally beautiful." Taken together, these passages indicate that the virtuous Gentile can indeed follow the law of nature, and, somehow, even the law of Moses.

In *Mos.* 2.44, Philo writes of his desire that "each nation would abandon its peculiar ways, and, throwing overboard their ancestral customs, turn to honouring our laws alone." David Hay argues that this passage points to a time when all people will follow the law of Moses in the eschatological future.[14] My reading of this passage indicates only Philo's hope for such a time, which could occur even in his lifetime. In any case, even apart from this hope, Philo's belief that a few virtuous people still follow the law of nature, and the fact that the law of Moses is in tune with the law of nature, opens up Philo's thought to a universality of law. The law is a means of following God and nature, which, for Philo, if not the Hellenistic world, is the same thing. It is how all humanity ought to live.

Josephus on the Law

Josephus's writing on the law is extensive, but much less philosophical than Philo's, though some of the same language and many of the same concerns appear. Josephus discusses the Torah extensively in 3.90-286 and 4.196-292 of the *Jewish Antiquities* and in *Against Apion* 2.164-219.[15] Geza Vermes states that Josephus characterizes the law "as a body of customs and statutes representing the constitution of the Jewish theocracy" that "assigns ultimate rule and

14. Hay, "Philo," 372.

15. Steve Mason, *Flavius Josephus on the Pharisees: A Composition-Critical Study* (StPB 39; Leiden: Brill, 1991), 96. The *TLG* returns a count of 517 uses of νόμος in Josephus.

authority to God."[16] For Josephus, "it is the means by which God governs his people and, Josephus argues, it is obeyed by the Jews in every detail."[17] Steve Mason, however, also demonstrates that while Josephus demanded scrupulous adherence to the law of Moses, he included in this law an "undifferentiated mass" of scriptural laws and subsequent traditions.[18] Nevertheless, the nation of the Jews was to obey and study all the laws (*Ant.* 4.309; *Ag. Ap.* 2.175, 257) and in Josephus's day would be loath to disobey the law (*Ant.* 3.317; *Ag. Ap.* 2.175). In fact, wisdom only resides with those who have precise knowledge of the law (*Ant.* 20.264).

And yet for Josephus the law of Moses is the best law in a limited way compared to Philo, for Josephus, like Lycurgus, is more open to granting that all peoples have laws they should follow. While Josephus claimed that people everywhere admired the laws of the Jews (*Ag. Ap.* 2.282), he says in *Ag. Ap.* 2.144 that "a wise man's duty is to be scrupulously faithful to the religious laws of his country, and to refrain from abuse of those of others."[19] Gentile nations have their own laws, which Josephus does not disdain (*Ant.* 4.139; *Ag. Ap.* 2.226, 257). Such limitations of purpose probably emerge from Josephus's own historical situation, which demands a vigorous apologetic defense of Jewish law and a light touch when discussing the laws of others.

The light touch is seen because Josephus tends to reflect kindly on the laws of others, omitting "any reference to idol-worship when he discusses the chastisements of the law with respect to breaking the commands of the Law of Moses" in *Ag. Ap.* 2.215-17 and 2.237, reporting that "Moses enjoined tolerance towards alien deities."[20] In Josephus's reflection on Exodus 22:27, Barclay shows that his caution might be part of a careful respect for Gentile sensibilities common among Jews at the time and perhaps dependent on Philo himself.[21]

16. Vermes, "Summary," 290-91.

17. Paul Spilsbury, "Josephus," in *Justification and Variegated Nomism*, vol. 1, *The Complexities of Second Temple Judaism* (ed. D. A. Carson, Peter T. O'Brien, and Mark A. Seifrid; WUNT II 140; Tübingen: Mohr Siebeck, 2001), 248.

18. Mason, *Flavius Josephus*, 103. See also Tessa Rajak, *Josephus: The Historian and His Society* (London: Duckworth, 1983), 168-69, who notes that many things that Josephus forbids, such as suicide, are not directly forbidden by scripture; cf. Sabrina Inowlocki, "'Neither Adding nor Omitting Anything': Josephus' Promise Not to Modify the Scriptures in Greek and Latin Context," *JJS* 56, no. 1 (2005): 48-65.

19. Mason, *Flavius Josephus*, 95 states that "scrupulous adherence to one's traditional laws is, for Josephus, a universal responsibility, binding on all nations."

20. Vermes, "Summary," 300-301.

21. John M. G. Barclay, *Flavius Josephus: Translation and Commentary*, vol. 10, *Against Apion* (Leiden: Brill, 2007), 306 n. 958.

Barclay shows that Philo in *Spec.* 1.53, *Mos.* 2.205, and *QE* 2.5 takes the same approach, and observes that "if Josephus does not take this point from Philo, he certainly shares with him a common tradition."[22] So, while Josephus touts the law of Moses for political and ethnic reasons, he desires to stamp out any tensions that might be inflamed.

Apologetic concerns do, however, lead Josephus to protect and advocate for the law against those who would deride it. Many types of anti-Semitic charges brought against the Jews are found in *Ag. Ap.* 1.223-320 and 2.1-296. On numerous occasions, therefore, Josephus will describe following the law in the context of "protecting" or "guarding" it (using forms of φυλακή or φυλάσσω), such as in *Ant.* 4.306, 309, 318 and *Ag. Ap.* 1.60, 212. Spilsbury states that "all of Josephus' works are aimed in one way or another at defending the Jews against various charges brought against them in Josephus' own time. This apologetic agenda colors everything Josephus wrote."[23] This extends to Josephus presenting the law of Moses as the best of all laws, emulated by the people of other nations, as in *Ag. Ap.* 2.145-56.

Apart from his desire to protect and guard the Mosaic law, Josephus understood the positive function of the law as a political and ethnic identity marker. The law of Moses is the best law, "and observance of the Mosaic Law indicated membership in the Jewish nation," but every nation must have its own law that grants membership in the polity of a nation.[24] Its cultural embodiment as a political and ethnic entity is the key element of the law for Josephus, not its philosophical or theological meaning.[25] The laws of Moses comprise a "constitution" (πολιτεία), as demonstrated in *Ant.* 3.332 and 4.198.[26] On more than thirty occasions by my count, Josephus speaks of the law in terms of the polity (πολιτεία) or the city (πόλις), and while Josephus's concerns were rarely religious, not concerned with topics such as "justification," "salvation," ritual cleanness, dietary laws, Sabbath observances, or liturgical rules, in *Ag. Ap.* 2.173-76 he stresses that Moses left for the people a "complete programme for living."[27] The political and ethnic nature of law in Josephus has become more

22. Barclay, *Against Apion,* 306 n. 958.

23. Spilsbury, "Josephus," 245-47.

24. Lucio Troiani, "The ΠΟΛΙΤΕΙΑ of Israel in the Graeco-Roman Age," in *Josephus and the History of the Greco-Roman World: Essays in Memory of Morton Smith* (ed. Fausto Parente and Joseph Sievers; Leiden: Brill, 1994), 17.

25. Spilsbury, "Josephus," 242.

26. Mason, *Flavius Josephus,* 97; Spilsbury, "Josephus," 242.

27. Spilsbury, "Josephus," 242; Mason, *Flavius Josephus,* 100.

apparent because the focus of scholars "on the Roman context has revealed Josephus' interest in the Judean constitution (πολιτεία)."[28]

There is also the odd reality, as many commentators have noted, regarding Josephus's presentation of the polity of the Jews, and that is his "notorious omission of all reference to the covenant."[29] Is this because of his desire to distance himself and Judaism from the land-oriented covenantal theology of Zealots?[30] Or is the idea of covenant replaced by that of divine providence (πρόνοια), in which God's support is made evident with those who prosper, as in *Ant.* 1.14?[31] Harold Attridge argues that any benefits the Israelites derive from God are "based not on any special relationship with God (as implied by the term 'covenant,' for instance), but on the Israelites' conformity to the will of God as spelled out in the Law of Moses."[32] Spilsbury sees the omission as arising from the "patron-client system of social relations prevalent in the Roman empire during the late first century," arguing that Josephus was indeed convinced of a special relationship between God and Israel (seen in *Ant.* 3.313, 4.114, and 7.380) even without the covenant language.[33] Whether we take the tack of Halpern-Amaru, Attridge, or Spilsbury with respect to the omission of covenant language in Josephus is of little concern for our discussion of the law, for "more important than God's alliance, however, is God's gift of the law which is described as the greatest of all God's benefactions" and gratitude for God's benefactions is most properly "expressed by obedience to the Law."[34] Israel's task, as Josephus expressed it, was to maintain "a life of piety which is defined explicitly as obedience to the Law of Moses."[35]

Is there a genuine universal dimension to the law of Moses in Josephus, however, as we saw in Philo? Does Josephus, apart from the apologetic aims

28. Zuleika Rodgers, "Josephus' *'Theokratia'* and Mosaic Discourse: The Actualization of the Revelation at Sinai," in *The Significance of Sinai: Traditions about Sinai and Divine Revelation in Judaism and Christianity* (ed. George J. Brooke, Hindy Najman, and Loren T. Stuckenbruck; Themes in Biblical Narrative 12; Leiden: Brill, 2008), 130.

29. Spilsbury, "Josephus," 248.

30. Betsy Halpern-Amaru, "Land Theology in Josephus' *Jewish Antiquities*," *JQR* 71, no. 4 (1981): 201-29.

31. Argued by Harold W. Attridge, *The Interpretation of Biblical History in the* Antiquitates Judaicae *of Flavius Josephus* (HDR 7; Missoula: Scholars, 1976), 86-87.

32. Spilsbury, "Josephus," 249.

33. Spilsbury, "Josephus," 249, and "God and Israel in Josephus: A Patron-Client Relationship," in *Understanding Josephus: Seven Perspectives* (ed. Steve Mason; JSPSup 32; Sheffield: Sheffield Academic, 1998), 172-91.

34. Spilsbury, "Josephus," 250.

35. Spilsbury, "Josephus," 250.

of his presentation and his guarding the law of the Jewish people, present a law that can be attractive to the Roman world and beyond? There are two aspects of these questions to explore here. Since the world is a "theocracy," all rule being placed in God's hands (*Ag. Ap.* 2.190), the Jews follow a law that represents God's eternal rule (*Ag. Ap.* 2.178, 184).[36] The "constitution," or polity, of the Jews is given by the ruler of the world and since Josephus does not discuss a special covenant relationship with the Jews, the special status for the Jews is that they have the law of Moses to guide them. While Josephus is most concerned to protect the polity of the Jews, he begins to evince a desire to have others participate in the law of the Jews in *Ag. Ap.* 2.209-12. John Barclay writes that "'friendly welcome' (active support) for those who wished to become proselytes may be presupposed by the fact that the phenomenon occurred at all, and with enough frequency (in Rome) to elicit hostile remarks from Tacitus (*Hist.* 5.5.1) and Juvenal (*Sat.* 14.96-106)."[37] According to Spilsbury, *Ant.* 5.97-113 demonstrates that

> ethnic descent from Abraham is subservient to obedience to the Mosaic Law when it comes to membership in the commonwealth of Israel. . . . [T]he position he is apparently countering here is one positing that outside of the land of Israel ethnic descent without detailed observance of the Law was a sufficient basis for continued Jewish identity.[38]

The relationship of the Jews with God is based on observance of the laws of Moses (*J.W.* 2.390-94), which is not required of other nations, but this reality also allows for anyone who follows the law of Moses to claim a place in the polity of the Jews. And if the laws of Moses reflect the laws of the universe (*Ag. Ap.* 2.284), and reveal the truth about God (*Ag. Ap.* 2.190-98), the one who follows God's law most fully lives according to the truth.[39] When you consider your law, revealed by the one, true God, to be in accord with the will of God, it is difficult to maintain your polity as simply one among many. While Josephus generally presents the law of Moses as simply the law for the Jewish polity, the practical apologist also hints at a universality underpinning the best of all laws.

But this hint leads us, finally, to Josephus's own discussion on the law of

36. Barclay, *Against Apion,* 262 nn. 637-38. Barclay states in note 637 that "as far as we know, Josephus coins the following term," that is, "theocracy," but discusses in note 638 the similar conceptions that were used by Plato and Cicero.

37. Barclay, *Against Apion,* 291 n. 846.

38. Spilsbury, "Josephus," 251.

39. Rodgers, "Josephus' '*Theokratia,*'" 132.

nature in his work, for which he might be dependent on Philo.[40] The phrase "law of nature" occurs on five occasions in Josephus (*Ant.* 4.332; 17.95; *J.W.* 3.370, 374; 4.382) with two additional, closely related phrases (*Ant.* 17.118; *Ag. Ap.* 2.199). Prior to examining the use of the phrase itself, it would be good to see how Josephus establishes the close relationship of law and nature in general. Josephus equates the law of Moses with nature in *Ant.* 1.24, in which he is most likely reliant on Philo's *De Opificio Mundi,* and in *Ant.* 1.19 he presents Moses as the best lawgiver, the one who emulated nature, probably dependent here, too, on Philo's *De Opificio Mundi* and *On the Life of Moses.* Josephus also claims that before the giving of the law the patriarchs were able to live according to God's law (*Ant.* 3.86-88) since the law of Moses is not just a collection of ordinances (*Ant.* 1.21), but "is also profoundly rational and in keeping with the natural laws of the universe,"[41] which means that law can be "accessed through reason *as well as* by the revelation to Moses."[42] What does this mean in Josephus's understanding, however, and how does he see the law of nature with respect to the law of Moses?

On a few occasions, the law of nature is synonymous with the will of God (*Ant.* 4.322; 17.95; *J.W.* 3.374),[43] but in each of these three instances this law of nature has to do with dying a natural death, as opposed to dying by suicide. It is a practical, not philosophical, argument based on what Josephus sees as the moral and natural way to end one's life, employed in an argument against the Zealots. In fact, Josephus claims that "suicide is repugnant to that nature which all creatures share and an act of impiety towards God who created us. Among the animals there is not one that deliberately seeks death or kills itself; so firmly rooted in all is nature's law — the will to live" (*J.W.* 3.370). Josephus is also highly critical with respect to Antipater's parricide, which he claims annuls "the law written against you . . . and the nature of justice" (*Ant.* 17.118). Josephus again criticizes the Zealots because they break the law of nature by not burying the dead (*J.W.* 4.381-82; cf. 3.377-78). Note that in all of these cases Josephus's understanding of the law of nature is related to death. It would seem that his concern with the law of nature is limited to criticizing immoral practices, mostly concerning the Zealots, related to death and dying.

This is the extent of the use of the actual phrase "law of nature," although

40. George P. Carras, "Philo's *Hypothetica,* Josephus' *Contra Apionem* and the Question of Sources," in *Society of Biblical Literature Seminar Papers 1990* (ed. David J. Lull; Atlanta: Scholars, 1990), 431-50.

41. Spilsbury, "Josephus," 248.

42. Rodgers, "Josephus' '*Theokratia,*'" 143.

43. Bockmuehl, *Jewish Law,* 109.

Markus Bockmuehl states that *Ag. Ap.* 2.184-89 and 190-219 offer the most extensive argument for the Torah's accordance to nature.[44] In *Ag. Ap.* 2.184, Josephus does describe the law of Moses as in "accordance with the will of God," which is language used elsewhere to describe the law of nature (*Ant.* 4.322; 17.95; *J.W.* 3.374), and in *Ag. Ap.* 2.199, sex is described as only natural among men and women, a common criticism of Greco-Roman sexual practices by Jews, but definitely based on Hellenistic views of nature as moral.[45] Elsewhere in *Against Apion* Josephus will say that although the Jews have no wealth or cities, "our law at least remains immortal (ἀθάνατος)" (*Ag. Ap.* 2.277) and "as God permeates the universe, so also the law has found its way among all mankind" (*Ag. Ap.* 2.284). It is also true to say that Josephus presents particular regulations of the Torah, especially related to the decoration of the temple, as reflecting the nature of the universe (e.g., *Ant.* 3.123, 180-87; *J.W.* 5.212-13). And yet it still seems clear that the law of nature is a limited concept for Josephus, related mostly to apologetic purposes.

Josephus seems genuinely to believe in the law of nature, but the concept is not developed philosophically but apologetically, especially with respect to practices regarding suicide and burial. Without question Josephus sees that nature is in accord with the law of Moses and the practices of the Jews, yet Josephus does not develop a theory of nature or law as does Philo. Josephus's view of the law of nature also does not impinge on his most basic understanding of how people should practice law: while the law of the Jews is the best, and Gentiles are welcome to observe it, it is still preferable for other nations to follow their own law, for that is what creates each polity and, ultimately, the law of Moses is the polity of the Jews.

Conclusion

While both Philo and Josephus consider the law of Moses God's gift to the Jews and invoke this law as an advantage for the Jews, Philo believes that the law of Moses ought to be followed by all those who cannot follow the law of nature, which would be the vast majority of people. Josephus is not as sophisticated philosophically or theologically, and he focuses more fully on the law of Moses

44. Bockmuehl, *Jewish Law,* 110.

45. John W. Martens, "'Do Not Sexually Abuse Children': The Language of Early Christian Sexual Ethics," in *Children in Late Ancient Christianity* (ed. Cornelia B. Horn and Robert R. Phenix; STAC 58; Tübingen: Mohr Siebeck, 2009), 227-54.

as a national law, a constitution for the Jewish people, which must be guarded and protected. This view depends not only on his temperament, which was less philosophical than Philo's, but also on his precarious position as defender and apologist for the Jewish people in Rome. Josephus would not mind if the Gentiles followed the law of Moses, but it is not essential for a true philosophical or good life. Philo offers us a far more robust view of the relationship of the law of Moses to other laws and the law of nature, which his philosophical and apologetic needs demanded. This reflection on the law of Moses was an unavoidable process of deliberation in a diverse and universal world. Was it basically one law among many (Josephus), essential for the Jewish people, or was it the universal law (Philo), given to a particular people, but available to the whole world as the truth had to be?

The questions with respect to the meaning and function of the law had to do in a profound way with their encounter with the complexity of the Greco-Roman world, but James Kugel indicates that some of the issues had to do also with something inherent in Judaism: it was a religion of laws.[46] When theological monotheism was confronted by philosophical universality, Judaism had to respond to these challenges, whether perceived as threats or opportunities. In light of Hellenistic speculation and application of new theories of higher law, it is clear that the law of Moses would have to be melded to or — at the very least — impacted by Hellenistic views of the universality of law in the guise of the law of nature, unwritten law, or living law. That Jewish thinkers were prepared and able to do so was due to the fact that they had an answer already in place: God gave us our law and since there is only one God, this law remains valid in some form, shape, or manifestation.

46. James L. Kugel, "Some Unanticipated Consequences of the Sinai Revelation: A Religion of Laws," in *The Significance of Sinai: Traditions About Sinai and Divine Revelation in Judaism and Christianity* (ed. George J. Brooke, Hindy Najman, and Loren T. Stuckenbruck; Themes in Biblical Narrative 12; Leiden: Brill, 2008), 6-7.

Torah Ethics and the New Testament

Jesus, the Eschatological Perfection of Torah, and the *imitatio Dei* in Matthew

Wesley G. Olmstead

In Matthew 19:16-22, an interlocutor approaches Jesus and poses a question of ultimate importance: "What good thing must I do to have life eternal?" (19:16). Jesus responds with his own question (19:17a), but his eventual answer — "If you wish to enter life, keep the commandments" (19:17b) — focuses squarely on Torah.

The pericope belongs to the Triple Tradition (cf. Mark 10:17-22; Luke 18:18-23) and, although the story proceeds along similar lines in all three Gospels, Matthew's distinctive shaping of the account both offers an important window onto Jesus' posture toward Torah in this Gospel and raises several important questions.[1] Even if it only makes explicit what is implicit in Mark, why does Matthew's Jesus say, "Keep the commandments" (19:17b)? Is obedience to Torah to be understood as a (or the?) condition of life? How does the inclusion of the command to love one's neighbor (19:19b) influence our understanding of the pericope and of Matthew's view of Torah? What is the intended rhetorical force of the young man's question, "What am I still lacking?" (19:20). How are we to understand Jesus' reference to "perfection" (19:21)? What is the relationship between attaining "perfection" and finding "life"?

Readers of Matthew's Gospel will know, of course, that this is not the first time Jesus has addressed issues like these. However else it functions here, Matthew's use of τέλειος ("perfect"; 19:21) seems designed to point readers

1. Stephen Westerholm, "Law and Gospel in Jesus and Paul," in *Jesus and Paul Reconnected: Fresh Pathways into an Old Debate* (ed. Todd D. Still; Grand Rapids: Eerdmans, 2007), 20, notes a prior question: why should the question even arise for a Jew in Jesus' day, who knew that "God had chosen Israel as his people. He had given them his law. He had told them, 'Do this and you will live'"? But, Westerholm suggests, "it is not strange at all that the issue became urgent, and its answer uncertain, for one who listened to the teaching of Jesus" (22).

back to its only other occurrence in the Gospel (5:48), where it stands at the climax of Jesus' programmatic treatment of Torah (5:17-48). In what follows, I take that cue and turn to a discussion of Matthew 5:17-48 before returning to Matthew 19.

Eschatological Perfection: Matthew 5:17-20

Matthew 5:17-20[2] opens with an abrupt correction: "Do not think that I came to abolish the law or the prophets" (5:17a). Matthew 5:17b emphatically echoes this denial ("I did not come to abolish") before correcting it ("but to fulfill"). That Jesus did not come to do away with the law and the prophets seems clear, but exactly what his positive statement entails is less obvious. Of the many interpretations of πληρῶσαι ("to fulfill") in 5:17, I restrict discussion here to the two I judge most likely.

Ulrich Luz is representative of those who think that in 5:17 πληρόω means "to accomplish completely," "to obey fully."[3] In favor of Luz's reading, there may be a parallel use of πληρόω in 3:15 where, as here, the voice of the verb is active.[4] Moreover, "to obey fully" (πληρῶσαι) follows naturally as a correction of "to abolish" (καταλῦσαι). And there are other early Christian texts in which we find a similar use of πληρόω (cf. Rom. 8:4, 13:8; Gal. 5:14). Nevertheless, this is not what Matthew typically means by πληρόω. More tellingly, Jesus' references to Torah in 5:21-48, the so-called antitheses, which are not merely about obeying the law, pose an important challenge to this understanding of πληρόω in 5:17.[5]

More probably, as John P. Meier has argued,[6] πληρόω has the sense here

2. On the challenges this text creates for contemporary scholarship, see Klyne R. Snodgrass, "Matthew and the Law," in *Treasures New and Old: Contributions to Matthean Studies* (ed. David R. Bauer and Mark Allan Powell; Atlanta: Scholars, 1996), 112.

3. Ulrich Luz, *Matthew 1–7: A Continental Commentary* (Minneapolis: Fortress, 1989), 260-65.

4. Only three of the sixteen occurrences of the verb in Matthew's Gospel are active in voice (3:15, πληρῶσαι; 5:17, πληρῶσαι; 23:32, πληρώσατε); all others are passive.

5. See Douglas J. Moo, "Jesus and the Authority of the Mosaic Law," *JSNT* 20 (1984): 25-26.

6. John P. Meier, *Law and History in Matthew's Gospel: A Redactional Study of Mt. 5:17-48* (Rome: Biblical Institute, 1976), 75-85; similarly, for example, Robert J. Banks, *Jesus and the Law in the Synoptic Tradition* (SNTSMS 28; Cambridge: Cambridge University Press, 1975), 207-10; Moo, "Mosaic Law," 24-30; W. D. Davies and Dale C. Allison, *A Critical and Exegetical Commentary on the Gospel according to Saint Matthew* (3 vols.; ICC; Edinburgh: T&T Clark, 1988-97), 1:485-87; Richard T. France, *The Gospel of Matthew* (NICNT; Grand Rapids: Eerdmans, 2007), 181-84.

that it typically does in Matthew — to answer the expectations of the prophets, "to bring to a designed end."[7] Not only is this by far the most common use of the word in Matthew's Gospel;[8] it is also the sense that has dominated the preceding chapters.[9] Matthew's readers have been prepared to understand the word in this prophetic sense. Moreover, this use of πληρόω is supported by the driving force of the narrative itself. Matthew 1:1–4:17 seems designed above all to announce that in Jesus the era of fulfillment has been launched. As Messiah, son of David, and son of Abraham (1:1), Jesus brings Israel's long and winding history to its climax (1:1-17). As Emmanuel, Jesus signals the returning presence of Israel's God (1:18-25). As king of the Jews (2:2), Jesus provokes opposition from the rival king (2:1-21) and, like Israel's first great deliverer, withdraws in the face of that violent opposition, only to return after the king's death (2:13; cf. Exod. 2:15, 20; 4:19). Recapitulating Israel's history, Jesus experiences both exodus (2:15; cf. Hos. 11:1) and exile (2:17-18; cf. Jer. 31:15). As successor to the eschatological Elijah (3:4; cf. 2 Kings 1:8) whose appearance signals the end of exile (3:3; cf. Isa. 40:3), Jesus announces the dawn of the eschatological kingdom (4:17; cf. 3:2). As the royal Son and Isaianic Servant upon whom the Spirit descends (3:17; cf. Ps. 2:7; Isa. 42:1), Jesus emerges from the Jordan. As the obedient Son, Jesus is tested for forty days in the wilderness, once more recapitulating Israel's history, but now with unwavering fidelity to the God of Israel (4:1-11; cf. Deut. 6:13, 16, and especially 8:1-5). In short, the use of πληρόω in Matthew 1–4 is anything but incidental. Instead, it punctuates these chapters, underscoring that to which the narrative persistently bears witness: in Jesus, God has answered his promises and Israel's history has reached its climax. The time of fulfillment has come and the long-awaited, eschatological kingdom has dawned. If we need further confirmation that this is how we should read πληρόω in 5:17, Matthew's distinctive formulation of the saying he records in 11:13 offers it: there, in the midst of his most explicit discussion of the Baptist's eschatological role, Jesus declares that "all the law and the prophets prophesied until John."[10] For

7. BDAG 828.4.

8. Twice πληρόω simply means "to fill up" — either a net (13:48) or a cup (23:32; cf. L&N 59.37; BDAG 828.1). Here in 5:17 and in 3:15 the force of the verb is disputed. Elsewhere, the word always means "to answer the expectations of the prophets" (1:22; 2:15, 17, 23; 4:14; 8:17; 12:17; 13:35; 21:4; 26:56; 27:9) or "of the scriptures" more broadly (26:54).

9. See 1:22; 2:15, 17, 23; 4:14. The use in 3:15 constitutes the only possible exception and even there Meier (*Law and History,* 79-80) makes a strong case in favor of the typical Matthean use of the word.

10. The key verb, ἐπροφήτευσαν, makes no appearance in the Lukan parallel (Luke 16:16).

Matthew, both the law and the prophets have a prophetic role. This is precisely Jesus' point in 5:17: he did not come to abolish the law and the prophets but as the one to whom they pointed all along. He was their eschatological goal. Finally, as we will see, this understanding of πληρόω is most capable of explaining the relationship between Jesus' teaching and Israel's scriptures as Matthew unfolds it in 5:21-48. There, as the one to whom the scriptures point, Jesus authoritatively declares how Torah is to be obeyed.

In 5:18, Jesus turns from his relationship to the law and the prophets (5:17) to the law's authority, addressing both its extent and its duration. We meet the former in the verse's hyperbolic central clause: the authority of the law extends to its smallest components[11] — Torah in its entirety is binding. The "until" clauses on either side take up the latter: for how long? But exactly how these temporal clauses answer this question remains disputed.

R. Banks insists that the second "until" clause is determinative and that "πάντα [NRSV, 'all'] here refers to the demands of the Law . . . not as mere imperatives but as signs which look forward to that which is now appearing in the teachings of Jesus. In it they are now about to 'come to pass' (v.18d) and consequently to 'find fulfilment' (v.17b)."[12]

In J. P. Meier's view, Jesus asserts that the law remains valid until a certain eschatological point (5:18b). Matthew 5:18d identifies this eschatological point — it is the entire career of Jesus that culminates in his death and resurrection: "In short, 18d says that 18b takes place at the death-resurrection of Jesus, which is the fulfillment of OT prophecies; vs. 18b says that 18d is the eschatological event ushering in the new aeon."[13] For Meier, then, "the binding force of the Mosaic Law . . . has passed with the passing of the old creation."[14] David Sim objects to Meier's reading (and, by implication, to Banks's as well) on the grounds that it flies in the face of the clear meaning of 5:17: "If the Matthean Jesus claims in 5:18 that the law does become invalid with his death or resurrection, then he obviously did come to abolish the law."[15] As we will see, however, 5:19 poses a more serious challenge to these readings than does 5:17.

The two "until" clauses are instead roughly synonymous, designed to em-

11. On the precise referents of ἰῶτα and κεραία, see John Nolland, *The Gospel of Matthew: A Commentary on the Greek Text* (NIGTC; Grand Rapids: Eerdmans, 2005), 220.

12. Banks, *Jesus and the Law,* 217.

13. Meier, *Law and History,* 64-65.

14. Meier, *Law and History,* 64.

15. David C. Sim, *The Gospel of Matthew and Christian Judaism: The History and Social Setting of the Matthean Community* (Edinburgh: T&T Clark, 1998), 125.

phasize the point that the law retains its authority until the end of the age.[16] As Davies and Allison observe, this does not mean that the two clauses are redundant; instead, the law remains binding until the end of the age (5:18b), when God's redemptive purposes are accomplished (5:18d).[17] In Jesus' argument, 5:18, introduced by γάρ ("for"), grounds 5:17: Jesus did not come to abolish the law or the prophets (5:17), *for* the law, in its entirety, remains binding until God's purposes are accomplished at the end of the age (5:18).

Just as γάρ binds 5:18 to 5:17, so an inferential οὖν ("therefore") links 5:19 to 5:18: *since* the law remains valid (5:18), those who break the least of its commands will themselves be called least (5:19). Here we meet the principal reason for rejecting the interpretations of 5:18 set out by Banks and Meier. While an attempt has sometimes been made to find in "these commandments" a reference to Jesus' own commands in the antitheses that follow (5:21-48),[18] the link between 5:18 and 5:19, secured by οὖν, makes this untenable: 5:19 envisions the ongoing authority of Torah for followers of Jesus. Nor is there any hint that this situation is temporary; in heaven's kingdom, the dawn of which John (3:2) and Jesus (4:17) announce, those who break the least of these commands will themselves be called least (5:19a). The future passive κληθήσεται ("will be called"; 5:19a, b) underscores the point.

Matthew 5:20, once more introduced by γάρ (cf. 5:18), draws the tightly linked pericope to its conclusion. The precise nature of the relationship between 5:19 and 5:20, however, is disputed. At issue is how we understand Jesus' reference to the "least" in heaven's kingdom (5:19). If, with the majority of Matthean scholars, we think that the least are assigned a lower rank in the kingdom, then Jesus' argument seems to be that deliberate violation of the least Old Testament commands (breaking them and teaching others to do the same) relegates one to a lesser position in the kingdom because entrance to the kingdom itself demands a lofty righteousness — one greater than that of the scribes and Pharisees. If, however, as some think,[19] the least are actually

16. So also, for example, Alan Hugh McNeile, *The Gospel according to St. Matthew* (London: Macmillan, 1915), 59; Moo, "Mosaic Law," 26-27; Davies and Allison, *Matthew*, 1:494-95; Snodgrass, "Matthew and the Law," 116.

17. Davies and Allison, *Matthew*, 1:494.

18. So, for example, Banks, *Jesus and the Law*, 220-23; Eduard Schweizer, *The Good News according to Matthew* (Atlanta: John Knox, 1975), 108.

19. For example, John Chrysostom, *Chrysostom: Homilies on the Gospel of Saint Matthew* (ed. Philip Schaff; *NPNF* 10; Peabody: Hendrickson, 1994), 16:5; Martin Luther, *The Sermon on the Mount and the Magnificat* (ed. Jaroslav Pelikan; Luther's Works; St. Louis: Concordia, 1956), 21:71; Schweizer, *Matthew*, 105; Moo, "Mosaic Law," 28.

excluded from the kingdom, then the argument is that deliberate violation of Torah excludes one from the kingdom because righteousness that exceeds that of the scribes and Pharisees is an entrance requirement. The theology that emerges from the Sermon on the Mount (e.g., 7:21-27) and from the wider gospel (e.g., 28:18-20) suggests that this minority view is probably to be preferred.

Matthew 5:17-20 comprises a potent affirmation of Torah and its abiding significance. Jesus did not come as the opponent of the law and the prophets but instead as their eschatological fulfillment (5:17). He defends this basic point by insisting on the law's abiding validity (5:18); his followers will therefore obey it (5:19), for entrance to the kingdom depends on it (5:20). At first glance, then, his treatment of Torah in the antitheses that follow seems puzzling.

Eschatological *Perfection:* Matthew 5:21-48

The conclusions we draw about Matthew's vision of the shaping influence of Torah on the ethical practices of Jesus' followers will turn, in large part, on our understanding of the relationship between Jesus' programmatic statement in 5:17-20 and the antitheses that follow in 5:21-48.[20] About this relationship, as we will see, we can draw at least two important conclusions. First, the antitheses begin to illustrate the nature of the surpassing righteousness that marks those who enter the kingdom (5:20). Second, they do so by giving examples of what fidelity to the law looks like in the new eschatological situation — after the Messiah, to whom the law and the prophets pointed, has come.

The first of Jesus' antitheses takes up the first command from the second tablet: "You shall not murder" (Exod. 20:13). Like the rest of the Sermon, the antitheses are carefully structured, the six antitheses arranged in two triads.[21] Five of the six antitheses begin with ἠκούσατε ὅτι ἐρρέθη,[22] but only the first antithesis in each of the triads features the full introductory formula: ἠκούσατε ὅτι ἐρρέθη τοῖς ἀρχαίοις ("You have heard that it was said to the people of old"; 5:21, 33). This full formula, assumed in the remaining antitheses, is particularly important. Τοῖς ἀρχαίοις identifies the original hearers — presumably the people of Moses' generation. Jesus' auditors have heard what was said to the ancients because this is how they encountered the ancient Torah — as it was

20. One of the tests of any exegesis of Matthew 5 is whether it is able to let both 5:17-20 and 5:21-48 have their full force.

21. See Dale C. Allison, *Studies in Matthew: Interpretation Past and Present* (Grand Rapids: Baker Academic, 2005), 173-215, especially 181-84.

22. The exception, in 5:31, is introduced simply by ἐρρέθη δέ.

read to them.[23] Jesus, that is, is not concerned here to contrast his teaching merely with contemporary interpretation of the law but with the law itself.[24]

A second formula, ἐγὼ δὲ λέγω ὑμῖν [ὅτι] ("But I say to you [that]"), introduces each of Jesus' responses to what they have heard. Δέ ("but") introduces the next step in Jesus' argument, in which he contrasts his own teaching (emphatic ἐγώ) with what was said to the ancients. Here then is a puzzle: Torah, which cannot be broken (5:18-19), nevertheless does not offer the final word (5:21-22). That honor goes to Jesus.

Matthew 5:23-26 draws out the implications of Jesus' eschatological fulfillment of Torah, as it relates to murder. If not only murder but also anger makes one liable to judgment, then (οὖν) the reconciliation of human relationships takes priority, temporally, over worship (5:23-24). What is particularly interesting here is that the worshiper is apparently not the one guilty of anger but is instead the one who has provoked anger; the logic seems to be that in offending his or her brother, Jesus' disciple has put that brother in the dangerous place in which anger would be a natural response. The situation is serious enough that worship in the temple should be interrupted; it can wait. In this context, 5:25-26 can hardly be read merely as a proverbial expression of wisdom: "it is better to settle than to be sent to prison." Instead, the point seems to be that settling with one's human adversary means not encountering the divine judge. This is what it means to be faithful to Torah, now that the Messiah has come and the kingdom has dawned.

We meet a similar intensification of Torah in the second, and perhaps also in the third and fourth antitheses;[25] the same cannot, however, be said of the

23. So too Chrys C. Caragounis, *The Development of Greek and the New Testament: Morphology, Syntax, Phonology, and Textual Transmission* (Grand Rapids: Baker Academic, 2006), 401.

24. So too Stephen Westerholm, "Law and the Early Christians," *Journal of Dharma* 22, no. 4 (1997): 415: "The suggestion that Jesus is here portrayed as merely offering his own interpretation of provisions in Torah comes to grief in those cases where he prohibits what Torah allowed. But it also fails to do justice to the contrast drawn in the antithetic formulation itself between ancient dictum and the authoritative declaration of Jesus." Contrast, for example, Matthias Konradt, *Israel, Church, and the Gentiles in the Gospel of Matthew* (BMSEC; Waco: Baylor University Press, 2014), 17 n. 2.

25. See Paul Foster, *Community, Law, and Mission in Matthew's Gospel* (WUNT II 177; Tübingen: Mohr Siebeck, 2004), 94-143, for the argument that the fourth, fifth, and sixth antitheses overturn, and do not merely, intensify Torah. Crispin H. T. Fletcher-Louis, "The Destruction of the Temple and the Relativization of the Old Covenant: Mark 13:31 and Matthew 5:18," in *"The Reader Must Understand": Eschatology in Bible and Theology* (ed. Kent E. Brower and Mark W. Elliott; Leicester: Apollos, 1997), 150, finds a relativization of Torah already in the third antithesis.

fifth antithesis in 5:38-39. When Jesus takes up the *lex talionis,* he does not merely extend the limitation on retaliation; he rejects the principle outright (5:39). Thus, in this fifth antithesis we can no longer speak of intensification of Torah; we can, however, still speak of intensification of demand. This is what it means to be faithful to Torah in the new age.

Like the fifth antithesis, the sixth and climactic one seems not to intensify the demands of the Hebrew scriptures, but to overturn them. While the first part of the citation comes directly from the pages of Torah (Lev. 19:18), the second ("and you shall hate your enemy") does not. Nevertheless, the notion that God's faithful people might hate their opponents (and his) is not a concept foreign to Israel's scriptures (e.g., Pss. 26:5; 119:113; 139:21-22).[26] Jesus calls his followers instead to love their enemies and appeals, for support, to the nature of Israel's God: those who love their enemies imitate their Father in heaven because he provides indiscriminately for his creatures, evil and good (5:45b, c). If they love only those who love them, they imitate instead the tax gatherers and pagans (5:46-47); if you only do this, what more have you done? Jesus asks rhetorically. But the rhetorical question (τί περισσὸν ποιεῖτε ["what *more* are you doing?"]; 5:47) is vital structurally, forming an inclusio with 5:20 (ἐὰν μὴ περισσεύσῃ ὑμῶν ἡ δικαιοσύνη πλεῖον ["unless your righteousness greatly *exceeds*"]) and signaling that each of the intervening antitheses illustrates the surpassing nature of Jesus' demand. Matthew 5:21-48, with its explication of Jesus' teaching vis-à-vis Torah in the era of fulfillment, has simultaneously been an exposition of the righteousness on which entrance to the kingdom depends. Torah remains binding for followers of Jesus, but now in light of its eschatological fulfillment in Jesus. What does it mean to be faithful to the law and the prophets now that the kingdom has dawned and the Messiah has come? Matthew 5:21-48 begins to illustrate precisely this. Jesus requires more than Torah.

Matthew 5:48 ("Therefore, you shall be perfect as your heavenly Father is perfect") draws the final antithesis to conclusion. If τέλειος means more, it cannot in this context mean less than the perfection in love to which Jesus calls his followers in imitation of their Father (5:44-46). The notion of the *imitatio Dei* that undergirds the final antithesis in its entirety receives powerful and explicit articulation here. And if it stands as the concluding imperative of the final antithesis, it probably functions similarly for the antitheses as a

26. Foster, *Community, Law, and Mission,* 132, suggests instead that "Matthew has stated what was for him the obvious corollary of the halakhic understanding of love of neighbours, namely hatred of enemies, and it is this implication that he rejects."

whole, standing over them all and drawing them to climactic conclusion. The antitheses, then, illustrate both the more that Jesus requires and the nature of fidelity to Torah in the era of fulfillment.

With respect to the commandments of Torah, we might summarize Matthew's conviction thus:

1. The commandments of Torah (indeed, the law and the prophets in their entirety) find their fulfillment in Jesus (5:17).
2. They remain authoritative and so are to be obeyed (5:18-19).
3. As the one to whom they pointed, Jesus determines how they are to be obeyed (5:17, 21-48).
4. Jesus requires more than Torah did (5:20, 21-48).
5. The more that Jesus requires is rooted in the love command (5:43-48; cf. 7:12; 22:34-40).
6. The more that Jesus requires consists of imitation of the Father in his indiscriminate display of love since, rightly understood, the love command is rooted in the character of Israel's God (5:48).

We are now in a position to return to our discussion of Matthew 19:16-22 and to observe that the parallels between the two texts extend well beyond their common use of τέλειος.

Matthew 5:17-48	**Parallel Motifs**	**Matthew 19:16-22**
5:20	In both texts, entrance to the kingdom is at stake.	19:16, 17, 23
5:18-19	Both passages demand obedience to Torah's commands.	19:17
5:21-26, 27-30, 43-48	Both texts refer explicitly to the commands about murder, adultery, and loving one's neighbor.	19:18 19:19
5:20, 46-47	In both Jesus demands more than obedience to Torah.	19:20-21
5:48	In both Jesus calls for "perfection."	19:21
5:48	In both Jesus calls for imitation.	19:21

Back, then, to the questions with which our discussion of Matthew 19 began. Why does Matthew's Jesus say, "Keep the commandments" (19:17b)? Is obedience to Torah to be understood as a (or the?) condition of life? If Jesus' teaching about Torah in Matthew 5 is to guide us, then Jesus invites the young man to keep the commandments because Torah remains binding in the era of fulfillment (5:18-19).[27] Rightly understood, obedience to Torah does remain a condition for entering the life of the age to come (5:20). But, as we have seen, obedience to Torah in the age of fulfillment must take that fulfillment into account. Matthew's distinctive inclusion of the love command (19:19), of the young man's question "What am I still lacking?" (19:20), and of Jesus' reference to "perfection" (19:21) all point toward Matthew 5 and remind readers of the fulfillment that has arrived with Jesus. The young man is lacking something because, however faithful he has been to Torah (19:20), the new eschatological situation requires something more. It requires fidelity to Jesus' own understanding of Torah, rooted as it is in the love command (19:19; cf. 5:43-48) and in the perfection that consists of imitation of the God of Israel in his indiscriminate kindness (19:21; cf. 5:48). It requires following Jesus himself (19:21). Jesus' call to "perfection," in 19:21 as in 5:48, is nothing other than a call to life. It responds directly to his young interlocutor's question (19:16).

The man's righteousness was inadequate, then, but not quite in the way so many post-Reformation exegetes have assumed. The problem is not best described as the self-righteous delusion of one who thought he could be perfect in his own merit. Instead, the man's righteousness was inadequate because he had failed to understand the more — the "greater righteousness" — that was required now that the Messiah had arrived, now that God's long-awaited kingdom had dawned. "Perfection" is the necessary human response to God's gracious kingdom initiative and was the goal to which the law pointed all along. Not surprisingly, this understanding of Torah that is grounded in the *imitatio Dei* shapes Jesus' encounters with both would-be followers and opponents throughout Matthew's Gospel.

Jesus, Torah, and the *imitatio Dei*

Twice in Matthew's Gospel, Jesus appeals to Hosea 6:6 ("I desire mercy, not sacrifice") in the face of Pharisaic critique: my mission, he argues, is rooted in the character of the God of Israel. The first of these appeals is found in Matthew 9.

27. This conclusion remains difficult for many exegetes. Ironically, Matthew's own redaction has inadvertently compounded the difficulty. When, for Christological reasons, Matthew turned the attributive adjective ἀγαθέ into a substantive, ἀγαθόν ("good thing"; 19:16), he opened the door for readings of the text that would focus on the young man's preoccupation with his own performance. NRSV and ESV exacerbate the problem by translating "what good *deed* must I do?"

Matthew 9:9-13

Matthew 5–9 consists of a carefully constructed synopsis of Jesus' Galilean mission (Matt. 4:23; cf. 9:35): Jesus teaches (Matthew 5–7) and acts (Matthew 8–9) with unique messianic authority. But Matthew 8–9 also depicts the posture Jesus adopts toward Israel's marginalized and it is this posture that becomes the point of dispute in 9:9-13.

The pericope recounts Jesus' call of Matthew, the dinner that follows, and the controversy that erupts over Jesus' scandalous dinner partners (9:10-11). As Davies and Allison note, Jesus' practice of table fellowship seems to have been informed by a particular eschatology and by a particular soteriology.[28] Both proved offensive. Since Jesus made frequent use of the banquet as an image of the kingdom (e.g., 8:11-12; 22:1-14; 25:1-13; 26:29) and since his own eschatology included a strong realized component (4:17; 12:28; et al.), it seems likely that both Jesus and his opponents saw in his table fellowship a deliberate anticipation of the final kingdom. If so, then this eschatological vision was simultaneously soteriological:

> [B]y eating with people who were outcasts Jesus was offering a prophetic symbol. He was announcing that the opportunity to receive God's mercy was being opened to all in Israel, including — perhaps especially? — those who had forsaken the covenant and were despised by most pious Jews. In Jesus' view the soteriological scheme of law and covenant had been relativized by his own person. . . . So the presence of God's eschatological envoy and the demand to respond to him and his cause gave a new opportunity to the outcasts and at the same time cut the old religious moorings of the "righteous."[29]

All of this seems helpful in understanding Matthew's Gospel, provided we understand the relativization of Torah and covenant of which Davies and Allison speak in terms of fulfillment. If Torah has been relativized, and 5:21-48 suggests that it has, that is only because, in God's design, the eschatological age has dawned — the Messiah to whom Torah pointed has come (5:17). He must inevitably take center stage. And he does: fidelity to the God of Israel is now defined in terms of response to Israel's Messiah (see, e.g., 7:21-27; 10:32-33, 37-39;

28. Davies and Allison, *Matthew,* 2:101.
29. Davies and Allison, *Matthew,* 2:101.

16:24-28). As important as these considerations are for our topic, however, at 9:9-13 my primary interest is in Jesus' response to the Jewish leaders' objection.

In Matthew, Jesus' distinctive appeal to Hosea highlights an otherwise mostly traditional response to his opponents. As in Mark, Jesus' answer begins proverbially: "Those who are well have no need of a physician, but those who are sick" (9:12). But before he turns explicitly to address his own mission, Jesus quotes the prophet: "Go and learn what this means: 'I desire mercy (ἔλεος) and not sacrifice'" (9:13a). Jesus does not, however, simply appeal to Israel's scriptures; more precisely, he appeals to the portrait of YHWH that is to be found there. He supports his own mission as physician to the sick by appeal to the God of Israel: YHWH himself delights in "mercy" and not sacrifice. Jesus' mission is rooted in the same delight; Jesus' mission is rooted, that is, in the *imitatio Dei*.

In its context, Hosea 6:6 explains why it is that YHWH's judgment "goes forth as the light" (6:5) against Ephraim and Judah (6:4). Judgment proceeds because YHWH delights in "mercy" and not sacrifice, in the knowledge of God rather than burnt offerings (6:6), but his people have instead "transgressed the covenant" and "dealt faithlessly with me" (6:7). Violence and infidelity have invaded the house of Israel (including the priesthood), defiling both Ephraim and Judah (6:8-10).

Several considerations, however, suggest that in Hosea 6:6 LXX ἔλεος denotes something more than kindness extended to other humans. First, as it often does in the LXX, ἔλεος here translates חֶסֶד.[30] חֶסֶד can of course be attributed either to God or to humans, who can in turn show חֶסֶד to other humans or to God.[31] Second, Hosea 6:6 takes up and echoes the complaint of 6:4, where the fleeting ἔλεος / חֶסֶד that YHWH laments is that which Israel offers her God: "What shall I do with you, O Ephraim? What shall I do with you, O Judah? Your ἔλεος / חֶסֶד is like a morning cloud, like the dew that goes away early." This link to 6:4 suggests that in the first instance the prophet's use of חֶסֶד in 6:6 also speaks to Israel's relationship with YHWH.[32] Third, when Hosea 6:6b, "and the knowledge of God rather than burnt offerings," follows 6:6a (cf. 4:1), the parallelism suggests again that ἔλεος / חֶסֶד, like

30. English translations of חֶסֶד in Hosea 6:6 vary (NRSV, ESV: "steadfast love"; NJB: "faithful love"; NET: "faithfulness"; NIV: "mercy"; HCSB: "loyalty"). As James Luther Mays, *Hosea: A Commentary* (OTL; Philadelphia: Westminster, 1969), 63, observes, "[n]o English word is a satisfactory equivalent for the Hebrew term."

31. BDB, 338-39; David A. Baer and Robert P. Gordon, "חסד," *NIDOTTE*, 2:211-18.

32. So too Hans Walter Wolff, *Hosea: A Commentary on the Book of the Prophet Hosea* (Hermeneia; Philadelphia: Fortress, 1974), 120.

ἐπίγνωσιν / דַּעַת ("knowledge"), has YHWH as its object. Fourth, we learn something about the ἔλεος / חֶסֶד in which YHWH delights by the contrast supplied in 6:7-10: what YHWH's people offered instead of ἔλεος / חֶסֶד was covenant infidelity (6:7-10; cf. 5:13). To be sure, Israel's covenant infidelity was expressed in human relationships (6:8-10) but, in the end, it meant "they dealt faithlessly with me" (6:7).[33] All of this suggests that in Hosea 6 ἔλεος / חֶסֶד describes faithful covenant love for YHWH himself. In this covenant fidelity YHWH delights.

In a 1977 article, David Hill drew attention to several of these matters. For him,

> [t]he entire message of Hosea is dominated by the theme of covenant-obligation, and when, in the midst of a denunciation of Israel's failure, the prophet expresses the divine demand as being for חסד rather than sacrifice there can be no doubt that he means covenant-loyalty, i.e. devotion and fidelity to Jahweh.[34]

For Hill, the point of the citation in Matthew's Gospel is not merely that God desires that humans show mercy, but instead (as in Hosea) that they express their fidelity to YHWH in concrete acts of mercy.[35] Hill thinks that Matthew was working directly from the Hebrew text,[36] but the LXX is also concerned primarily with covenant fidelity. The Greek ἔλεος, like the Hebrew חֶסֶד, is in both Hosea 6:4 and 6 directed in the first instance toward YHWH. No less significant, when we turn to Matthew, it is Jesus' own fidelity to YHWH and his covenant that comes under implicit critique in 9:9-13. In response, Jesus appeals to what YHWH himself delights in to defend his association with tax gatherers and sinners. But perhaps we can say more.

ἔλεος / חֶסֶד features so consistently in descriptions of Israel's God that when it is used as a covenant term for what YHWH requires from Israel (as in

33. In his classic study, *Hesed in the Bible* (Cincinnati: Hebrew Union College Press, 1967), 56, Nelson Glueck argued that in the prophets "one cannot discuss *hesed* as the conduct of men corresponding to a mutual relationship without looking at *hesed* at the same time as the conduct of men toward God."

34. David Hill, "On the Use and Meaning of Hosea vi. 6 in Matthew's Gospel," *NTS* 24, no. 1 (1977): 109.

35. Hill, "Use and Meaning," 110.

36. Hill, "Use and Meaning," 108; see further Robert H. Gundry, *The Use of the Old Testament in St. Matthew's Gospel with Special Reference to the Messianic Hope* (NovTSup 18; Leiden: Brill, 1967), 111, on whose argument Hill depends.

Hosea 6), it inevitably recalls the character of the covenant God. Of the many dozens of texts that demonstrate this, we pause to cite three:

> I the LORD your God am a jealous God . . . but showing steadfast love (ποιῶν ἔλεος / וְעֹשֶׂה חֶסֶד) to the thousandth generation of those who love me and keep my commandments. (Exod. 20:5-6)

> The LORD passed before him, and proclaimed, "The LORD, the LORD, a God merciful and gracious, slow to anger, and abounding in steadfast love and faithfulness (καὶ πολυέλεος καὶ ἀληθινὸς / וְרַב־חֶסֶד וֶאֱמֶת), keeping steadfast love (ποιῶν ἔλεος / נֹצֵר חֶסֶד) for the thousandth generation." (Exod. 34:6-7)[37]

> For the LORD is good; his steadfast love (τὸ ἔλεος αὐτοῦ / חַסְדּוֹ) endures forever (Ps. 100:5; cf. 1 Chron. 16:34, 41; 2 Chron. 5:13; 7:3, 6; 20:21; Ezra 3:11; Pss. 106:1; 107:1; Jer. 33:11)

Of the refrain ("his ἔλεος / חֶסֶד endures forever")[38] that runs through this last group of texts, Baer and Gordon comment: "This statement seems to have taken on an almost credal status by the time these texts were worked into the canonical framework."[39] Israel's God is the God of ἔλεος / חֶסֶד. Thus, when YHWH calls for ἔλεος / חֶסֶד, as he does in Hosea 6:6, he calls for a reflection of his own character. That this is in fact how we should read Hosea 6:6a is confirmed by Hosea 6:6b: the steadfast, loyal love in which YHWH delights is in fact rooted in the knowledge of God himself, the God who maintains steadfast, loyal love to his people.

All of this is particularly relevant for Jesus' defense of his mission in Matthew 9:13.[40] Like a physician drawn to the sick, Jesus embraces Israel's tax collectors and sinners; he does so, however, not only out of compassion or only because covenant fidelity is expressed in mercy (so Hill), but also (and more fundamentally) because the steadfast love in which YHWH delights is a response to YHWH's own steadfast, covenant love. In his messianic mis-

37. Cf. Num. 14:18; Neh. 9:17; Pss. 86:15; 103:8; 145:8; Joel 2:13; Jonah 4:2.

38. Often preceded by ὅτι ἀγαθόν (or χρηστός) / כִּי־טוֹב (so, e.g., 1 Chron. 16:34; 2 Chron. 5:13; 7:3; Ezra 3:11; Pss. 106:1; 107:1; Jer. 33:11).

39. Baer and Gordon, "חסד," 2:215.

40. *Pace* J. Andrew Dearman, *The Book of Hosea* (NICOT; Grand Rapids: Eerdmans, 2010), 196, who thinks that Hosea 6:6 is employed proverbially, "as a saying apart from its Hosean context, in the Gospel of Matthew (9:13; 12:7)."

sion, Jesus perfectly reflects YHWH's own covenant faithfulness. The point is driven home once more in Matthew 12:1-8, this time with even more specific reference to Torah.

Matthew 12:1-8

In Matthew 12:1-8, the evangelist once again depicts Jesus embroiled in controversy, though here it is his disciples' action that provokes critique: "Look, your disciples are doing what is not lawful to do on the Sabbath" (12:2). Thus, this Sabbath controversy is explicitly a challenge to Jesus' disciples', and by extension to Jesus' own, fidelity to Torah.[41]

In Matthew's account, Jesus responds to the Pharisees' charge by appealing to two biblical examples: the story of David requesting bread from Ahimelech (1 Samuel 21) and the responsibility of the priests to offer sacrifice on the Sabbath (see Num. 28:9-10). The first of these parallels the incident in Matthew 12 in that both actions are precipitated by hunger[42] and that both involve the followers of Israel's anointed (1 Samuel 16; cf. Matt. 3:13-17) but not, apparently, because both happened on the Sabbath.[43] No explicit conclusion is drawn from the first example. The second example is unique to Matthew and notes that the priests profane the Sabbath but are innocent because their responsibility in the temple supersedes their responsibility to the Sabbath command. Here Matthew does turn to explanatory conclusion: "Something greater than the temple is here" (12:6). The argument moves from lesser to greater (*qal va-homer*): if the priests profane the Sabbath but are innocent because of the greater importance of the temple and the cult (12:5), then Jesus' disciples are also innocent since the Messiah,[44] greater than the temple (12:6), is necessarily also greater than

41. On the precise nature of the disciples' offense, from a halakic point of view, see Isaac W. Oliver, *Torah Praxis after 70 CE: Reading Matthew and Luke-Acts as Jewish Texts* (WUNT II 355; Tübingen: Mohr Siebeck, 2013), 87-91.

42. Only Matthew explicitly notes the hunger of the disciples (12:1), strengthening the link to David's situation, as depicted in 12:3.

43. But see Ulrich Luz, *Das Evangelium nach Matthäus* (4 vols.; EKKNT; Zürich: Benziger, 1985-2002), 2:230, for the suggestion, based on Leviticus 24:8, that the incident did take place on the Sabbath.

44. Some have found in μεῖζον ("something greater") reference to the kingdom of God (C. H. Dodd, *The Parables of the Kingdom* [New York: Charles Scribner's Sons, 1961], 31; Oliver, *Torah Praxis*, 96-97) and others "more generally to the phenomena of the ministry of Jesus and the disciples and the reality of the dawning kingdom" (Donald A. Hagner, *Matthew 1–13* [WBC 33A; Dallas: Word, 1993], 330) or, on the basis of 12:7, to mercy (Luz, *Matthäus*, 2:232; Konradt,

the Sabbath.[45] That a Christological explanation is offered for the second appeal to Israel's scriptures perhaps suggests a similar logic at work in the first. The disciples' action is vindicated not so much by their need as by the presence of "something greater than David" — the messianic son of David.[46]

In 12:7, Matthew's Jesus continues his distinctive response by appealing once more to Hosea: "And if you had known what this means — I desire ἔλεος and not sacrifice — you would not have condemned the innocent." Jesus indicts his opponents not principally on humanitarian grounds but instead on theological, covenantal ones. Jesus finds fault with the Pharisees who charge his disciples with infidelity toward Torah not because they refuse to offer the mercy that overlooks human failings[47] — in Jesus' view, after all, like the priests in the temple on the Sabbath (12:5), his disciples are innocent (12:7c) — but because they fail to understand Israel's scriptures (12:7a). As in 9:13, what Jesus' opponents have failed to understand is the steadfast love for YHWH that expresses itself in mercy toward his people and is rooted in the knowledge of the God of Israel. The God who delights in steadfast, covenant love is the God of steadfast, covenant love. Preoccupied with fidelity to Torah (12:2), Israel's leaders have, in Matthew's view, lost sight of fidelity to YHWH himself (12:7). In his imitation of the God of steadfast love, Jesus embodies this fidelity.

As we have seen, for Matthew, Jesus is the Messiah to whom the law and the prophets point (5:17) and who determines how Torah, which remains binding (5:18-19), is to be obeyed (5:21-48). As there, so here, Jesus insists that Torah must be understood in the light of the character of the covenant God himself. Obedience to Torah in the age of fulfillment is rooted in the *imitatio Dei*.

Israel, Church, and the Gentiles, 111). But the neuter, which can elsewhere refer to persons (Daniel B. Wallace, *Greek Grammar beyond the Basics: An Exegetical Syntax of the New Testament* [Grand Rapids: Zondervan, 1996], 295 n. 7), probably does here too. Matthew may employ the neuter because it is Jesus' role rather than his person that is primarily in view (France, *Matthew,* 461), but more probably because he thought such a provocative self-reference was best couched in allusive and indirect language (Caragounis, *Development of Greek,* 235-40).

45. The parallel is not exact, of course, since there is no indication that the disciples serve Jesus in picking grain.

46. Several lines of evidence support this conclusion: (1) Matthew eliminates Mark's reference to David's need (Mark 2:25); (2) Matthew also omits one of Jesus' two concluding comments in Mark: the one that focuses on human need (Mark 2:27); (3) the concluding sentence that he retains from Mark focuses on Jesus' authority over the Sabbath as "Son of Man" (12.8); (4) twice more in this chapter, the evangelist depicts Jesus as "something greater" — ἰδοὺ πλεῖον Ἰωνᾶ ὧδε (12:41); ἰδοὺ πλεῖον Σολομῶνος ὧδε (12:42) — encouraging readers to reflect on the ways that Israel's history finds its climax in Jesus.

47. *Pace* Oliver, *Torah Praxis,* 97.

Torah, Jesus, and the Kingdom of God in the Gospel of Mark

S. A. Cummins

Consideration of Jesus and the Mosaic law in the Gospel of Mark has been undertaken in various ways, usually by employing detailed tradition-historical and redactional analyses. Discussions typically concern the extent to which Mark's Jesus, tradition, and Gospel in their final form reflect first-century Judaism, including halakic debates, and may be said to reject, revoke, relativize, or revise the law or aspects thereof, even as they otherwise fulfill, intensify, and universalize the Torah (e.g., in terms of principles, values, and ethics).[1] The approach taken in this essay is to offer a narrative and theological reading of Mark's presentation of Jesus, first briefly in terms of the prevailing perspectives in play and the participants involved, and then more fully, if necessarily selectively, in terms of Jesus' enactment of the kingdom of God in relation to the role of the Torah and the people of God. It will be argued that throughout Jesus is committed to and concerned about the Torah (and also the temple), and that the covenant life it seeks to effect in Israel is affirmed, taken up, and

1. All this often has in view Mark's audience and the Gentile mission. Among many studies, see William Loader, *Jesus' Attitude towards the Law: A Study of the Gospels* (WUNT II 97; Tübingen: Mohr Siebeck, 1997; repr., Grand Rapids: Eerdmans, 2002), especially 9-136 on Mark, and his more recent "Jesus and the Law," in *Handbook for the Study of the Historical Jesus* (ed. Tom Holmén and Stanley E. Porter; 4 vols.; Leiden: Brill, 2011), 3:2745-72. See also James G. Crossley, *The Date of Mark's Gospel: Insight from the Law in Earliest Christianity* (JSNTSup 266; London: T&T Clark, 2004), 82-124, 159-205; Heikki Sariola, *Markus und das Gesetz: Eine redaktionskritische Untersuchung* (Helsinki: Suomalainen Tiedeakatemia, 1990); John P. Meier, *Law and Love* (A Marginal Jew: Rethinking the Historical Jesus 4; New Haven: Yale University Press, 2009).

This essay is offered in appreciation for the significant contribution of Professor Stephen Westerholm to our understanding of Torah in Second Temple Judaism and early Christianity.

transposed in his own life and mission, death and resurrection, and thence in the common life and practice of the Christ-believers addressed in this Gospel. In this way its faithful readers may live truly human lives within the economy of God.

Perspectives Human and Divine: Mark's Narrative

Appreciating the role of the Torah within the Jesus-centered drama disclosed in Mark's narrative involves the reader's ongoing correlation and consideration of two overarching and interrelated levels: (a) a transcendent and apocalyptic perspective, operative throughout but especially in view at certain revealing "high points";[2] and (b) the earthly public ministry of Jesus from Galilee to Jerusalem, as his remarkable words and deeds announce and enact the kingdom of God, and provoke a range of responses from his Jewish contemporaries as they try to understand who he is and what he is doing. Moreover, with these two spheres in play, Mark's narrative can also be read (i) prospectively, as the reader journeys alongside Jesus, puzzling over and interacting with all that is involved, including the Torah- and temple-related events that develop and climax, and (ii) retrospectively, from the standpoint of its dramatic ending, with (iii) both of these dimensions located in relation to an advancing eschatological horizon yet to be fully and finally realized (in view, for example, in chapter 13).

Together these interrelated perspectives disclose a Jesus whose Spirit-empowered identity and mission, continuing and culminating that of Israel, entails the heavenly and earthly realms; encompasses the past, present, and future; and, indeed, functions within the entire unfolding work and will of God. Within all of this Jesus' role is not only that of teacher and prophet,[3] but also that of Messiah-King and Son of God who is a suffering Son of Man, crucified and risen, and ultimately that of glorified Lord.[4] It is as such that Jesus

2. Foremost among these are the prologue (1:1-15), Jesus' transfiguration (9:2-8), and the crucifixion (15:21-41) and resurrection (16:1-8).

3. Jesus is widely recognized as a teacher by his disciples (4:38; 9:38; 10:35; 13:1; cf. 14:14); people at large (5:35); needy individuals (9:17; 10:51) and other inquirers (10:17, 20; 12:32); and the Pharisees, Herodians, and Sadducees (12:14, 19). He is deemed a prophet by some (6:15; 8:28), though not all accept him as such (6:4; cf. 14:65).

4. On Jesus as "Christ," see 1:1; 8:29; 14:61; 15:32 (and see 9:41; 12:35); "Christ" in 15:32 is synonymous with "King of Israel" (see also "King of the Jews" in 15:2, 9, 12, 18, 26); on "Son of God," see 1:1; 3:11; 5:7; 14:61; 15:39; and on "Son of Man," see 2:10, 28; 8:31, 38; 9:9, 12, 31; 10:33, 45;

fulfills the Torah (and temple), and brings about the redemption and renewal of Israel and the world under God.

Participants: The Composition and Condition of the People of God

As will be detailed in the third section of this chapter, Mark's narrative indicates that Jesus takes up Torah in conjunction with a fundamental commitment to a varied Israel that collectively, if problematically, comprises the covenant people of God. Jesus' interaction with his Jewish contemporaries — encompassing his family, the crowds, needy individuals, leading groups, and first followers — involves a complex and often contested range of interests, expectations, and aspirations. And as his mission unfolds, the seriousness of Israel's situation, which is representative of humanity as a whole, comes increasingly into view.

Taken together, the nation is ill and infirm (1:32-34; 6:53-56), beset by unclean spirits and demons,[5] lacking leadership (6:34), and in need of provision and care (8:1-3). This is accompanied by an inability to hear, see, and understand aright (e.g., 4:1-20; 6:52; 7:14-23; 8:14-21; 9:30-32) and a vain seeking after signs, which lacks receptivity and faith (8:11-12, 38; 9:19). These characteristics attest to an underlying and intractable condition characterized as "hardness of heart" (compare 3:5; 6:52; 10:5). Too often occupied by sin and Satan, rather than the Spirit, Israel is divided and variously compromised (3:20-30), unable to comprehend Jesus' identity and align itself with his mission.[6] This condition evokes a range of responses from Jesus. He is, for example, "incensed" (1:41),[7]

13:26; 14:21, 41, 62. On Jesus as "Lord," see Daniel Johansson, "*Kyrios* in the Gospel of Mark," *JSNT* 33, no. 1 (2010): 101-24, discussing pertinent instances of the term, and arguing that Mark "claims that Jesus shares the identity of being κύριος with the God of Israel" (101). Note that all biblical citations in this essay follow the NRSV unless otherwise noted.

5. They, unlike human participants, identify Jesus' divine authority and power (see 1:23-24; 3:11; 5:6-8).

6. Correlation of the Beelzebub controversy (3:20-30) and the ensuing parables section (4:1-34) suggests that receptivity and understanding is bound up with God's overall purposes (4:10-12) and is a function of alignment with Jesus rather than Satan; unchecked, the latter leads to an increasingly intractable condition, with judgment its eschatological outcome (4:26-29). Israel's situation is symptomatic of a worldwide condition and struggle, as indicated by Jesus' encounter with the Gerasene demoniac in predominantly Gentile territory (5:1-20).

7. Here reading ὀργισθείς in 1:41, in conjunction with the force of ἐμβριμησάμενος in 1:43, on which see Joel Marcus, *Mark 1–8: A New Translation with Introduction and Commentary* (AB 27; New Haven: Yale University Press, 2000), 206, 209; similarly, Richard T. France, *The*

angry (3:5), astonished at their unbelief (6:6), upset in his spirit (8:12), ready to rebuke (8:33; 9:25), and, in Gethsemane, "distressed and agitated . . . deeply grieved" (14:33-34). Thus, the reader recognizes the crucial and continuing nature of Jesus' call to repent and receive the kingdom of God (1:14-15).

Performance: Jesus, Israel, and the Torah

This section explores Mark's presentation of Jesus' identity and mission, focusing on his interaction with his fellow Jews on the role of the Torah (and temple) for Israel within the purposes of God. In turn, consideration is given briefly to the prologue, which sets the parameters and agenda; the contested question as to what is (and is not) lawful and life-giving; purity as essentially a Torah-obedient pattern of life among and on behalf of the people of God; Jesus' transfiguration as signifying his embodiment of the Torah; and Jesus' last days teaching in Jerusalem, culminating in the realization and recasting of the Torah (and temple) through his death and resurrection.

The Prologue: God's Gospel, Israel's Story, and Jesus' Identity and Mission

The Torah operates within the wider framework of Israel's God-governed story as taken up in Jesus and the Spirit. This is evident from the outset in a prologue (1:1-15), which provides a privileged perspective on, and interpretative lens for, the dramatic narrative that follows. The title (1:1) and immediately ensuing composite Old Testament citation (1:2-3; Exod. 23:20; Mal. 3:1; Isa. 40:3)[8] indicate that Mark's Gospel concerns God's good news, anticipated in the law and the prophets (with exodus and exile associations especially in play), as announced by and centered on Jesus. This Jesus is Israel's Messiah, Son of God (see Exod. 4:22-23), and ultimately Lord, and he invites all to experience redemption and the end of estrangement by repenting, believing, and participating in the kingdom of God (1:1-3, 14-15). As the baptism by John

---

Gospel of Mark: A Commentary on the Greek Text (NIGTC; Grand Rapids: Eerdmans, 2002), 115, 117-18.

8. On this much discussed citation and its programmatic role in Mark, see Steve Moyise, *Evoking Scripture: Seeing the Old Testament in the New* (London: T&T Clark, 2008), 6-20. Among many studies on scripture in Mark overall, see Rikk E. Watts, "Mark," in *Commentary on the New Testament Use of the Old Testament* (ed. G. K. Beale and D. A. Carson; Grand Rapids: Baker Academic, 2007), 111-249.

and the temptation by Satan attest, this is to be accomplished by a self-giving Jesus who, in the face of testing, not least in relation to the Torah (and temple), remains faithful to his God-affirmed identity and Spirit-empowered mission.[9]

Synagogue, Sabbath, and What Is Lawful and Life-Giving

Much of Jesus' Galilean mission revolves around the synagogue, the Sabbath, and questions concerning what is (or is not) lawful — a matter which, as we will see, persists until his last days in Jerusalem.[10] So, for example, at Capernaum on the Sabbath (1:21-28) he astounds all present with his new teaching ("and not as the scribes," 1:22), and by powerfully healing a man with an unclean spirit. This command performance, authoritatively and innovatively addressing from within an instance of Israel's infirmity, is immediately broadcast around Galilee (1:28) and indeed typifies Jesus' mission throughout the area (1:39).

That Jesus' practice and pattern indicates a critical commitment to and concern for the well-being of the Jewish people and their way of life is again evident in his cleansing of a leper (1:40-45), whose condition also epitomizes a needy Israel. Incensed at the situation, Jesus reaches out, addresses, heals, and commands.[11] Significantly, and evidently integral to the scenario, he then follows the Torah by instructing the healed man to "show yourself to the priest, and offer for your cleansing what Moses commanded" (1:44; see Leviticus 13–14). While Jesus follows Torah (and temple) practice, as the additional "as a testimony to them" intimates, there may be a polemical element in play too: Jesus is highlighting the need for purity in Israel and its leaders, while also attesting to the cleansing being accomplished in his own mission.[12] Jesus

9. Certain features of the baptism — for example, "the heavens torn apart" (1:10; cf. Isa. 64:1); the descending Spirit and divine affirmation of Jesus as Son (1:11; cf. Ps. 2:7 and Isa. 42:1) — anticipate the ensuing narrative: God is powerfully at work in Jesus as Israel's anointed Messiah-King, who is appointed as a (suffering) servant to bring justice, light, and healing.

10. On Jesus and Sabbath, see, for example, Lutz Doering, "Sabbath Laws in the New Testament Gospels," in *The New Testament and Rabbinic Literature* (ed. Reimund Bieringer et al.; JSJSup 136; Leiden: Brill, 2010), 207-53; and his comprehensive study *Schabbat: Sabbathalacha und -praxis im antiken Judentum und Urchristentum* (TSAJ 78; Tübingen: Mohr Siebeck, 1999).

11. For arguments countering the view that Jesus' touching the leper necessarily rendered him impure and was contrary to biblical law, see Crossley, *Date*, 87-92.

12. On this reading Jesus' instruction is not simply a ploy designed to confront and dismiss the Jewish authorities (see further the discussion in Loader, *Law*, 21-22), but rather exemplifies a fundamental concern for a Torah-obedient way of life in Israel, not least among its leaders.

upholds the Torah, and urges even as he engenders its efficacious outworking in Israel.

The seriousness of Israel's situation is pressed further in the healing of a paralytic (2:1-12), though in Jesus' home rather than the synagogue. Noting the faith of those acting on the man's behalf (2:3-5a), Jesus first declares his sins forgiven (2:5b). This incurs the charge of blasphemy from some of the scribes who are present and questioning in their hearts (2:6-8), an indictment on which Jesus is eventually convicted by the Sanhedrin (14:64). His rhetorical response to these experts in the Torah presses back: that he commands ("Stand up and take your mat and walk," 2:9) and can heal indicates that he can also forgive. Jesus seeks among the scribes an alignment in their understanding of the law and of his identity and mission as authoritative Son of Man (2:12).

This is also attested in Jesus' response to certain Pharisees who question why his disciples do not fast (2:18-22). Jesus has just shared a meal with "sinners and tax collectors," been critiqued by "the scribes of the Pharisees" for the unclean company he keeps, and replied proverbially that he is reaching out to sick sinners and not the healthy righteous (2:16-17).[13] Now the meal becomes a wedding banquet (2:19-20), quickly followed by complementary illustrations involving the unlikely pairings of an old cloak/new cloth and old wineskin/new wine (2:21-22), which together indicate that fasting is not appropriate while in the presence of the newly unfolding and irrepressible kingdom of God. Jesus is not rejecting the role of fasting in its proper place, but rather intimating that what is envisaged by the Torah is now present in Jesus-centered association, participation, and celebration.

In the next scene, certain Pharisees declare it unlawful for Jesus' disciples to pluck grain on the Sabbath (2:23-28; see Exod. 20:8-11; 34:21; Deut. 5:12-15),[14] perhaps neglecting to note that the Torah also teaches compassionate allowance for the needy (see Deut. 23:25), because everyone within the covenant community should have benefit of the Torah's protection. Covenant-keeping and care are also implied in Jesus' ensuing example of David's expedient use of the tabernacle holy bread to meet the needs of his companions (2:25-26; see Exod. 25:30; Lev. 24:5-9; 1 Sam. 21:1-6). The implied realignment of perspective required of the Pharisees is then pressed by Jesus' ensuing remark, "The

13. Jesus is concerned for all of Israel, for everyone is in need. Yet the sick, mindful of their condition, may be the more receptive, while the purportedly righteous, perhaps inured to their need, may be less so.

14. Crossley, *Date*, 159-66, offers a sustained argument that Mark's Jesus in 2:23-28 does not condone non-observance or abrogation of the Sabbath, and his intra-Jewish dispute with the Pharisees is over their halakic expansion of biblical law on the matter at hand.

Sabbath was made for humankind, and not humankind for the Sabbath" (2:27; cf. Exod. 16:29), and taken even further with "so the Son of Man is lord even of the Sabbath" (2:28). This episode is not adequately or entirely explained as Jesus showing indifference, countering expansionist applications of the law to merely minor matters, arguing for one law overruling another, setting aside the Sabbath and Torah as such, or dismissively placing himself over and above the law.[15] Rather, the context indicates that the observance of the commandment demands that it be properly located within a Torah that is itself read in relation to Israel's redemption out of Egypt (Deut. 5:12-15), framed within God's design for all of humanity and creation (Gen. 2:1-3; Exod. 20:8-11), and then finally located in relation to Jesus himself who as "the Son of Man is lord even of the Sabbath" (2:28).

Similar themes are involved in the synagogue and Sabbath scene involving Jesus healing a man with a withered hand (3:1-6). Jesus turns the tables and asks, "Is it lawful to do good or to do harm on the Sabbath, to save life or to kill?" (3:4).[16] The onlookers' studied silence in the face of the law's own intent — Torah obedience leading to life over disobedience resulting in death (Deut. 30:11-20) — incurs Jesus' anger at their hardness of heart, as he restores the man's hand. This leads certain Pharisees to plot with the Herodians concerning how to destroy Jesus (3:6; cf. 8:15), placing themselves under the condemnation rather than the blessing of the Torah (see Deut. 26:16–30:20), and ironically foreshadowing Jesus' later self-giving, which is designed to deal with the fundamental issue (hardened human hearts) and achieve the ultimate end (human life renewed).

15. See further the discussions in Loader, "Jesus and the Law," 2749-50, and especially *Law*, 33-38. Note also Markus Bockmuehl, *Jewish Law in Gentile Churches: Halakhah and the Beginning of Christian Public Ethics* (Edinburgh: T&T Clark, 2000), 13-14, who cautions that a Christological reading of 2:27-28, even at a redactional level, needs to take adequate account of the original Palestinian context of these verses as pertaining to the Sabbath being for humankind's need and enjoyment, and the fact that the only two instances of "son of man" prior to the first passion prediction (8:31), namely, at 2:10, 28, "arguably carry none of this meaning but should be taken as a reference to humankind in general (as is the case for the plural υἱοῖς τῶν ἀνθρώπων in 3.28)" (13). See also, though, the discussion of 2:10-12 in France, *Mark*, 127-29, who argues that the healing (performed by Jesus in particular) and the unique power and authority at work suggest that "the dynamics of the passage are such that the title must be understood not primarily as identifying Jesus with the rest of humanity, but precisely as setting him apart" (128).

16. Precedent for acting to save life on the Sabbath may be found in 1 Maccabees 2:29-41; cf. *m. Yoma* 8:6; *b. Yoma* 85b. See the discussions and explanations offered in Loader, *Law*, 36-38, and Bockmuehl, *Jewish Law*, 7.

This sequence of remarkable episodes illustrates Jesus' early mission among his needy fellow Jews. It extends from those at the margins to others at the very center of public life, and shows his constant commitment to and concern for all of Israel. This includes upholding and fulfilling the Torah and covenant life, not least when pressed and tested thereon, by means of his authoritative and powerful words and deeds, which actualize the in-breaking of the kingdom of God. As difficult as it is to conceptualize and articulate, this would appear to entail more than saying Mark's Jesus "stands beside" even as (e.g., in 2:10, 28) he authoritatively and independently "moves[s] beyond" the Torah.[17] Rather, the commandments and the Torah function within — indeed, are taken up into — the dynamic unfolding of a Jesus-centered rescue and renewal of the people of God.

Jesus and Purity: Leadership and Covenant Life among the People of God

From the foregoing it is evident that Jesus is concerned that leadership — in the form of guidance, direction, and living by example — is lacking in Israel. A stark instance of this is seen in the retrospective account of the death of John the Baptist, who is executed on the orders of Herod Antipas (6:14-29). Notably, the event is precipitated by John's public condemnation of Herod's unlawful marriage to his sister-in-law (6:18; see Lev. 18:16). And the episode, which illustrates a conflicted Herod's misrule over his household and kingdom, is symptomatic of a wider malaise (see 3:24-25).

Purity and holiness are the foci of a complex, challenging, and contested passage in Mark 7:1-23.[18] The Pharisees and certain scribes observe some of Jesus' disciples eating with unwashed and thus ritually impure hands (7:1-2; see Lev. 15:11), and their concern and practice is explained parenthetically by Mark (7:3-4).[19] Jesus is asked why his disciples do not "live [walk] according

17. See Loader, *Law,* 37, who employs such terms in trying to express the continuity and newness entailed.

18. See Loader, *Law,* 65-69, for a structural analysis of Mark 7:1-23 within 6:7–8:26, and detailed analysis of the passage on 71-79; Loader identifies Jesus' authoritative declaration in 7:15 as the "punch line," subsequently explained by Mark in 7:19 (so "Jesus and the Law," 2751). On purity and this passage, see especially Meier, *Law and Love,* 342-477.

19. Mark's explanation — including connecting handwashing with various traditions of "all the Jews" (7:3) — has been variously viewed as generalized, hyperbolic, lacking in evidence, and disparaging (compare Loader, *Law,* 71-72). Crossley, *Date,* 183-88, allows that Mark generalizes and exaggerates, but argues that the report in 7:3-4 is not a complete invention and explains

to the tradition of the elders, but eat with defiled hands" (7:5). He responds by citing Isaiah in rebuking their hypocrisy for abandoning God's commandments for their own merely human tradition (7:6-8; Isa. 29:13 LXX). Not to be missed here are the wider Isaianic associations implying leaders who lack understanding (e.g., Isa. 29:9-16). The critique continues in 7:9-13 with Jesus' reference to the commandment to honor father and mother (Exod. 20:12; Deut. 5:16), which the Pharisees and scribes undermine by misapplying the practice of Corban.[20]

At this point Jesus turns to the crowd and urges them to listen and understand: defilement is not a matter of what is outside but rather lies inside a person — collectively, all people (7:14-15). This compressed comment is then explicated in private and in a more literal fashion for his disciples, who are also struggling to understand (7:17-23), in the midst of which is Mark's parenthetical and summary statement: "Thus he declared all foods clean" (7:19c). Loader contends that for Mark's Jesus the declaration in 7:15 is absolute, indicating an exclusive contrast, and it seriously contradicts the Torah.[21] Likewise, in the generalizing parenthetical remark in 7:19c, aiming to remove food laws as an impediment to Gentile inclusion, Mark declares what he knows "was contrary to the Law."[22] Thus, whereas to this point Jesus has been depicted as authoritatively "beside and beyond Torah," it now becomes evident that the ultimate outworking of this "may include permanently setting

---

aspects of Jewish halakah unfamiliar to Mark's readers. Meier, *Law and Love*, 399-405, regards 7:1-5 to be of "dubious historical character" (400) — and, apart from verses 10-12, sees little in 7:6-23 as traceable to the historical Jesus.

20. For a discussion of this practice, see, for example, Meier, *Law and Love*, 376-84; Crossley, *Date*, 188-91.

21. See "Jesus and the Law," 2751-53, and *Law*, especially 74-78. Loader notes that "[a]rguably, Mark (and perhaps Mark's tradition) gave the saying an absolute meaning which it did not originally have," and that if traceable back to Jesus it is likely to have had a rhetorically antithetical pattern such as in Hosea 6:6 wherein mercy is strongly preferred, though sacrifice is not rejected out of hand ("Jesus and the Law," 2752). Meier, *Law and Love*, 384-97, contends that 7:15 is an absolute statement — and not, alternatively, a dialectical and relative remark — and unlikely to have been made by the historical Jesus.

22. Loader, *Law*, 77; see also 125-26. Cf. Crossley, *Date*, 193, who argues that "Mark 7.15 does not reject defilement as described in the biblical Torah, but rather external defilement through handwashing," and that "Mark 7.19 does *not* accept that prohibited foods can now be eaten, but rather those foods eaten with unwashed hands can be eaten" (italics original). Crossley views 7:1-23 as concerned with handwashing only; he argues that it "should be read wholly in the context of intra-Jewish halakic disputes" (*Date*, 182-205, citation on 204), not as opposing biblical food laws.

aside specific Torah provisions and demeaning them as worthless!"[23] For Mark what matters is not mere external rituals and religious tradition, but human attitudes and ethics.[24]

The context suggests, however, that this may be an unnecessarily excessive and rather reductionist evaluation. Mark's Jesus criticizes what is in view in 7:1-13 only insofar as, in his estimation, it is hypocritical, abandons the commandments, and fails to worship God truly. The "word of God" (7:13) is being rendered void, undermining Israel's ability to live well together as the holy people of God. It is with this in view that he presses hard to the heart of the matter: fundamentally, it is that which is at the very center (heart) of a person and a people, and emerges in their actions, which can defile (7:15; cf. 7:6, 19a).[25] The situation is serious and so the language is stark; but the use of "there is nothing" (7:15a) and "Thus he declared all foods clean" (7:19c) need not be taken as a wholesale setting aside of the Torah, but rather as pressing down deeply into its essence, which is God's love and concern for the heart of Israel. Viewed from this essential standpoint, a range of interrelated elements may be kept in play, each having their own proper place. All foods are in themselves clean, whether as approved by the law or as otherwise sanctioned (among the Gentiles); in the case of Jewish food laws, Torah observance must function within the framework of a cleansed and covenant faithful heart (otherwise it will issue in defilement),[26] just as all human conduct must avoid every form of evil (7:20-23). Here, as elsewhere, Jesus is fundamentally concerned to uphold the life-giving intent of the Torah as well as the welfare of the entire person, all of Israel, and, by extension, the whole of humanity.

It is not incidental that the above episode is immediately followed by Jesus' encounter with a Gentile Syrophoenician woman, whose daughter has an unclean spirit (7:24-30). This episode reinforces what real uncleanness entails: being possessed by evil demons instead of God's Spirit. It also indicates that such uncleanness is found among both Jews and Gentiles, and that while Jesus recognizes the Israel-specific focus of his life and mission, he acknowledges

23. Loader, *Law*, 78.

24. Loader, *Law*, 78-79; cf. 94, 125-26.

25. In the course of his analysis of 7:1-23, Stephen Westerholm, *Jesus and Scribal Authority* (ConBNT 10; Lund: Gleerup, 1978), 84, observes in connection with 7:15 "that there is no suggestion on the part of Jesus that he intended to enunciate a new principle, institute a new law, or consciously revoke an old one. He was concerned only with defining the true nature of impurity."

26. The Jewish people can follow an approved list for their purposes, as long as this does not override what is essentially the case: everything is God's and what really counts is not the kind of food that enters a person (and passes out), but what it is that exists (and remains) in that person's heart in relation to God.

that its outworking also extends to the Gentiles. Both John the Baptist and Jesus uphold the nature and intent of the Torah, not least when it is violated, impeded, or misappropriated by leading figures within Israel, and even though this carries considerable cost. The end in view, shared by the Torah and its faithful interpreters, is an Israel and a world that is pure and holy.

Jesus' Transfiguration and a Turning Point: Embodying Torah

Jesus' transfiguration (9:2-8) is one of the high points in Mark's narrative, rich with various associations. Three interrelated observations may be made. First, the mountain location, the visitation of Moses and Elijah, and the dwelling that Peter wants to make all variously evoke Mount Sinai, the law and the prophets, and the festival of Tabernacles (cf. Exod. 25:1-9; Lev. 23:33-43);[27] in short, Torah (and temple) are very much in view. Second, Jesus' dazzling white clothes (evincing Adam),[28] his conversation with Moses and Elijah who are alive in the heavenly realm (see 12:24-27), and the overshadowing cloud and attending affirmation of Jesus as beloved Son all evoke a Jesus-focused divine self-disclosure (cf. Exod. 24:15-18). Third, that Peter, James, and John (9:2; see 5:37; 14:33) — the inner circle of disciples — are privileged if fearful participants in all of this suggests that they comprise the core of a continuing Israel constituted around Jesus, Son of God (see 1:1, 11; cf. Ps. 2:7). In sum, Jesus embodies and enacts all that Torah (and temple) seeks to effect in Israel: God's redemptive presence, the redressing of Adam's lost glory, and covenant life within the people of God. All this underwrites the divine charge, "listen to him!" (9:7d; cf. Deut. 18:15, 18). Notably, the first instruction issued by Jesus is to command his disciples not to tell what they had seen, for even the transfiguration is to be understood in relation to Jesus' yet forthcoming role as suffering Son of Man, and only thence his resurrection (9:9-13).

A turning point occurs as Jesus moves from Galilee toward Judea and Jerusalem (10:1; cf. 10:32), marked by another episode involving the Torah and its interpretation (10:2-12).[29] Jesus is tested by some Pharisees who ask, "Is it

27. Joel Marcus, *Mark 8–16: A New Translation with Introduction and Commentary* (AB 27A; New Haven: Yale University Press, 2009), 1118, concludes that "the most important backgrounds for the Markan transfiguration are traditions about Moses, the Feast of Tabernacles, and royal epiphanies." Note also Watts, "Mark," 185-88, detailing and developing many of the elements briefly identified here.

28. On Adam and the transfiguration, see Marcus, *Mark 8–16*, 636-40; cf. 1113-14.

29. Meier, *Law and Love*, 119-28, is among those who conclude that Mark 10:2-12 is an ide-

lawful for a man to divorce his wife?" (10:2). Given John the Baptist's earlier fate for condemning Herod Antipas's unlawful marriage (6:14-29; cf. Josephus, *Ant.* 18.109-36), and Jesus' prior exchange with the Pharisees and scribes on purity and the human heart (7:1-23), Jesus' twofold interpretation of the pertinent divorce regulation (Deut. 24:1-4) is both daring and telling. First, he argues that Moses wrote this commandment as a concession to their hardness of heart, perhaps mindful that the set of rulings in which it was contained were intended to enhance rather than hinder Israel's life together as the people of God (see, e.g., Deut. 24:6-15). Second, referencing the creation accounts,[30] Jesus pointedly locates the commandment — and, by extension, the entire Torah — within God's wider intent for image-bearing humanity as a whole.[31]

Jesus' commitment to the Torah's commandments and their continuing role in relation to the kingdom of God is once again evident in his ensuing interaction with a rich man (10:17-22), who wants to know from this "good teacher" how he may inherit eternal life (10:17). In response, Jesus cites and endorses several of the Ten Commandments (Exod. 20:12-16; Deut. 5:16-20).[32] However, love compels Jesus to add that this man must also remove anything — in this case, riches (cf. 4:18-20) — that impedes keeping the Torah, and the freedom to fulfill it by following Jesus himself, not least in actions on behalf of the poor that betoken treasure in heaven (10:20-22). Torah taken up in Jesus must be embodied and enacted; such is the challenge and cost of the kingdom of God (10:23-31).

Jesus in Jerusalem: Torah and Temple Transposed

Jesus' last days in Jerusalem are marked by his authoritative Torah-centered teaching in the temple (14:49).[33] That he enters the city to public acclaim on

---

alized Christian composition, but he nevertheless regards it as reflecting the sort of interaction entailed when Jesus engaged in halakic debates on divorce (124).

30. Cf. Mark 10:6 and Gen. 1:27; 5:2; and Mark 10:7-8 and Gen. 2:24.

31. Bockmuehl, *Jewish Law,* 6, rightly regards Jesus' response as affirming "the priority of a more foundational practice based on an earlier, positive principle within the Torah, namely the Creator's intention for the permanence of marriage," and views this in relation to contemporary halakic debate. Yet, by extension, this may be further located within God's purposes for the entire range of human relationships in Israel and the wider world.

32. While "You shall not defraud" is not among the Ten Commandments, see Deuteronomy 24:14-15. Loader, *Law,* 91, rightly regards Jesus' response here as "thoroughly Jewish," echoing the Shema (in 10:18) and affirming the commandments.

33. The position taken here, even if it cannot be pursued at any length, is that in Mark, Jesus' view of the Torah and his view of the temple are analogous: in and of themselves they

a lowly donkey (11:1-11; cf. Zech. 9:9-10), intimates his ironic identity and role as a Messiah-King who will suffer humiliation. The ensuing combined fig tree and temple incident (11:12-25; cf. Isa. 56:7; Jer. 7:11) indicates the fruitless and faithless situation at the center of Israel, where worship of God is being displaced by a merely human economy, and the origin and operation of Jesus' authority is under serious dispute (11:27-33). And this, together with a parable (12:1-12; cf. Isa. 5:1-7 LXX), which summarizes the story so far in a series of telling symbols that culminate with the sent Son,[34] precipitates and provides perspective on the climactic events that follow.

As in Galilee, so in Jerusalem the Jewish authorities test Jesus on the Torah and his commitment to Israel (12:13-17), now asking: "Is it lawful to pay taxes to the emperor, or not?" (12:14). Again recognizing hypocrisy in play, Jesus offers his own provocative question and instruction, which focuses on the interrelated issues of image-bearing, authority, and allegiance. That is, to whom do Israel and, indeed, the entire world belong? Torah — "what is lawful" — turns on covenant faithfulness consonant with the creation-wide purposes of God.

Then some of the Sadducees try to test Jesus the teacher with an involved argument drawing from the Torah on Levirate marriage (12:18-27; see Deut. 25:5-6) and designed to discredit resurrection. This incurs Jesus' sharp critique — they "know neither the scriptures nor the power of God" (12:24) — and counterargument. He first asserts that post-resurrection there is no marriage; indeed, resurrected humans are themselves transformed and so are "like angels in heaven" (12:25). Then follows his own startling two-part proof of resurrection from the Torah: (a) God identified himself to Moses as the God of Abraham, Isaac, and Jacob (see Exod. 3:6, 13-16), thereby intimating that they are still alive; and (b) more fundamentally, Israel's God "is God not of the dead, but of the living" (12:27). The God whose name was disclosed to Moses — "I AM WHO I AM" (Exod. 3:14) — is one who has always acted on

---

are together central, if variously compromised, symbols of God's covenant relationship with Israel that find their fulfillment in and through Jesus. While conceptualizing this is challenging, construal in terms of continuity and transposition is to be preferred over language of "replacement." For the use of the latter, see, for example, Loader, *Law,* 95-108, applied variously to both the temple (e.g., "replaced by the community of prayer and faith," which is "made without hands") and the Torah (e.g., "[t]o replace the temple by a community is to replace substantial sections of Torah") (104).

34. Principally, a man/owner (God), vineyard (Israel), tenants (Israel's leaders), servants (prophets), and beloved son and cornerstone (Jesus); see, for example, the detailed analyses in Marcus, *Mark 8–16,* 801-15; and John R. Donahue and Daniel J. Harrington, *The Gospel of Mark* (SP 2; Collegeville: Liturgical, 2002), 337-43.

behalf of Israel, to reveal, rescue, and covenant, and is now doing so in Jesus' powerful teaching and activity. Torah is not to be appropriated in self-serving and restrictive ways (only "to/for us," 12:19), but interpreted in service of the living God, whose presence, purposes, and power are evidently operative in Jesus' life and mission for Israel and the world.

The essential and life-giving intent of the Torah is again immediately evident in Jesus' interaction with one of the scribes (12:28-34), who, impressed by his response to the Sadducees, now asks which commandment is first of all.[35] Jesus replies with a slightly amplified rendering of the Shema (12:29b-30; cf. Deut. 6:4-5):[36] central to Torah obedience is Israel's love of God, responding to God's immeasurable redeeming love of Israel (see Deut. 10:12-22). Again drawing from the Torah, Jesus adds a second commandment as a corollary: "You shall love your neighbor as yourself" (12:31; cf. Lev. 19:18b) — entailing care for others as the holy people of God (see Lev. 19:1-37). The scribe affirms Jesus' response, adding that love of God and neighbor is "much more important than all whole burnt offerings and sacrifices" (12:33; cf. 1 Sam. 15:22; Hos. 6:6).[37] In view is the realization, rather than the exploitation and frustration, of the Torah and temple in service of the love of God and his people.[38] Recognizing his wise reply, Jesus declares that the man is close to the kingdom of God (12:34).

Teaching in the temple, Jesus handles scripture in a way that both questions the interpretation of the scribes and provocatively intimates his own identity (so 12:35-37). Here, on one level he seems to be addressing as inadequate the scribes' view that the Messiah is merely the Son of David. On another level he is aligning the respective identities and roles of King David, the Messiah, and the Lord of all, with implied reference to his own life and mission. Also briefly in view is a Jesus-centered apocalyptic scenario (12:36). This is subsequently envisaged on a grand scale in a temple-focused (13:1-3), Israel-centered, yet wider apocalyptic scenario depicted in Jesus' so-called eschatological discourse (13:1-37). The climax is the coming of the Son of Man in power and glory (13:26; cf. Dan. 7:13-14), and the gathering of the elect from across creation (13:27;

35. See Meier, *Law and Love,* 478-528, on the structure, exegesis, and arguments for the historicity of 12:28-34.

36. Jesus adds "with all your mind" to Deuteronomy 6:4-5.

37. Crossley, *Date,* 83, cites Old Testament prophetic texts critiquing sacrifices: for example, Isa. 1:10-17; Jer. 6:20; 7:21-28; Amos 5:21-27.

38. Thus to suggest that this episode involving the two commandments and offerings/sacrifices is essentially a contrast "between attitude and ethical behavior, on the one hand, and [external] cultic activity on the other" (Loader, *Law,* 101) appears too reductionist and dualistic.

cf. Deut. 30:4; Zech. 2:6). As anticipated in the law and the prophets, God is faithful to his chosen, scattered, covenant people, and return and restoration is ultimately realized with the appearance of the glorious Son of Man. At this point a now fruitful fig tree (13:28-31) is invoked to illustrate the nearness of all this, its imminent outworking assured by Jesus' words, which will not pass away. Torah taken up in Jesus' teaching and exaltation endures to the end.

The pivotal point in all of this is Jesus' death. The antecedent Passover meal with his disciples (14:12-26; see Exod. 12:1-20; Deut. 16:1-8), which reflects Torah observance, is highlighted by his dramatic declaration "this is my body. . . . [T]his is my blood of the covenant" (14:22-24), signifying that his self-sacrifice will enact the ultimate in Torah obedience, covenantal commitment, and divine deliverance.[39] His anticipation of Judas's betrayal, the disciples' desertion, and Peter's denial (see 14:17-21, 27-31), and the ensuing Gethsemane scene in which even the inner circle abandons a distressed Jesus (14:32-42), collectively indicate the intractable condition of Israel (and the world), and that Torah-obedient covenant life is to be realized through Jesus. He rebukes his captors for arresting him like a bandit, when every day he had been "with [them] in the temple teaching" (14:49a). His commitment to Torah and temple has been misunderstood and he himself rejected, though ironically his arrest and death are the way in which the scriptures are to be fulfilled (14:49b).

False testimony before the Sanhedrin claims that Jesus said "I will destroy this temple that is made with hands, and in three days I will build another, not made with hands" (14:58). Complete conceptual clarity on all that is entailed here remains elusive. But it might be inferred that Jesus' purported demolition and rebuilding of the temple — whose operation is regulated by the Torah — actually entails their recasting or transposition by means of his death and resurrection, this brought about not by human hands, but by the handiwork of God.[40] Indeed, in response to the high priest who asks directly, "Are you the Messiah, the Son of the Blessed One?" (14:61c), Jesus utters a revelatory "I am," and again elaborates by reference to a glorified and coming Son of Man (14:62; cf. Ps. 110:1; Dan. 7:13-14; also Mark 8:38; 13:26). This is deemed blasphemy deserving of death (see Lev. 24:16), the charge reframed for Pilate as insurrection (see 14:64; 15:1-5), and he plays his part in relation to the "King of the Jews." Thus the temple and Torah are invoked against Jesus, yet they will be taken up

39. Loader, *Law,* 118, observes that there is no indication here that Mark exploits this atoning event (or the earlier reference to Jesus' atoning death in 10:45) over and against the temple system.

40. And this is to be located within the renewal of the entirety of God's good creation, co-opted and corrupted by evil, now rescued and realized via Jesus and the Spirit.

and transformed by his dying and rising as Israel's Messiah, Son of God, and glorious Son of Man. Indeed, the temple is again invoked against Jesus during the crucifixion (15:29-30); yet upon his dying the torn temple curtain (15:38; cf. 1:11) signals the self-manifestation of God's glory, thence also powerfully displayed in the ensuing resurrection of Jesus (16:6). In the interim, we see a reconstituted people of God, signified in the coming together around Jesus of both the well-positioned and those from afar: Joseph of Arimathea, who buries Jesus according to Sabbath law (15:42-46), and the covenant faithful women who had followed him from Galilee to Jerusalem (15:47; cf. 15:40-41), the latter including the first witnesses to the resurrection (16:1-8).

The Gospel of Mark and Life Together

Readers of Mark's narrative may see that the Torah (and temple), so constitutive of the life and mission of Israel, is affirmed, taken up, and transposed in the life and mission, and atoning death and resurrection of Jesus, who has brought about the kingdom of God. And in this way it continues to be constitutive of life together for the Spirit-empowered covenant people of God. Walking together according to the unfolding work and will of God means loving God and neighbor; and the latter encompasses the whole of humanity, not least those in the background and on the margins. It involves hearing, embodying, and enacting — and not impeding — the gospel of God, its commandments, teachings, and scripture. A transformative and ethical life together needs forgiveness and cleansing, renewed hearts and minds, and faith in the face of testing. It involves invitation and hospitality; care and compassion; protection, assistance, and guidance. In the midst of conflict and destruction, it requires truth over falsehood, bearing witness and watchfulness, as those fitted for the final ingathering. And its ultimate end is glory.

Reading Law as Prophecy: Torah Ethics in Acts

David M. Miller

Stephen Westerholm once remarked that "controversy surrounding the Jewish 'law'" was the single biggest internal issue that "tested and shaped the self-understanding of the nascent church."[1] The controversy is on full display in pivotal scenes in Acts, and its complexity is reflected in modern scholarly attempts to make sense of them. As we will see, Jewish Christians in Acts are depicted as faithful to the law, though they are never instructed to follow its requirements. Gentile Christians, conversely, are viewed as not under the law's "yoke," but commanded to observe four requirements that resemble its demands. Some readers conclude from this portrayal that all Christians are freed from the law;[2] others infer that the law is in some sense still binding as law on Jewish and Gentile Christ-believers.[3] There is also disagreement about whether the law was still a live issue in Luke's context or — to mention one of several alternatives — whether polemic about the law within the narrative had already

1. Stephen Westerholm, "Law and the Early Christians," *Journal of Dharma* 22, no. 4 (1997): 396.

2. See Craig L. Blomberg, "The Law in Luke-Acts," *JSNT* 22 (1984): 62, 69-71; Mark A. Seifrid, "Jesus and the Law in Acts," *JSNT* 30 (1987): 40, 51-52; François Bovon, "The Law in Luke-Acts," in *Studies in Early Christianity* (Grand Rapids: Baker Academic, 2005), 68; Daniel Marguerat, "Paul and the Torah in the Acts of the Apostles," in *Torah in the New Testament: Papers Delivered at the Manchester-Lausanne Seminar of June 2008* (ed. Michael Tait and Peter Oakes; LNTS 401; London: T&T Clark, 2009), 106.

3. For the view that Jews remain obligated to the whole law, and Gentiles to part of it, see Jacob Jervell, *Luke and the People of God: A New Look at Luke-Acts* (Minneapolis: Augsburg, 1972), 133-51.

I would like to thank Tenyia Miller, Michael Pahl, Steve Walton, and Susan J. Wendel for their helpful comments on earlier versions of this essay.

become an outsider condemnation of Jews by Gentile Christians.[4] For our purposes, the most important question is whether or not there is a Torah ethic in Acts. That is, does Luke indicate or take for granted that the law should play an ongoing role in guiding the ethical reflection of both Jewish and Gentile Christ-believers?[5]

That Luke links the law with prophecy is widely recognized within scholarship on the law in Luke-Acts, but because prophecy is often assumed to be synonymous with prediction, the prophetic character of the law is commonly treated as a curiosity unrelated to other passages where "law" refers to a collection of commandments.[6] Yet what seems to be an anomaly may, on further inspection, point to a solution. Recognizing how Luke reads law and prophecy together enables us to see more clearly that Luke links Jewish — but not Gentile — Christ-believers to Torah, and why he does so: Luke ties both law and prophets to the covenant with Israel, which for Luke, is limited to Jews. In Acts, Luke introduces the law primarily to support his claim that Torah-observant Jewish Christians are faithful to the covenant with Israel. Once the actual function of the law within the narrative argument of Acts has been established, it is possible to tease out what Luke thought about how the law should function to inform the ethical practices of Gentile Christ-believers. Here connections between Torah and prophecy are again instructive: the way Luke applies the biblical prophets to his own day suggests how he might have applied the Torah to Gentile believers not subject to the covenant requirements of Torah.

4. For different conclusions about the ethnic makeup of Luke's audience, cf. Stephen G. Wilson, *Luke and the Law* (SNTSMS 50; Cambridge: Cambridge University Press, 1983), 105, and Isaac W. Oliver, *Torah Praxis after 70 CE: Reading Matthew and Luke-Acts as Jewish Texts* (WUNT II 355; Tübingen: Mohr Siebeck, 2013), 39.

5. See Richard A. Burridge, *Imitating Jesus: An Inclusive Approach to New Testament Ethics* (Grand Rapids: Eerdmans, 2007), 258: "in the end, for Luke the law provides neither ethics nor salvation."

6. According to Wilson, *Law*, 27, there is in Luke-Acts "no attempt to correlate the two." Cf. Jervell, *Luke*, 137; Seifrid, "Law," 51-52; Kalervo Salo, *Luke's Treatment of the Law: A Redaction-Critical Investigation* (Helsinki: Suomalainen Tiedeakatemia, 1991), 23; Bovon, "Law," 61-62. Notable exceptions include Matthias Klinghardt, *Gesetz und Volk Gottes: das lukanische Verständnis des Gesetzes nach Herkunft, Funktion und seinem Ort in der Geschichte des Urchristentums* (WUNT II 32; Tübingen: Mohr Siebeck, 1988), 11, 121-23; William Loader, *Jesus' Attitude towards the Law: A Study of the Gospels* (WUNT II 97; Tübingen: Mohr Siebeck, 1997; repr., Grand Rapids: Eerdmans, 2002), 381.

The Law and Jewish Christ-Believers

Readers of Acts often wonder why Jewish Christ-believers remain Torah observant even after Paul and Peter declare that salvation is by faith not by observing the law.[7] In my view, preoccupation with this question tends to obscure Luke's actual reasons for stressing Jewish-Christian Torah observance, which have to do with the identity of the covenant people and the legitimacy of the Gentile mission.[8] Luke's question is not why Jewish Christ-believers, who are saved by faith, still keep the law, but how the Jewish early Jesus movement, as heirs of the covenant promises contained in the law and prophets, can extend the offer of salvation to Gentiles apart from the law, without violating the law.

The Law, the Prophets, and the Covenant with Israel

Though they have different labels, the law and prophets in Luke-Acts speak with one voice — as Hans Conzelmann observed, "both prophesy and . . . both command"[9] — and they support the same covenant with Israel. From Luke's perspective, Moses was not only the lawgiver par excellence, he was also the first in a line of prophets. In Acts 3:21-26, Peter quotes Moses' prediction that "[t]he Lord your God will raise up from your brothers a prophet like me" (Deut. 18:15) as an example of what the "prophets from of old" had foretold. After this one specific example from Moses, Peter generalizes that all the other prophets "from Samuel and those who came after him" also proclaimed "these days" (Acts 3:24). The sequence of prophets listed after Moses indicates that Luke, like some of his Jewish contemporaries, regarded Moses as a prophetic prototype and understood Deuteronomy 18:15 as regulations about the required response to prophets in general.[10]

Luke portrays the biblical prophets, in turn, acting in continuity with Mo-

7. Acts 13:38-39; 15:11. For a clear statement of the question, see Marguerat, "Torah," 99-100.

8. See Jervell, *Luke*, 133-51.

9. Hans Conzelmann, *The Theology of St Luke* (New York: Harper & Row, 1961), 159 n. 1; cf. Klinghardt, *Gesetz*, 122.

10. Josephus presents Joshua as Moses' successor in connection with prophecies (ἐπὶ . . . ταῖς προφητείαις) (*Ant.* 4.165); he says that Joshua "prophesied" (προεφήτευσε) (*Ant.* 4.311); and in *Ant.* 5.20, he refers to Joshua unequivocally as "the prophet"; cf. *Ant.* 4.218. Ben Sira 46:1, similarly, presents Joshua as Moses' successor (διάδοχος) in prophecy (προφητεία). An eschatological interpretation of Deuteronomy 18:15 also existed (see 4QTest and 1QS IX 11). Luke held both together.

ses. Global references to law and prophecy show that Luke regarded scripture in its entirety as a collection that pointed forward to Jesus and the resurrection.[11] But Luke recognizes that the prophets of old were sent to call their ancient contemporaries to repentance as well as to predict the more distant future, and he emphasizes that, like Moses, they were persecuted and rejected as a result.[12] For Luke, prophets, like Moses their prototype, are those who speak for God, whose messages must be heard. When Peter proclaims in Jesus the final fulfillment of Deuteronomy 18:15, the fulfilled prediction comes with a command to listen and a warning that those who refuse to do so will be excluded from the people (Acts 3:22-23).

The penalty for failing to listen to the prophets in general, and to Jesus in particular, brings the prophets within the orbit of the law and the Mount Sinai covenant, which emphasized not only hearing God but also listening to Moses. The covenantal implications of listening to Jesus[13] are reinforced by Luke's transfiguration account (Luke 9:28-36), where references to the mountain, overshadowing cloud, and heavenly voice recall the Sinai theophanies of Exodus and Deuteronomy, and expose the significance of the transfiguration's concluding imperative. Just as hearing Moses, according to Exodus and Deuteronomy, is central to the covenant God made with Israel at Sinai,[14] so Luke's transfiguration presents Jesus, the "chosen son," as the one whose words, like Moses', must now also be heard and obeyed as a condition for membership in the people of God.[15]

The Mosaic covenant evoked by the transfiguration is, for Luke, combined with the covenant God made with Abraham. In Acts, circumcision is the sign of the covenant with Abraham (7:8) and carries with it an obligation to obey the law of Moses (15:5). Within Stephen's speech, the exodus (7:17) links the covenant (7:7-8) to the "living words" of the law (7:35-38). "Worshiping" (λατρεύειν), which is the Abrahamic covenant's purpose (7:6-8; cf. Luke 1:72-75), is also the goal of the giving of the law (7:38-53).[16]

11. Luke 24:27, 44; Acts 26:22; cf. 24:14.

12. See Luke 6:23, 26; 10:24; 11:47, 50; 13:28, 34; Acts 7:52.

13. Luke 6:47, 49; 8:11-15; 8:21; 10:16; 10:24; 10:39; 11:28; 11:31; 16:29, 31.

14. Exod. 19:5-9; 20:18-21; Deut. 5:1-5, 23-29; 18:15-19.

15. See David M. Miller, "Seeing the Glory, Hearing the Son: The Function of the Wilderness Theophany Narratives in Luke 9:28-36," *CBQ* 72, no. 3 (2010): 498-517.

16. See Miller, "Luke 9:28-36," 515-16. For connections between the Abrahamic and Mosaic covenants in early Judaism, see James M. Scott, "Covenant," in *The Eerdmans Dictionary of Early Judaism* (ed. John J. Collins and Daniel C. Harlow; Grand Rapids: Eerdmans, 2010), 491-94.

Luke's conceptions of law and prophecy are thus so tightly intertwined that they cannot be separated without damage to our understanding of both. The prophets predicted the future, to be sure, but they also reinforced the demands of Moses and defended the same Mosaic covenant. As we will see, these connections between law, prophecy, and covenant help explain why Jewish Christ-believers in Acts remain faithful to the law.

Jewish-Christian Orientation to the Law

As there is general agreement that Jewish Christ-believers in Acts remain Torah observant, we need not labor the point here.[17] Although no character in Acts specifically instructs Jewish Christ-believers to keep the law, the Jesus of Luke's Gospel commends obedience to the law (10:28; cf. Mark 12:34), and suggests that those who listen to Moses will respond positively to Jesus as well (16:29-31). In the first century, some Jews sought to root their legal decisions in exegesis of the written Torah, others accepted authoritative tradition, while still others justified their regulations by appeal to the prophetic inspiration of the interpreter.[18] Against such a variegated backdrop, stories about Jesus' authority to offer new and surprising interpretations of Torah form part of a larger legal debate rather than a direct attack on the law.[19] More important, according to Luke and Acts, Jesus' Jewish followers continue to observe specific Torah requirements, such as Sabbath observance,[20] which indicates that — whatever their traditional thrust — Luke did not understand the controversy stories in his Gospel as changing or criticizing the law itself.

Rather than moving away from strict adherence to the law, the church that Paul encounters on his final visit to Jerusalem is filled with "myriads" of believing Jews who "are zealous for the law" (Acts 21:20). The Paul of Acts

17. Stephen Westerholm, "Law in the NT," *NIDB*, 3:597, represents the consensus.

18. See Jonathan Klawans, *Josephus and the Theologies of Ancient Judaism* (Oxford: Oxford University Press, 2012), 177. Klawans associates the first approach with the Sadducees, the second with the Pharisees, and the third with the Qumran community.

19. Contrast Wilson, *Law*, 35, 45, 47, who argues that Jesus' prohibition of divorce in Luke 16:18 contradicts the law by adding to it, and that Jesus' claim to authority over the Sabbath in Luke 6:5 implies that he is free to break it.

20. However we interpret the Sabbath controversies earlier in Luke, the women who witnessed Jesus' burial still keep the Sabbath laws, for Luke adds to his Markan source that they "rested on the Sabbath according to the commandment" (Luke 23:56). Acts emphasizes synagogue attendance (13:14; 16:13; 17:2; 18:4). Most likely, the command to rest on the Sabbath was simply assumed. See Acts 1:12 on a Sabbath day's walk.

participates in temple worship to show that he "guards the law" (21:24); he also denies that he has done anything against the law (25:8) or his people's ancestral customs (28:17). According to Acts 24, Paul's faith in the law's predictions goes hand in hand with his own continued Torah observance: hope in the resurrection (vv. 14-15) motivates Paul to live with a clear conscience (v. 16), which is illustrated by almsgiving, maintaining ritual purity, and offering sacrifices (vv. 17-18). Since the elaborate defense narrative in Acts 21–26 responds to charges that Paul violated the law and taught other Jews to do the same (21:21, 28), repeated statements about Paul's innocence would be disingenuous if they meant that Paul only observed the Torah during his visit to Jerusalem or that his motive was merely to avoid offense.

Luke certainly thought that Jesus was more important than Moses and that "salvation" was not available in the law (Acts 13:38-39; 15:11). In this sense, Luke limits the role of the law and makes it subordinate to Jesus. Also, faith, not law, is the defining characteristic of the early Jesus movement, and in this respect there is no distinction between Jews and Gentiles.[21] But when Peter affirms that both Jews and Gentiles "believe in order to be saved" (Acts 15:11),[22] it does not follow that law observance is optional for the covenant people.[23] Just as the four terms of the apostolic decree (Acts 15:20) were imposed on Gentiles as requirements for those saved by faith, so we may conclude in light of the trajectory of Acts that, from Luke's perspective, the law remained obligatory for Christ-believing Jews.

How Peter's noonday vision fits into this otherwise consistent pattern of Jewish Torah observance is unclear. Luke explicitly applies the vision to the purity of people (Acts 10:28; cf. 10:14, 34-35), not to the status of the unclean food on the sheet let down from heaven, and the primary function of the Cornelius account within Acts is to demonstrate that "God has granted even the Gentiles repentance that leads to life."[24] Yet Luke recognizes that the extension of salvation to Gentiles may impinge on Jewish Torah observance. Called to account for staying with uncircumcised people and eating with them (11:3), Peter responds by telling a story about food that concludes with the declaration, "what God has cleansed, do not regard as defiled" (11:9). What this means on a practical level becomes apparent when the conversion of Cornelius's house-

21. Acts 2:44; 4:32; 5:14; 6:7; 9:42; 10:43; 11:17; 13:39; 14:1, 22; 15:11; 16:31; 17:12; 19:4; 20:21; 26:18; cf. 15:5; 21:20.

22. For this translation, see John Nolland, "A Fresh Look at Acts 15:10," *NTS* 27, no. 1 (1980): 112-13.

23. See Nolland, "Acts 15:10," 110 n. 16; Oliver, *Torah Praxis*, 450.

24. Acts 11:18; cf. 10:34-35, 47; 11:1; 15:7-8.

hold in Acts 10–11 is compared with that of the Philippian jailor in Acts 16. In the former account, Peter and company agree to stay with Cornelius — and, one assumes, to eat his food — after he has received the Holy Spirit and been baptized (10:48). In the latter, the Philippian jailor believes and is baptized before providing Paul and Silas with food (16:33-34). In both cases baptism precedes table fellowship between Christ-believing Jews and Gentiles,[25] and eating together recalls "the fellowship, breaking of bread, and prayers" characteristic of the Jerusalem church in the early chapters of Acts (2:42; cf. 6:1-6). Although Luke does not focus on the practical social ramifications of the Cornelius narrative, the way he tells the story indicates that, as a result of the gift of the Spirit and the moral "cleansing" of Gentile hearts (15:9), Christ-believing Jews may dine in the houses of baptized Gentiles.

But would eating with baptized Gentiles necessarily entail a violation of the food laws?[26] Isaac Oliver supposes that believing Gentiles would serve "kosher" food to their Jewish guests, so that no change in *kashrut* is in view.[27] It is perhaps more likely that Christ-believing Jews who ate with baptized Gentiles selected kosher food from the menu. On the one hand, while Cornelius and other God-fearing Gentiles may well have observed the food laws, Luke shows no interest in the kind of food the Philippian jailor set before Paul and Silas.[28] On the other hand, after Luke's narration of the apostolic decree (Acts

25. See Oliver, *Torah Praxis*, 317, 361-62.

26. I assume that the central legal issue concerned the food laws of Leviticus 11 and Deuteronomy 14, not merely associating with Gentiles, although it is true that Acts 10–11 also emphasizes Peter's entering into Cornelius's house (Acts 10:25, 27; 11:3, 12). Since Gentiles were not normally considered part of the purity system and so did not transmit ritual impurity, most Jews did not think mere interaction with Gentiles contravened the Torah. See Jonathan Klawans, "Notions of Gentile Impurity in Ancient Judaism," *AJS Review* 20, no. 2 (1995): 287, 290, 292; cf. Beverly Roberts Gaventa, *The Acts of the Apostles* (ANTC; Nashville: Abingdon, 2003), 168. Peter's problem, according to Acts 10:28, is not that it was "*unlawful* (ἀθέμιτος) for a Jew to associate with or to visit a Gentile," as most English translations have it. The word, ἀθέμιτος "refers prim[arily] to violation of tradition or common recognition of what is seemly or proper" (BDAG 24), and is better rendered "taboo" here (F. F. Bruce, *The Book of the Acts* [rev. ed.; NICNT; Grand Rapids: Eerdmans, 1988], 209). For an opposing view, see, for example, Jervell, *Luke*, 149 n. 24; cf. 189; Philip Francis Esler, *Community and Gospel in Luke-Acts: The Social and Political Motivations of Lucan Theology* (SNTSMS 57; Cambridge: Cambridge University Press, 1987), 71-109.

27. Oliver, *Torah Praxis*, 317-18, 362-64, 397-98; cf. Loader, *Law*, 369-71, 377-78.

28. Against Jacob Jervell, "The Church of Jews and Godfearers," in *Luke-Acts and the Jewish People: Eight Critical Perspectives* (ed. Joseph B. Tyson; Minneapolis: Augsburg, 1988), 11-20, Luke does not present Cornelius's Torah observance as the paradigm for Gentile converts because the Philippian jailor can hardly have been a God-fearer (see Jervell, "Godfearers,"

15:20, 29) we must envisage Paul and Silas always being careful to avoid food sacrificed to idols and meat with blood in it when dining with recently baptized converts; the same considerations could apply to kosher requirements. Even if Peter's vision means in effect that Jews should eat whatever is set before them, this change in halakah would not indicate that the law in general, or the food laws in particular, have been abolished or set aside because it would be limited to meals with baptized Gentiles. In any case, the description of Torah-observant Jewish believers at the beginning and end of Acts indicates that Luke could affirm both Peter's faithfulness to the law and his practice of table fellowship with Gentile Christians.[29] Jewish Christ-believers, as Luke describes them, remain oriented toward Torah observance.

The Narrative Function of Jewish-Christian Torah Observance

The function of Luke's portrayal of Jewish Christ-believers as Torah observant is related to the overlap between law, prophecy, and the covenant with Israel. If the promises to Israel stated in the law and the prophets are fulfilled in a community characterized by its remarkable piety as shown by its Torah observance, the non-Christ-believing Jerusalem leadership serves as its literary foil.[30] For example, after reviewing Israel's tragic failure to observe the "living words" that Moses received on Mount Sinai (Acts 7:38, 53) and of persecuting the prophets (7:52), Stephen accuses his auditors of violating the law by betraying and murdering the prophet and "righteous one" whom Moses (7:37) and the prophets (7:52-53) predicted. In response, the council demonstrates their "uncircumcised ears" when they cover them and rush at Stephen (7:51, 57). For Luke, obedience to the law's prescriptions also requires a response to the law's prediction; failure to respond to Jesus shows that one does not keep the law.

Luke reinforces the contrast between Jesus' Jewish followers and their Jewish opponents by charging the latter with violating the law's prescriptions. Paul, for example, accuses the high priest of breaking the law by commanding that Paul be struck (23:3). The sequel shows Paul's opponents twice attempting to kill him before a trial (23:12-22; 25:3) — in violation of both Jewish and Roman law. The effect is to present Paul and other Jewish Christ-believers as faithful

17). Other Gentile converts who are not depicted as God-fearers include those at Lystra (Acts 14:20) and Athens (Acts 17:34).

29. See Loader, *Law,* 377-78.

30. For this general point, see Conzelmann, *Theology,* 159-60; cf. 142, 146; Esler, *Luke-Acts,* 122-28.

to the terms of the covenant — as those who listen to Moses and Jesus, and who thereby inherit the promises to Abraham.

Luke's portrayal of a law-observant Paul also functions to present the mission to Gentiles as a legitimate Jewish activity. In the same way that Paul's evangelism among Gentiles in Acts 13–14 raises questions that are addressed at the Jerusalem council in Acts 15, the depiction of a combined Jewish and Gentile Diaspora church in Acts 16–20 prepares for and is explained by the Judean trial narrative in Acts 21–26,[31] where the specific charges against Paul confuse his instructions to Gentile converts with his instructions to Jews. Although Christ-believing Jews in Jerusalem suspect Paul of teaching "apostasy from Moses" and of telling Diaspora Jews "not to circumcise their children or to walk in the customs" (21:21), readers of Acts know from Paul's circumcision of Timothy (16:3) that Paul affirmed circumcision as a Jewish practice.[32] When Paul is finally arrested for defiling the temple and, like Stephen, for "teaching everyone everywhere against the people, the law, and this place" (21:28; cf. 6:13), Luke makes it clear that the charge was false. Yet this charge too was based on the mistaken belief that Paul had brought the Gentile Trophimus into the sanctuary (21:29). In Acts, Christ-believing and non-Christ-believing Jews alike regard the ambiguous identity of Gentile Christ-believers as a problem that threatens to undermine the law. Luke responds by depicting the most famous proponent of the Gentile mission as a faithful law-abiding Jew to show that the incorporation of Gentiles without requiring circumcision need not affect traditional Jewish practice.[33]

Instead of marginalizing the law, Luke uses it to advance his narrative aims: the law's predictions operate along with the demands of the covenant to iden-

31. Along similar lines, see Richard P. Thompson, "'Say It Ain't So, Paul!': The Accusations against Paul in Acts 21 in Light of His Ministry in Acts 16–20," *BR* 45 (2000): 34-50.

32. That the Paul of Acts circumcised Timothy "because of the Jews who were in those places" (16:3) does not mean that he thought circumcision was optional for other Jews. Luke signals that Timothy's identity is problematic by introducing him as the son of a Jewish mother and a Greek father (16:1). Since there is no (other) first-century evidence for the matrilineal principle, Jews would most likely have regarded Timothy as Greek, or at least, as not fully Jewish. Circumcision removed the ambiguity. See especially Shaye J. D. Cohen, *The Beginnings of Jewishness: Boundaries, Varieties, Uncertainties* (Berkeley: University of California Press, 1999), 263-307, 363-77; Christopher Bryan, "A Further Look at Acts 16:1-3," *JBL* 107, no. 2 (1988): 292-94.

33. The point, then, is the legitimacy of the Gentile mission, not the possibility of salvation. Contrast Jervell, who maintains that "the church as the restored Israel cannot lay claim to the promises and salvation" if its founding Jewish members abandon the law (*Luke*, 189; cf. 147, 172).

tify the Jewish sectarian group made up of Jesus' followers as the heirs of God's promises to Abraham,[34] and to demonstrate that Paul's Gentile mission does not contravene the law.

Gentile Christ-Believers and Torah Ethics

If, as I have argued, Luke presents the message of Jesus in continuity with, and not as a replacement of, the requirements of God's covenant with Israel expressed in the law of Moses, it would be natural for Luke to insist that Gentiles undergo complete conversion to the Jewish *ethnos*. This position Luke rejects. According to Acts 15, Gentiles are not required to be circumcised or to take on the full "yoke" of Torah (v. 10). On what basis, then, do Gentiles share in the effects of the covenant blessings promised to Abraham, and what is their obligation to the covenant law? If Luke thinks Christ-believing Jews must listen to Jesus and obey Moses, does it follow that Gentile believers need only listen to Jesus? To what extent does the Torah — understood in its usual Lukan sense as "the sum of commandments given to Israel through Moses on Mount Sinai"[35] — still function authoritatively for Gentile Christ-believers?

In what follows, I consider two common ways of explaining what Luke says about Gentiles and the law. I then propose an explanation that takes its cue from the law's connection to the covenant and Luke's understanding of prophecy.

Gentile Christ-Believers as "Resident Aliens"

According to Jacob Jervell, Luke presents Gentile Christ-believers as an "associate people" who belong to Israel and are incorporated into the "true Israel" without being Israel.[36] They are thus obligated to the laws that the Torah orig-

34. Contrast Gerald F. Downing, "Law and Custom: Luke-Acts and Late Hellenism," in *Law and Religion: Essays on the Place of the Law in Israel and Early Christianity* (ed. Barnabas Lindars; Cambridge: James Clarke, 1988), 153, 157-58, who argues that Luke links the church to ancient Jewish customs in order to present Christianity in the Roman world as a legitimate religious alternative. Downing is followed by Bovon, "Law," 72-73; Marguerat, "Torah," 116-17. Cf. Esler, *Luke-Acts*, 67-69.

35. Westerholm, "Law in the NT," 594. When the referent can be discerned from the context, terms for the law in Luke-Acts normally denote its commands.

36. Jervell, *Luke*, 64, 67, 143.

inally applied to Gentile resident aliens, laws that are restated in the apostolic decree of Acts 15:20 (cf. 15:29; 21:25).[37]

This explanation rightly insists that the apostolic decree imposes part of the Torah on Gentile Christ-believers. Despite the absence of chapter and verse references, Luke's readers would have connected the prohibitions against things defiled by idols, blood, what is strangled, and sexual immorality (15:20) to the Torah.[38] It is also clear enough that in contrast to the "yoke" of the law assumed by Jews (15:10), the decree only placed four requirements on Christ-believing Gentiles.[39] Subsequent references to the decree indicate that Luke believed it was incumbent on all Gentile Christ-believers.[40]

Nevertheless, the four requirements of the decree are not authorized by Moses. While they are connected to the law of Moses (15:21), James formulates the terms of the decree as his judgment (15:19).[41] In the letter the "apostles and elders" send to the Gentiles, the requirements are authorized by the Holy Spirit and the Jerusalem apostles and elders, not Moses (15:28; cf. 16:4).[42] When the decree is mentioned again in Acts 21, the Jerusalem elders contrast the commandments that "we sent to the believing Gentiles" with Paul's full adherence to the law (21:24-25). In this passage too an appeal to Moses for authorization is absent. Nor can the prohibitions simply be derived by compiling everything that the Torah says about resident aliens. The decree does not explicitly prohibit blasphemy or murder, for example, both of which are applied to non-Israelites in Leviticus 24:10-24; Leviticus 16:29 also extends the prohibition of work on

37. Jervell, *Luke*, 144; cf. 190-91. This understanding of the decree's origins is common. See, for example, Ernst Haenchen, *The Acts of the Apostles: A Commentary* (Hermeneia; Philadelphia: Westminster, 1971), 469. More recent defenses include Richard Bauckham, "James and the Gentiles (Acts 15.13-21)," in *History, Literature and Society in the Book of Acts* (ed. Ben Witherington III; Cambridge: Cambridge University Press, 1996), 172-78; Oliver, *Torah Praxis*, 365-98.

38. For prohibitions against blood and sexual immorality, see Lev. 17:10-14 and Leviticus 18. For references to food sacrificed to other gods, see Exod. 34:15; Num. 25:1-2; cf. 2 Macc. 6:21; 4 Macc. 5:2. "Strangled things" (πνικτός) is obscure (see Wilson, *Law*, 88-92).

39. To suggest that the decree lists only a selection of the legal requirements to which Gentiles were also subject (see Klinghardt, *Gesetz*, 205) ignores the issue that gave rise to it: instead of being required to be circumcised and to keep the law of Moses as the Christian Pharisees insisted (15:5), the Gentiles are not to be troubled or burdened by anything except for the requirements of the decree (15:19, 24, 28).

40. Acts 15:23 (Syria and Cilicia); 16:1-4 (the Lyconian cities of Lystra and Derbe); 21:25 ("the believing Gentiles").

41. Acts 15:21 indicates that the decree in verse 20 is related to the Torah, not that the decree is binding because it is contained in the law (contrast Oliver, *Torah Praxis*, 213-14; cf. Jervell, *Luke*, 144). Instead, "the relationship between the two is left unstated" (Gaventa, *Acts*, 223).

42. See Wilson, *Law*, 102.

the day of atonement to non-Israelites.[43] Whatever its origin, Luke does not indicate that the reason for imposing these four requirements on Gentiles was based on exegesis of the Torah.[44] The four regulations, which obligate Gentiles to four Torah requirements, are authorized by apostolic decree, not Torah.

Gentiles and the "Moral Law"

Distinguishing between ritual and moral law is an alternative way to defend an ongoing role for Torah among Gentile Christ-believers.[45] In its support, one may note that Jesus valued "justice and the love of God" over tithing mint, rue, and garden herbs (Luke 11:42), and that the legal expert in Luke 10 boiled the law down to love for God and neighbor (vv. 25-27). In addition, general ethical statements in Acts, such as "fearing God and working righteousness" (10:35), having "a clear conscience before God and people" (24:16), and "turn[ing] to God and practicing works worthy of repentance" (26:20; cf. 20:21), resemble Hellenistic Jewish summaries of the law, such as Philo's "holiness to God and justice to people" or Josephus's "piety" and "friendly relations with each other."[46] No doubt, ethical summaries of Torah were phrased in this way to appeal to Gentile audiences, such as Cornelius (Acts 10) and Felix (Acts 24), and thus to carry moral force without distracting audiences with practices peculiar to Jews.

Yet it is one thing to summarize the law in a way that would appeal to outsiders by listing commands ancient readers would universally regard as exemplary, and quite another to say that Gentiles are obligated to some but not all of the Mosaic law, on the authority of the law itself or on the supposition that the moral law is rooted in a covenant between God and humanity in general. While ancient Jews debated how best to epitomize the law, and distinguished between lesser and greater commandments, the overlap between these prac-

43. See Markus Bockmuehl, *Jewish Law in Gentile Churches: Halakhah and the Beginning of Christian Public Ethics* (Edinburgh: T&T Clark, 2000), 153; Wilson, *Law,* 86.

44. The first part of the decree — that Gentiles need not be "troubled" by any other Mosaic requirement (Acts 15:19; cf. 15:28) — is of course supported by James's interpretation of Amos 9:11 (Acts 15:15-17). The prohibitions, however, are not supported by explicit exegesis of Torah or any scriptural passage. Bauckham admits that "the exegetical basis" that he proposes "for the four prohibitions" is missing from Acts ("James," 183-84).

45. For the view that the moral law is still binding on Gentile Christ-believers, but that the ritual law has been set aside, see Bovon, "Law," 68-71; cf. Klinghardt, *Gesetz,* 10-11 n. 24; Loader, *Law,* 386-89; Marguerat, "Torah," 105.

46. Philo, *Abr.* 208, and Josephus, *Ag. Ap.* 2.146. See Wilson, *Law,* 70-71, 124 n. 22.

tices and our conventional modern categories of ritual law and moral law is only partial, and the potential for distortion is high. In modern usage, ritual law tends to be defined in outsider terms as anything that distinguished Jews from Gentiles, but what outsiders identify as merely ritual — such as the prohibition against ingesting blood (Lev. 17:10-14) — would most likely have been regarded as a moral requirement by ancient Jews.[47]

The absence of separate terminology for the categories of moral and ritual law confirms that the distinction was foreign to Luke. In Luke-Acts, "law" (νόμος) can be epitomized as love for God and neighbor (Luke 10:25-27), and basically equated with circumcision (Acts 15:5). The Lukan Jesus criticizes a preoccupation with legal minutiae that neglects justice and the love of God, but adds that it is necessary to practice both (11:42). The faithful Torah observance of Zechariah and Elizabeth in Luke (1:5) and Ananias of Damascus in Acts (22:12) demonstrates their piety because under normal circumstances ritual observance and moral behavior go together. At best, "ritual" and "moral" are modern categories that simply restate the problem: Gentiles are expected to order their lives in a way that accords with some, but not all, of the Torah's demands. The categories do not, however, provide a solution because they do not explain why some laws appear to apply while others do not.[48]

Gentiles and the Covenant

Both explanations considered so far suffer from an additional weakness: claiming that Gentile Christ-believers are subject to the Mosaic law when it is "moral law" or when it addresses "resident aliens" does not square with Luke's portrayal of Gentile Christ-believers. While Luke explicitly refers to the law in his description of faithful Christ-believing Jews, the law is almost completely absent from his description of Gentiles.[49] With one exception discussed below, Acts never mentions νόμος in connection with Gentiles. Instead, references to the law and the "prophet like Moses" are limited to Jewish contexts, where,

47. For this example, see Kirsopp Lake, "The Apostolic Council of Jerusalem," in *The Beginnings of Christianity Part I: The Acts of the Apostles* (ed. Henry J. Cadbury and Kirsopp Lake; 5 vols.; London: Macmillan, 1933), 5:207. Cf. W. A. Strange, *The Problem of the Text of Acts* (SNTSMS 71; Cambridge: Cambridge University Press, 1992), 93-96; E. P. Sanders, *Judaism: Practice and Belief: 63 BCE–66 CE* (Philadelphia: Trinity Press International, 1992), 194-95.

48. According to Wilson, *Law,* 107, "Luke . . . hardly seems aware of the problem let alone in a position to offer a solution."

49. Bovon, "Law," 68, observes that the law is "curiously absent from the book of Acts."

as we have seen, there is often a polemical contrast between Christ-believing and non-Christ-believing Jewish groups.[50]

The exception proves the rule. According to Acts 15:1, 5, the council in Jerusalem was convened to address a Jewish-Christian demand that Gentiles "must be circumcised and commanded to keep the law of Moses" in order "to be saved." Taken together, the speeches of Peter and James conclude — on the basis of Gentile reception of the Spirit and the testimony of scripture — that the demand must be rejected. Gentiles do not have to be circumcised or take on the "yoke" of Torah (15:6-11, 19). With this basic conclusion in place, the additional decision that Gentiles are, nevertheless, still obligated to four Mosaic stipulations requires special authorization by James, the apostles and elders, and the Holy Spirit (15:19, 23, 28). Unlike Peter and his Jewish companions who needed divine prompting before engaging in table fellowship with Gentiles, Gentiles appear to require authorization from outside the Torah if they are to adopt any of its practices as law. There is, then, a fundamental difference in orientation between Gentiles, who are not "under law" (to borrow a Pauline expression), and Jewish Christ-believers, who are portrayed as oriented toward the law.

The law is mentioned in connection with Jewish Christ-believers not only because it contributes to Luke's narrative argument, but also because, from Luke's perspective, it is the law of Israel, not that of another nation. The law of Moses can also be designated as "the custom (ἔθος) of Moses" (Acts 15:1), "the customs of the Jews" (Acts 26:3), or "the ancestral customs" (Acts 28:17). This is not because νόμος, for Luke, has been relegated to the level of mere custom, but because the law is "the *ethos* of a particular *ethnos*."[51] Because they do not become members of the Jewish *ethnos,* Gentiles are not subject to the laws of Israel.[52] Nor do Gentile believers become participants in the covenant with Israel. To be sure, Gentiles share along with Jews in the results of the Messiah's resurrection, which appears in Acts as shorthand for the covenant blessings promised to Israel,[53] but Gentiles receive the Holy Spirit and are granted "re-

50. See Susan J. Wendel, *Scriptural Interpretation and Community Self-Definition in Luke-Acts and the Writings of Justin Martyr* (NovTSup 139; Leiden: Brill, 2011), 143: Luke "reports numerous conflicts over how the scriptures ought to be interpreted and obeyed, but these reflect a struggle between Christ-believing and non-Christ-believing Jews."

51. Wilson, *Law,* 103.

52. See Jervell, *Luke,* 137; Wilson, *Law,* 104.

53. Acts 23:6; 24:14-16; 26:6-8, 22-23. See Robert C. Tannehill, *The Narrative Unity of Luke-Acts: A Literary Interpretation,* vol. 2, *The Acts of the Apostles* (Philadelphia: Fortress, 1990), 318-20, for the connection between "resurrection" and the promises to Israel. The "covenant" (διαθήκη) is connected to promises in Luke 1:72-75 and Acts 3:25; cf. 2:39; 3:18.

pentance unto life" (11:18) as "a people from the Gentiles for his name" (15:14).[54] Luke never refers to Gentile Christ-believers as Israel,[55] and he never includes them within the covenant with Abraham and with Israel at Mount Sinai.[56]

So far our conclusions about the possibility of a Torah ethic for Gentile Christ-believers have been negative: Luke neither thinks in terms of "moral law" nor indicates that Gentiles correspond directly to the Torah's "resident aliens," and because the Torah is the law of the covenant people, it does not apply, as law, to Gentiles.

Reading Torah as Prophecy

Luke's conception of prophecy points, finally, to another way of explaining the relationship between the ethical practices expected of Gentile Christ-believers and the authority of the Mosaic law. Even though the prophets, like the law, are connected to the Sinaitic covenant, and their messages, like the law, are addressed to the covenant people, not Gentiles, there is a sense in which the law (as well as the prophets' messages) would have continued to be received as prophecy by Gentile Christ-believers: the words of Moses no less than the words of the prophets were believed to be spoken under divine inspiration.[57] Viewing Torah as prophecy in this sense helps explain why the writings included in the Torah were regarded as sacred, and why they were believed to be relevant to the present, but it also suggests how Luke might have assumed the Torah applied to Gentiles.

When we consider how Luke read the biblical prophets — both their messages and stories about them — as prophecy, we discover an implicit sense of historical distance. Although the words of the prophets remained applicable to the present, Luke recognized that at least part of their message was not directly addressed, in the first place, to his own contemporaries. In these cases, Luke

54. See Wendel, *Scriptural Interpretation*, 261-66.

55. See Nils Alstrup Dahl, "'A People for His Name' (Acts XV. 14)," *NTS* 4 (1957): 324-27.

56. Again, for Luke, the Abrahamic and Mosaic covenants are combined (see p. 78 above). However the "new covenant" of Luke 22:20 is to be understood — assuming the longer text of Luke 22:19-20 is original — it does not make Gentiles part of the Abrahamic people, and it need not mean that the covenant with Israel is obsolete or that Jewish followers of Jesus are no longer obligated to the law.

57. On this point, see especially John Barton, *Oracles of God: Perceptions of Ancient Prophecy in Israel after the Exile* (London: Darton, Longman and Todd, 1986; repr., New York: Oxford University Press, 1988), 103; cf. 54-55.

treats both their lives and their message paradigmatically. In Luke 4, for example, the reception of Elijah and Elisha by people from outside their homeland contrasts with the rejection Jesus faced in his hometown (vv. 24-30). And in Luke 11, the sign of Jonah that is now given to Jesus' audience (v. 29) consists of an analogy between Jonah and the Son of Man (v. 30) and the latent threat that unless they too repent Jesus' contemporaries will experience the judgment once held in store for Nineveh (v. 32; cf. 13:3).

And so with law. In Acts 4:34, the statement that "there was no needy person among" Jesus' Jewish followers recalls Deuteronomy's prediction that "there will be no needy person among you" (15:4), and contributes to Luke's depiction of the Jewish church as the law-observant community in which the promises to Israel are fulfilled. Here the connection between law and ethical practice is direct. Later in Acts, however, when Paul reminds the Ephesian elders of the importance of generosity, he appeals to the words of Jesus, not to the law (20:35). Nevertheless, although the Torah is not cited directly as an authority in Gentile contexts, it is not far from view — Paul's claim that he did not "covet" echoes the tenth commandment[58] — and it still informs Gentile ethical practice, but it does so indirectly. For example, (1) Luke's description of the Jewish church in the early chapters of Acts is programmatic for the Gentile church later in Acts. Just as the reception of the Spirit by non-Jews recalls the arrival of the Spirit at Pentecost and confirms that salvation has reached the Gentiles, so also the generosity of the Gentile church in Antioch recalls the law-observant generosity of the Jewish church in Jerusalem.[59] (2) The teaching of Jesus about possessions to which Paul directs his Gentile audience in Acts 20:35 is, in Luke's Gospel, closely connected to the law.[60] These examples suggest that Luke would have wanted Gentile readers among his audience to apply Jesus' words and the Torah's commands by analogy to their own different situations outside the covenant in much the same way that characters in Luke's narrative apply the prophets by analogy in different historical contexts.[61]

58. Acts 20:33; Exod. 20:17; cf. 1 Sam. 12:3.

59. Acts 11:27-30; cf. Acts 2:42-47; 4:32–5:11. See Gaventa, *Acts,* 181: "Just as the first *ekklēsia* acts for its poor, the new *ekklēsia* in Antioch acts on behalf of fellow-believers in Judea." For a related argument about the paradigmatic function of possessions, see Luke Timothy Johnson, *The Literary Function of Possessions in Luke-Acts* (SBLDS 39; Missoula: Scholars, 1977).

60. For example, Luke 10:25-37; 16:19-31.

61. For a suggestive discussion of the role of metaphor and analogy in New Testament ethics, see Richard B. Hays, *The Moral Vision of the New Testament: Community, Cross, New Creation: A Contemporary Introduction to New Testament Ethics* (New York: HarperCollins, 1996), 293-304.

Conclusion

Elements of an implicit but generally consistent approach to Torah ethics may be discerned in Luke's second volume when law and prophecy are viewed together, and when Luke's depictions of Jewish and Gentile Christ-believers are treated separately. In Acts, Jews are depicted as consistently Torah observant; Gentiles, by contrast, are directly obligated to only four requirements of the law, as authorized by the apostolic decree. Yet although Luke did not think that Gentile Christ-believers encountered the Torah in the context of God's covenant with Israel, he presumably took for granted that the law — and controversy stories about the law in Luke's Gospel — remains authoritative and relevant for Gentile Christ-believers when it is read as prophecy and applied by analogy.

That we have to work so hard piecing together what Luke probably assumed about the place of Torah in forming Gentile ethical practices is itself instructive. The law in Luke's writings plays a supporting role behind his overwhelming interest in Jesus. While Luke does not think they conflict, it is the example of Jesus, much more than the demands of Torah, that serves as the primary paradigm for the main characters in Acts, and hence for Luke's Gentile readers.

Reproach and Revelation: Ethics in John 11:1-44

Adele Reinhartz

Jesus' Jewishness should be obvious to any reader of the Gospels, yet it is only in the past fifty years that the implications of Jesus' Jewish identity have been taken seriously by historians, exegetes, and theologians of the New Testament and early Christianity. One area of inquiry to which Jesus' Jewish context is particularly relevant is ethics. As Jesus was a Jew, it is reasonable to suppose that his ethics as well as his own behavior toward others would have been shaped at least in part by Jewish ethical principles and precepts.

Whether this assumption is true cannot be known for certain, for the historical Jesus is accessible only through the New Testament accounts written down some decades after his death. Yet it is supported in large measure by the Synoptic Gospels, in which Jesus occasionally makes explicit reference to biblical passages in support of his ethical positions. Perhaps the clearest example can be found in Luke 10:25-28, in which a lawyer tests Jesus with the question: "What must I do to inherit eternal life?" Jesus answers the question with a question: "What is written in the law? What do you read there?" In response, the lawyer combines Deuteronomy 6:5 and Leviticus 19:18: "You shall love the Lord your God with all your heart, and with all your soul, and with all your strength, and with all your mind; and your neighbor as yourself." Jesus commends him for this response: "You have given the right answer; do this, and you will live."[1]

To be sure, the Synoptics' Jesus challenges the boundaries of some funda-

1. All scriptural quotations are from the NRSV, unless otherwise noted.

This essay is dedicated with affection and respect to my dear colleague and friend Steve Westerholm.

mental aspects of Jewish law. When confronted by the Pharisees after his disciples pluck grain on the Sabbath, Jesus proclaims the principle "the Sabbath was made for humankind, and not humankind for the Sabbath" and on that basis declares that "the Son of Man is lord even of the Sabbath" (Mark 2:23-28). According to Matthew, Jesus also contextualized Jewish dietary rituals by declaring that "it is not what goes into the mouth that defiles a person, but it is what comes out of the mouth that defiles." He explains this principle in ethical terms: "Do you not see," he tells his disciples, "that whatever goes into the mouth enters the stomach, and goes out into the sewer? But what comes out of the mouth proceeds from the heart, and this is what defiles. For out of the heart come evil intentions, murder, adultery, fornication, theft, false witness, slander. These are what defile a person, but to eat with unwashed hands does not defile" (Matt. 15:11-20; see also Mark 7:18-23). The Synoptics' Jesus also, however, upholds the observance of the ethical precepts of the Decalogue, as in Matthew 19:16-19, in which he enumerates the good things that one must do to have eternal life: "If you wish to enter into life, keep the commandments. . . . You shall not murder; You shall not commit adultery; You shall not steal; You shall not bear false witness; Honor your father and mother; also, You shall love your neighbor as yourself."

By contrast, the Johannine Jesus nowhere urges observance of the Decalogue or other biblical precepts. Although he observes some aspects of Jewish law such as the blessing over bread before eating (6:11) and pilgrimage to Jerusalem (e.g., 2:13; 5:1), the Gospel narrative includes a number of stories in which Jesus' behavior contravenes Jewish and biblical ethical norms. In this essay, I focus on one such story, the raising of Lazarus in John 11, in which Jesus not only disregards a fundamental ethical precept but is also reproached for doing so by other characters in the narrative.

Jesus' ethical breach takes place at the very beginning of John 11. When he receives word from Mary and Martha that their brother Lazarus is ill, he lingers for two more days instead of rushing to Bethany, as the sisters — and perhaps most readers — would have expected. Most commentators on the ethical implications of this story focus on its magnificent resolution: Lazarus's resurrection. Ruben Zimmermann suggests that Lazarus becomes a model for ethics in that he follows Jesus' call: "He hears the voice, comes out, and, most important, starts to live in a new way!"[2] Lazarus therefore demonstrates

2. Ruben Zimmermann, "Is There Ethics in the Gospel of John? Challenging an Outdated Consensus," in *Rethinking the Ethics of John: "Implicit Ethics" in the Johannine Writings* (ed. Jan G. van der Watt and Ruben Zimmermann; WUNT I 291; Tübingen: Mohr Siebeck, 2012),

that "the right way of living is to abide in the life received through Jesus."[3] For Volker Rabens, Jesus' behavior at Lazarus's tomb provides insight into the Johannine understanding of love and friendship.[4] According to Keener, "assurance that Jesus did care, that God did have long-range purposes in the suffering, even that Jesus joined in weeping with the bereaved as well as ultimately held power over life and death, would mean much to believers facing that universal human predicament of death, whether or not related to persecution."[5]

My own emphasis is on the beginning of the story, Jesus' decision to delay his departure after hearing the news of Lazarus's illness. I argue (a) that in delaying his departure for Bethany, Jesus is behaving in a manner that is contrary to first-century biblically based Jewish ethical norms; (b) that the narrator as well as the characters within the story are acutely aware of this ethical breach; and (c) that this behavior is consistent with the Gospel's Christology, according to which Jesus, as God's Son, is not bound by the obligations and ethical norms prescribed by or derived from the Hebrew Bible. In developing the analysis, I engage in a resistant reading that actively questions the attempts by the narrator, the implied author, and most modern commentators to justify Jesus' ethical breach on the grounds of the story's joyful resolution.

Ethics in the Gospel of John?

The interest in Johannine ethics is a relatively recent development and many scholars remain skeptical about the importance or even the presence of ethics in the Fourth Gospel.[6] Wayne Meeks's article "The Ethics of the Fourth Evan-

68. Zimmermann contrasts Jesus' call to Lazarus with the people's call for Jesus' death in the passion narrative ("Is There Ethics in the Gospel of John?" 87). A closer parallel, however, may be John 5:25, in which Jesus prophesies that "the hour is coming, and is now here, when the dead will hear the voice of the Son of God, and those who hear will live," as well as 10:1-5 in which the sheep know the voice of the shepherd and follow him out of the sheepfold. For detailed discussion, see Adele Reinhartz, *The Word in the World: The Cosmological Tale in the Fourth Gospel* (SBLMS 45; Atlanta: Scholars, 1992), 41.

3. Zimmermann, "Is There Ethics in the Gospel of John?" 68.

4. Volker Rabens, "Johannine Perspectives on Ethical Enabling in the Context of Stoic and Philonic Ethics," in *Rethinking the Ethics of John: "Implicit Ethics" in the Johannine Writings* (ed. Jan G. van der Watt and Ruben Zimmermann; WUNT I 291; Tübingen: Mohr Siebeck, 2012), 129.

5. Craig S. Keener, *The Gospel of John: A Commentary* (2 vols.; Peabody: Hendrickson, 2003), 839.

6. It must be noted, however, that to some extent the question of whether the Gospel of

gelist" is perhaps the most persuasive expression of this perspective.[7] Meeks frames the topic as an inquiry into the usefulness of the Gospel of John as an instrument of moral formation. From a historical point of view, Meeks argues, "the kind of ethos that the narrative of the Fourth Gospel seems designed to reinforce . . . is not one that many of us would happily call 'Christian' in a normative sense."[8] When Christians have political power, "and when they are tempted to identify the enemies of Jesus and of his Johannine disciples with those whom they dislike and whom they have power to harm, the results are likely to be perverse."[9] Meeks's analysis of John's ethics is consistent with his understanding of the Johannine community as an isolated and closed sectarian group that sees itself as a bastion of resistance against a dark and hostile world.[10]

Other scholars are much more optimistic about finding ethics in John, whether such ethics are seen as operative only within the Johannine community or more broadly.[11] These scholars view the "love commandment" (13:34-35; 15:12) as the foundation of Johannine ethics,[12] but they acknowledge that

---

John "contains" ethics, implies an ethics, or can be used as the basis of moral formation depends on the definition of ethics that one adopts. Most scholars who concern themselves with Johannine ethics adopt a relational definition. Labahn, for example, proposes a common-sense definition that views ethics as the relationships among or between Christian believers, as well as between those inside and those outside. In his view, ethics can be defined as a theory of human behavior according to which individuals are responsible subjects able to make effective judgments about their own deeds. This theory provides a "reflective orientation" toward one's "actual way of life" by "defining how to behave and act" in accordance with a value system and in relation to either members of one's own group or society at large. Furthermore, he proposes that ethical texts attempt to "persuade the reader to embrace the norms that they promote as normative." Michael Labahn, "'It's Only Love' — Is That All? Limits and Potentials of Johannine 'Ethic' — A Critical Evaluation of Research," in *Rethinking the Ethics of John: "Implicit Ethics" in the Johannine Writings* (ed. Jan G. van der Watt and Ruben Zimmermann; WUNT I 291; Tübingen: Mohr Siebeck, 2012), 6-7.

7. Wayne A. Meeks, "The Ethics of the Gospel of John," in *Exploring the Gospel of John: In Honor of D. Moody Smith* (ed. R. Alan Culpepper and C. Clifton Black; Louisville: Westminster John Knox, 1996), 317-26.

8. Meeks, "Ethics," 317.

9. Meeks, "Ethics," 325.

10. Meeks, "Ethics," 323. For his detailed analysis of Johannine community, see Wayne A. Meeks, "Man from Heaven in Johannine Sectarianism," *JBL* 91, no. 1 (1972): 44-72.

11. Labahn, "It's Only Love," 41.

12. Labahn, "It's Only Love," 27. See also Johannes Nissen, "Community and Ethics in the Gospel of John," in *New Readings in John: Literary and Theological Perspectives. Essays from the Scandinavian Conference on the Fourth Gospel in Århus 1997* (ed. Johannes Nissen and Sigfred Pedersen; JSNTSup 182; Sheffield: Sheffield Academic, 1999), 194-212; Francis J. Molo-

John offers little additional material that explicitly addresses ethical matters. Nevertheless, by looking for the values and behaviors that underlie the Gospel narratives and discourses, and by situating them within Jewish and Hellenistic moral traditions, they discern a broader set of ethical precepts that extend beyond interpersonal relationships to the moral vision of the community as a whole.[13]

Ruben Zimmermann, for example, argues that the absence of a systematic exposition of ethical norms and principles does not in itself signal the absence of ethical engagement. On the contrary, the New Testament presents an "implicit ethics," which Zimmermann defines as a "rational system of morality" evident in stories or arguments that explain, require, or prescribe particular actions.[14] In his view, the Fourth Gospel draws on Jewish narrative tradition to offer "the story of God in Jesus Christ" as "the master narrative for the narratively-constituted ethical identity of the audience."[15]

Jan van der Watt considers the Gospel's performative dimensions: the ways in which stories such as the wedding at Cana (John 2) and the footwashing (John 13) lead readers to faith and thereby create a foundation for ethical action.[16] Underlying the Gospel's narrative ethics is the Decalogue, nine commandments of which are referred or alluded to in the Gospel of John.[17] Important as the Bible is, however, the foundation of all ethical action is faith in Jesus as the one who mediates the relationship between the believer and God.[18]

---

ney, *Love in the Gospel of John: An Exegetical, Theological, and Literary Study* (Grand Rapids: Baker Academic, 2013).

13. On the broadening of moral vision and friendship, see Nissen, "Community and Ethics," 199, 205.

14. Ruben Zimmermann, "The 'Implicit Ethics' of New Testament Writings: A Draft on a New Methodology for Analysing New Testament Ethics," *Neot* 43, no. 2 (2009): 403.

15. Zimmermann, "Is There Ethics in the Gospel of John?" 66.

16. Jan G. van der Watt, "Ethics through the Power of Language: Some Explorations in the Gospel according to John," in *Moral Language in the New Testament: The Interrelatedness of Language and Ethics in Early Christian Writings* (ed. Ruben Zimmermann and Jan G. van der Watt in cooperation with Suzanne Luther; WUNT II 296; Tübingen: Mohr Siebeck, 2010), 140. See also Jan G. van der Watt, "Radical Social Redefinition and Radical Love: Ethics and Ethos in the Gospel according to John," in *Identity, Ethics, and Ethos in the New Testament* (ed. Jan G. van der Watt; BZNW 141; Berlin: De Gruyter, 2006), 109.

17. Van der Watt, "Radical Social Redefinition," 110; Van der Watt, "Ethics through the Power of Language," 140. Cf. Jey J. Kanagaraj, "The Implied Ethics of the Fourth Gospel: A Reinterpretation of the Decalogue," *TynBul* 52, no. 1 (2001): 33-60.

18. Van der Watt, "Ethics through the Power of Language," 140; Zimmermann, "Is There Ethics in the Gospel of John?" 73.

Like Zimmerman and Van der Watt, I view John's narrative as the starting point for a consideration of Johannine ethics, and I agree that the Fourth Gospel's version of the life of Jesus implicitly reflects on Jewish ethical norms, the sources of which are found in the Hebrew scriptures. Where I differ from their perspective is in my evaluation of Jesus as an ethical actor, and in the role of ethics in the Gospel's overall program, as evidenced in particular by John 11.

John 11:1-6: Jesus' Ethical Breach

The opening verses of John 11 introduce the main players (Mary, Martha, Lazarus) and the core problem (Lazarus's illness).

> Now a certain man was ill, Lazarus of Bethany, the village of Mary and her sister Martha. Mary was the one who anointed the Lord with perfume and wiped his feet with her hair; her brother Lazarus was ill. (vv. 1-2)

The flash forward to the anointing story in John 12 implies that, in contrast to most other characters in John 1–12, this family has a prior and close relationship with Jesus.

The ethical conundrum posed by the story occurs in verses 3-6:

> So the sisters sent a message to Jesus, "Lord, he whom you love is ill." But when Jesus heard it, he said, "This illness does not lead to death; rather it is for God's glory, so that the Son of God may be glorified through it." Accordingly, though Jesus loved Martha and her sister and Lazarus, after having heard that Lazarus was ill, he stayed two days longer in the place where he was.

In verse 3, the phrasing of the sisters' message implies their belief that (a) Jesus has the ability to heal Lazarus, and (b) his love for Lazarus creates an ethical obligation for him to do so. On these grounds their expectation is reasonable, for in verse 5 the narrator affirms Jesus' love for Martha and her siblings. By placing Jesus' comment that "this illness does not lead to death" (v. 4) before Jesus' decision to delay (v. 6), the Gospel implies an awareness of and discomfort with Jesus' breach of ethical norms. Underlying this discomfort is the unacceptable notion that by delaying, Jesus bears some responsibility for Lazarus's death.

The Gospel preemptively addresses this issue by inserting Jesus' comment that Lazarus's illness serves an important purpose: the glorification of the Son of God. Jesus expands on this comment in his conversation with the disciples prior to his departure for Judea. The disciples worry that returning to Judea poses a danger to Jesus: "Rabbi, the Jews were just now trying to stone you, and are you going there again?" (v. 8). Jesus explains why he must go: "Our friend Lazarus has fallen asleep, but I am going there to awaken him" (v. 11). The disciples are puzzled by the euphemism: "Lord, if he has fallen asleep, he will be all right" (v. 12). "Then Jesus told them plainly, 'Lazarus is dead. For your sake I am glad I was not there, so that you may believe. But let us go to him'" (vv. 14-15). Jesus thereby reassures the disciples, and the readers, that contrary to the impression created by his delay, he does intend to come to Lazarus's assistance, if not at the time and in the manner that the sisters expected. His obligation to Lazarus overrides the disciples' concerns about his, and their, personal safety.[19] This exchange suggests that Jesus is not denying the ethical obligation of friendship but that he has relativized it: his obligation to help Lazarus is important enough to risk his own life, and perhaps that of his disciples, but less important than the opportunity to glorify God and his own sonship.[20]

Excusing Jesus' Ethical Breach

In justifying Jesus' delay, the implied author attempts to deflect the sisters' ethical reproach. Most scholarly readings of this chapter do the same.[21] This is

19. Danger to the disciples is suggested by Thomas's statement to his fellow disciples, "Let us also go, that we may die with him" (v. 16).

20. The same had occurred at the wedding at Cana, when Jesus initially seemed to refuse to alleviate the wine shortage (2:4), and again for the second Cana sign, when he refused to come down to Capernaum to heal the nobleman's son (4:48). In both cases he resolved the issues at hand, but not in the manner that the petitioners had imagined. Yet the stakes are greater in John 11 than in either of the previous passages. It is one thing to cope with a wine shortage. It is, of course, more serious to prevent a death. But to miss the opportunity to heal a beloved friend seems a far more serious ethical breach. The ethical question is whether the eventual result justifies the pain and trauma that was caused to the sisters and, of course, to Lazarus himself. For detailed discussion of this narrative pattern in the Johannine sign-stories, see Adele Reinhartz, "Great Expectations: A Reader-Oriented Approach to Johannine Christology and Eschatology," *Literature and Theology* 3, no. 1 (1989): 61-76.

21. These readings are compliant in the sense that they comply with the implied author's interpretation of the events. For a discussion of the concept of the compliant reading, see Adele Reinhartz, *Befriending The Beloved Disciple: A Jewish Reading of the Gospel of John* (New York: Continuum, 2001), 26-28.

not to say that all commentators ignore the problem raised by Jesus' decision to delay. R. Alan Culpepper refers to Jesus' answer in 11:4 as an "enigmatic response."[22] Raymond E. Brown goes beyond puzzlement to suggest that the narrator's parenthetical statement creates a paradox, for love should have led to immediate action.[23] Wendy Sproston North calls this

> one of the strangest moments in the entire Gospel. Instead of setting off immediately for Bethany, which is what we would expect, Jesus stays where he is for two more days. No explanation is offered for this. There is only the general assurance in v. 5 of Jesus' affection for the whole family, which looks designed to ward off any suggestion that his behaviour in v. 6 was due to indifference.[24]

Craig Keener too acknowledges that the delay creates a negative impression: "Given the urgency of the request for a miracle worker, Jesus' delaying could appear to dishonor the family and trivialize its suffering; even if Lazarus would have died before his arrival, the family was counting on his rapid arrival."[25]

Malina and Rohrbach provide a social-scientific explanation rooted in the honor/shame dynamic often associated with Mediterranean cultures. They argue that the fact that Jesus did not leave immediately for Bethany would have been a source of shame and as such required explanation: "People were normally expected to fulfill the symbolic contract implied in friendship by dropping everything and going immediately when summoned. Friends belonged to the in-group of collectivist society. They stood in privileged relationships with other group members and had the 'right' to immediate assistance."[26]

Some go further to consider why the Gospel includes this detail if it is so problematic. Sproston North suggests a literary reason: to emphasize that Lazarus was indeed dead.[27] The delay therefore removes doubt from the miracle, as there can be no suggestion that he awoke from a coma or otherwise

22. R. Alan Culpepper, *The Gospel and Letters of John* (Nashville: Abingdon, 1998), 186.

23. Raymond E. Brown, *The Gospel according to John: A New Translation with Introduction and Commentary* (2 vols.; AB 29; Garden City: Doubleday, 1966-70), 1:423.

24. Wendy E. Sproston North, *The Lazarus Story within the Johannine Tradition* (JSNTSup 212; Sheffield: Sheffield Academic, 2001), 136-37.

25. Keener, *John*, 839.

26. Bruce J. Malina and Richard L. Rohrbaugh, *Social-Science Commentary on the Gospel of John* (Minneapolis: Fortress, 1998), 195.

27. Sproston North, *Lazarus Story*, 138.

spontaneously revived. Zimmermann agrees with Sproston North, commenting that Jesus "deliberately stayed where he was, so that death became inevitable."[28] This point is important for two reasons: to demonstrate Jesus' glorification, and to emphasize the reality of death.[29]

Craig Keener objects to this line of interpretation. He suggests that Lazarus would have died even if Jesus had departed for Bethany immediately on hearing the news. Indeed, Lazarus may well have been dead before the message had even reached Jesus. Given that Lazarus had died four days before Jesus' arrival, and given that Bethany is a day's travel from the Galilee, there is at most a three-day interval between the time Jesus learns of his friend's illness and the time he arrives at the house of mourning. If so, Lazarus must have died on the day that the messenger(s) set off for the Jordan.[30]

Keener's calculations may be correct but they do not bear on the ethical question. Furthermore, they do not seem to cohere with the chapter's importance in John's narrative. Jesus' delay sets in motion the series of events that culminate in his own death and resurrection. Without the delay, Lazarus may not have died. Without his death, there would be no need for a resurrection. Without the resurrection, there would be no controversy among the Jewish witnesses, no concern among the council, no plan to put Jesus to death, and therefore no betrayal or crucifixion. The delay, and the likelihood that it resulted in Lazarus's death, are therefore crucial to the dramatic climax of the story, and to the salvation narrative that is central to John's Christology.

The question remains, however: from an ethical perspective, was Jesus' delay justified in light of the spectacular life-giving miracle that he later performed? Most scholars argue that it was. Christos Karakolis comments that "on the ethical level, the story of Lazarus shows the love and care that the members of the divine family should have for each other."[31] In this light, it is wrong to interpret Jesus' delay as waiting for Lazarus to die in order to perform

28. Ruben Zimmermann, "The Narrative Hermeneutics of John 11: Learning with Lazarus How to Understand Death, Life, and Resurrection," in *The Resurrection of Jesus in the Gospel of John* (ed. Craig R. Koester and Reimund Bieringer; WUNT I 222; Tübingen: Mohr Siebeck, 2008), 99.

29. Zimmermann, "John 11," 99. On this point, see also Philip Francis Esler and Ronald A. Piper, *Lazarus, Mary and Martha: Social-Scientific Approaches to the Gospel of John* (Minneapolis: Fortress, 2006), 111.

30. Keener, *John*, 839.

31. Christos Karakolis, "Semeia Conveying Ethics in the Gospel according to John," in *Rethinking the Ethics of John: "Implicit Ethics" in the Johannine Writings* (ed. Jan G. van der Watt and Ruben Zimmermann; WUNT I 291; Tübingen: Mohr Siebeck, 2012), 208.

a resurrection instead of a healing. "This interpretation is incompatible with the express love of Jesus towards Lazarus and his two sisters (11:5, 36) as well as with his strong emotions due to Lazarus' death and to the pain it had caused to those close to him."[32]

Lazarus's resurrection is therefore seen as benefiting not only himself and his family but also humanity as a whole. For John's Gospel, the resurrection of Lazarus is the catalyst for the Jewish authorities' plot against Jesus' life and his subsequent resurrection. Consequently, Lazarus's death is essential to human salvation. As Moody Smith points out, although Jesus' delay allowed Lazarus to die, "precisely through this death life will be revealed."[33] Keener explains:

> Lest readers misunderstand the reason for Jesus' delay (11:6), John explicitly emphasizes Jesus' love for the family. . . . Assurance that Jesus did care, that God did have long-range purposes in the suffering, even that Jesus joined in weeping with the bereaved as well as ultimately held power over life and death, would mean much to believers facing that universal human predicament of death, whether or not related to persecution.[34]

These comments suggest that the short-term suffering of the Bethany family was regrettable but in the end justified and indeed worthwhile in light of the opportunity that Lazarus's death offered for Jesus to demonstrate his glory to humankind as a whole.

One might wonder what Lazarus himself might have thought. Although his illness, death, and restoration are the main plot elements, Lazarus himself is given short shrift by many commentators on this chapter. A notable exception is Ruben Zimmermann. He notes that Lazarus might seem to be passive in the story (not surprising as he is dying or dead when we first hear of him) but in reacting to Jesus' call to life, Lazarus demonstrates that "the right way of living is to abide in the life received through Jesus."[35] From this episode, Zimmermann generalizes to the Gospel as a whole. Although the Fourth Gospel at first glance exhibits a "lack of concrete ethical advice," a closer look shows that "John enables different readers in various situations to act concretely."[36]

Zimmermann's interpretation suggests that Lazarus's restored life was qualitatively different from and superior to the life he enjoyed before his illness.

32. Karakolis, "Semeia," 208 n. 62.
33. D. Moody Smith, *John* (ANTC; Nashville: Abingdon, 1999), 219.
34. Keener, *John*, 839.
35. Zimmermann, "Is There Ethics in the Gospel of John?" 68.
36. Zimmermann, "Is There Ethics in the Gospel of John?" 79.

This might well have been the case, but the narrative does not say so. Indeed, the Gospel is silent about Lazarus's post-resurrection existence aside from a brief note of his presence at dinner in 12:2. He then disappears from the Gospel as completely as if he had remained in the grave after all.

A Resistant Reading of John 11

The characters within the story call Jesus to account. According to their ethical norms, as well as those of the narrator and implied author, Jesus' decision to delay his departure for Bethany by two days violated the obligations of friendship. The story hints at the need for both the characters and the narrator simply to accept Jesus' behavior. (Whether the story really occurred, or whether Jesus did or would really have behaved in this way is not relevant.) It is the narrator and implied author's view that the pain — to Lazarus, of course, but also to his sisters — caused by the delay was justified in view of the subsequent resurrection.

The scholarly interpretations reviewed above follow the Gospel's lead in justifying Jesus' "strange" or "paradoxical" or "enigmatic" behavior in light of the story's glorious resolution. In this respect, they constitute compliant readings of John 11:1-44. A compliant interpretation is consistent with the Christology of the Gospel and reinforces the broader Christian understanding of Jesus' own ethical perfection by resolving the tension created by the reference to his delay. It is also satisfying in that it appeals to human emotion, and the universal experience of grief and the hope of restoration.[37]

A resistant reading does not negate or diminish the joy that we naturally attribute to Lazarus, Martha, and Mary. Rather, it questions whether, from an ethical perspective, the end justifies the means, that is, whether the successful outcome erases Jesus' ethical breach.

In resisting the Gospel's affirmative answer, I would like to make three points. First, according to the Gospel account itself, Jesus' eventual action in restoring Lazarus to life is itself not ethically motivated. Although Jesus seems distressed by his friend's death, and/or by Martha and Mary's grief, he does not raise Lazarus in order to bring relief and joy to the dead man and his family, but to demonstrate his divine sonship to the disciples (11:15), to the siblings

37. One is reminded, for example, of Psalm 30: "You have turned my mourning into dancing; you have taken off my sackcloth and clothed me with joy, so that my soul may praise you and not be silent. O LORD my God, I will give thanks to you forever" (vv. 11-12).

(11:40), and to the crowd (11:42). To the disciples he says, "For your sake I am glad I was not there, so that you may believe" (11:15). To Martha he says, "Did I not tell you that if you believed, you would see the glory of God?" (11:40). About the crowd he tells God, "Father, I thank you for having heard me. I knew that you always hear me, but I have said this for the sake of the crowd standing here, so that they may believe that you sent me" (11:41-42). As with the other signs, the benefit to the individual whose need has been addressed seems to be a consequence rather than a goal of the sign.

Second, and more important, Jesus' violation of accepted ethical norms is not an isolated incident but occurs in at least two other passages: the Cana wedding (John 2) and the feast of Tabernacles (John 7). These examples return us to the relationship of Jesus' behavior in the Gospel of John to the ethical norms of Jewish and biblical tradition.

At the Cana wedding, Jesus' mother notes that the wine has run out. When she mentions this to Jesus, he replies, "Woman, what concern is that to you and to me? My hour has not yet come" (2:4). As in John 11, Jesus' initial refusal to engage with the problem is followed by performance of a miracle or sign that exceeds that which was requested in the first place: Jesus does not go out to purchase wine, but turns water into wine. To be sure, his use of the term "woman" here, while sounding disrespectful, is also a marker of revelation; Jesus uses it to preface revelatory statements to the Samaritan woman (4:21) and to Mary Magdalene at the empty tomb (20:15).[38] Nevertheless, at the very least this passage is ethically ambiguous; in John 2:4, it sounds very much like Jesus violates the command to honor (or at least be polite to) one's parents (Exod. 20:12).[39]

A second example of ethical ambiguity occurs in John 7:8-10. Prior to the feast of Tabernacles, Jesus' brothers urge him to go up to Jerusalem "so that your disciples also may see the works you are doing; for no one who wants to be widely known acts in secret" (7:3-4). The narrator interprets their comment as hostile, adding parenthetically: "For not even his brothers believed in him" (7:5). By this point in the narrative, the implied author has already established that Jesus does indeed go to Jerusalem for most, if not all, of the pilgrimage festivals (see 2:13; 5:1), the exception being the previous Passover

38. See briefly Adele Reinhartz, "The Gospel according to John," in *The Jewish Annotated New Testament* (ed. Amy-Jill Levine and Marc Z. Brettler; Oxford: Oxford University Press, 2011), 161.

39. Although they portray Jesus as upholding the commandment to honor one's parents (e.g., Mark 7:10-13), the Synoptics too portray Jesus as distancing himself from his mother. See, for example, Mark 3:31-35.

when he stayed in the Galilee, fed the multitudes, and delivered the Bread of Life discourse (chapter 6).[40] In John 7, Jesus tells his brothers that he will not join them for the festival: "Go to the festival yourselves. I am not going to this festival, for my time has not yet fully come" (7:8). Yet after his brothers departed, Jesus also went "not publicly but as it were in secret" (7:10). While lying and deceit are not direct violations of the Decalogue, they are proscribed in other biblical passages such as Exodus 23:7 ("Keep far from a false charge") and Leviticus 19:11 ("You shall not steal; you shall not deal falsely; and you shall not lie to one another").

John 11 too can be understood in the context of Jewish ethical norms. In the Lazarus story, the principle at stake is *pikuach nefesh,* according to which the preservation of human life overrides all other considerations, religious or otherwise. This rabbinic principle is articulated in the Babylonian Talmud tractate *Yoma* 84b, which, commenting on a *baraita,* states that "the possibility of danger to human life renders inoperative the laws of the Sabbath." If the obligation to save a life overrides even the Sabbath — one of the most important commandments — then by extension, it is paramount above almost all other considerations. The principle is not stated directly in the Bible but is associated in rabbinic discussion with several biblical verses, including Leviticus 18:5 ("You shall keep my statutes and my ordinances; by doing so one shall live: I am the Lord") and Leviticus 19:16 ("You shall not profit by the blood of your neighbor: I am the Lord"). Rabbinic development of this principle postdates the writing of the Gospel of John, but it echoes Hellenistic views about the obligations of friendship that date back as far as Aristotle.[41] The comments of Mary, Martha, and the Jews, and the narrator's haste to explain Jesus' delay, imply that this principle was known and accepted as important to the first-century audience for which the Gospel was written.

The key to understanding the Gospel's stance toward Jesus' interpersonal ethical breaches and their relationship to biblically based law and practice is to be found in chapter 5. Jesus is in Jerusalem at an unnamed festival. On the Sabbath, he heals a man who has been ill for thirty-eight years, and tells him to pick up his mat and walk (v. 8). The Jewish authorities confront the man: "It is the Sabbath; it is not lawful for you to carry your mat" (v. 10). But the man points out that he is simply obeying the one who made him well,

40. Adele Reinhartz, "Jesus as Prophet: Predictive Prolepses in the Fourth Gospel," *JSNT* 36 (1989): 3-16.

41. On the development of and primary sources for *pikuach nefesh,* see Hayim Yitshak Abramovitz, *Va-hai bahem: pikuah nefesh ba-halakhah: leket mekorot meforashim me-rishone ha-tanaim ve-'ad aharone ha-poskim* (Jerusalem: Orot, 1957).

who had told him to "Take up your mat and walk" (v. 11). For this reason, "the Jews started persecuting Jesus, because he was doing such things on the Sabbath" (v. 16). Jesus does not deny the violation but asserts that the Sabbath law does not apply to him because he is God's Son: "My Father is still working, and I also am working" (v. 17). Just as God's creative and healing activity continues on the Sabbath, so too does the work of the Son, who acts in his Father's name.

The healed man implicitly acknowledges the same point as he accepts the authority of the healer who told him to take up his mat.[42] Nevertheless, the Gospel is not directly concerned with the question of whether believers in Christ should or should not observe Jewish or biblical law. The main point is rather that laws that govern human behavior, though divinely given, do not apply to God or God's family. As God's Son, Jesus behaves as God does. Jesus' statement in 5:17 echoes discussions in Hellenistic Jewish literature, on God's own non-observance of the Sabbath in conjunction with Genesis 2:2-3.[43]

I suggest that this same understanding of the relationship of the divine to human behavior underlies the Gospel stories in which Jesus' behavior violates ethical laws such as honoring parents, refraining from lies and deceit, and the obligation to save a life. As in the case of Sabbath law, the Gospel of John is not making a statement about the value of these laws. Rather, it is declaring that, for Jesus, observance of these laws and norms is secondary to the requirements and responsibilities of his identity as the Messiah and Son of God. The need to glorify God and be glorified by God overrides other concerns. The Johannine Jesus may not always be at ease with the need to choose between the human and divine claims on him — this much would be suggested by his mournful behavior on arriving in Bethany — but it is clear where his primary obligation lies. The consolation is that in complying with the demands of his divine identity, he is ultimately working toward the salvation, and therefore, the good of others.

42. On the question of whether the Gospel is implicitly saying that Sabbath observance is no longer necessary for believers, see William Loader, "The Law and Ethics in John's Gospel," in *Rethinking the Ethics of John: "Implicit Ethics" in the Johannine Writings* (ed. Jan G. van der Watt and Ruben Zimmermann; WUNT I 291; Tübingen: Mohr Siebeck, 2012), 143-58.

43. Peder Borgen, *The Gospel of John: More Light from Philo, Paul and Archaeology: The Scriptures, Tradition, Exposition, Settings, Meaning* (NovTSup 154; Leiden: Brill, 2014), 179-91. For ancient discussion, see Aristobulus 5.11; Philo, *Leg.* 1.5-6, 18.

Reflections on Torah and Ethics in the Gospel of John

The analysis of John 11 and related passages suggests that ethics in the Gospel of John is not so much implicit — lying beneath the surface of its narratives and discourses — as inferred — derived from the Gospel by exegetes and theologians who wish to bring this Gospel to bear on the topic of Christian ethics more generally. Nevertheless, to say that the Gospel can be used as a resource for ethics does not mean that the Gospel "contains" ethics.[44]

The key to understanding the Gospel's willingness to show Jesus' ethical shortcomings may lie in the prologue, which presents Jesus as the divine Logos who takes on flesh to dwell among humankind. As the Logos, Jesus is not only the Son of God but also divine revelation, one that supersedes the Torah as the "text" that mediates the covenantal relationship between God and humankind. Just as the Torah was given to humankind and not the angels (Shabbat 88b) so too did the Logos take on flesh for the sake of humankind. Neither God nor God's Logos is bound by the laws of the Torah or by the norms that make human relationships both possible and satisfying.[45]

The Gospel's portrayal of Jesus as breaching ethical norms does not mean that the historical Jesus himself did so. Nor does it mean that the Gospel encouraged believers in Jesus to do so, or that the Gospel's audience rejected the Hebrew Bible as authoritative and formative in terms of its own ethical norms. It does suggest, however, that the Gospel writer is not attempting to set Jesus up as a model for human ethics, or, one might add, to prescribe an ethical system for the sake of the Gospel's audiences. On the contrary, he is asserting that as the Son of God Jesus disregards or overrides the accepted ethical norms for a higher purpose.

44. These two points seem to be conflated in Zimmermann, "Is There Ethics in the Gospel of John?" 44 and *passim*.

45. This conclusion is consistent with the analysis presented by Loader, "Law and Ethics."

The Law of the Laws: James, Wisdom, and the Law

Scot McKnight

Scholarship on how the Jewish scriptures were used among various Jewish groups continues to grow,[1] but my focus in this study is on law, the letter of James, and how the law is understood and used by the author, whom I consider to be the brother of Jesus.[2] In particular, there is reason to focus on James's appropriation of what can be called the Jesus Creed. By this I mean Jesus combined the Shema of Deuteronomy 6:5-9 with Leviticus 19:18 to form a kingdom-shaped Shema (the Jesus Creed), and this can be seen in Mark 12:28-32 (and parallels), which shows a presence in other parts of the New Testament, most notably Paul (Rom. 13:9; Gal. 5:14), not to ignore the pervasive presence of the same in 1 John. If the Old Testament plays an important part in the theology of the earliest Christians from Jesus on, that same movement also learned to read its scriptures at the feet of Jesus, and if Jesus can be said to have "reduced" Torah to the Jesus Creed, we cannot be surprised to find it in the letter of James.

In a suggestive move for investigating James's use of the Old Testament,[3] Luke Timothy Johnson probed the presence, mostly implicit, of Leviticus 19

1. There is no need here to provide a listing of that scholarship, but one cannot move on without mentioning the brilliant work on how the Hebrew Bible's own authors and editors were at work on earlier texts and how those methods formed later hermeneutics by Michael Fishbane, *Biblical Interpretation in Ancient Israel* (Oxford: Clarendon, 1985).

2. Scot McKnight, *The Letter of James* (NICNT; Grand Rapids: Eerdmans, 2011), 13-38. Others have argued the same, including Luke Timothy Johnson, *The Letter of James: A New Translation with Introduction and Commentary* (AB 37A; New York: Doubleday, 1995). Not all agree, of course, and the most recent robust defense of alternative authorship is Dale C. Allison, *A Critical and Exegetical Commentary on the Epistle of James* (ICC; New York: Bloomsbury T&T Clark, 2013), 3-32.

3. I am aware that use of "Old Testament" is a Christian perception of what Jews often call Tanak or what scholars call the Hebrew Bible.

in the letter of James.[4] Provoked into a consideration of the pervasive use of Leviticus 19 in James by a similar source at work in *The Sentences of Pseudo-Phocylides,* Johnson finds Leviticus 19 where others have not looked, or have looked but not seen it. Clearly, James cites Leviticus 19:18b in James 2:8, and apparently James is quoting from the LXX itself, though one has to wonder if a similar translation might not have come from anyone who can read Hebrew and Greek. Johnson contends that the context for James's use of Leviticus 19:18b deals with partiality, a theme found in Leviticus 19:15,[5] and that James's connection of Leviticus 19:18b to lines in the Ten Commandments (James 2:11; citing Exod. 20:13-14; Deut. 5:17-18) also finds substantive parallel in *Pseudo-Phocylides.* Johnson adds James 5:4's evocation of the unpaid workers as an almost certain use of Leviticus 19 inasmuch as Leviticus 19:13 seems to be melded to Isaiah 5:9, though he admits that James 5:4 has close, even closer, parallels in Malachi 3:5 and Deuteronomy 24:14. The presence of Leviticus 19 already in James tips a consideration in favor of the same text's influence in James 5:4. With no more than a twinkle in my eye, one might say Johnson then stretches the skin of the fox over other texts to show the presence of Leviticus 19 in James 4:11; 5:12, and 5:20. I am less concerned with whether or not Johnson is right than that he has pointed us forward to a discussion of James's use of the law as seen through his citation of Leviticus 19:18 in James 2:8.

How then does James understand and use the law?[6]

Logos Is *Nomos*

First, I contend for James that λόγος is νόμος, the Logos is the Torah. One of the more intriguing shifts in James can be seen in James 1:22-25, which I quote in order to italicize the shift:

4. Luke Timothy Johnson, *Brother of Jesus, Friend of God: Studies in the Letter of James* (Grand Rapids: Eerdmans, 2004), 123-35.

5. Where the LXX has οὐ λήμψῃ πρόσωπον and James has προσωπολημψίαις in 2:1.

6. Some of what follows expands and extends sections from three other studies of mine, including a forthcoming festschrift study for Bruce Chilton, a paper presented at Rochester College, and "James' Secret: Wisdom in James in the Mode of Receptive Reverence," in *Preaching Character: Reclaiming Wisdom's Paradigmatic Imagination for Transformation* (ed. Dave Bland and David Fleer; Abilene: Abilene Christian University Press, 2010), 201-16. An excellent probing study of James's use of the Old Testament is D. A. Carson, "James," in *Commentary on the New Testament Use of the Old Testament* (ed. G. K. Beale and D. A. Carson; Grand Rapids: Baker Academic, 2007), 997-1013.

> Do not merely listen to the *word* [λόγος], and so deceive yourselves. Do what it says. Anyone who listens to the *word* [λόγος] but does not do what it says is like someone who looks at his face in a mirror and, after looking at himself, goes away and immediately forgets what he looks like. But whoever looks intently into the perfect *law* [νόμος] that gives freedom, and continues in it — not forgetting what they have heard, but doing it — they will be blessed in what they do. (NIV)

James also uses νόμος in 2:8, where he cites Leviticus 19:18b; in 2:9, where the νόμος condemns the sinner for favoritism (alluding perhaps to Lev. 19:15); in 2:10, where the whole law (an expression sometimes used for the Jesus Creed in the New Testament) must be kept; and in 2:11, where two specific commandments are cited and that furthers the condemning role of the νόμος. The same function of the νόμος is at work, with new nuance and rhetorical significance, in James 4:11: slandering a brother or sister in the messianic community "speaks against the νόμος and judges it." When judging the νόμος, he adds, "you are not keeping it [words used in James 1:23-25 for λόγος], but sitting in judgment on it."

In James 2:12, a new stage is reached: "Speak and act as those who are going to be judged by the νόμος," but he adds that this νόμος "gives freedom." Once again we are drawn back to the paradigmatic terms in James 1:23-25, cited above, where we learn that λόγος is νόμος and this λόγος-νόμος creates "freedom." As I sorted out in another context, this expression about freedom in James 1:25 has three possible meanings: the Hellenistic Judaism view that sees here a life in accordance with reason (e.g., Philo, *Prob.* 45-46); the more nomistic Judaism view, where the observant Jew finds freedom in obeying God (Ps. 19:7-11; Sir. 6:23-31); and what I call "Christian Judaism," by which I mean Jesus-as-Messiah Judaism, where it refers to the Torah of Moses as understood and interpreted by Jesus.[7] This is my next point.

The *Logos-Nomos* Is Shema Revised

The Torah, or the νόμος, is comprehended by James through the hermeneutics of Jesus. My contention is that however often James quotes Leviticus 19 in his letter, the more important point is that James has absorbed Jesus' hermeneutic of love in seeing the entire Torah through the lens of love of God and love of

7. McKnight, *James*, 155-58.

neighbor. To be sure, loving others is important in the Jewish tradition, so I am not contending that Jesus was the first Jew to discover the importance of loving others alongside loving God. One finds this neighbor love especially in the *Testaments of the Twelve Patriarchs,* but the parallel is clearly not as formal as many have suggested. Here is what we find in *Testament of Issachar* 5:2: "Love the Lord and your neighbor." Two chapters later the same author can say of himself: "The Lord I loved with all my strength; likewise, I loved every human being as I love my children" (7:6). *Testament of Dan* 5:3 echoes the same: "Throughout all your life love the Lord, and one another with a true heart." We add also *Letter of Aristeas* 229: "The King . . . 'What deserves to be regarded as beauty?' He replied, 'Piety, for this is the preeminent form of beauty. Its dynamic is love.'"[8] What I am arguing, then, is that Jesus attached the explicit command to love others from Leviticus 19:18 to the daily recitation of the Shema, not that Jesus was the first Jew to have thought loving God needed to be complemented with loving others.[9]

I outline the case that the Shema as interpreted or amended by Jesus is at work in the letter of James in a number of places. The essence of the Shema is to love God by observing the commands of God, while the essence of the Jesus Creed is to love God and to love others — both, at the same time, always. What is often unnoted is that James has both ends of the Jesus Creed, and that this Jesus Creed is how James comprehended the λόγος-νόμος as God's will for the messianic community. In the final section of this chapter, I baptize his Torah comprehension in his apprehension of the wisdom of Jesus the Sage.

First, in James 1:12 we read, "Blessed is anyone who endures temptation. Such a one has stood the test and will receive the crown of life that the Lord has promised to those who love him." Love (ἀγαπάω)[10] in this context reexpresses and engulfs what James has already advocated for the messianic community: to believe and to endure (1:3-4). The formative point for Jews of the first century

8. On this, see W. D. Davies and Dale C. Allison, *A Critical and Exegetical Commentary on the Gospel according to Saint Matthew* (3 vols.; ICC; Edinburgh: T&T Clark, 1988-97), 3:237-38.

9. For an investigation of the Golden Rule, which is structurally parallel to the Jesus Creed, in Jesus and Judaism, see Philip S. Alexander, "Jesus and the Golden Rule," in *Hillel and Jesus: Comparative Studies of Two Major Religious Leaders* (ed. James H. Charlesworth and Loren L. Johns; Minneapolis: Fortress, 1997), 363-88.

10. See Ceslas Spicq, *Theological Lexicon of the New Testament* (trans. James D. Ernest; 3 vols.; Peabody: Hendrickson, 1994), 1:8-22. See also Leon Morris, *Testaments of Love: A Study of Love in the Bible* (Grand Rapids: Eerdmans, 1981), 169-72.

came from the daily recitation of the Shema,[11] a daily creedal prayer commitment that reminded the observant Jew that the essential command was to love God entirely. When we read that the daily routine of the Essene was to "enter the Covenant of God" (1QS X, 10), this most likely (as Sanders observes) refers to the recitation and praxis of the Shema's central command. We can assume that James, as a son of Mary and Joseph, brother and devoted follower of Jesus, recited the Shema daily and, if you agree with me, in the form taught by Jesus (the Jesus Creed). If, as many historians have concluded, the daily recitation of the Shema entailed also the recitation of the Ten Words (see *m. Tamid* 5:1; Nash Papyrus), then we have one more connection of Shema recitation to James 1:12: in the Ten Commandments God's "steadfast love" (חֶסֶד) is extended to those who "love me (לְאֹהֲבַי) and keep my commandments" (Exod. 20:6; cf. Deut. 5:10). Law, then, is less a sense of duty than the expression of what loving God looks like. That is, law is God's revelation to God's people who love him and who want to remain in fellowship with God. The focus on Shema is as mediated to James through his Judaism as it is through his brother, but the focus Jesus gives to the Jesus Creed makes me think James 1:12 could have come to James as much through Jesus as his Jewish world.

Second, James, like the apostle Paul of his day (Rom. 13:9; Gal. 5:14), has more emphasis on loving others than he does on loving God. Two texts — James 1:25 and 2:8 — need to be brought into connection because it is here that we see both what James makes of the νόμος and how dependent he is on how Jesus interpreted that νόμος.

> But those who look into the perfect law, the law of liberty, and persevere, being not hearers who forget but doers who act — they will be blessed in their doing. (1:25 NRSV)

> You do well if you really fulfill the royal law according to the scripture, "You shall love your neighbor as yourself." But if you show partiality, you commit sin and are convicted by the law as transgressors. For whoever keeps the whole law but fails in one point has become accountable for all of it. (2:8-10 NRSV)

The person James has in mind is the one who both looks and perseveres in what one sees. What they look at and persevere in is "the perfect law, the law

11. E. P. Sanders, *Judaism: Practice and Belief: 63 BCE–66 CE* (Philadelphia: Trinity Press International, 1992), 195-96.

of liberty." It surprises some to see the word "law" in this location: James has been using the term "word" (λόγος) up to this point (see 1:18, 21, 22, 23). There would seem to be only one real possibility here for James: he is referring to the Torah of Moses. But a variety of observations lead to the conclusion that James has a Jesus-shaped Christian hermeneutic of the Torah in mind in his "perfect law, the law of liberty." In the first place, Jesus connected his interpretation of the Torah with the word "perfection" on two occasions: Matthew 5:17-20, 48 and 19:16-21.[12] Now it so happens that in early Christian traditions both of these terms are connected to the Torah as taught by Jesus (see Matt. 5:17-20, 48; Gal. 5:13-14). Second, when James refers to the "law of liberty" the best interpretation is that he is referring to observance through the formative element of love. This becomes clear in James 2:8-11, where love leads in the observance of the commandments. An echo of 1:23-25 is found in 2:12 in the word "freedom." Put together, then, 1:23-25 is tied to 2:8-12 in a way that suggests the law of freedom is the second half of the Jesus Creed, or Leviticus 19:18b — the law of loving one's neighbor as oneself. This comes into the world of James through his older brother Jesus. Jesus "hermeneuts" the νόμος through the dual commands of loving God and loving others. The λόγος-νόμος for James is the Shema revised by Jesus.[13]

Third, we must repeat the point: James 2:8-10 explicitly cites the second half of the Jesus Creed, a text (Lev. 19:18b) not tied to the Shema by anyone in the Jewish world (known to me) prior to Jesus. If we linked the first of our texts above (James 1:12) to James 2:8-10, we have a full citation of both elements of Jesus' revision of the Shema. James 2:8 reads, "If you really do fulfill the royal law. . . ."[14] James here speaks next of their need to "fulfill the royal law," or the "royal command," or the "capital command."[15] In what sense is the law "royal" and how does this factor into the Jesus-shaped reading of the Torah? A few components come into play and need not exclude one another. It could

12. On τέλειον, see James 1:4 and 1:17. On this term, see Allison, *James*, 154-58; Douglas J. Moo, *The Letter of James* (PNTC; Grand Rapids: Eerdmans, 2000).

13. See Carson, "James," 1000, who sees "law" here as "rightly summarized" in the Jesus Creed.

14. Εἰ μέντοι νόμον τελεῖτε βασιλικόν. The particle μέντοι must be taken together with 2:9; the two verses in 2:8-9 as a whole form a contrast with what James has advocated in 2:1-7 because 2:9 (manifesting partiality) is the true condition of the community. But, the assumption of the truth of 2:8 needs to be connected to the obviously similar idea in 1:25 and its practices in 1:26-27. Thus, 2:8 itself contrasts with 2:2-7 and therefore needs a positive counterpart like what is seen in 1:25-27.

15. McKnight, *James*, 206-9; Allison, *James*, 401-5.

refer to the "capital," or "preeminent," of all the laws, which would suggest a connection of "royal law" to Leviticus 19:18 and thus that the law of loving others is that preeminent law. James would then be agreeing with Jesus (Mark 12:28-32), Paul (Rom. 12:19; 13:9; Gal. 5:14), John (1 John 3:11, 23; 4:17), and Peter (1 Pet. 4:8). But, inasmuch as Jesus is the Messiah and the Messiah is the royal king and the Messiah's rule is the kingdom, then the Messiah's law is royal and designed for his kingdom (see James 2:1). We can extend this slightly to another consideration: if the law is the Messiah's (royal) law, then the law itself is the royal law for the king's subjects as they live in the kingdom. I suggest, then, that "royal law" refers (1) to Jesus' highlighting of Leviticus 19:18 as the preeminent command alongside loving God; (2) to this interpretation of the Torah bringing the Torah to its destined completion (1:25); (3) to this law of love actually creating freedom for the messianic community; and (4) to the empowering implanted presence of word and Spirit in the messianic community, the people of the king who live the royal way of love. We confirm, then, that the λόγος-νόμος is the Shema revised by Jesus.

To back up before we see the import of the fourth text: we are arguing that James read the Torah through the grid given him by his older brother Jesus. That is, he learned to see all the *mitzvoth* as expressions of either loving God or loving others. The center of his brother's hermeneutics of the Torah is found in Jesus' own amendment to the standard recitation of the Shema, namely, Jesus added Leviticus 19:18 to Deuteronomy 6:5-9. The Shema, then, is the core of the earliest followers of Jesus' formation.

James 2:18-19 is our fourth text.[16]

> But someone will say, "You have faith and I have works." Show me your faith apart from your works, and I by my works will show you my faith. You believe that God is one; you do well. Even the demons believe — and shudder. (NRSV)

What matters here is not all the debates this specific text, along with 2:20-26, has generated, but the obviousness of James's citation of the opening for the Shema: "Hear O Israel, the Lord our God, the Lord is one." If we add James 1:12 and 2:8-10 to 2:18-19, we have the Shema as Jesus revised it. Put differently, the Shema locates James in observant Judaism; the addition of 2:8 locates James in Jesus-based Judaism. James comprehends the Torah in a Jewish world in which loving God and loving others forms the core command. Jesus is giving to his

16. See McKnight, *James,* 233-42; Allison, *James,* 468-78.

followers a way of comprehending the Torah: through love. James follows the path cut by Jesus.

Finally, I stretch the skin of the fox of the Shema revised over James 4:12 as well: "There is one lawgiver and judge who is able to save and to destroy. So who, then, are you to judge your neighbor?" Two points lead us to think that James may have picked this up from the Shema as revised by Jesus. First, the term πλησίον, or "neighbor," which is found seventeen times in the New Testament. Most noticeably, there are only two exceptions in the New Testament to the presence of this term not deriving from Leviticus 19:18.[17] A second consideration is that if we read James 3:1–4:12 as a unit, as I do, and as directed to teachers, as I do, then the completion of that section is in 4:11-12. This means the terms of that last paragraph — speaking slanderously of one's brothers, doing the law, and neighbor — take us right back to 1:23-25, to 2:8-12, and to the Shema as revised by Jesus. But the point here is not as weighty as the previous observations. Yet one more less-than-weighty consideration is the term "one" with "Lawgiver" in 4:12. One should not think that the term "one" by itself evokes the Shema, but in a letter already established as resonating with the Shema as revised by Jesus, I am inclined to see it once again here. For the one formed by the daily recitation of the Shema in the Jesus Creed form, there is only one to whom this "one" might refer: the One God of Israel. Add "neighbor" in the same verse (4:12) and one has at least a suggestion that James is listening to his brother.

Our summary then is that James comprehends the Torah through the grid of his older brother, who taught him to be Torah observant by loving God and loving one's neighbor as oneself. Where does James fit along the spectrum of Jewish groups? I want to suggest that he is not moving us toward Rabbinic Judaism but into the wisdom tradition, and here the work of Richard Bauckham is instructive.[18]

Jesus, James, Wisdom, and Law

The νόμος of James emerges from the context of the wisdom tradition. James surely saw God as the one true lawgiver (4:12), but our contention is that James

17. See Matt. 5:43; 19:19; 22:39; Mark 12:31, 33; Luke 10:27, 29, 36; Rom. 13:9-10; 15:2; Gal. 5:14; perhaps Eph. 4:25; James 2:8 and our text. Exceptions are John 4:5; Acts 7:27.

18. Richard Bauckham, *James: Wisdom of James, Disciple of Jesus the Sage* (New Testament Readings; London: Routledge, 1999).

saw Jesus as the sage whose wisdom he absorbed. Had James seen Jesus as the New Moses or as the New Lawgiver, I am suggesting, he would have quoted Jesus more often. But instead James has absorbed Jesus' teaching in such a way that his teachings emerge in every paragraph; apart from one lone exception he never quotes Jesus![19] And, in spite of the multitudinous parallels to the Old Testament one finds in the Nestle-Aland Greek text's margins to James, there are few explicit quotations (2:8, 11, 23; 4:6; 5:4, 5). In other words, James is not a name-dropper or a quoter, but an absorber of the wisdom of Jesus.

But what is wisdom? Ellen Davis says wisdom is "living in the world in such a way that God, and God's intentions for the world, are acknowledged in all that we do." This, as she wisely points out, is for all: "The fruit of wisdom, a well-ordered life and a peaceful mind, results not from a high IQ but from a disposition of the heart that the sages (wisdom teachers) of Israel most often called 'fear of the LORD.'"[20] One of my favorite lines of hers, a wise one indeed, is this: "the sages of Israel teach that those who would be wise must aim, not at power, but at goodness."[21] We turn next to another veteran wisdom scholar, Leo Perdue, who emphasizes wisdom as human construction. Perdue lands upon three elements to wisdom:

> First, wisdom is a body of knowledge, a tradition that sets forth an understanding of God, the world and nature, humanity, and human society.
>
> Second, wisdom is understood as discipline . . . that is, both a curriculum of study and a structured form of behavior designed to lead to the formation of character.
>
> Third, wisdom was moral discourse and behavior that constructed and legitimated a cosmology in which righteousness, both correct and just behavior as well as proper decorum, ordered the world, society, and individual existence.[22]

19. The exception is James 5:12, on which see McKnight, *James*, 423-29; Allison, *James*, 722-39.

20. Ellen F. Davis, *Proverbs, Ecclesiastes, and the Song of Songs* (Westminster Bible Companion; Louisville: Westminster John Knox, 2000), 1.

21. Davis, *Proverbs, Ecclesiastes, and the Song of Songs*, 27.

22. Leo G. Perdue, *Wisdom Literature: A Theological History* (Louisville: Westminster John Knox, 2007), 29-30. See also Douglas F. Estes, "Wisdom and Biblical Theology," in *Dictionary of the Old Testament: Wisdom, Poetry and Writings* (ed. Peter Enns and Tremper Longman III; Downers Grove: IVP Academic, 2008), 854. A good exposition of this inductive approach has been outlined by Walter Brueggemann, *Theology of the Old Testament* (Minneapolis: Fortress, 1997), 680-82.

In light of Proverbs 1:1-7, and from the angle of James (not Jesus the Sage), I contend that we need to see James's use of the Old Testament, his disposition toward the Torah, and his relationship to Jesus' teachings as "receptive reverence." Notice the words italicized in Proverbs 1:3:

> The proverbs of Solomon son of David, king of Israel:
> For learning about wisdom and instruction,
>   for understanding words of insight,
> *for gaining instruction in wise dealing,*
>   *righteousness, justice, and equity;*
> to teach shrewdness to the simple,
>   knowledge and prudence to the young —
> Let the wise also hear and gain in learning,
>   and the discerning acquire skill,
> to understand a proverb and a figure,
>   the words of the wise and their riddles.
>
> The fear of the LORD is the beginning of knowledge;
>   fools despise wisdom and instruction.

I want simply to sketch four themes from these verses for approaching what James does with law. First, a wise person, Proverbs informs us, "gains" instruction, or correction, in wise dealing (1:3a); second, the wise person has the attributes of righteousness, justice, and equity (צֶדֶק, מִשְׁפָּט, מֵישָׁרִים; 1:3b), which is about what James says in 3:13-18; third, the wise person is prudent and has discretion (עָרְמָה, מְזִמָּה; 1:4; cf. 8:12); and, fourth, the wise person possesses skill to know and practice these various attributes (1:5b).[23] No one could reasonably dispute that James draws on each of these, even if those themes do not morph his letter into the genre of wisdom.

But when we view wisdom from the angle of the student, wisdom shifts. I contend that wisdom is experienced by the willing and believing student as "receptive reverence" toward one's wise elders. "Receptive reverence" is my translation of the Hebrew לָקַחַת מוּסַר הַשְׂכֵּל in Proverbs 1:3a: "to take, or receive, or absorb the instruction/correction of insight [or 'discipline']."[24] Alongside scholarly studies of the origins of wisdom, we need a similar focus on the necessity of its absorption by the student, that is, on the posture of the

23. A good summary can be found in Proverbs 9:7-12.

24. On "discipline" (מוּסָר), see also 1:8; 4:13; 8:10; 23:23; 24:32.

student.[25] More directly, we put it like this: a wise person is receptive, malleable, and submissive in a reverent and respectful manner of the wisdom of one's teachers.

James, I contend, had absorbed the wisdom of Jesus[26] and the wise of his day, and it was his intent to incarnate that wisdom as he addressed the messianic community. His comprehension of Torah then is subsumed under his comprehension, yea apprehension, of wisdom. In making this claim, I am simultaneously making the claim that James did not (simply) treat the words of Moses or of Jesus as *halakah* but as *hokmah,* not simply as "law and ruling" but as "wisdom."[27] My contention, then, is that James's use of the Jesus tradition is parallel to his use of the Torah tradition in the mode of receptive reverence that he passes on in a legal-wisdom rhetoric.

Scholars have produced and reproduced such lists of James's use of the Jesus tradition many times and in many ways, but at least the following deserve consideration as they will introduce us to how James used and comprehended the Torah:[28]

25. See Joseph Blenkinsopp, *Sage, Priest, Prophet: Religious and Intellectual Leadership in Ancient Israel* (Louisville: Westminster John Knox, 1995), 9-65; Perdue, *Wisdom Literature,* 1-36.

26. I do not mean to argue here that James primarily understands Jesus through the lens of a sage or that his primary Christology is sapiential. In fact, I do not believe that; what we know from James is that Jesus is the Messiah (1:1) and the Glorious Lord (2:1). Anyone who is Messiah and Glorious Lord is surely a sage, but the issue here is one of priority: Messiah and Lord are prior to Sage. I like what Bauckham does with this; see *James,* 97-108, where he surfaces the central elements of Jesus' teachings (like radicality) and then compares those to James and concludes that James operates as did Jesus.

27. I would not classify the genre of James as a halakic use of Jesus, even if Peter Davids preferred that term (but only "loosely") in his important article on this theme. See Peter H. Davids, "James and Jesus," in *The Jesus Tradition outside the Gospels* (ed. David Wenham; Gospel Perspectives 5; Sheffield: JSOT, 1985), 74. Wesley Hiram Wachob, *The Voice of Jesus in the Social Rhetoric of James* (SNTSMS 106; Cambridge: Cambridge University Press, 2000), explores the Greco-Roman rhetorical context to find a similar conclusion for James.

28. This section is taken from my *James,* 25-26. See also Allison, *James,* 56-62; James B. Adamson, *James: The Man and His Message* (Grand Rapids: Eerdmans, 1989), 169-94; John S. Kloppenborg, "The Reception of the Jesus Tradition in James," in *The Catholic Epistles and the Tradition* (ed. Jacques Schlosser; BETL 176; Leuven: Peeters, 2004), 91-139, and "The Emulation of the Jesus Tradition in the Letter of James," in *Reading James with New Eyes: Methodological Reassessments of the Letter of James* (ed. John S. Kloppenborg and Robert L. Webb; LNTS 342; London: T&T Clark, 2007), 121-50; Patrick J. Hartin, *James and the Q Sayings of Jesus* (JSNTSup 47; Sheffield: JSOT, 1991); "James and the Q Sermon on the Mount/Plain," in *Society of Biblical Literature 1989 Seminar Papers* (ed. David J. Lull; Atlanta: Scholars, 1989), 440-57.

The theme of joy in trial/testing is found in **James 1:2** and Matthew 5:10-12 par. Luke 6:22-23.

The word "perfection" in **1:4** finds an important parallel in Matthew 5:48 (cf. Luke 6:36) and 19:21 (cf. Luke 18:21).

The generosity of God for those in need is found in **1:5** and Matthew 7:7-9 par. Luke 11:9-11.

The call to suspend anger in **1:20** connects to Matthew 5:22.

The important theme of being a doer of the word, not just hearing the word, as seen in **1:22-25** reminds one of Matthew 7:24-27 par. Luke 6:47-49.

The demand to do all the law in **2:10** is matched in part by a similar demand in Matthew 5:19.

The paramount significance of mercy in **2:13** finds something similar in Matthew 5:7.

The call to peace in **3:18** is also matched by a Beatitude in Matthew 5:9.

James's concern with the either-or of love/friendship with God or the world in **4:4** finds something similar in Matthew 6:24 par. Luke 16:13.

The connection of humility and eschatological exaltation in **4:10** finds a substantive connection with yet another Beatitude in Matthew 5:5.

The theme of not judging in **4:11-12**, which in many ways brings to completion what has been said in 3:1–4:10, not to mention other subtle connections in other parts of James, is also important to the Jesus traditions, as seen in Matthew 7:1-5 par. Luke 6:37-38, 41-42.

The hostile reaction to rich oppressors in **5:2-6** finds close associations with Matthew 6:24, 25-34 par. Luke 16:13; 12:22-31.

The patience of the prophets in **5:10** matches Matthew 5:12 par. Luke 6:23.

> Most notably, the statement about oaths in 5:12 must be connected to Matthew 5:33-37 as a nearly explicit quotation of a Jesus saying.[29]

Did James use Matthew, Q, or simply the Jesus tradition? The truth is that we do not know; the truth is the ambiguity of that connection. Explicit citation by James is rare and we stand on sure footings when we conclude that James acts like others in the wisdom tradition because he has made Jesus' teachings his own. It is entirely appropriate to describe these observations with the words that James is "emulating" Jesus' words,[30] and I contend this points us toward what I am calling "receptive reverence" in the wisdom tradition. Where James most explicitly quotes the Torah he is clearly quoting the Torah as he was taught it, or as it was hermeneuted, by Jesus. In other words, Torah is not just command for James: it is the wisdom of Messiah Jesus. The law for James is mediated through Jesus the Sage.

Conclusion

Law is about God's commands for his people, while prophecy is a message from God through a prophet to the people of God. History renders events into a meaningful narrative that drives the people of God to what God is doing in

29. There are other possible parallels but at least these can also be mentioned: James 1:6 (Mark 11:22; Matt. 21:21); James 2:8 (Mark 12:31; Matt. 22:39; Luke 10:27); James 3:1 (Matt. 23:8-12); James 3:2-3 (Matt. 12:36-37); James 5:9 (Mark 13:29; Matt. 24:33; Luke 21:31). See Virgil V. Porter Jr., "The Sermon on the Mount in the Book of James," *BSac* 162, nos. 647-48 (2005): 344-60, 470-82; Massey H. Shepherd, "The Epistle of James and the Gospel of Matthew," *JBL* 75, no. 1 (1956): 40-51, who famously argued that James was pervaded by Matthean parallels.

30. Bauckham, *James*, 35-56, sketches formal parallels in aphorisms (beatitudes, "who-ever" and "the one who is" sayings, conditional sayings, synonymous couplets, antitheses and paradoxes, wisdom admonitions with motive clause, aphoristic sentences, statements of reciprocity, and debate sayings) and similitudes/parables (nine different forms). On James's reformulation of wisdom sayings, see 83-93; for the shaping of Jesus on James, see 97-108. See also Kloppenborg, "Reception," and his "Emulation of the Jesus Tradition," 133-42. James's use of the "Old Testament" is similar in the style of emulation and intertexture; see Richard Bauckham, "James, 1 and 2 Peter, Jude," in *It Is Written: Scripture Citing Scripture: Essays in Honour of Barnabas Lindars, SSF* (ed. D. A. Carson and H. G. M. Williamson; Cambridge: Cambridge University Press, 1988), 306-9; Wiard Popkes, "James and Scripture: An Exercise in Intertextuality," *NTS* 45, no. 2 (1999): 213-29; Wesley Hiram Wachob, "The Epistle of James and the Book of Psalms: A Socio-Rhetorical Perspective of Intertexture, Culture, and Ideology in Religious Discourse," in *Fabrics of Discourse: Essays in Honor of Vernon K. Robbins* (Harrisburg: Trinity Press International, 2003), 264-80.

this world, while apocalyptic divulges the secrets of heaven to God's people. The Gospels and the Acts of the Apostles draw us into the narrative world of Jesus and the early Christians to learn what happened, while the epistles provide for us one end of a phone call from an early Christian leader to a church or from churches to another leader. But wisdom is a sage's experience-derived truths of the way the world works when God's people live before God. Law must be memorized and interpreted; prophecy must be heeded and directions changed; history needs to be heard and entered into; apocalyptic asks its hearers to take due warning; the epistles guide us in similar circumstances and give us major ideas for theology; wisdom petitions its listeners to absorb, pass on, and reformulate. If we have to choose one of these genres to describe James, wisdom works best.[31] A fundamental characteristic of wisdom is to listen to, absorb, and rearticulate what you have learned. The entire letter is soaked in receptive reverence of what Jesus taught. James's theory of the Torah, the λόγος-νόμος, is mediated to him through Jesus as the sage who interpreted the Torah itself through the Shema revised.

31. This paragraph was generated by comments by Bauckham, *James*, 31, 74-83. It is taken from McKnight, "James' Secret," 209.

Questions about *Nomos*, Answers about *Christos*: Romans 10:4 in Context

Beverly Roberts Gaventa

In Romans 10:4, Paul writes that "Christ is the τέλος of the law." This passage is a deep exegetical rut, created by our efforts to identify the nuance of the word τέλος with precision. On this point, as on numerous others, our interpretive vehicles are stuck in the mud. We attempt first to power forward, gunning the accelerator for all it's worth. When that strategy fails, we throw the vehicle into reverse, only to find that we gain perhaps inches but no more. No traction, no leverage, no release. So we rock back and forth, back and forth, seldom pausing to ask whether we might need some help, or even how we got into this mess in the first place.[1]

Traction can be gained. Getting out of the rut requires attending more closely to the larger context of Paul's remarks. When we do that we find that, however we translate 10:4 (whether Christ is the termination, the goal, or the fulfillment of the law), on any translation, the cumulative effect of the larger argument in 9:30–10:13 is that of dethroning νόμος as *the* or even *a* defining element in God's dealings with Israel post-Χριστός. However we translate 10:4, the questions the text raises about νόμος are answered with Χριστός. That means in effect that Christ undermines the law.

1. The literature on Romans 10:4 is voluminous; instructive orientations to the debate appear in C. E. B. Cranfield, *A Critical and Exegetical Commentary on the Epistle to the Romans* (2 vols.; ICC; Edinburgh: T&T Clark, 1975-79), 2:515-20; Robert Badenas, *Christ the End of the Law: Romans 10.4 in Pauline Perspective* (JSNTSup 10; Sheffield: JSOT, 1985), 7-37; and Gerbern S. Oegema, *Für Israel und die Völker: Studien zum alttestamentlich-jüdischen Hintergrund der paulinischen Theologie* (NovTSup 95; Leiden: Brill, 1999), 222-30.

I am pleased to offer this small contribution in appreciation of Stephen Westerholm, whose scholarship has both enlightened and enlivened the study of Paul.

A few preliminary observations are in order. The questions raised in this essay are limited and specific; they concern primarily what Paul has to say in the letter to the Romans. My conclusions are not intended as a statement about the place of the law in the whole of the Christian canon or the whole of Christian tradition. Paul does not always sing in unison with other voices in the canon. Sometimes, in fact, he is not even in harmony with other canonical voices but seems to be on a different page of the songbook altogether. The role of interpreters is not to compel all the voices to sing in unison, but to listen to them all and be instructed by their rich variety.

Second, I want to distinguish our readings of these ancient texts from our contemporary understandings of relations between Christians and Jews. To "distinguish" is not the same thing as to "separate" or "disconnect." On any scholarly reconstruction, the situation Paul confronts regarding Jews, Gentiles, and Christian mission in the first century is dramatically different from that of the twenty-first century. To say that Paul's letters are authoritative for Christians does not mean Christians are obligated to replicate each and every one of his views and practices. That would be a highly un-Pauline way to read scripture (not to mention that it also does not appear to have been the evangelists' method of reading scripture). To name only the most obvious example, we utterly reject slavery, although scripture assumes and accepts that practice. We can and we must faithfully read and interpret Paul's letters for our own time, and that will sometimes mean that our teachings and practices differ from those reflected in his letters.

Third, I hope that we can disentangle our answers to this question and other issues involved in the discussion of Paul and Judaism from charges of supersessionism, of anti-Judaism, or of dejudaizing the New Testament. The question of supersessionism is far too important to be treated in a facile manner or reduced to a matter of mere name calling, as unfortunately happens from time to time in the academy.[2] At best, it discourages people from saying

2. See also my comments on this question in my "The Character of God's Faithfulness: A Response to N. T. Wright," *Journal for the Study of Paul and His Letters* 4, no. 1 (2014): 71-80. Richard B. Hays comments similarly: "This complex retrospective hermeneutical reconfiguration of 'the Israel of God' complicates any attempt at simple judgment about whether Paul is or is not a supersessionist. A corollary of this point is that Pauline interpreters ought to quit lobbing the accusation of 'supersessionism' at one another" (see "Apocalyptic *Poiēsis* in Galatians: Paternity, Passion, and Participation," in *Galatians and Christian Theology: Justification, the Gospel, and Ethics in Paul's Letter* [ed. Mark W. Elliott et al.; Grand Rapids: Baker Academic, 2014], 200-219, quotation on p. 216). On the definition of supersessionism, see R. Kendall Soulen, "Supersessionism," in *A Dictionary of Jewish-Christian Relations* (ed. Edward Kessler and Neil Wenborn; Cambridge: Cambridge University Press, 2005), 413-14.

what they really think and reinforces the disturbing practice of talking only with those people with whom we already agree.

To return to my opening observation: Romans 10:4 is an exegetical rut. We have dug it deeply by piling up arguments about the positive or negative valence of τέλος.[3] We have isolated 10:4 from the larger argument Paul is making in chapters 9–11, to say nothing of chapters 1–8. And sometimes we have further isolated it by demanding that it serve as the sum and substance of Paul's instruction about the law of Moses. What we need to do first is to attend to the surprisingly complex account of the law developed in chapters 1–8, before looking more closely at 9:30–10:13.

The Law and Sin

The word νόμος first appears in Romans 2, where it serves to identify Jews as distinct from Gentiles, or at least Paul plays with the notion that the law marks the boundary between Jew and Gentile. Jews are said to have the law, while Gentiles do not, except that some Gentiles may keep the law without having it and some Jews may dishonor the law they have. The result is that, by the end of chapter 2, Paul has severely undermined the line between Jew and Gentile and driven his audience to the question of 3:1: "Is there any benefit to being a Jew?"[4]

Beginning with chapter 3, as he builds his argument about God's intervention to rescue humanity from its captivity to Sin, Paul includes comments about the law. (By stating it that way, I suggest that the law is not Paul's central concern here; it is an issue he knows must be addressed, but he does not write Romans 1–8 primarily in order to give an account of the law.)[5] The comments about the law veer back and forth between claims that seem "positive"[6] or at least untroubling and those that are quite provocative. After concluding that the law speaks so that ev-

3. Perhaps New Testament scholars need to revisit James Barr's comments on word study every few years (in *The Semantics of Biblical Language* [London: Oxford University Press, 1961], especially 1-45, 206-62).

4. On this point we are helped by John M. G. Barclay's discussion of the redefining of categories in Romans 2 in "Paul and Philo on Circumcision: Romans 2:25-29 in Social and Cultural Context," in *Pauline Churches and Diaspora Jews* (WUNT I 275; Tübingen: Mohr Siebeck, 2011), 61-79, especially 68-70.

5. For a distinctly different reading, see Thomas H. Tobin, *Paul's Rhetoric in Its Contexts: The Argument of Romans* (Peabody: Hendrickson, 2004), especially 70-78.

6. I use the terms "negative" and "positive" as shorthand, but I place them in scare quotes because they oversimplify greatly what is anything but simple in the text.

ery human mouth may be closed (3:19), and that God's rectification (δικαιοσύνη) does not come through law observance, Paul will nonetheless affirm that the law and the prophets confirm God's rectification (3:21).[7] In 3:31, Paul insists that he is not nullifying but upholding the law, yet his very next references to the law (in 4:13 and 15) separate it from the promise to Abraham and from Abraham's heirs:

> It was not through the law that the promise came to Abraham or to his offspring . . . (4:13)

> The law produces wrath. Where there is no law there is also no transgression. (4:15)

Paul is walking an argumentative tightrope. Although he does not make overtly "negative" claims about the law, he nonetheless sprinkles the argument with highly provocative assertions and associations. Especially if his reputation as a critic of Gentile law observance has already arrived at Rome prior to his letter,[8] these assertions will be troublesome.

With chapters 5 and 6, Paul increases the volume on the provocation meter. In the context of discussing the reign of Sin and Death, he repeatedly introduces references to the law that associate it with Sin.

> Sin does not count without the law. (5:13)

> The law slipped in, in order to increase the trespass. (5:20)

These statements may be regarded as ambiguous, but in 6:14-15 Paul comes quite close to identifying the law with Sin itself:

> Sin will not rule over you as a king, because you are not under the law but under grace. So what? Should we sin, because we are not under the law but under grace?
>
> Of course not!

7. I agree with Stephen Westerholm's comment that "*it is not legitimate to apply what Paul says of the Scriptures in general to the Sinaitic laws without further ado,*" in *Perspectives Old and New on Paul: The "Lutheran" Paul and His Critics* (Grand Rapids: Eerdmans, 2004), 300 (emphasis original). In this particular instance, however, the use of the phrase "law and prophets" in such close proximity to other, more provocative, comments about the law is surely part of Paul's argumentative strategy.

8. As Tobin, *Paul's Rhetoric,* assumes (see note 5 above).

Paul makes no distinction at this point between being under Sin's power and being under the power of the law. This point repeats forcefully in the early verses of chapter 7:

> The law lords it over (κυριεύω) a person for life. (7:1)

Earlier he has written about Christ that "Death no longer lords it over him" (6:9), and he has assured the Roman auditors that "Sin will no longer lord it over you" (6:14). This attribution of lordship to Death, Sin, and now the law forces finally the question of 7:7: is the law the same thing as Sin? "Of course not!" again comes the answer. The law is God's good, holy, and right gift, but it has turned out that God's enemy Sin is even more powerful than God's own law. It is not just that the law reveals Sin to be Sin, but that Sin has made use of the law in order to produce death (as in 7:8, 9, 11, 13, 17, 20). That is to say: Sin has proven to be more powerful than the law. It has produced a kind of fissure within the law. On the one hand, there is the law that is ruled by Sin and Death; on the other, the law that is taken under the rule of the spirit of life in Christ Jesus (8:2). The sending of the Son condemns Sin and liberates humanity.[9]

To pull together these observations: in Romans 1–6, then, Paul affirms the Mosaic law but he simultaneously inserts provocative statements about it, statements that raise profound questions. When finally in chapter 7 he directly addresses the question he has raised, he answers the question in terms of Sin. Despite the questions he has raised about the law, the problem is not the law; instead, the problem is Sin. And he answers the question in terms of God's actions in Jesus Christ. Questions that are asked about the law are addressed in terms, first, of Sin and then of Christ.

This complex account of the law needs to be kept in mind as we turn to chapters 9–11. It is not enough to invoke 3:21 and 31 as evidence that Paul understands the law positively. The larger story is that the law, while good and holy, has been overtaken by Sin, that the law even stands in forced partnership with Sin. My contention is that, when we turn to Romans 9–11, a similar

9. Here I am drawing heavily on the work of Paul W. Meyer, "The Worm at the Core of the Apple: Exegetical Reflections on Romans 7," in *The Word in This World: Essays in New Testament Exegesis and Theology* (Louisville: Westminster John Knox, 2004), 57-77. And see also J. Louis Martyn, "*Nomos* Plus Genitive Noun in Paul: The History of God's Law," in *Early Christianity and Classical Culture: Comparative Studies in Honor of Abraham J. Malherbe* (ed. John T. Fitzgerald, Thomas H. Olbricht, and L. Michael White; NovTSup 110; Leiden: Brill, 2003), 575-87.

pattern emerges. Paul raises questions about the law, but he answers those questions in terms of Christ.

The Law and Christ

When we read Romans 9–11 in light of this account of the law in chapters 1–8, what stands out is Paul's relative silence concerning the law. He does, of course, list the "giving of the law" among the other gifts God has bestowed on Israel. Yet in the argument that follows, Paul makes little reference to the law. He traces God's creation of Israel in the miraculous birth of Isaac (9:7-9), he narrates God's action in the divided Israel of the present (11:1-10), and he anticipates the salvation of all Israel (11:26), but at none of these crucial junctures in the account of God's dealings with Israel does Paul identify the law as an active part of Israel's present or future. Put another way, after 9:4, whatever it is that Paul has to say about the law, his remarks are not crucial for his understanding of Israel. The single place in which Paul writes about the law in these chapters is in 9:30–10:13, an important exception, to be sure.

The Centrality of God's Action in 9:30–10:13

Throughout Romans 9–11, Paul limns God's astonishing, even offensive, way of dealing with Israel. God calls Israel into being, God sustains Israel, and God will always be faithful to Israel. This way of putting the subject matter is crucial. When we describe chapters 9–11 as concerned about Israel's disobedience or Israel's disbelief, we put ourselves on the wrong path from the outset. Even the opening verses of chapter 9, in which Paul identifies the Israelites, emphasize gifts bestowed by God (with the possible exception of λατρεία, which is of course worshipful service rendered to God). And with 9:6a, the thesis of the three chapters is stated succinctly: God's word has not failed. The end of chapter 11 corresponds to this theocentric beginning: it is God who confined all to disobedience, God whose ways are not known, and God to whom all glory is due. We know, then, that whatever else Paul has to say in this passage, Israel stands "between God and God."[10]

10. This expression comes from Gerhard Ebeling, "Existenz zwischen Gott und Gott: ein Beitrag zur Frage nach der Existenz Gottes," *ZTK* 62, no. 1 (1965): 86-113; cited by J. Louis Martyn, *Theological Issues in the Letters of Paul* (Nashville: Abingdon, 1997), 44.

That observation about the centrality of God holds also for 9:30–10:13, although the footrace posited at the outset of the passage might lead us to think otherwise. When Paul writes that Gentiles have arrived at the finish line for a race they never entered, while Israel has entered and run without ever arriving, he appears to suggest human achievement or failure. And, indeed, many treatments of 9:30–10:13 refer to Israel's "failure," or "disbelief" or "rejection." On closer examination, however, it emerges that this surprising state of affairs exists by virtue of an even more surprising intrusion: God has rigged the race.

Of course, Paul does also affirm that the rectification Gentiles "overtook" is rectification ἐκ πίστεως, which could mean that the Gentiles believed, that they took an action. The context, however, strongly suggests otherwise. Paul has just astonishingly turned Hosea's words about Israel into words about Gentiles. God has called Gentiles something they were not (i.e., called them into being as a people, 9:24-25).[11] The assertion that Gentiles finished a race for which they were not even registered underscores this conclusion. Πίστις scarcely refers to a Gentile decision. It must necessarily be something God has done on their behalf, namely, to generate faith among them, to call them into faith.[12]

And this reference to Gentiles who win a race they never entered requires the conclusion that Paul is talking about the present time. This is not a reference to Gentile faith in the period of Aristotle or Plato, but in the Christ time.[13] *Mutatis mutandis,* this observation governs the argument that follows. What Paul has to say here about Israel not completing the race necessarily refers to the present time. In the present, God has rigged the race.

Israel's situation, like that of the Gentiles, results from God's action. Israel has not finished the race because it has tripped over a stumbling stone God put in place. Verse 33 makes this clear, "Behold I put in Zion. . . ."[14] Below I argue that the ignorance Paul attributes to Israel in the opening lines of chapter 10

11. See also J. Ross Wagner, *Heralds of the Good News: Isaiah and Paul "in Concert" in the Letter to the Romans* (NovTSup 101; Leiden: Brill, 2002), 121.

12. This suggestion, of course, touches on the much larger debate about πίστις Χριστοῦ. Increasingly, I regard this phrase, particularly in Romans 3:26, as a shorthand expression for those who have been grasped by the gospel of Jesus Christ.

13. This discussion in 9:30 is to be distinguished from the theoretical discussion in chapter 2 about Gentiles who somehow keep the law even though it is not theirs "by nature." Chapter 2 has nothing to say about Gentiles and πίστις.

14. Admittedly, this point about God's activity would be stronger if Paul had included the independent pronoun ἐγώ found in Isaiah 28:16 LXX, on which he is drawing (along with Isa. 8:14a LXX). Since he also substitutes (or appears to, as questions of this sort are extremely difficult) τίθημι for ἐμβαλῶ, however, the entire phrase differs in Romans from the form found in Isaiah.

also derives from God's action, but for the moment I set that point aside. The main concern at present is to establish that this central section of Romans 9–11 coheres with what precedes and what follows in its preoccupation with the activity of God. If at any point we forget that preoccupation, we are in danger of a serious distortion of the text.[15]

Israel's Situation

Alongside comments about divine activity, however, in 9:30–10:13 Paul also remarks on Israel's actions or standing.[16] First, unlike the Gentiles, Israel does pursue what Paul refers to as νόμος δικαιοσύνης, "the law of rectification or righteousness," often rendered as "the law that leads to righteousness."[17] Instructed by an important essay of J. Louis Martyn, however, we see that in Romans νόμος with the genitive repeatedly means the law under the power of another agent, as in 8:2 and elsewhere.[18] That same pattern holds here: what Israel pursues (at the present time) is "the law under the power of rectification," probably here to be understood as God's own rectification. At the present time Israel is pursuing that law, the good and right and holy law of 7:12, but Israel has not arrived at that law. Nothing here suggests either a problem inherent in the law or a problem in Israel's behavior.[19] Again, this is the present time; it is not a generalized argument about either Jewish "legalism" or Jewish national prerogatives.

When Paul begins in verse 32 to explain how it happens that Israel did

15. See the illuminating comments of J. Louis Martyn: "God's election, being free of all presuppositions, cannot be traced through the generations of Israel on any basis other than the act of God himself, the one who issues the promise *newly* in each generation and solely on the basis of his own faithful perdurance" (*Galatians: A New Translation with Introduction and Commentary* [AB 33A; New York: Doubleday, 1997], 350-51).

16. One neglected feature of 9:30–10:21 is that it speaks consistently of Israel as a whole (with the possible exception in v. 16). This generalized naming of Israel stands at odds with 9:24 and with the discussion of the "remnant" and the "rest" in chapter 11. Paul uses a kind of hyperbole here that he will undermine in the beginning of chapter 11, where he insists that not all of Israel is in the same situation.

17. See Wagner, *Heralds*, 122 and the literature cited there. Wagner translates this phrase as "the law that leads to righteousness"; that is, Israel is running after the law on the assumption that it leads to, it promises, it produces righteousness.

18. Martyn, "*Nomos* Plus Genitive."

19. Similarly, Stanley K. Stowers, *A Rereading of Romans: Justice, Jews and Gentiles* (New Haven: Yale University Press, 1994), 304.

not reach the finish line, he writes that Israel ran after the law, God's own law, not "from faith" but as if it were "from works."[20] "Faith" here is almost certainly again shorthand for the faith/trust/confidence generated by God in Jesus Christ (as in v. 30). It is not strength of conviction or trust in God in some abstract sense but present confidence in the God who has now raised Jesus Christ from the dead. If that is the case, then what is to be made of the term set in opposition to faith: "works"? At least as early as the second corrector(s) of Sinaiticus, readers of Paul's text have found it necessary to come to his assistance by supplying the genitive "of the law," that is, law observance, doing the law. The problem, then, is understood to be doing the law. At several points in Romans, Paul has used the expression ἔργα νόμου (2:15; 3:20, 28), which makes this a reasonable deduction. Yet that is not the move Paul makes in 9:32.

What Paul contrasts with πίστις, confidence generated by God's act in Jesus Christ, is not "works of the law," however those "works" are to be construed (whether as boundary markers or something more comprehensive). Instead, he contrasts the divinely generated πίστις with human effort. This we learn from the context. To begin with, the last use of the phrase "works of the law" was in 3:28. Closer to hand is the discussion of God's dealings with Jacob and Esau in 9:10-13. Paul writes that God acted "before they were born or did anything good or evil." God did this so that the initiative would remain with God, "not ἐξ ἔργων but ἐκ τοῦ καλοῦντος," "not by human action but by the one who called them into being." Contrary to both Jewish and later Christian exegesis, Paul insists that God's choice had nothing to do with any action or disposition on the part of Jacob or Esau. In the case of these unborn twins, whose lives antedated the giving of the law, this "work" cannot be a reference to the observance of Mosaic law. Instead it refers to human effort, and in a context in which many interpreters of Genesis insisted that there must have been some "reason" for God's decision, a reason based on what God knew the two would become. Here also "works" refers to human action, human effort.[21]

The entire argument of 9:6-29 confirms this point: Paul is arguing, relentlessly so, that God brought Israel into being. God brought Isaac into being, God brought the twins into being and chose Jacob, God brought Pharaoh into being and hardened him, and God has now called not only Jews but also Gentiles. To be sure, the "works" to which Paul refers may well be works that

20. The Greek here is notoriously elliptical, as both "Israel" and a verb have to be supplied.

21. See my "On the Calling-Into-Being of Israel: Romans 9:6-29," in *Between Gospel and Election: Explorations in the Interpretation of Romans 9–11* (ed. Florian Wilk and J. Ross Wagner with the assistance of Frank Schleritt; WUNT I 257; Tübingen: Mohr Siebeck, 2010), 255-69, especially 26-63, and the literature cited there.

conform to the law, but the emphasis falls not on the law as such, but on the action of human beings, on the notion that human action is effective.[22]

Thus: Israel ran a race, not based on faith (faith again generated by God) but as if they could run by their own effort. Verse 32b intensifies the argument: worse than not getting to the goal, they stumbled. Paul takes Isaiah's words to explain why they stumbled: God ("I") put in place a stumbling stone, and the one who trusts in it [him] will not be ashamed.[23] In view of the repetition of Isaiah 28:16 just a few lines later ("The one who trusts in him will not be ashamed"),[24] it seems clear that the "stone" here is Christ. But this is not Christ the "corner stone" or "sure foundation," but Christ whom God puts in place in order to trip Israel. That is to say, the "problem" Israel has is Christological, and it is generated by God. That point bears repeating since below I argue that Paul himself repeats it in 10:1-13 (and he will develop it in chapter 11): Israel's "problem," or better Israel's current situation, is Christological[25] and it is generated by God.

This interpretation, which emphasizes not Israel's reliance on the law as such but Israel's perception about human action, finds reinforcement in chapter 10. Following 10:1, with its reiteration of concern for his kinfolk, Paul writes: "I witness on their behalf that they have zeal for God but it is not informed, because they do not know God's rectification."

He goes on to say that "they" sought to establish their own rectification and not to submit to God's rectification, but these statements explicate the initial statement about not knowing. Their zeal for God is not informed; it is ignorant. These are statements about perception, understanding, and they recast in a more general way the claim of verse 32 that Israel acted based on "doing" rather than on πίστις. The problem with Israel is that Israel has not been shown where God's action is. The problem here is knowledge, perception,

22. Westerholm remarks similarly: "nothing in this passage suggests that Israel is pursuing the wrong *kind* of 'works.' What is emphatically excluded is consideration of *any* human work in the granting of divine favour" ("Paul and the Law in Romans 9–11," in *Paul and the Mosaic Law* [ed. James D. G. Dunn; WUNT I 89; Tübingen: Mohr Siebeck, 1996], 228).

23. On the conflation of Isaiah 8:14 and 28:16 in 9:33, see the instructive discussion in Wagner, *Heralds*, 126-31.

24. Notice 1:16 and Paul's use of shame and glory language in eschatological contexts. See αἰσχύνω (Phil. 1:20); ἐπαισχύνομαι (Rom. 1:16); καταισχύνω (Rom. 5:5; 9:33; 10:11); αἰσχύνη (Phil. 3:19); καυχάομαι (Rom. 2:17, 23; 5:2, 3, 11; 1 Cor. 1:31; 2 Cor. 10:13, 15-17; Gal. 6:14; Phil. 3:3); and καύχησις (Rom. 15:17; 1 Cor. 15:31; 2 Cor. 1:12; 7:4; 11:10; 1 Thess. 2:19).

25. See E. P. Sanders, who agrees that the problem here is Christological, although he does not draw attention to God's role at this point (*Paul, the Law, and the Jewish People* [Minneapolis: Fortress, 1983], 37-38).

understanding.[26] Much of the second half of chapter 10 will twist around this comment about not understanding, not knowing. That concern coheres with issues of perception that appear later in the letter (e.g., 12:2, 3, 16; 13:11), and it coheres with a large strand of the Corinthian correspondence having to do with epistemology.[27]

In addition, just as Paul comments in 9:32-33 that Israel stumbled over the stone because God put it in place, so here he leaves open the possibility that God has produced Israel's (temporary) ignorance. The point is implicit rather than explicit; however, it is worth observing that Paul does not say that Israel refused to know or to acknowledge God (by contrast with 1:18-32). And in 11:7-8, he will claim that the current hardening of part of Israel is the result of God's action.

What is it that Israel does not know? Because they do not know (having been blinded for now), they undertake to establish their own rectification (doing things, effort) and do not submit to God's, namely, Christ (as in 10:4). This "doing" is almost certainly that of law observance, yet what Paul observes is not a problem with the law or even a problem with Israel's view of the law, but ignorance about it brought on by God (to which Paul will return in Romans 11).

It may seem by now that the νόμος of my title has gone missing. In order to see what Paul is doing with this issue, however, it was necessary to establish, first, the dominance of his concern for God's role throughout Romans 9–11. It was also necessary to see what exactly Paul says and does not say about Israel. And it was also important to see how little the argument of 9–11 depends on any understanding of νόμος.

Nomos

As throughout 9–11, then, in 9:30–10:13 Paul argues that God creates and sustains Israel. If Israel has fallen down, it is because God put the stone in place.

26. See Shane Berg, "Sin's Corruption of the Knowledge of God and the Law in Romans 1–8," in *The Unrelenting God: Essays on God's Action in Scripture in Honor of Beverly Roberts Gaventa* (ed. David J. Downs and Matthew L. Skinner; Grand Rapids: Eerdmans, 2013), 119-38, especially 137.

27. See especially J. Louis Martyn, "Epistemology at the Turn of the Ages," in *Theological Issues in the Letters of Paul* (Nashville: Abingdon, 1997), 89-110; and Alexandra R. Brown, *The Cross and Human Transformation: Paul's Apocalyptic Word in 1 Corinthians* (Minneapolis: Fortress, 1995).

If Israel does not understand and is confused, it is because God has covered their eyes.

But what does that mean about the law? In particular, what is to be made of 10:4? Is Christ the law's termination or the law's fulfillment? Its goal? Its end? And what nuance is to be given to any of these terms? Examinations of the use of τέλος elsewhere, whether in Paul or otherwise, will not resolve this question.[28] If anything is clear about this verse, it is that understanding it depends entirely on the context. This is not a slogan or a proposition to be unpacked outside the context. Instead, we need to attend to the way in which Paul explicates 10:4 in what follows. In fact, it may be better to say that Paul does not so much explicate 10:4 as he directs attention away from it.

First, in verse 5, Paul enlists the authority of Moses and the text of Leviticus 18:5 to declare regarding the law that "[t]he person who does these things will live by means of them." When Paul cites this same text in Galatians 3:11, he does so in order to separate Gentile believers from the notion that they must add Torah practice to their lives in Christ. We know that, but there is scant reason to think that the Romans would know it, although they may well recall Paul's opening association in 1:17 of life with πίστις rather than νόμος. In Leviticus, nonetheless, this statement straightforwardly promises life to those who keep the law, and so for the moment we may imagine that Paul is simply recalling that promise.[29]

Then we arrive at verses 6-8:

> the rectification that comes through πίστις says this: "Do not say in your heart, 'Who will go up into heaven?' which means, 'to bring Christ down,' or 'Who will go down into the abyss?' which means, 'to bring Christ up from the dead.'" What does it say instead? "The word is near; it is in your mouth and in your heart," which means the word of πίστις that we preach.

I have deliberately avoided translating the δέ at the beginning of verse 6; whether the δέ is read conjunctively or disjunctively, Paul here introduces a second speaker. Alongside or possibly over against the first voice, the rectification that comes through the law, we have a second voice, the rectification

28. See Badenas, *Christ the End of the Law,* 4, for various scholarly judgments about the pivotal character of this verse.

29. Francis Watson has argued that Paul is picking up the word ποιήσας from Leviticus 18:5 and emphasizing the "doing" (i.e., working) of the law (*Paul and the Hermeneutics of Faith* [London: T&T Clark, 2004], 329-41). That line of argument is close to my own, although I wonder whether Paul's audience would have detected that emphasis.

that comes through faith. Richard Hays and Ross Wagner have made strong arguments that these two voices sing in harmony rather than dissonance.[30] Although I confess that I have a very hard time reading the passage that way, at present I will grant that point.

Even granting that point, however, what Paul suggests is that it is Christ who is near. Assuming that the auditors know at least enough about scripture to catch Paul's use of Deuteronomy 30 and that they associate these texts with the nearness of the law, then what they hear will be that the Christ is the one who is near (vv. 6b, 7b). The word that is preached by "us" has to do with Christ, and no mention is made of the law. Everything in the passage from 10:6 onward concerns the Christ, the confession of Christ, and the inclusion of both Jew and Gentile in that confession. Νόμος never enters the Israel story again.

However we read 10:4, then — even if we read it as asserting that the law reaches its fulfillment — the argument Paul builds after that point implies the end of the law. He hints at it; he shows it; and he leaves it to his auditors to come to this conclusion. Paul does not have to make a definitive statement about the end of the law or its temporary standing. In effect, the question of the law is answered with Christ, just as chapter 7 answers the question about the law by means of Sin's powerful act. Paul does not have to criticize either the law or Israel. What he has to do is announce God's action in Jesus Christ.

The question about God's dealing with Israel through the law is answered by the claim that God deals with Jew and Gentile alike through the Christ. Chapter 11 confirms that understanding: Israel's "problem" is that God has divided it in the present time; God has blinded part of Israel in order to bring in Gentiles and then redeem all. Chapter 11 presents interpreters with a host of challenging issues, but the law is not one of them. In Romans 9, Israel is God's creation quite apart from the law. In Romans 11, Israel continues as God's beloved, quite apart from the law.

This reading of Paul's strategy finds confirmation in the remainder of the letter, in what is usually referred to as the "ethical," or "parenetic," section of the letter. Paul mentions the law only once: "The one who loves the other has fulfilled the law . . . love is the fulfillment of the law" (13:8-10). Here too Paul is highly elusive. Fulfillment of the law by means of loving the other is a good, but that good appears to be defined first by Paul's understanding of the body

30. Richard B. Hays, *Echoes of Scripture in the Letters of Paul* (New Haven: Yale University Press, 1989), 73-83; Wagner, *Heralds*, 159-65. They are not alone; see the survey in Preston M. Sprinkle, *Law and Life: The Interpretation of Leviticus 18:5 in Early Judaism and in Paul* (WUNT II 241; Tübingen: Mohr Siebeck, 2008), 168-73. And see the important criticisms by Westerholm, *Perspectives*, 327-28.

of Christ (12:5) rather than prescribed by the commandment as such.[31] And the discussion of the observance or non-observance of the law as it pertains to food in chapter 14 is stunningly dismissive of such obligations: if "the kingdom of God is not food and drink," it can scarcely be concerned with observing the Mosaic law.[32]

Students who first encounter the scholarly debate around Romans 10:4 (among other exegetical cruces) are tempted to roll their eyes, even to suspect that the debate says more about conflicting theological traditions (or scholarly ambitions) than it does about Paul's letter. What I have argued is that the prolonged quarrel actually reflects the obliqueness of Paul's argument. Perhaps because of his own uncertainty about his reception in Rome (and space does not permit reflection on that question), Paul takes up the question of the law but tells it "slant."[33] In Romans 1–8, that means depicting the law as God's holy, right, and good creation, which has nonetheless been conscripted by Sin itself. And in Romans 9–11, that means depicting God's creation and maintenance of Israel, even God's unchanging call of Israel, without reference to an ongoing role for the Mosaic law.

31. "[W]hen Paul speaks of Christians 'fulfilling' the law, he is describing, not prescribing, their behavior" (Westerholm, *Perspectives*, 434). And see also his "Law and Christian Ethics," in *Law in Religious Communities in the Roman Period: The Debate Over* Torah *and* Nomos *in Post-Biblical Judaism and Early Christianity* (ed. Peter Richardson and Stephen Westerholm; SCJ 4; Waterloo: Wilfrid Laurier University Press, 1991), 75-91, especially 87, 89.

32. On this point, see John M. G. Barclay, "'Do We Undermine the Law?' A Study of Romans 14.1–15.6," in *Paul and the Mosaic Law* (ed. James D. G. Dunn; WUNT I 89; Tübingen: Mohr Siebeck, 1996), 287-308.

33. Emily Dickinson, "Tell All the Truth."

Paul, Abraham's Gentile "Offspring," and the Torah

Terence L. Donaldson

Paul presents us with more than his share of puzzles, one of the most puzzling of which is the profile he constructs for Gentile believers in Christ. On the one hand, such *ethnē*-in-Christ (as we might call them)[1] are categorically forbidden to undergo circumcision.[2] Submit to the circumcising knife, Paul says to his Galatian readers, and you will ipso facto be "cut off from Christ" (5:2-4). On the other hand, however, Paul insists that, precisely by being in Christ, non-Jewish believers are part of Abraham's "seed" (σπέρμα). Summing up a major section of his argument, Paul says to the Galatians, "If you are Christ's, then you are Abraham's seed (σπέρμα), heirs according to the promise" (3:29). Likewise in Romans, Paul makes the claim that the promise is "guaranteed to all his [Abraham's] seed (σπέρματι)," including those uncircumcised ἔθνη who "share the faith of Abraham," who is "the father of all of us, as it is written, 'I have made you the father of many nations (ἐθνῶν)'" (4:16-17; also v. 13).

The first aspect of the profile is well known. Every reader of Paul knows of his adamant opposition to circumcision; it is a defining characteristic of

1. While I do not object to the term "Gentile Christians," both components of the term are problematical in a discussion about Paul and potentially misleading. See my article "'Gentile Christianity' as a Category in the Study of Christian Origins," *HTR* 106, no. 4 (2013): 433-58.

2. The males among them, at least. One wonders what Paul's view would have been about their wives and daughters.

I remain grateful to this volume's honoree, Stephen Westerholm, for his close, careful, and perceptive reading of my work, and also for his collegial friendship over the past thirty years. I am delighted to have this opportunity to applaud him for his distinguished career and to wish him many more years of fruitful scholarship.

the gospel that he "proclaim[s] among the ἔθνη" (Gal. 2:2). The other aspect, however, requires a bit more consideration.

Looking first at general usage, throughout Israel's scripture and subsequent Jewish literature the term "seed" (σπέρμα in Greek, זרע in Hebrew)[3] is characteristically and consistently used as a designation for the people of Israel: "O seed (σπέρμα) of his servant Abraham, children of Jacob, his chosen ones" (Ps. 105[104]:6); "On the day when I chose Israel, I swore to the seed (σπέρμα) of the house of Jacob" (Ezek. 20:5); "A holy people (λαόν) and a blameless seed (σπέρμα) wisdom delivered from a nation of oppressors" (Wis. 10:15). To put a sharper point on it, the term is frequently set in binary contrast with the "nations" (ἔθνη, גוים). In Genesis 22:18, a passage to which we will return, God declares to Abraham, "by your seed (σπέρματι) shall all the nations (ἔθνη) of the earth be blessed." "The LORD set his heart in love on your ancestors alone," Moses says to the people in Deuteronomy 10:15, "and chose you, their seed (τὸ σπέρμα αὐτῶν) after them, out of all the nations (πάντα τὰ ἔθνη)." The theme is echoed in *Psalms of Solomon* 9.9: "For you chose the seed (σπέρμα) of Abraham above all the nations (ἔθνη)." Both uses appear frequently and examples could be multiplied indefinitely.

Most important for our purposes, however, is the whole discourse in Genesis 17, where Abraham's "seed" (σπέρμα appears seven times) are categorically defined in terms of circumcision:

> God said to Abraham, "As for you, you shall keep my covenant, you and your seed (σπέρμα) after you throughout their generations. This is my covenant, which you shall keep, between me and you and your seed (σπέρματος) after you: Every male among you shall be circumcised. . . . Any uncircumcised male who is not circumcised in the flesh of his foreskin[4] shall be cut off from his people (γένους); he has broken my covenant. (Gen. 17:9-10, 14)

Here we encounter a significant step beyond the more general use of the term; here "seed of Abraham" is defined in such a way as to make circumcision a *sine qua non*. Abraham's σπέρμα are circumcised — end of discussion. Read

3. For present purposes it will be sufficient to focus on Greek usage, though σπέρμα is consistently used to render זרע.

4. Here the LXX has the additional phrase "on the eighth day," perhaps under the influence of verse 12; for an argument in support of this as the preferred reading, see Matthew Thiessen, *Contesting Conversion: Genealogy, Circumcision, and Identity in Ancient Judaism and Christianity* (Oxford: Oxford University Press, 2011), 17-30.

alongside Genesis 17, then, Paul's insistence that uncircumcised ἔθνη belong to Abraham's σπέρμα by virtue of their being in Christ — and, even more, his insistence that this is according to "scripture" (see Gal. 3:8; Rom. 4:3) — would seem to be a flat-out contradiction in terms, an attempt to square the covenantal circle. One can only imagine what exegetical hay the rival teachers in Galatia would have made of Paul's assertion.

If the assertion were limited to Galatians, we might be able to see it simply as a rash statement made in the heat of the moment. It reappears, however, in the calmer context of Romans, where Paul reworks the argument in a more measured and reflective way. Paul cannot have been unaware of what he was doing, for he cites a sentence from Genesis 17 in the process: "as it is written, 'I have made you the father of many nations (ἐθνῶν)'" (4:17, citing Gen. 17:5). The contra-scriptural move he makes here is clearly deliberate.

The most important thing to note, however, is that the text he does cite offers him a simpler and smoother way of linking uncircumcised *ethnē*-in-Christ with Abraham. It was not necessary to turn uncircumcised ἔθνη into σπέρμα Αβραάμ in order to bring them into a positive relationship with Abraham. The divine promise to Abraham made at the start of the Genesis narrative was not only that "I will make of you a great nation," but also that "in you all the families of the earth shall be blessed" (12:2, 3). The promise is repeated in Genesis 22:18, this time in terms of σπέρμα and ἔθνη: "and by your seed (σπέρματι) shall all the nations (ἔθνη) of the earth gain blessing for themselves," and again in 26:4 ("all the nations [ἔθνη] of the earth shall gain blessing for themselves through your seed [σπέρματι]").[5] This promise includes blessing for the ἔθνη, but without compromising the distinction between ἔθνη and σπέρμα. Paul would have had a much easier exegetical time of it if he had simply argued that his *ethnē*-in-Christ represented the fulfillment of the promise to Abraham that "all the nations" would be blessed through Abraham's "seed" — blessed, that is, as ἔθνη and thus in their uncircumcised state. Indeed, even if he felt constrained to argue on the basis of Genesis 17, he could have identified the "multitude of ἔθνη" of 17:4-5 with the nations of the earth who would be blessed through Abraham's "seed." But Paul rejected this easier route, apparently feeling constrained to identify his *ethnē*-in-Christ as members of "Abraham's seed," even as he rejected the scripturally prescribed terms of membership. What are we to make of this?

5. See also Gen. 18:18; 28:14; Sir. 44:21.

In a previous work on Paul,[6] I attempted to make sense of this puzzling identity construal within the context of a larger question: how are we to understand the convictional shift involved in Paul's transformation from a "zealot for the traditions of [his] fathers" (Gal. 1:14) to an "apostle to the ἔθνη" (Rom. 11:13)? Here I will need to be content with a brief description of the parameters within which I pursued the question and the kind of answer that emerged.[7]

Working within the framework of Sanders's *Paul and Palestinian Judaism,*[8] I accepted his argument that for Paul the "solution preceded the problem." That is, I started with these assumptions: that Paul's new adherence to Christ was not driven by any prior dissatisfaction with Torah-centered Judaism; that prior to his Damascus experience Paul's symbolic world corresponded (more or less) to what Sanders described as "covenantal nomism"; that his apostolic discourse, including his various discussions of the Mosaic law, was driven by his new, Christ-centered convictions; and that these convictions are to be seen as a reconfiguration, rather than an abandonment, of his native Jewish convictions. With respect to his convictions about the ἔθνη, this meant that I wanted to understand them not as reflecting an abandonment of the Jewish symbolic world with its "particularism," but instead as a revised version of some form of what I called its "universalism" — the various ways in which Jews conceived of a positive place for non-Jews in its covenant-centered, symbolic world.

These various "patterns of universalism" as I called them (though the term is perhaps inadequate) can be differentiated for the most part by the role played by the Torah with respect to non-Jews. One such pattern was that of proselytism, in which non-Jews could "have a share in the age to come" by fully embracing the Torah and becoming members of the Jewish people. Another was characterized by a two-level understanding of the Torah, where a portion of it was taken to pertain to all humankind (Jews as well as non-Jews) while some of it pertained exclusively and distinctively to Jews. In this pattern, non-Jews who lived in conformity to the "Torah for non-Jews" could be considered as standing in a right relationship with God ("righteous Gentiles"). A third pattern, which overlaps considerably with the second, is one in which the Torah is seen as a particular manifestation

6. *Paul and the Gentiles: Remapping the Apostle's Convictional World* (Minneapolis: Fortress, 1997).

7. The clearest summary I have seen is that of Stephen Westerholm, *Perspectives Old and New on Paul: The "Lutheran" Paul and His Critics* (Grand Rapids: Eerdmans, 2004), 194-200.

8. E. P. Sanders, *Paul and Palestinian Judaism: A Comparison of Patterns of Religion* (Philadelphia: Fortress, 1977).

of a natural law, accessible (at least in theory) to non-Jews as well (what I called "ethical monotheism"). The fourth pattern, which anticipates a mass turning to the God of Israel on the part of non-Jews in the eschatological future ("participants in the end-time redemption of Israel"), is not characterized by a single view of Torah, but (apparently) could be combined with any of them.[9]

In my attempts to understand Paul within this framework, his characterization of non-Jewish Christ-believers as members of Abraham's σπέρμα came to play an important role.[10] After exploring various possibilities, I eventually came to the following reconstruction.

1. Prior to his Damascus experience, Paul believed that the only possibility for Gentiles to have a share in the age to come was by becoming proselytes in this age. That is, unlike (say) King Izates's adviser Ananias, who, while seeing proselytism as preferable, nevertheless thought that Izates could be acceptable to God without it, Paul took the more stringent position characterized by the king's other adviser, Eleazar (Josephus, *Ant.* 20.38-46). In his own words, prior to his Damascus experience he "preached circumcision" (Gal. 5:11).[11]

9. For a full collection of pertinent material, with commentary and analysis, see my *Judaism and the Gentiles: Jewish Patterns of Universalism (to 135 CE)* (Waco: Baylor University Press, 2007).

10. Another important aspect was Paul's eschatological scenario, which seemed to turn typical "Gentile pilgrimage" expectations on their head: "salvation has come to the Gentiles" not, as was typically expected, as a by-product of Israel's redemption, but as the result of Israel's "stumbling," "defeat," or "rejection" (Rom. 11:11-12, 15); while "all Israel" will eventually be "saved," Israel's redemption will bring to an end (rather than precipitate) the period of time in which "the fullness of the Gentiles" will be able to "come in" (Rom. 11:25-26). For more on this, see my response chapter in Mark D. Nanos and Magnus Zetterholm, eds., *Paul within Judaism: Restoring the First-Century Context to the Apostle* (Minneapolis: Fortress, 2015), which is a kind of companion piece to this one.

11. Douglas Campbell has recently argued, forcefully, that Galatians 5:11 refers to an early stage of Paul's post-Damascus apostolic ministry; Douglas A. Campbell, "Galatians 5.11: Evidence of an Early Law-Observant Mission by Paul?" *NTS* 57, no. 3 (2011): 325-47. If he were right, it would not affect my reconstruction in any fundamental way. If immediately after his Damascus experience he "preached circumcision," this would almost certainly be a continuation of his pre-Damascus pattern of Torah adherence. As for Paul's convictional reconfiguration, Campbell's reading would simply imply that the process was worked out over a somewhat longer period. The sentence remains difficult on any reading of it, however (especially the two appearances of ἔτι, which logically cannot represent contemporaneous periods of time). On balance, I continue to prefer the pre-Damascus reading of the verse.

2. Connected with this, Paul also shared the view that for non-Jews — those who existed outside the covenant and apart from the people of Israel — the Torah functioned only to condemn. (I will return to this point below.)
3. Since the Jewish tradition of "zeal" was centered on a readiness to use violence to protect the Torah- and temple-centered way of life, Paul's activity as a persecutor — "as to zeal, a persecutor of the church" (Phil. 3:6) — was driven by a perception that the Christ message represented a threat (of some kind) to Torah religion.
4. While there are several ways in which this threat has been construed, my conclusion was that Paul perceived Christ and Torah as representing rival ways of identifying the people of God — that is, rival ways of marking out (in the present) the community of the righteous that would be vindicated by the Messiah at his coming (in the future). In traditional Jewish eschatology, there was no necessary tension between the present role of the Torah (to demarcate the community of the righteous) and the future role of the Messiah (to vindicate the righteous and establish the future age). But the more complex, two-stage messianic work of Christ — who had effected the decisive work of salvation already in the past, but was still coming in the future to bring it to consummation — served to complicate the roles of Torah and Messiah and to bring them into (at least potential) rivalry.
5. The cognitive effect of the Damascus experience was the new conviction that the crucified Jesus had been raised by God and was therefore God's appointed Messiah and agent of salvation.
6. This new conviction did nothing to resolve the tension between Christ and Torah that Paul had already perceived in his pre-Damascus existence; the temporal overlap remained fully intact. The effect of the new conviction, however, was to make Christ, rather than Torah, the boundary around the community of the righteous.
7. Nevertheless, Paul could not simply invert Torah and Christ; the Torah remained something given by God, and thus must have a part to play. Likewise, God's election of Israel was not negated by the coming of Christ; for Paul, Israel (necessarily identified by the Torah as a mark of membership) could not simply be abandoned or absorbed into a more amorphous collection of the ἔθνη.
8. Finally, Paul continued to believe that non-Jews needed to become full members of Abraham's σπέρμα in order to share in the blessings of the age to come. What changed for him was the new conviction that

Christ had replaced Torah as the means by which such incorporation took place.[12]

Since this essay is part of a volume honoring Stephen Westerholm, my claim that Paul perceived Christ and Torah as representing rival ways of marking out the community of the righteous calls for a short excursus. Westerholm has, of course, raised strong objections to the idea that "righteousness" functions in Pauline discourse primarily as a membership term.[13] To use the terms in which Westerholm sums up the issue, Paul's language of "justification by faith, not by works of the law," has to do not with "erasing ethnic boundaries" but with "grace abounding to sinners."[14] He points out that the basic sense of the term, both in common usage and in Israel's scripture, has to do with doing what is right: "The 'righteous' are thus those who *do* what they *ought to do* (i.e., righteousness)"; those who do not are sinners.[15] Thus, on the basis of a survey of scriptural usage, he asserts: "the language of 'righteousness' can hardly designate membership in God's covenant people"; "'righteousness' does not mean, and by its very nature *cannot* mean, membership in a covenant."[16] Turning to Paul specifically, he argues that the term retains this basic sense in his usage as well.[17] Since, for Paul, all are sinners, in this basic sense of the term "there is not one who is righteous, not even one" (Rom. 3:10). Of course, Paul also uses the term in a second sense: sinners who believe in Christ are nevertheless declared righteous. In order to differentiate these two senses of the term, Westerholm suggests a distinction between "ordinary righteousness" and "extraordinary righteousness."

I accept the point that in the ordinary scriptural sense of the term "righteousness" has to do with conformity to a moral standard, with the corollary that those who fall short can be described as sinners. Westerholm has convinced me that one should not speak as if the term simply designated the status of a covenant member in good standing, directly and without remainder. However, if one is going to make a distinction between "ordinary" and

12. For the full argument, readers are referred to the pertinent sections of my *Paul and the Gentiles*.

13. Especially in his major work *Perspectives* and in a recent follow-up, *Justification Reconsidered: Rethinking a Pauline Theme* (Grand Rapids: Eerdmans, 2013).

14. See the title of chapter 20: "Grace Abounding to Sinners or Erasing Ethnic Boundaries?" in Westerholm, *Perspectives*.

15. Westerholm, *Justification*, 61 (emphasis original).

16. Westerholm, *Justification*, 62-63 (emphasis original).

17. "Paul no doubt had his idiosyncrasies, but using ordinary words in a sense peculiarly his own was not among them" (Westerholm, *Justification*, 65).

"extraordinary righteousness," then the Mosaic covenant, taken on its own terms, needs to be understood as a means of "extraordinary righteousness" as well. For the simple fact is that, despite an awareness of sin, Israel's scripture frequently describes people as righteous. The contrast between "the righteous" and "the sinners" permeates the Psalms, for example, the psalmists leaving no doubt that those who fear the Lord (31:17-19), delight in the law (1:1-6), worship in the temple (5:7-8, 12), and so on, belong to the company of the righteous.

The point can be illustrated economically on the basis of two psalms quoted by Paul himself. In Romans 3:10-12, Paul cites Psalm 14:2-3[18] to make the point that "there is no one who is righteous, not even one." While the verse taken on its own might appear to represent God's assessment of the whole of humankind (see also v. 2), the psalm goes on to identify a separate group, the "company of the righteous" (v. 5), identified as "his people" Israel (v. 7). A little later in Romans (4:7-8), Paul adduces Psalm 32:1-2 as a witness for righteousness by faith: "Blessed are those whose iniquities are forgiven and whose sins are covered; blessed is the one against whom the Lord will not reckon sin." The psalmist clearly considers himself to be one of the blessed, and addresses the psalm to a whole company of the righteous (vv. 5, 10-11). If the existence of "justified sinners" is an indicator of "extraordinary righteousness," then, on the basis of the use of the term in Israel's scripture, it is clearly applicable as well to those who are members in good standing of the covenant people Israel.

My point, then, is that, viewed from the outside, the "extraordinary righteousness" that for Paul the apostle had been accomplished by Christ was structurally similar to the "extraordinary righteousness" that for Israel had been provided by the Torah and the covenant. Put in other terms, both before and after his Damascus experience, Paul could well have perceived Christ and Torah as rival instruments for producing and marking off the community of the righteous. Further, both before and after his Damascus experience, Paul believed that for non-Jews to have a share in the age to come, it was necessary for them to become part of the σπέρμα Αβραάμ in this age.

Returning to my main line of argument, my primary purpose in this chapter is to build on this observation, with a view to shedding some light on what Paul has to say about the place of the Torah with respect to the life of the *ethnē*-in-Christ. Even if he sees his converts as σπέρμα Αβραάμ, they are patently not proselytes in any material sense of the term. While there might be some formal similarity between the two — that is, between the identity structure of the *ethnē*-in-Christ as Paul conceives it in his post-Damascus situation

18. Perhaps with some influence from Ecclesiastes 7:20.

and his prior proselyte-only stance — the *ethnē*-in-Christ are not proselytes to the Jewish people. Indeed, Paul categorically forbids them from becoming proselytes: circumcision, which would bring with it the obligation to observe "the whole law" (Gal. 5:3), would at the same time sever them from Christ.

This, of course, does not exhaust what Paul has to say about the role of the Torah with respect to Gentile Christ-believers. Those who live "according to the Spirit" thereby "have the just requirement of the law fulfilled in" them (Rom. 8:4). "The whole law" is "summed up" in the commandment to love one's neighbor as oneself (Rom. 13:9; Gal. 5:14), a commandment that Paul enjoins on his readers. On occasion he can appeal to specific legal texts for guidance on ethical matters (Rom. 13:9; 1 Cor. 9:8; 14:21, 34; more generally, Rom. 15:4; 1 Cor. 10:11).[19]

Can we, then, shed some light on this aspect of Paul's discourse by looking at it from the perspective of my proposed starting point — namely, the idea that before his Damascus experience Paul had shared that strand of Jewish thought according to which the only way in which non-Jews might have a share in the age to come was by becoming proselytes (i.e., by becoming part of the "seed of Abraham") in the present age?

Guilty of the Greatest Offense against the Law

In Josephus's account of the conversion of King Izates, the king wavered between the counsel of two advisers: Ananias, who was of the opinion that the king "could worship God even without being circumcised"; and Eleazar, known "for being extremely strict when it came to the ancestral laws," who told the king that, by ignoring what the law commanded, he was committing an act of unrighteousness (ἀδικῶν) against both the law and God (*Ant.* 20.41-44). In Eleazar's view, the Torah was binding on the whole of humankind — the Torah in its entirety, including the commandment of circumcision. The only way for a non-Jew such as Izates to be acceptable to God — to do what was "right" (cf. ἀδικῶν) — was to "do what was commanded in [the Torah]" and to be circumcised.

To explore further the view represented by Eleazar, I would like to place it in the context of what might be termed a "spectrum of pessimism" with respect

19. On the latter point, see Peter J. Tomson, *Paul and the Jewish Law: Halakha in the Letters of the Apostle to the Gentiles* (CRINT 3/1; Assen: Van Gorcum, 1990), 68-95, where he deals with these passages in the context of a larger discussion of Paul's halakah.

to the non-Jewish world. At the most pessimistic end of the spectrum is the book of *Jubilees,* which declares that "anyone who is not circumcised on the eighth day . . . [will] be destroyed and annihilated from the earth . . . because he has broken the covenant of the Lord our God" (*Jub.* 15.26). Such a position, requiring not only circumcision but circumcision on the eighth day, amounts to a categorical exclusion of non-Jews from the outset. Equally pessimistic, though less categorically so, are passages in the *Testament of Moses* (1.11-13), Pseudo-Philo's *Biblical Antiquities* (11.1-2), and the *Apocalypse of Abraham* (31.1-8), which hold out no hope for the non-Jewish nations and envision their ultimate annihilation. Except for a few enigmatic references to the presence of *gerim* (גרים: sojourners, "proselytes"),[20] the sectarian literature from Qumran is equally pessimistic, with its deterministic division of humankind into the "men of the lot of God" and the "men of the lot of Belial" and its anticipation of the ultimate destruction of the latter.[21] *Fourth Ezra* is almost as gloomy, though the author does envisage the possibility that God "will find individual men who have kept your commandments" (however, "nations you will not find"; *4 Ezra* 3.36). *Second Baruch* is more sanguine, envisaging a considerable number of those from the nations "who left behind their vanity and who have fled under your wings," described a little later as "those who first did not know life and who later knew it exactly and who mingled with the seed of the people" (*2 Bar.* 41.4; 42.5). Still, those "who do not keep the statutes of the Most High" will in the end pass away like smoke (*2 Bar.* 82.6).[22]

What is of particular interest in this (and related) material is a persistent theodical concern.[23] The conviction that, except for the righteous who keep the law, the "whole multitude" of Adam and Eve's descendants are "going to corruption" (*2 Bar.* 48.43) seems to have raised questions about divine justice. Without backing away from the conviction that all outside the covenant are destined for destruction, this literature evidences a concern to justify God's final judgment of those "who do not keep the statutes of the Most High."

20. CD VI, 21; XIV, 6; 4QpNah 3-4 II, 9; 11QT[a] XL, 6; 4QFlor I, 4; 4Q159 Frags. 2-4, 1; 4Q279 Frag. 5, 6.

21. 1QS II, 1-10; also, for example, 1QM I, 10; III, 9.

22. Also in *2 Baruch,* there are two more positive references to the nations in the Cloud and Waters Apocalypse (chapters 53–74; see 68.5-6 and 72.2-6). This section of *2 Baruch,* however, is distinct from the rest of the work in several respects and appears to be an already existing apocalypse that has been incorporated into the larger work; for a more thorough discussion, see Donaldson, *Judaism and the Gentiles,* 189-93.

23. Except for *Jubilees,* which, without any hint of an uneasy conscience, maintains that God has deliberately allowed the other nations to be misled into destruction (*Jub.* 15.31).

In some cases, Gentile culpability results simply from the fact that they "did not know my Law" (2 *Bar.* 48.40) or that "they have not learned my Law" (*L.A.B.* 11.2). While these statements seem to assume that non-Jews should have "known" and "learned" the Torah,[24] how this knowledge should have been acquired is left unspecified. Elsewhere in 2 *Baruch* it is said that non-Jews "despised my Law" (51.4), which implies that they did have at least some awareness of the law's existence. This line of thought is especially prominent in *4 Ezra:*

> For God strictly commanded those who came into the world, when they came, what they should do to live, and what they should observe to avoid punishment. Nevertheless they were not obedient, and spoke against him; they devised for themselves vain thoughts, and proposed to themselves wicked frauds; they even declared that the Most High does not exist, and they ignored his ways! They scorned his Law, and denied his covenants; they have been unfaithful to his statutes and have not performed his works. (7.21-24; see also 7.72-74; 8.55-61; 9.9-12)

How this strict commandment was communicated, however, and how it was that they "obtained the Law" (7.72) is not made clear, though some of the language (e.g., "who came into the world") is suggestive of a line of thought that is more important for my purposes here.

According to this line of thought, some basic knowledge of God and of God's commandments is discernible from the created order itself. This theme appears clearly at one point in 2 *Baruch* (54.13-19). In support of the statement that "those who do not love your Law are justly perishing" (v. 14), Baruch declares: "For his works have not taught you, nor has the artful work of his creation which has existed always persuaded you" (v. 18). The fault, however, lies not with God's "works" but with the "unrighteous ones" themselves, who willfully "rejected the understanding of the Most High" (v. 17).[25] The theme appears as well in the *Apocalypse of Abraham*. Although the example of Abraham demonstrated that it was possible to recognize the folly of idolatry and to perceive from the created order that there is a "God who created all things" (7.10), the Gentiles have spurned this opportunity for repentance:

24. Given as "a light to the world," according to *L.A.B.* 11.1

25. In 2 *Baruch* 48.40, even though the unrighteous did not know God's law, each one nevertheless "knew when he acted unrighteously."

"For I waited so that they might come to me, and they did not deign to" (*Apoc. Ab.* 31.6).[26]

What emerges in this latter set of texts, then, is a kind of natural theology in a pessimistic key. The created order itself bore witness to the Creator God and to some fundamental ethical injunctions, which should have led human beings to seek the God who had been revealed more fully in the Torah and the covenant. While this did happen in some cases (those "who left behind their vanity and who have fled under your wings"; *2 Bar.* 41.4), for the most part the witness of the natural order simply justified the judgment to come.

Here this "spectrum of pessimism" links up with that larger collection of Jewish texts in which we find a more positive view of natural revelation and natural law.[27] In this strand of tradition, the law of Moses is presented as a particular — and more explicit — substantiation of a fundamental law that is embedded in the created order itself and capable of being discovered and followed by right-minded human beings. What comes to expression here is a form of "ethical monotheism," characterized by belief in the one Creator God (and thus by rejection of idolatry; *Apoc. Ab.* 1–8) and by a set of basic ethical norms (having to do with sexual immorality, murder, theft, and the like; *Apoc. Ab.* 24–25). Most of this literature downplays those aspects of the Mosaic law that serve to differentiate Jews from non-Jews and displays an optimism that non-Jews will be able to recognize, desire, and conform to this more fundamental ethical monotheism. The Wisdom of Solomon, which begins with an optimistic universalism but ends with a more pessimistic assessment of the possibility of achieving righteousness outside the covenant,[28] might be taken as representing the point at which two strands of tradition link up.

While this material deserves much more detailed treatment than can be given here, the preceding discussion is sufficient to establish two observations. First, there was a place in the stringent "proselytism-only" position taken by such first-century Jews as Eleazar — and (I argue) Paul in his "earlier life" (Gal. 1:13) — for a form of natural theology and natural law. The form is largely pessimistic. Only in the case of those non-Jews who choose to move beyond

26. See also *T. Mos.* 1.11-13: "He created the world on behalf of his people, but he did not make this purpose of creation openly known from the beginning of the world so that the nations might be found guilty, indeed that they might abjectly declare themselves guilty by their own . . . discussions." While the sentence is obscure, it could be read as implying that something should have been known about God from the created order.

27. For a full collection of these texts, with commentary, see the pertinent sections in Donaldson, *Judaism and the Gentiles*.

28. See Donaldson, *Judaism and the Gentiles*, 62-68.

these natural perceptions to fully embrace the law of Moses and worship the God of Israel does this natural theology have any positive role to play, and then simply a preliminary one. Otherwise, it functions simply to justify their ultimate condemnation and destruction.

Second, this condemnation is based not simply on the natural law that was spurned but the written law of Moses to which it should have led. Baruch, for example, speaking of the unrighteous "inhabitants of the earth," declares that "your Law, which they transgressed, will repay them on your day" (*2 Bar.* 48.47). Similarly in *4 Ezra*, God declares that "as many as scorned my Law while they still had freedom . . . these must in torment acknowledge it after death" (*4 Ezra* 9.11-12). In Pseudo-Philo's *Biblical Antiquities*, God says to Moses: "I have given an everlasting Law into your hands and by this I will judge the whole world." This means that the law, then, has a dual function: "For them ['my people'] I will bring out the eternal statutes that are for those in the light but for the ungodly a punishment" (*L.A.B.* 11.1-2). In other words, for those within the covenant the Torah served as a means of righteousness; for those outside, however, it functioned simply to condemn.[29]

The Torah and the *Ethnē*-in-Christ

What light can be shed, then, on Paul's discourse about the Gentiles, the Torah, and Christ, on the assumption that, prior to his Damascus experience, he shared the position of those Jews who believed that only by becoming proselytes (σπέρμα Αβραάμ) in this age would ἔθνη be acceptable to God and have a share in the age to come?

On the basis of the preceding examination of this "proselyte-only" position, an important observation can be made at the outset. Two characteristic features of this position — the idea that outside the covenant the Torah functions simply to condemn, and the theodical use of a natural law in a negative key — correspond with distinctive features of Paul's own discourse. First, Paul's insistence that, apart from Christ, all the law can do is to reveal sin (e.g., Rom. 3:20; 4:15; 5:13; 7:7-13) and thus to condemn sinners (e.g., Rom. 3:19-20; 4:15) has long puzzled Jewish and sympathetic non-Jewish scholars alike. What happened to the central Jewish theme of "God's forgiveness and man's repen-

29. This point has been made by Lloyd Gaston, *Paul and the Torah* (Vancouver: University of British Columbia Press, 1987), 28.

tance," whose "outward symbol was the Day of Atonement"?[30] The absence of these covenantal features is less puzzling, however, if one places the Pauline discourse alongside the view examined in the previous section, in which, for Gentiles outside the covenant, the role of the Torah is simply to condemn.[31] Second, commentators have often noted the similarities between Paul's discourse in Romans 1:18-32 and "standard Hellenistic Jewish polemic" against Gentile sinfulness, such as is found in Wisdom 11–15.[32] His argument — that knowledge about God was accessible "ever since the creation of the world . . . through the things he has made" (1:20), and that this knowledge leaves people "without excuse" and subject to judgment — is of a piece with the pessimistic theodical natural theology described above.[33] These correspondences are at least consistent with our assumption about Paul's pre-Damascus position.

But what happens if in addition we assume the transformation postulated above — that is, that as a result of his Damascus experience, Paul came to view Christ as replacing Torah in its role as the foundation and boundary marker for the community of the righteous? Specifically, what insight might this provide into the relationship between the law and the *ethnē*-in-Christ, a relationship that he construes positively as well as negatively?

If my preceding analysis is correct, although the "proselyte-only" position is characterized by a universal and unitary view of the Torah — to have a share in the age to come, non-Jews must embrace the Torah as a whole and enter the covenant — there is nevertheless a kind of bifurcation. A role is assigned, albeit a secondary one, for an awareness of God and God's basic moral expectation that is deducible from the created order itself. For a more positive strand of Jewish tradition, such ethical monotheism seems to have functioned, at least

30. Claude G. Montefiore, *Judaism and St. Paul: Two Essays* (London: Max Goschen, 1914), 75; see the discussion of Montefiore in Stefan Meissner, *Die Heimholung des Ketzers: Studien zur jüdischen Auseinandersetzung mit Paulus* (WUNT II 87; Tübingen: Mohr Siebeck, 1996), 40-45.

31. While Paul certainly does not dissolve the Torah-based distinction between the Jews and the ἔθνη, I believe that he saw the Torah as playing this role for Jews as well. The point is not essential for the purposes of this essay, however, and so will not be discussed directly. But see also note 35.

32. For example, James D. G. Dunn, *Romans* (2 vols.; WBC; Waco: Word, 1988), 1:53; see also Ernst Käsemann, *Commentary on Romans* (London: SCM, 1980), 39-41.

33. To be sure, in the continuation of the discourse, Paul seems to shift to a more positive key, suggesting that it is possible for Gentiles to "do instinctively what the law requires" (Rom. 2:14), a notion that seems to undercut the argument that "all, both Jews and Greeks, are under the power of sin" (3:9) and will "be held accountable to God" (3:19). See the discussion in Donaldson, *Paul and the Gentiles*, 140.

in principle, as an alternative route to God.[34] For the more negative strand of tradition described above, however, such a creation-based natural theology in and of itself had only a negative function. Only in the case of those who began with this preliminary *in nuce* glimpse of God and of the divine commands and then went on to embrace the Torah as a whole, did natural theology function in a more positive way.

But what if this second step had been replaced? What if — as I have argued in the case of Paul — the Torah had been replaced by Christ as the means by which non-Jews are to come into a positive relationship with the God who is discernible through the created order? One could well imagine a shift of perception by which the universal and unitary view of the Torah, characteristic of his former life, fell into two parts — the law of Moses, the distinctive possession of "the Israelites" (Rom. 9:4);[35] and the "truth about God" and God's "righteous requirements" (δικαίωμα; Rom. 1:32), apparent in the created order itself. In such a shift, then, this natural law, or ethical monotheism, would no longer function simply as subsidiary to the Mosaic Torah — that is, either as a preliminary step toward full proselytism or as a standard justifying divine punishment. Rather, even in a situation where Christ had replaced Torah, such a natural law could continue to have an important part to play for those ἔθνη who had come to be "in Christ." Those "who are in Christ Jesus," who "walk . . . according to the Spirit," are those in whom the "righteous requirement (δικαίωμα) of the law"[36] is "fulfilled" (Rom. 8:1-4).

What does this "righteous requirement" look like? On two occasions, Paul can sum it up in the law of love: "The whole law is summed up in a single commandment, 'You shall love your neighbor as yourself'" (Gal. 5:14; also Rom. 13:8-10). Where he provides more extensive descriptions,[37] his ethical injunctions have to do with monotheistic worship, rejection of idolatry, sexual immorality, bloodshed, lack of self-control, and so on — precisely the kinds of

34. See chapter 12, "Ethical Monotheism," in Donaldson, *Judaism and the Gentiles.*

35. Clearly for Paul the Torah continues to have a role in identifying Israel as a distinctive people. Further, given his assertion that those who are circumcised "are obliged to obey the entire law" (Gal. 5:3) and his injunction that believers are to "remain in the condition in which [they] were called" (1 Cor. 7:20), it appears that he expects *Ioudaioi*-in-Christ to continue to observe the Torah.

36. While *ethnē*-in-Christ can fulfill the "righteous requirement (δικαίωμα)" of God (see Rom. 1:32) without embracing the whole law of Moses, Paul here can still describe this δικαίωμα as the δικαίωμα "of the law." In other words, even though this δικαίωμα stands on its own as a kind of natural law apart from the written law, Paul does not deny that it is discernible in the law of Moses as well.

37. In addition to Rom. 1:18-32, see, for example, 1 Cor. 5:10-11; 6:9-10; Gal. 5:19-21.

vices and virtues common in the ethical monotheistic tradition (*Apocalypse of Abraham,* Wisdom of Solomon, *Letter of Aristeas, Sibylline Oracles* 3–5, Philo, and the like).

All of this deserves to be unpacked in greater detail. For present purposes, however, my point is that what Paul has to say about the role of "the law" with respect to the ἔθνη, especially the *ethnē*-in-Christ, can be accounted for on the assumption that his Damascus experience precipitated the kind of transformation of Paul's convictions such as I proposed in *Paul and the Gentiles* and summarized above. Indeed, I suggest that, rather than simply accounting for it, such an understanding of the convictional consequences of Paul's Damascus experience puts his apostolic discourse about the ἔθνη into a framework in which it can be better understood. This is especially true with respect to what I have described as the puzzling profile of Paul's *ethnē*-in-Christ — that is, non-Jews, who are said to fulfill the "righteous requirement" of the law, who do so without being circumcised, but who nevertheless can be described as belonging to the "seed of Abraham."[38]

38. A number of scholars have argued that Paul thinks of the *ethnē*-in-Christ as "righteous Gentiles"; that is, they are bound to observe those aspects of the Torah that pertain to non-Jews; so Tomson, *Paul and the Jewish Law;* Markus Bockmuehl, *Jewish Law in Gentile Churches: Halakhah and the Beginning of Christian Public Ethics* (Edinburgh: T&T Clark, 2000), 85-173, especially 127-40; Alan F. Segal, *Paul the Convert: The Apostolate and Apostasy of Saul the Pharisee* (New Haven: Yale University Press, 1990), 204. It is true that Paul's *ethnē*-in-Christ resemble such "righteous Gentiles" in significant respects. However, given his insistence that they are also σπέρμα Αβραάμ, I believe Paul got to this point by a different route. The resemblance can be accounted for on the basis of the fact that, as far as ethical behavior is concerned, the profiles of the "ethical monotheist" and of the "righteous Gentile" also resemble each other in significant respects.

The Conversion of the Imagination: Scripture and Eschatology in 1 Corinthians

Richard B. Hays

What role did Israel's Torah play in Paul's letters as he sought to reshape the consciousness and identity of the small communities of Gentile converts that he had founded, communities that were scattered around the Mediterranean world in the middle of the first century? Most discussions of this question, both in traditional Christian theology and in academic New Testament scholarship, have focused on Paul's statements about the soteriological inefficacy of the law's commandments, in contrast to the spiritual power of the gospel of the crucified and risen Jesus. But this way of framing the issue may occlude certain key elements of Paul's message. While he argues urgently that the law, taken by itself, cannot offer deliverance from the powers of sin and death (e.g., Rom. 8:3-4), Paul nonetheless insists that Israel's scripture tells the true story of the world and thereby provides the moral and existential framework within which the emergent *ekklēsia* lives and moves. For Paul, the Torah — read as narrative — configures the identity of his Gentile communities as the divinely intended, eschatologically revealed expansion of the people of Israel.

In light of this hermeneutical posture, it is no surprise that Paul appropriates the Torah not chiefly as a source of rules but as a typological prefiguration of the church. This essay seeks to explore the surprising ways in which Paul's pastoral advice to the church in Corinth depends pervasively on his figural

This essay first appeared in *NTS* 45, no. 3 (1999): 391-412, and was subsequently incorporated as the title essay in Richard B. Hays, *The Conversion of the Imagination: Paul as Interpreter of Israel's Scripture* (Grand Rapids: Eerdmans, 2005), 1-24. I am pleased that the editors of the present volume have invited its inclusion in this collection of essays in honor of Stephen Westerholm, whose scholarly work I have long admired as a model of sound research, judicious judgment, and gracious clarity. I am grateful to Cambridge University Press for permission to reprint the essay in its current slightly abridged form.

interpretation of Torah for a Gentile community, a community that he was exhorting to read the story of Israel as their own story. Within such a story-shaped world, the Mosaic law can continue to speak directly to God's people in an eschatologically transformed context.

This way of approaching the question of Torah in Paul's thought casts fresh light on several important matters. Not least, it shows that the dichotomy between "apocalyptic" and "covenant theology" in Paul is misconceived. It is precisely the apocalyptic message of cross and resurrection that drives Paul's hermeneutically transformative affirmation of narrative continuity between the story of Israel and the identity of the church.

Were the Corinthians Performing Isaiah's Script (1 Cor. 14:25)?

At the conclusion of a long argument urging the Corinthians to practice intelligible prophecy rather than unintelligible speech in tongues, Paul asks them to consider the effects of their speech on outsiders who may be present in their worship assembly. "If, therefore, the whole church comes together and all speak in tongues, and outsiders or unbelievers enter, will they not say that you are out of your mind? But if all prophesy, and an unbeliever or outsider enters, he is reproved by all, called to account by all. The hidden things of his heart are disclosed, and thus, he will fall on his face and worship God, declaring, 'Truly, God is among you'" (1 Cor. 14:23-25). Although there is no explicit citation formula here signaling an Old Testament quotation, it has been widely recognized that Paul's imagined description of the unbeliever's reaction alludes to at least two passages from the prophets, Isaiah 45:14 and Zechariah 8:23. Nestle-Aland, in fact, treats the words ὁ θεὸς ἐν ὑμῖν ἐστιν as a direct quotation of the Isaiah passage,[1] with a marginal notation indicating an allusion to Zechariah. The possible significance of these intertextual connections, however, has rarely received sustained consideration.[2] The

1. Nestle-Aland also italicizes ὄντως as part of the quotation, although this word is lacking in the LXX. See, however, the MT of 45:15, in which אכן is the first word.

2. Commentators who briefly note the Old Testament reference include Heinz-Dietrich Wendland, *Die Briefe an die Korinther* (NTD 7; Göttingen: Vandenhoeck & Ruprecht, 1954), 113; C. K. Barrett, *The First Epistle to the Corinthians* (HNTC; New York: Harper & Row, 1954), 327; Hans Conzelmann, *1 Corinthians* (Hermeneia; Philadelphia: Fortress, 1975), 244 n. 35; Gordon D. Fee, *The First Epistle to the Corinthians* (NICNT; Grand Rapids: Eerdmans, 1987), 687. The most extensive treatment known to me is Florian Wilk, *Die Bedeutung des Jesajabuches für Paulus* (FRLANT 179; Göttingen: Vandenhoeck & Ruprecht, 1998), 331-33.

two most comprehensive recent studies of Paul's citation technique, those of Dietrich-Alex Koch and Christopher D. Stanley, explicitly decline to treat 1 Corinthians 14:25c as an Old Testament quotation and offer no discussion of the passage.[3]

In the absence of a citation formula, some scholars remain skeptical that Paul intends to remind his readers of any Old Testament passage.[4] Allusions and echoes are for those who have ears to hear. Nonetheless, as a heuristic exercise, let us pose the following question: if in fact 1 Corinthians 14:25 does echo the language of Israel's prophets, how would this echo affect our interpretation of the text?

In *Echoes of Scripture in the Letters of Paul,* I sought to show that Paul's Old Testament allusions and echoes frequently exemplify the literary trope of metalepsis. Metalepsis is a rhetorical and poetic device in which one text alludes to an earlier text in a way that evokes resonances of the early text beyond those explicitly cited. The result is that the interpretation of metalepsis requires the reader to recover unstated or suppressed correspondences between the two texts.[5] If Paul's phrasing in 1 Corinthians 14:25 is, as I believe, an instance of metalepsis, we must go back and examine the wider contexts in the scriptural precursors to understand the figurative effects produced by the intertextual connections.

3. Koch does not discuss the passage, commenting that the relation of Paul's formulation to the alleged Old Testament source is "wesentlich lockerer" than other cases where he does acknowledge an unmarked quotation (*Die Schrift als Zeuge des Evangeliums: Untersuchungen zur Verwendung und zum Verständnis der Schrift bei Paulus* [BHT 69; Tübingen: Mohr Siebeck, 1986], 18). Stanley excludes the passage from consideration because he is following "strict guidelines that limit the investigation to passages that offer explicit indication to the reader that a citation is being offered" (*Paul and the Language of Scripture: Citation Technique in the Pauline Epistles and Contemporary Literature* [SNTSMS 69; Cambridge: Cambridge University Press, 1992], 206 n. 85).

4. Everyone acknowledges that within the same paragraph, in 1 Corinthians 14:21, Paul explicitly quotes Isaiah 28:11-12. His interpretation of this passage is so obscure that most critical attention has focused on the explicit quotation. On 14:21, see Richard B. Hays, *First Corinthians* (Interpretation; Louisville: John Knox, 1997), 238-40. The presence of an explicit Isaiah quotation in the paragraph enhances the likelihood that Paul is alluding to another passage from Isaiah in 14:25.

5. For fuller explanation of this approach to reading Paul's intertextual echoes, see Richard B. Hays, *Echoes of Scripture in the Letters of Paul* (New Haven: Yale University Press, 1989), 14-21. For a full discussion of the trope in literature ancient and modern, see John Hollander, *The Figure of Echo: A Mode of Allusion in Milton and After* (Berkeley: University of California Press, 1981). A similar literary phenomenon has been traced within the Hebrew Bible by Michael Fishbane, *Biblical Interpretation in Ancient Israel* (Oxford: Clarendon, 1985).

Isaiah 45 is part of Deutero-Isaiah's prophecy concerning the end of Israel's exile and the restoration of Jerusalem. As a result of this dramatic turn in Israel's fortunes, the Gentile nations will be moved to recognize the glory of Israel's God (cf. Isa. 49:23; 60:1-16). "And they shall bow down (προσκυνήσουσιν) before you and pray to you, because God is among you (ἐν σοὶ ὁ θεός ἐστιν), and they shall say, 'There is no God besides you; for you are God, and we did not know it, the God of Israel, the Savior'" (Isa. 45:14b-15 LXX). Paul echoes the verb προσκυνήσουσιν, changing it to the singular προσκυνήσει since he is talking about a single Gentile unbeliever, and he repeats the quotation "God is among you," changing the pronoun from singular σοὶ to plural ὑμῖν because he is referring not to Israel as a nation but to the assembled community of worshipers in Corinth.[6] Thus, Paul subtly pictures the conversion of Gentile unbelievers through the prophetic activity of Corinthian Christians as a fulfillment of Isaiah's eschatological vision: the Gentiles will recognize the presence of God in the midst of God's people.

Similar motifs appear in Zechariah 8:20-23 and Daniel 2:46-47.[7] The strongest verbal connection, however, is to Isaiah 45:14. In all three of these Old Testament subtexts, we see a common pattern: through the mediating witness of the people of God, the Gentile outsider is brought to offer worship to Israel's God. This way of formulating the matter, however, immediately exposes the novelty of Paul's metaleptic evocation of Isaiah in 1 Corinthians 14:25. In Paul's scenario it is the church — itself a predominantly Gentile community — through which God will accomplish the eschatological conversion of outsiders. The Gentile Christian "understudies" seem now to have stepped into the role originally assigned to Israel in Isaiah's eschatological drama. Using the scriptural imagery in a metaphorical manner, Paul has clothed his depiction of the conversion of "outsiders" in language that originally had been used by Isaiah to portray the response of Gentiles to an eschatologically restored Israel.

6. As Koch and Stanley have shown, adaptations of this sort are a standard feature of Paul's quotation practice: he tailors the grammar and syntax of the quotation to fit the application he is giving it.

7. The Daniel passage, though overlooked by Nestle-Aland, is noted by Wendland, *Briefe an die Korinther,* 113; Barrett, *First Epistle,* 327; Hans Hübner, *Biblische Theologie des Neuen Testaments* (vol. 2; Göttingen: Vandenhoeck & Ruprecht, 1993), 197; Wilk, *Bedeutung des Jesajabuches,* 331.

Theses concerning Apocalyptic Eschatology and Scripture in 1 Corinthians

I offer these preliminary remarks about 1 Corinthians 14:25 as a "teaser," a way of reopening the question of scripture and eschatology in 1 Corinthians. We have become so thoroughly accustomed to thinking of Paul as "Apostle to the Gentiles" that we may be in danger of overlooking what this self-designation suggests: Paul understood himself as a Jew sent by the God of Israel to the world of Gentile "outsiders" for the purpose of declaring to them the message of eschatological salvation promised in Israel's scriptures — preeminently Isaiah — to the whole world.

In Galatians 1:15-16, Paul describes his own call to this apostolic ministry in language that echoes the vocation of the "servant" of Isaiah 49, whom God sends as "a light to the nations, that my salvation may reach to the end of the earth" (49:6; see the parallel between Gal. 1:15 and Isa. 49:1). This means that Paul understands his apostolic vocation to be inseparable from his apocalyptic interpretation of certain biblical texts that prefigure the events of the end-time. His gospel proclaims that through the death and resurrection of Jesus this end-time has broken in upon the world. It is no accident that in 2 Corinthians 6:2 Paul articulates his λόγος τῆς καταλλαγῆς by first quoting from Isaiah 49:8 ("At an acceptable time I have listened to you, and on the day of salvation I have helped you"), and then declaring, "Behold, now is the well-favored time; behold, now is the day of salvation!" This passage nicely illustrates the way in which Paul's apostolic self-understanding as Christ's ambassador (2 Cor. 5:20) is woven together with an eschatological hermeneutic that produces startling new readings of Israel's scripture.

The integral connection between Paul's gospel and an apocalyptic worldview has been widely recognized. This insight was championed in different ways by Albert Schweitzer[8] and Ernst Käsemann,[9] and it has been developed in the English-speaking world — again in interestingly different ways — by J. Christiaan Beker[10] and J. Louis Martyn.[11] What has not always been equally

8. Albert Schweitzer, *Die Mystik des Apostels Paulus* (Tübingen: Mohr Siebeck, 1930).

9. The seminal essays by Käsemann are "Zum Thema der urchristlichen Apokalyptik" and "Gottesgerechtigkeit bei Paulus," in *Exegetische Versuche und Besinnungen* (vol. 2; Göttingen: Vandenhoeck & Ruprecht, 1964), 104-31, 181-93.

10. J. Christiaan Beker, *Paul the Apostle: The Triumph of God in Life and Thought* (Philadelphia: Fortress, 1980).

11. J. Louis Martyn, *Theological Issues in the Letters of Paul* (Nashville: Abingdon, 1997); see also the extended note "Apocalyptic Theology in Galatians," in *Galatians: A New Translation with Introduction and Commentary* (AB 33A; New York: Doubleday, 1997), 97-105.

clear, however, is how Paul's missionary strategy in his confrontation with pagan culture repeatedly draws on eschatologically interpreted scripture texts to clarify the identity of the church and to remake the minds of his congregations. This essay examines Paul's use of scripture in 1 Corinthians as a test case.

In 1 Corinthians, we find Paul calling his readers and hearers to a conversion of the imagination. He was calling Gentiles to understand their identity anew in light of the gospel of Jesus Christ — a gospel message comprehensible only in relation to the larger narrative of God's dealing with Israel. Terence L. Donaldson has recently argued that "the shape of Paul's rhetoric concerning Gentile salvation can best be accounted for in terms of an underlying pattern of convictions in which Gentiles are thought of as proselytes to an Israel reconfigured around Christ."[12] This seems to me to be exactly correct. We must emphasize, as Donaldson does, the word "reconfigured" in order to make it clear that Paul was not promulgating a linear *Heilsgeschichte* in which Gentiles were simply absorbed into a Torah-observant Jewish Christianity. Rather, the "Israel" into which Paul's Corinthian converts were embraced was an Israel whose story had been hermeneutically reconfigured by the cross and resurrection. The result was that Jew and Gentile alike found themselves summoned by the gospel story to a sweeping reevaluation of their identities, an imaginative paradigm shift so comprehensive that it can only be described as a "conversion of the imagination."[13] Such a thoroughgoing conversion could be fostered and sustained only by a continuous process of bringing the community's believers and practices into critical confrontation with the gospel story.

This hermeneutical confrontation is nowhere more visible than in 1 Corinthians. A careful consideration of this letter leads to the formulation of two major theses:

1. Paul was trying to teach the Corinthian church to think eschatologically.
2. Paul was trying to teach the Corinthian church to reshape its identity in light of Israel's scripture.

These two theses are necessarily intertwined: Paul read scripture through the lens of an eschatological hermeneutic, and conversely, he "read" the identity of the eschatological community through the lens of scripture.

12. Terence L. Donaldson, *Paul and the Gentiles: Remapping the Apostle's Convictional World* (Minneapolis: Fortress, 1997), 236.

13. Wayne Meeks and other social historians of the Pauline communities have used the term "resocialization" to point to social dimensions of the phenomenon I am describing here. See, for example, Wayne A. Meeks, *The Moral World of the First Christians* (Philadelphia: Westminster, 1986), 13-14, 126, 129.

The critical cutting edge of these two theses may be clarified if I state polemically two negative corollaries.

1. The Corinthians did not have an "over-realized eschatology." Instead, they employed categories of self-understanding derived from a decidedly non-eschatological Greco-Roman cultural environment. Their particular form of "enthusiasm" seems to have been a hybrid of Stoic and Cynic philosophical influences, popular sophistic rhetoric, and charismatic spiritual fervor. Paul keeps injecting future apocalyptic language[14] into his argument to gain critical leverage against various problematical practices of the Corinthians; this in no way demonstrates, however, that the source of the Corinthian errors was a premature eschatological timetable.

2. Adolf von Harnack was badly mistaken about Paul's use of scripture in his mission to the Gentiles. Harnack, as is well known, contended that "Paulus das A.T. nicht als das christliche Quellen- und Erbauungsbuch von vornherein den jungen Gemeinden gegeben . . . hat," and that he engaged with them in arguments about the interpretation of the Old Testament "nur . . . wenn sie in Gefahr standen, dem judaistischen Irrtum zu verfallen," i.e., only when his hand was forced by Judaizing opponents.[15] This account simply fails to do justice to Paul's varied and rich uses of scripture in 1 Corinthians, where the problems have nothing to do with "Judaizing"[16] or with outside opponents. This letter gives evidence that Origen was right when he wrote, in his *Homilies on Exodus* 5.1, that the apostle Paul, "'teacher of the Gentiles,' taught the church which he had gathered from among the Gentiles, how to understand the books of the Law."

Recent scholarship has shown, from many angles, how problematical are both the "over-realized eschatology" hypothesis and the view that Paul did not

14. For thorough studies of Paul's pastoral use of such language, see David W. Kuck, *Judgment and Community Conflict: Paul's Use of Apocalyptic Judgment Language in 1 Corinthians 3:5–4:5* (NovTSup 66; Leiden: Brill, 1992); Matthias Konradt, *Gericht und Gemeinde: Eine Studie zur Bedeutung und Funktion von Gerichtsaussagen im Rahmen der paulinischen Ekklesiologie und Ethik im 1 Thess und 1 Kor* (BZNW 117; Berlin: De Gruyter, 2003).

15. Adolf von Harnack, "Das Alte Testament in den Paulinischen Briefen und in den Paulinischen Gemeinden," *SPAW* (1928): 124-41; the passages quoted here are from 137, 130. By way of contrast, see the findings of Andreas Lindemann ("Die Schrift als Tradition: Beobachtungen zu den biblischen Zitaten im Ersten Korintherbrief," in *Schrift und Tradition: Festschrift für Josef Ernst zum 70. Geburtstag* [ed. Knut Backhaus and Franz Georg Untergassmair; Paderborn: Ferdinand Schöningh, 1996], 225), who concludes that "Paulus selbst im Zuge der Heidenmission die jüdische Bibel als die authoritative Tradition des Christentums eingeführt hat."

16. Despite the arguments of M. D. Goulder, "ΣΟΦΙΑ in 1 Corinthians," *NTS* 37, no. 4 (1991): 516-34.

teach scripture to his churches. Yet, one continues to find such views in print.[17] Therefore, a fresh examination of these issues is necessary.

One final word of preliminary clarification: I am by no means suggesting that scripture and Jewish apocalyptic eschatology were the only tools Paul used in his efforts to reshape the minds of his congregations. Paul drew on a wide range of resources to accomplish his pastoral ends, appealing at times to the conventions of Greco-Roman moral philosophy[18] and pervasively to Christology and early Christian confessional and liturgical traditions — many of which were also strongly eschatological in character. I do not presume in this short essay to give a comprehensive account of the strategies Paul employed in seeking to transform the thinking of his readers; rather, I aim to concentrate attention on the two themes I have identified and to trace their outworking in selected passages of a single letter.

Written for Our Instruction, upon Whom the Ends of the Ages Have Met (1 Cor. 10:1-22)

In 1 Corinthians 10, Paul sets forth an extended typological correspondence between Israel in the wilderness and the situation of the Corinthian church as it confronts the issue of eating meat sacrificed to idols. Even though Paul explicitly quotes just one biblical verse (Exod. 32:6, in 1 Cor. 10:7), his argument alludes to several episodes narrated in Exodus and Numbers[19] and presupposes that his Corinthian readers are familiar with the story.[20] Indeed, the people's central act of infidelity, the worship of the golden calf in Exodus 32, is not explicitly described at all; instead, it is suggestively evoked by the oblique

17. The most thorough and nuanced recent defense of the "over-realized eschatology" hypothesis is to be found in C. M. Tuckett, "The Corinthians Who Say 'There Is No Resurrection of the Dead' (1 Cor 15,12)," in *The Corinthian Correspondence* (ed. Reimund Bieringer; BETL 125; Louvain: Leuven University Press, 1996), 247-75; Tuckett's notes offer a survey of the literature on this question. The view that Paul did not teach scripture in his churches is perhaps less widely held, but see, for example, the carefully formulated comments of Martyn, *Theological Issues,* 159. More common is the view that Paul's use of scripture is simply "proof texting," without regard for original context.

18. See, for example, Abraham J. Malherbe, *Paul and the Popular Philosophers* (Minneapolis: Fortress, 1989); Hans Dieter Betz, *Der Apostel Paulus und die sokratische Tradition: Eine exegetische Untersuchung zu seiner Apologie 2 Korinther, 10–13* (BHT 45; Tübingen: Mohr Siebeck, 1972).

19. See, for example, Num. 14:26-35; 25:1-9; 26:62; 21:5-9; 16:41-50.

20. As rightly observed by Lindemann, "Schrift als Tradition," 215.

quotation of Exodus 32:6, which connects idolatry with sitting down to "eat and drink" — a connection that has considerable rhetorical force in Paul's argument against eating and drinking in pagan temples. This is a wonderful example of the figurative device of metalepsis: the full force of the quotation is apparent only to a reader who recognizes its original narrative context. Paul is arguing from the story, not narrating it as something new to his audience. The thing that is new here is the way he brings the narrative of Israel into metaphorical conjunction with the issues the Corinthians face.[21]

Paul's first important hermeneutical move is to introduce the Israel of the wilderness generation as "our fathers" (οἱ πατέρες ἡμῶν, 10:1). For the predominantly Gentile Corinthian church, this is already an important gesture. Israel's story is not somebody else's history;[22] rather, Paul addresses the Gentile Corinthians as though they have become part of Israel.[23] They are invited to understand themselves now as descendants of the characters who appear in the pages of scripture.

This interpretation is confused by Paul's passing reference to the Corinthians' past life as idol worshipers in 1 Corinthians 12:2. "You know," he writes, "that when you used to be Gentiles (ὅτε ἔθνη ἦτε), you were carried away to dumb idols." This formulation implies that he considers them ἔθνη no longer. Within Paul's symbolic world, they are no longer among the *goyim* because they have been taken up into the story of Israel.[24] It should be noted that Paul is not trying to convince his Gentile readers to accept this identity description as a novel claim; rather, he assumes their identification with Israel as a given and tries to reshape their behavior in light of this identification.

In this case Paul's concern is that the "strong" Corinthians were participating in festive meals held in the temples of pagan gods (8:10) and thereby

21. See my *Echoes*, 91-104. See also Richard B. Hays, "The Role of Scripture in Paul's Ethics," in *Theology and Ethics in Paul and His Interpreters: Essays in Honor of Victor Paul Furnish* (ed. Eugene H. Lovering and Jerry L. Sumney; Nashville: Abingdon, 1996), 30-47; reprinted in *Conversion of the Imagination*, 143-62.

22. By contrast, we might recall the notorious remarks of Rudolf Bultmann: "For the person who stands within the Church the history of Israel is a closed chapter. . . . Israel's history is not our history, and in so far as God has shown grace in that history, such grace is not meant for us. . . . The events which meant something for Israel, which were God's Word, mean nothing more to us" ("The Significance of the Old Testament for the Christian Faith," in *The Old Testament and Christian Faith: A Theological Discussion* [ed. Bernhard W. Anderson; New York: Harper & Row, 1963], 8-35, here 14).

23. See Rom. 11:17-24.

24. Thus, Paul's offhand expressions in 10:1 and 12:2 support Donaldson's thesis (note 12, above) that Paul thinks of his converts as proselytes to an eschatologically reconfigured Israel.

dangerously "partaking of the table of demons" (10:21). Within the discipline of New Testament studies there has been a long history of speculative reconstructions of the Corinthians as proto-Gnostic sacramentalists.[25] There is, however, no clear evidence in the text that the "strong" Corinthians justified their behavior on the basis of some sort of realized eschatology or magical sacramentalism.[26] In the immediate context, the more obvious basis for their behavior is the simple slogan πάντα ἔξεστιν (10:23). As many commentators have noted, the closest parallels to this language are to be found in Stoic/Cynic thought.[27] The slogan claims that the σοφός is free to do whatever he chooses because he possesses the knowledge (see 8:1) that sets him above the petty taboos of social convention; he possesses ἐξουσία — philosophically informed inner freedom.

Against this line of thought, Paul poses several arguments in 8:1–11:1; in 10:1-22, he urges the Corinthians to understand themselves as standing in typological relationship to Israel.[28] He is calling for a conversion of the imagination — an imaginative projection of their lives into the framework of the

25. This theory was articulated in an influential essay by Hans von Soden, "Sakrament und Ethik bei Paulus," in *Urchristentum und Geschichte: Gesammelte Aufsätze und Vorträge* (vol. 1; Tübingen: Mohr Siebeck, 1951), 239-75. For a recent summary of various reconstructions and proposals, see Wolfgang Schrage, *Der erste Brief an die Korinther* (EKKNT 7/2; Neukirchen-Vluyn: Neukirchener, 1995), 385-86.

26. For a recent challenge to the "sacramentalist" interpretation, see Karl-Gustav Sandelin, "Does Paul Argue against Sacramentalism and Over-Confidence in 1 Cor 10.1-14?" in *The New Testament and Hellenistic Judaism* (ed. Peder Borgen and Søren Giversen; Aarhus: Aarhus University Press, 1995), 165-82.

27. Conzelmann (*1 Corinthians,* 108) remarks that "only the Stoics and Cynics provide material for comparison." For references, see Johannes Weiss, *Der erste Korintherbrief* (MeyerK; Göttingen: Vandenhoeck & Ruprecht, 1925), 157-58; Robert M. Grant, "The Wisdom of the Corinthians," in *The Joy of Study: Papers on New Testament and Related Subjects Presented to Honor Frederick Clifton Grant* (ed. Sherman E. Johnson; New York: Macmillan, 1951), 51-55; Jacques Dupont, *Gnosis. La connaissance religieuse dans les Épîtres de Saint Paul* (Paris: Gabalda, 1949), 298-308; Kuck, *Judgment and Community Conflict,* 217 n. 348.

28. The suggestion that Paul is here drawing on a preformulated Jewish Christian midrash continues to find defenders (e.g., Wayne A. Meeks, "'And Rose up to Play': Midrash and Paraenesis in 1 Corinthians 10:1-22," *JSNT,* no. 16 [1982]: 64-78; Koch, *Schrift als Zeuge,* 214-16). Richard Horsley, while regarding the passage as a Pauline composition, has suggested that Paul is "echoing the language of the Corinthian spirituals" and seeking to counteract interpretations of the Exodus narrative that they had learned from Alexandrian traditions of allegorical exegesis introduced into the community by Apollos (Richard A. Horsley, *1 Corinthians* [ANTC; Nashville: Abingdon, 1998], 134-37). In my judgment this hypothesis goes beyond the evidence of the passage. Paul gives no indication that he is rebutting any other interpretation of the story; he is simply alluding to the biblical narrative for his own parenetic purposes.

Pentateuchal narrative. The Pentateuchal imagery is not confined to verses 1-13; Paul sustains it through verse 22. The phrase "they sacrificed to demons and not to God" (10:20) is taken directly from the Song of Moses in Deuteronomy 32:17 (and thus it refers, contrary to many English translations, not to "pagans" but to unfaithful Israel), and Paul's rhetorical question in 10:22 loudly echoes the language of Deuteronomy 32:21: "Or shall we provoke the LORD to jealousy (παραζηλοῦμεν)?"[29] Paul picks up this language in 1 Corinthians 10:14-22 to warn the Corinthians not to recapitulate Israel's error, not to provoke God's jealousy as the wilderness generation did by their idolatry. His hortatory point depends on the reader's act of imaginative identification with Israel.

In the course of the argument Paul provides an explicit hermeneutical warrant for this act of imaginative identification: "These things happened to them τυπικῶς, and they were written for our instruction, on whom the ends of the ages have met" (10:11). Here we see how Paul's eschatological hermeneutic informs his reading and application of scripture. He calls his converts to understand that they live at the turning point of the ages, so that all the scriptural narratives and promises must be understood to point forward to the crucial eschatological moment in which he and his churches now find themselves. His eschatological reasoning calls on the Corinthians to perform a complex imaginative act. On the one hand, they are to see in their own experience the typological fulfillment of the biblical narrative. The events narrated in scripture "happened as τύποι ἡμῶν" (10:6). The phrase does not mean — despite many translations — "warnings for us." It means "types of us," prefigurations of the *ekklēsia.* For Paul, scripture, rightly read, prefigures the formation of the eschatological community of the church. This is what I sought to emphasize in *Echoes of Scripture in the Letters of Paul* by speaking of Paul's "ecclesiocentric hermeneutics."

But this is only the first half of the complex imaginative act to which Paul summons his readers. The Corinthians are not only to see how scripture points to its fulfillment in their own community, but also to see that God's final judgment stands over their present experience. The prospect of future apocalyptic judgment, symbolized by the destruction that came upon the idolatrous Israelites in the wilderness, hovers over the entire passage. If the "strong" persist in provoking God's jealousy, they will suffer loss and destruction (cf. 3:10-17; 4:1-5; 5:1-5; 6:9-10; 11:27-32). Because Paul and his readers stand at the turn of

29. On the importance of Deuteronomy 32 in 1 Corinthians 10:14-22, see Hays, *Echoes,* 93-94. See also Richard H. Bell, *Provoked to Jealousy: The Origin and Purpose of the Jealousy Motif in Romans 9–11* (WUNT II 63; Tübingen: Mohr Siebeck, 1994).

the ages, they must envision their present experience both as the fulfillment of the scriptural figures and, at the same time, as a hint of the eschatological consummation that is still to come. Thus, Paul's reading of scripture is "bifocal," corresponding to the dialectical ("already/not yet") character of his eschatology.

Paul does not deal with the idol meat problem in halakic fashion[30] by finding a pertinent rule or commandment in the Old Testament. For example, he does not quote commandments against idol worship (e.g., Exod. 20:4-6; Deut. 17:2-7). This is the correct insight underlying Harnack's observation that Paul did not treat the Old Testament as an *Erbauungsbuch* for his Gentile churches: he did not treat it as a rulebook. Instead, he sketches a broad narrative and invites his readers to undertake the metaphorical leap of finding their own circumstances figured in the narrative.[31]

By offering explicit reflection about how to read scripture as an eschatological community-forming word for a Gentile congregation grafted into Israel, 1 Corinthians 10 lays bare the hermeneutical assumptions that govern Paul's references to scripture throughout the letter. Thus, we can employ this passage as a lens to bring several other texts more sharply into focus. Since a single essay cannot survey all the passages in 1 Corinthians where we see the interplay of scripture and apocalyptic eschatology, let us consider two significant blocks of the text in which we see these motifs at work: the opening attack on "wisdom" (1:18-31) and Paul's first specific response to Corinthian misbehavior, the case of the incestuous man (5:1-13).

I Will Destroy the Wisdom of the Wise (1 Cor. 1:18-31)

After the opening appeal for unity in the church (1:10-17), Paul launches into a long deliberative argument against factionalism.[32] The first major unit of

30. *Pace* Peter J. Tomson, *Paul and the Jewish Law: Halakha in the Letters of the Apostle to the Gentiles* (CRINT 3/1; Assen: Van Gorcum, 1990), 187-220.

31. See Hays, "The Role of Scripture in Paul's Ethics," 39-42. For a broader discussion of the metaphorical use of scriptural narrative in moral judgment, see Richard B. Hays, *The Moral Vision of the New Testament: Community, Cross, New Creation: A Contemporary Introduction to New Testament Ethics* (New York: HarperCollins, 1996), 298-304.

32. Margaret M. Mitchell (*Paul and the Rhetoric of Reconciliation: An Exegetical Investigation of the Language and Composition of 1 Corinthians* [HUT 28; Tübingen: Mohr Siebeck, 1991]) has shown definitively that 1 Corinthians should be read as a unified deliberative composition appealing for concord.

the letter (1:18–4:21) is directed, as recent studies have convincingly demonstrated, against the Corinthians' infatuation with popular sophistic rhetoric and against their resultant arrogance and competitiveness.[33] The expression σοφίᾳ λόγου in 1:17 refers to the eloquent rhetorical presentation of wisdom (cf. 2:4). Against slickly packaged philosophical rhetoric, Paul sets in stark antithesis ὁ λόγος ὁ τοῦ σταυροῦ, which is "foolishness to those who are perishing but, to us who are being saved, the power of God" (1:18). Already in this antithesis Paul has introduced an apocalyptic motif, the division of humanity into two groups: those who are to be destroyed along with the present evil age and those who are rescued by God's intervention. Those who are being saved are called to live in the light of another wisdom — defined precisely by the shocking form of the cross — that subverts everything the Corinthians had previously counted as σοφία. Paul is seeking to reshape their consciousness into this apocalyptic mode so that they will find their primary identification with fellow believers rather than seeking legitimacy according to the status-defining standards of their native civic culture.

The backbone of the discussion in 1:18–3:23 is a series of six Old Testament quotations (1:19; 1:31; 2:9; 2:16; 3:19; 3:20), all taken from passages that depict God as one who acts to judge and save his people in ways that defy human imagination. Paul thus links his gospel of the cross to the older message of judgment and grace proclaimed in Israel's scripture, and he challenges the boastful pretensions of his readers.

The first quotation (1:19), taken from Isaiah 29:14, declares God's eschatological annihilation of human wisdom. Clearly, Paul has selected this quotation because it pronounces God's sentence of judgment on σοφία. The impact of Paul's intertextual link becomes clearer when we listen to the oracle of Isaiah 29:13-14 in its entirety.

> The LORD said:
> Because these people draw near *with their mouths*

33. See especially Peter Marshall, *Enmity in Corinth: Social Conventions in Paul's Relations with the Corinthians* (WUNT II 23; Tübingen: Mohr Siebeck, 1987); Timothy H. Lim, "Not in Persuasive Words of Wisdom, but in the Demonstration of the Spirit and Power," *NovT* 29, no. 2 (1987): 137-49; Stephen M. Pogoloff, *Logos and Sophia: The Rhetorical Situation of 1 Corinthians* (SBLDS 134; Atlanta: Scholars, 1992); A. Duane Litfin, *St. Paul's Theology of Proclamation: 1 Corinthians 1–4 and Greco-Roman Rhetoric* (SNTSMS 79; Cambridge: Cambridge University Press, 1994); Ben W. Witherington III, *Conflict and Community in Corinth: A Socio-Rhetorical Commentary on 1 and 2 Corinthians* (Grand Rapids: Eerdmans, 1995); Bruce W. Winter, *Philo and Paul among the Sophists* (SNTSMS 79; Cambridge: Cambridge University Press, 1997).

> and honor me *with their lips*,
> while their hearts are far from me,
> and their worship of me is a human commandment
> learned by rote;
> so I will again do
> amazing things with this people,
> shocking and amazing.
> *The wisdom of their wise shall perish*
> *and the discernment of the discerning shall be hidden.*[34]

The Isaiah text pointedly associates σοφία with "lip service," a purely verbal show of piety — the very thing for which Paul will chastise the Corinthians, not only in 1:18-31 but also throughout the letter. Furthermore, Isaiah 29:14a suggests that God will do away with "the wisdom of the wise" by doing "shocking and amazing" things, precisely as Paul now declares God has done through using the ignominious death of Jesus on a cross to overturn human wisdom. Even Paul's choice of the expression τοῖς ἀπολλυμένοις in 1 Corinthians 1:18 anticipates the strong verb ἀπολῶ in the Isaiah quotation. For this reason we should perhaps read the participle as a true passive voice construction: those who regard the cross as foolishness are not just "perishing" but are actually "being destroyed" by God. God's eschatological judgment is taking effect precisely in their incomprehension of God's saving action. (See Rom. 1:18-32 for a close parallel.)

Here again we see Paul trying to teach the Corinthians to perceive reality within the framework of a dialectical "already/not yet" eschatology. God has already put the wise to shame through the foolishness of the cross, the apocalyptic event that has shattered the old order of human wisdom. The σοφός and the γραμματεύς and the rhetorician of this age have all been effectively brought to nothing (1 Cor. 1:20; cf. 1:28: καταργήσῃ) by the cross; therefore, "this age" no longer has power or pertinence. The Corinthians who still prize σοφία λόγου are oblivious to God's apocalyptic delegitimation of their symbolic world. On the other hand, the present participles ἀπολλυμένοις and σῳζομένοις in 1:18 show that Paul regards the unfolding of the eschatological scenario as still in progress, not yet complete.

Can it be merely fortuitous that Paul introduces his exposition of the "word

34. Isaiah 29:13-14 NRSV (emphasis added). Paul's citation of 29:14b follows the LXX precisely except for the last word, where he substitutes ἀθετήσω for κρύψω. As Stanley notes (*Paul*, 186), this is a Pauline modification to strengthen the description of God's scandalous action.

of the cross" with a scripture quotation (1:19)? The conversion of the imagination that Paul demands is fostered by placing σοφία in a scriptural framework of God's judgment; in light of scripture, Paul is calling on the Corinthians to reevaluate their prizing of rhetoric. Paul does not read Isaiah 29:14 merely as a general maxim about how God always regards human wisdom. Rather, the argument takes its particular force from Paul's conviction that the transforming action of God prophesied by Isaiah has now taken place in the crucifixion of Jesus. Consequently, Paul and his readers now stand in the new eschatological situation where Isaiah's words must be read not merely as a judgment on ancient Judean leaders but also as an indictment of the rhetorical affectations of the Corinthians — and simultaneously as a warning of the destruction that is coming on "the day of our Lord Jesus Christ" (1 Cor. 1:8) for those who do not live according to the word of the cross.

This call for scriptural reevaluation is made even more explicit in 1:26-31, as Paul shifts the focus from Isaiah 29 to another biblical passage: "Let the one who boasts boast in the Lord." The text is usually identified as Jeremiah 9:24 (Jer. 9:23 LXX), but J. Ross Wagner has recently argued that an equally good case can be made for finding the source of the quotation in the closely parallel passage 1 Kingdoms 2:10 LXX (1 Sam. 2:10).[35] Happily, we are not forced to choose between these two Old Testament passages as the background for 1 Corinthians 1:26-31. Significant writing often mingles the echoes of multiple precursors. Both passages provide rich subtexts for Paul's argument.

The threefold reference in 1 Corinthians 1:26 to the Corinthians' lowly status before their calling ("not many were wise [σοφοί]. . . not many were powerful [δυνατοί], not many were of noble birth [εὐγενεῖς]") mirrors the threefold warning against boasting in Jeremiah 9:22 LXX (9:23): "Let the wise man (σοφός) not boast in his wisdom, let the strong man (ἰσχυρός) not boast in his strength, and let the rich man (πλούσιος) not boast in his riches."[36] In Jeremiah, this warning occurs in the context of a series of judgment oracles: because the people are caught up in lies, iniquity, oppression, and idolatry, God's judgment is coming upon Jerusalem and Judah (Jer. 8:3–9:26). A repeated theme of this unit is that people who claim to be "wise" will soon incur God's judgment (e.g., 8:9: "The wise shall be put to shame, they shall be

35. J. Ross Wagner, "'Not beyond the Things Which Are Written': A Call to Boast Only in the Lord (1 Cor 4.6)," *NTS* 44, no. 2 (1998): 279-87. This possibility is noted by Koch (*Schrift als Zeuge*, 35-36) and Schrage (*Der erste Brief an die Korinther* [EKKNT 7/1; Neukirchen-Vluyn: Neukirchener, 1991], 205) but overlooked by Stanley (*Paul*, 186-88).

36. See Gail R. O'Day, "Jeremiah 9:22-23 and 1 Corinthians 1:26-31: A Study in Intertextuality," *JBL* 109, no. 2 (1990): 259-67.

dismayed and taken; since they have rejected the word of the Lord, what wisdom is in them?"). Jeremiah 9:23-24 brings this section to a climax by warning against all boasting and reaffirming that God will act with "steadfast love, justice, and righteousness in the earth." If Paul is thinking of this passage, he has elaborated Jeremiah's admonitions in his proclamation that God has now shamed the wise and the strong (τοὺς σοφούς and τὰ ἰσχυρά, 1 Cor. 1:27), and he has condensed Jeremiah 9:24 into a pithy maxim: "Let the one who boasts boast in the Lord."[37] The scriptural quotation — as Paul has hermeneutically reformulated it — is primarily a warning of eschatological judgment.

If Paul is thinking of 1 Samuel 2:10, on the other hand, he is alluding to Hannah's song of praise, a song that extols God for having reversed the fortunes of the poor and the downtrodden. The theme of eschatological judgment is still present, but the emphasis lies more on the startling reversal brought about by God's gracious power. This motif resonates with Paul's exposition of paradoxical status reversal through the foolishness of the cross, the fundamental theme of 1 Corinthians 1:18-31. The entire Song of Hannah leaves lingering echoes as we listen to Paul's critique of the Corinthian fascination with rhetoric. Consider the following admonition in 1 Samuel 2:3: "Do not boast (μὴ καυχᾶσθε), and do not speak lofty things; do not let grandiloquence (μεγαλορρημοσύνη) come out of your mouth, because the Lord is a God of knowledge, and God prepares his own designs." The pertinence of this passage to Paul's epistolary purposes hardly requires comment. Finally, the climactic admonition to boast in the Lord in 1 Samuel 2:10 is virtually identical to the parallel in Jeremiah 9:24: ἀλλ᾽ ἢ ἐν τούτῳ καυχάσθω ὁ καυχώμενος συνίειν καὶ γινώσκειν τὸν κύριον.

Some critics have contended that in 1 Corinthians 1:31 Paul is merely quoting a common early Christian maxim without direct awareness of any scriptural context. Otherwise, so the argument goes, how could he have passed up the chance to quote Jeremiah 9:22 LXX explicitly (μὴ καυχάσθω ὁ σοφὸς ἐν τῇ σοφίᾳ αὐτοῦ)?[38] I am afraid that this line of reasoning merely illustrates our guild's characteristic resistance to the rhetorical effect of literary allusion. Allusions are often most powerful when least explicit. This remains true even

37. The same shortened quotation shows up in identical form in 2 Corinthians 10:17 without a citation formula. Rather than showing that Paul does not regard the sentence as a scriptural quotation, this shows that he regards it — by the time he wrote 2 Corinthians 10–13 — as thoroughly familiar to his readers. If I quote or paraphrase "Blessed are the meek, for they shall inherit the earth" in a sermon, I do not need to insert a citation formula to explain to the congregation that I am quoting a saying of Jesus.

38. Koch, *Schrift als Zeuge*, 36; Traugott Holtz, "Zum Selbstverständnis des Apostels Paulus," *TLZ* 91, no. 5 (1966): 326.

if some readers are slow of heart to discern the metalepsis. Paul's argument is perfectly intelligible at the surface level with or without the Old Testament echoes,[39] but the reader who overhears the original context of these citations will be all the more deeply affected by the hearing.

In either case we see that Paul is once again drawing on scripture in an effort to reshape the identity of the Corinthian community. He has imaginatively projected the σοφοί at Corinth into the role of the "wise" and boastful leaders of Israel and Judah who were admonished by the prophetic oracles of Isaiah and Jeremiah. Like those leaders, the Corinthians stand under a warning of God's coming judgment and a summons to change their ways. They can respond appropriately to Paul's letter only if they hear God's word to Israel as a word spoken directly to them. Furthermore, when scripture says ὁ καυχώμενος ἐν κυρίῳ καυχάσθω, Paul understands the κύριος to be the κύριος Ἰησοῦς Χριστός. Consequently, when he tells them to "boast in the Lord," he is summoning the Corinthians to reconfigure their self-understanding and conduct in light of Jesus Christ crucified (2:2), the figure to whom scripture points.

If we are correct that Paul's argument aims fundamentally at calling the contentious Corinthians to reevaluate themselves by the standard of scripture, then it follows that there really should be no further dispute about the meaning of the slogan in 1 Corinthians 4:6: μὴ ὑπὲρ ἃ γέγραπται. It means that Paul is trying to teach the puffed-up Corinthians not to transgress these specific scriptural warnings against arrogance. He has conducted the extended *synkrisis* of himself and Apollos (3:5–4:5) with this goal in mind. Wagner has shown how the entire argument of 1:18–4:21 focuses on the biblical admonition against boasting, which is explicitly repeated in 3:21 after two more biblical quotations (Job 5:13 and Ps. 93:11 LXX) that reinforce the same lesson.[40] A more thoroughgoing examination of the Old Testament quotations in 1 Corinthians 2:9, 2:16, 3:19, and 3:20 would only underscore the point: Paul is trying to remake the minds of his readers by teaching them to interpret their lives in light of an eschatologically interpreted scripture.

This leads to one further observation. If Paul was trying to teach the Corinthians to think in eschatological terms, it hardly makes sense to suppose

39. Lindemann ("Schrift als Tradition," 205) comments: "[D]ie Tatsache, dass es sich um ein Schriftwort handelt, hat für den Inhalt der Aussage von 1,31 kein grundsätzlich entscheidendes Gewicht."

40. Wagner, "Not beyond," 283-85. Wagner's argument fills out and supports the interpretation set forth by Morna D. Hooker, "'Beyond the Things Which Are Written': An Examination of 1 Cor. IV.6," *NTS* 10, no. 1 (1963): 127-32.

that they had an "over-realized eschatology."[41] The over-realized eschatology hypothesis rests on only the scantiest evidence in the letter. One bit of purported evidence is 1 Corinthians 15:12, interpreted to mean that some Corinthians whom Paul describes as denying the resurrection were in fact claiming that they had already experienced it (on the analogy of 2 Tim. 2:17-18). This tortuous interpretation, which requires us to suppose that Paul misunderstands or misrepresents the Corinthians' actual opinions, has been decisively undermined by more recent studies.[42] An apparently stronger textual basis for the over-realized eschatology hypothesis is 1 Corinthians 4:8, where Paul flings at the Corinthians an ironic word of reproach: "Already you are filled! Already you are rich! Apart from us you have become kings!" As many scholars have pointed out, however, while these status attributions

41. The origin of this idea in modern scholarship appears to be von Soden's essay "Sakrament und Ethik bei Paulus" (note 25 above), originally published in 1931. Whatever one may make of von Soden's proposal to understand the Corinthians as "überspannte Enthusiasten des Pneumaglaubens," the exegetical basis for the proposal that their enthusiasm was rooted in realized eschatology was exceedingly slender. For instance, von Soden's suggestion that 15:12 should be interpreted to mean that some Corinthians believed the resurrection was already past — quoted repeatedly by subsequent scholars — appears in a single footnote (259-60 n. 28) as a bare assertion with no exegetical argumentation. The depiction of the Corinthians as "Gnostics" with a realized eschatology was "canonized" in Bultmann's *Theologie des Neuen Testaments* (Tübingen: Mohr Siebeck, 1953), 168. In the English-speaking world this hypothesis became influential through the translation of Bultmann, through the translated essays of Käsemann (especially "On the Subject of Primitive Christian Apocalyptic," in *New Testament Questions of Today* [Philadelphia: Fortress, 1969], 108-37), through C. K. Barrett's commentary (e.g., 109), and through James M. Robinson and Helmut Koester, *Trajectories through Early Christianity* (Philadelphia: Fortress, 1971), 30-40, 148-52. The most systematic attempt to defend the hypothesis exegetically was made by Anthony C. Thiselton, "Realized Eschatology at Corinth," *NTS* 24, no. 4 (1978): 510-26. In fact, however, Thiselton's argument depends on showing repeatedly that Paul appeals to future eschatology in his arguments to correct the Corinthians' behavior; but this does not prove that the Corinthians had a realized eschatology! It merely shows that Paul was trying, with some difficulty, to teach them to think in eschatological categories.

42. Particularly noteworthy are the following: Birger A. Pearson, *The Pneumatikos-Psychikos Terminology in 1 Corinthians: A Study in the Theology of the Corinthian Opponents of Paul and Its Relation to Gnosticism* (SBLDS 12; Missoula: Scholars, 1973); Gerhard Sellin, *Der Streit um die Auferstehung der Toten: eine religionsgeschichtliche und exegetische Untersuchung von 1 Korinther 15* (FRLANT 138; Göttingen: Vandenhoeck & Ruprecht, 1986); Alexander J. M. Wedderburn, *Baptism and Resurrection: Studies in Pauline Theology against Its Graeco-Roman Background* (WUNT 44; Tübingen: Mohr Siebeck, 1987); Martinus C. de Boer, *The Defeat of Death: Apocalyptic Eschatology in 1 Corinthians 15 and Romans 5* (JSNTSup 22; Sheffield: Sheffield Academic, 1988); and Kuck, *Judgment and Community Conflict*, especially 214-20.

no doubt reflect the Corinthians' self-description, the temporal framework supplied by the adverb ἤδη represents Paul's own perspective, not theirs, just as the phrase χωρὶς ἡμῶν also represents Paul's own ironic commentary on the Corinthians' boasting.[43]

The evidence is overwhelming that the claim to possess all things and to be self-sufficient and kingly was a distinguishing mark of Stoic and Cynic thought. Two familiar examples will suffice. According to Epictetus, the true Cynic can say, "Who, when he lays eyes upon me, does not feel that he is seeing his king and master?" (*Dissertationes* 3.22.49). Or again, Plutarch comments wryly, "But some think the Stoics are jesting when they hear that in their sect the σοφός is termed not only prudent and just and brave, but also *an orator,* a poet, a general, *a rich man,* and *a king*; and then they count themselves worthy of all these titles, and if they fail to get them, are vexed" (*De tranquillitate animi* 472A, emphasis added). Of course, neither Stoics nor Cynics were led to such views because of an excess of eschatological enthusiasm! Instead, they claimed a superior philosophical knowledge and personal discipline. There is no reason to think that the Corinthians were any different; they were simply absorbing such attitudes from the popular philosophers and rhetoricians around them and "baptizing" them into Christian discourse. Paul, horrified at their posturing, responds by appealing again and again to apocalyptic warrants to get theological leverage against such boastful claims.

Their boasting is wrong not because it prematurely claims eschatological fulfillment but because it leaves eschatology out of consideration altogether. It foolishly ignores that all human actions stand under the final judgment of the Lord, "who will bring to light the things now hidden in darkness and disclose the purposes of the heart" (1 Cor. 4:5). It is God alone who retains the power to judge and to render rewards. In the present time, however, Christian existence is to be lived under the sign of the cross as exemplified by Paul's own apostolic suffering (4:9-13).

If Paul was seeking to correct the Corinthians' over-realized eschatology,

43. Richard A. Horsley, "How Can Some of You Say That There Is No Resurrection of the Dead? Spiritual Elitism in Corinth," *NovT* 20, no. 3 (1978): 203-5. See especially the convincing discussion of Kuck (*Judgment and Community Conflict,* 214-20), who, following Horsley, argues that the words of 4:8 are "Paul's own *reduction ad absurdum* of the Corinthian way of thinking." These expressions "do not mean that they think they have already experienced the eschaton which Paul still awaits, but rather that they think they have advanced to maturity on a faster track than Paul. Paul is sarcastically accusing them of thinking that they have advanced spiritually and ethically beyond their teacher" (216). This explains why Paul moves into a discussion of his own suffering in verses 9-13; see especially the ironic *synkrisis* in verse 10.

he committed a colossal pastoral blunder when he wrote to them later, in 2 Corinthians 6:2, "Now is the day of salvation." We gain far more insight into the issues driving 1 Corinthians when we recognize that Paul is seeking to redefine their identity — which has been shaped by non-eschatological ideas indigenous to their culture — within an apocalyptic narrative that locates present existence in the interval between cross and parousia (cf. 1 Cor. 11:26). Within that interval he calls the Gentile Corinthians to shape their behavior in accordance with scripture's admonitions, to act like the eschatological Israel he believes them to be.

Clean Out the Old Leaven (1 Cor. 5:1-13)

Finally, a brief glance at 1 Corinthians 5 will illustrate how Paul's appeals to scripture and eschatology operate in shaping his specific behavioral directives to the church.

When Paul begins to scold the Corinthian church for failing to discipline a man involved in an incestuous relationship, he complains that this kind of πορνεία is not to be found even ἐν τοῖς ἔθνεσιν (5:1). Once again, as in 12:2, this formulation implies that he considers his Gentile Corinthian converts to belong no longer to the category of the ἔθνη. While Paul regards the offending behavior as a violation even of pagan morality, it is also, more specifically, a violation of Jewish law. The most immediately pertinent text is Deuteronomy 27:20: "Cursed be anyone who lies with his father's wife" (see also Deut. 23:1[22:30]; Lev. 18:8; 20:11). Probably, Paul does not cite the Old Testament warrant because he sees no need to argue the point; he thinks such conduct should be self-evidently abhorrent to his Gentile converts. Nonetheless, the fact that the offender has violated Israel's covenant law turns out to be highly relevant for understanding Paul's response. His directive to the congregation (1 Cor. 5:13) is a quotation of the formula used repeatedly in Deuteronomy to prescribe the death penalty for offenses that lead the community into idolatry or flagrant impurity: ἐξάρατε τὸν πονηρὸν ἐξ ὑμῶν αὐτῶν.[44] Most commentaries, following the notation in

44. The formula appears, with minor variations, in Deut. 13:5; 17:7, 12; 19:19; 21:21; 22:21, 22, 24; 24:7. In 17:12 and 22:22, it reads ἐξαρεῖς τὸν πονηρὸν ἐξ Ἰσραηλ. In Paul's citation he tailors the verb to address the Corinthian situation by changing the LXX's ἐξαρεῖς to ἐξάρατε. It should be emphasized that Paul does not envision the church actually executing capital punishment on the offender; he reinterprets the formula to require exclusion of the offender from the community, in this respect paralleling the common interpretation of these texts in

the Nestle-Aland margin, list this as a citation of Deuteronomy 17:7, a passage that prescribes the stoning of idolaters. Because this seems unrelated to the situation Paul is addressing, few commentators see the Old Testament quotation as having any particular significance for Paul's argument.[45]

Once we recognize, however, that the same formula appears in other contexts in Deuteronomy, we can hardly overlook the fact that one of the offenses requiring the death penalty is adultery. In Deuteronomy 22:22, 24, Moses prescribes capital punishment for adulterers and then invokes the purgation formula: ἐξαρεῖς τὸν πονηρὸν ἐξ Ισραηλ/ἐξ ὑμῶν αὐτῶν. Precisely within this immediate context, we also find a commandment forbidding a man to "take" his father's wife (23:1).[46] The inference lies readily at hand that Paul, who knows the Torah inside and out, has categorized the case of Corinthian incest as a violation of the law articulated in Deuteronomy 27:20 and 23:1. Having so categorized the offense, he calls for the punishment associated with it in Deuteronomy 22, and he cites the Deuteronomic formula as a direct command to the church. This helps to explain why he feels it necessary to call for the drastic punishment of "destruction of the flesh" of the offender (5:5). Thus, rather than regarding 1 Corinthians 5:13 as a quotation of Deuteronomy 17:7, we should see the subtext as Deuteronomy 22:22–23:1.[47]

This analysis demonstrates once again that Paul thinks of his Gentile Corinthian readers as having been taken up into Israel in such a way that they now share in Israel's covenant privileges and obligations. The unmarked quotation in 1 Corinthians 5:13 functions as a metaphor that figuratively transfers the Corinthians into the shoes of the Israel to whom Moses proclaimed, "Hear,

---

Second Temple Judaism (see William Horbury, "Extirpation and Excommunication," *VT* 35, no. 1 [1985]: 13-38).

45. Once again, Stanley does not treat the passage because Paul does not introduce the quotation with a citation formula. In *Echoes* (97), I also followed the convention of treating 1 Corinthians 5:13 as a quotation of Deuteronomy 17:7. For reasons explained here, I now regard this identification as imprecise; the more relevant textual precursor is Deuteronomy 22:22–23:1.

46. Many translations, recognizing the connection of Deuteronomy 23:1 to the preceding context, number it as Deuteronomy 22:30.

47. This analysis follows Brian S. Rosner, *Paul, Scripture and Ethics: A Study of 1 Corinthians 5-7* (AGJU 22; Leiden: Brill, 1994), 82-83. (Rosner [61-93] offers a wide-ranging discussion of other possible scriptural backgrounds to 1 Corinthians 5.) The fact that Paul cites the formula as "Remove the evil person ἐξ ὑμῶν αὐτῶν" rather than "ἐξ Ἰσραηλ" (Deut. 22:22) is of no special significance. He is merely quoting the formula as it appears in seven of its nine occurrences in Deuteronomy, including in 22:24, the instance in closest proximity to 23:1. The two formulations are synonymous, a point of some importance for understanding Paul's metaphorical transference of this language to the Corinthian congregation.

O Israel, the statutes and ordinances that I am addressing to you today" (Deut. 5:1). Paul does not regard the whole Torah as binding on these Gentiles (that is a topic for another day),[48] but he does, nonetheless, address them as participants in the covenant community, using the language of scripture. He is trying to reshape their consciousness so that they take corporate responsibility for the holiness of their community; he does this by using scripture to address them as Israel.

Is this rhetorical device too subtle? Might the Corinthians have been oblivious to the original context of the Old Testament quotation? One feature of this passage suggests that Paul's invocation of the Torah might not have been totally wasted on his Corinthian readers. In verses 6-8, he once again castigates the community for boasting and restates the demand for community discipline by using the story of Passover as a metaphor. Because Christ has already been slain as the Passover lamb, he says, it is time to purify the lump of dough, time to celebrate the festival of unleavened bread rightly by removing all leaven from the house (Exod. 12:14-15).

The extraordinary thing about Paul's use of this metaphor is how little he explains. He does not quote Exodus 12, he does not explain his striking Christological typology that links Jesus with the Passover lamb, and he does not describe the Jewish custom of removing all leaven from the home in preparation for the feast. Yet he seems to expect his readers to understand the argument. How are we to assess this? Is this simply a rhetorical miscalculation, a failed act of communication? Or did Paul expect that his emissaries, such as Timothy (1 Cor. 4:17), would explain this passage to the Corinthians? Or, alternatively, should we infer that the implied readers of this letter have been taught more about scripture than we might suppose? Paul treats them as readers able to discern the allusion to Exodus 12 (or Deut. 16:1-8), to recover the original context, and to interpret the figurative linkage between Israel and the Corinthian congregation. The text makes sense if and only if the readers of the letter embrace the typological identification between themselves and Israel.

For readers who do make the link, the metaphor is complex and illuminating. Sexual immorality, like leaven, can spread and contaminate the whole community; therefore, the evil influence must be purged. The result is that the community itself will be like the unleavened bread prepared for the feast. Christ's death as Passover lamb marks the community's deliverance from bondage and passage to freedom. The community, then, is metaphorically

48. On this topic, see Markus Bockmuehl, *Jewish Law in Gentile Churches: Halakhah and the Beginning of Christian Public Ethics* (Edinburgh: T&T Clark, 2000).

portrayed not only as the unleavened bread but also as the journeying people of the exodus, called to celebrate the feast and to live in ways appropriate to their identity as a people rescued by God from the power of evil and death. The incestuous man, on the other hand, is to be excluded from the household whose door is marked by the blood of Jesus, the Passover lamb; that is, he is left outside, exposed to the power of the destroyer (1 Cor. 5:5; cf. Exod. 12:12-13).

The Passover imagery, in this typological reading, is interpreted eschatologically. The death of Jesus as paschal lamb rescues the community from the wrath that is coming, and the community is called to maintain its purity and integrity, leaving God to deal with outsiders in the eschatological judgment (1 Cor. 5:12-13).

All of this is only suggested, not explained, by Paul's allusion to Passover tradition. His metaphorical evocation of that tradition leaves much to the imagination of the readers. Precisely for that reason, 1 Corinthians 5 exemplifies the way Paul employs scripture to foster the conversion of the imagination.

Beyond the New Testament

Torah Obedience and Early Christian Ethical Practices in Justin Martyr

Susan J. Wendel

Scholars of early Christian origins often focus on the role that doctrine played in establishing the boundaries of early Christ-believing communities. In the words of Daniel Boyarin, "'[i]n' was to be defined by correct belief; 'out' by adherence via an alleged choice to false belief."[1] Other researchers have similarly framed their questions about the development of early Christian identity with reference to "distinctions that hold sway in the theoretical and theological realm."[2] According to Keith Hopkins, for example, "the very existence, from early on in Christian history, of brief statements of Christian beliefs set Christianity apart from Judaism and paganism. . . . Christianity became a religion of belief, whereas Judaism and paganism were religions predominantly of traditional practice, with settled adherents."[3] In explicit and implicit ways, such discussions portray early Christ-believing groups as holding a faith-based religious system over against the supposedly more praxis-based systems of other groups, especially Judaism.

Against this general trend, Denise Kimber Buell and others have drawn attention to the frequency with which early Christians draw on "existing social practices," along with existing interpretations of these practices, to define their groups.[4] Buell's helpful corrective should not lead to the conclusion that

1. Daniel Boyarin, *Border Lines: The Partition of Judaeo-Christianity* (Philadelphia: University of Philadelphia Press, 2004), 17.

2. Nina E. Livesey, "Theological Identity Making: Justin's Use of Circumcision to Create Jews and Christians," *JECS* 18, no. 1 (2010): 51-79.

3. Keith Hopkins, *A World Full of Gods: The Strange Triumph of Christianity* (New York: Free Press, 1999), 80.

4. Denise Kimber Buell, *Why This New Race: Ethnic Reasoning in Early Christianity* (New York: Columbia University Press, 2005), 37; cf. Judith Lieu, "The Race of the God-Fearers," *JTS* 46, no. 2 (1995): 483-501.

doctrinal matters were not significant for early Christians. Rather, it should invite us to explore the relationship between early Christian beliefs and social practices, and to consider how early Christian identity was articulated, in part, through interaction with existing social practices and their interpretation.

Following this trajectory, my essay focuses on how early Christian apologists drew on an existing social practice — Jewish observance of the Mosaic law — to formulate a theological explanation for the ethical conduct of Christians.[5] To do so, I first explore Justin Martyr's use of the Mosaic law to assert the superiority of the ethical practices of the Christ-believing community over other groups. This will entail a consideration of two important dimensions of his references to the Mosaic code: (1) his presentation of the moral conduct of Christians as a pattern of covenantal faithfulness that represents an alternative to that of Jewish Torah observance (first section), and (2) his use of the Mosaic law to depict the knowledge and behavior of Christians as superior to non-Jewish beliefs and practices (second section). Subsequently, I offer a brief consideration of parallel treatments of the Mosaic law in the writings of other second-century Christian apologists (third section). I argue that although Justin and other early apologists do not promote the adoption of the Mosaic law in its entirety, they nonetheless use this ancient code as a positive reference point for highlighting the superiority of Christian knowledge and practices.[6]

Justin's Use of the Mosaic Law to Describe Covenantal Faithfulness

A cursory reading of Justin Martyr's *Dialogue with Trypho* would seem to support the view that Justin promotes a belief-based religious system over against a praxis-based Torah observance.[7] At the end of Justin's lengthy pro-

5. Scholars of early Judaism and Christianity frequently discuss the difficulties associated with identifying some ancient writings as "apologetic" literature. I use "apology" and its cognates in this essay to refer to authors or works that defend or compete for the recognition of their groups in relation to non-Jewish traditions within the Greco-Roman world. For an insightful discussion of the use of the category of "apology" to describe early Christian writings, see Sara Parvis, "Justin Martyr and the Apologetic Tradition," in *Justin Martyr and His Worlds* (ed. Sara Parvis and Paul Foster; Minneapolis: Fortress, 2007), 115-17.

6. Although the early Christian apologists' treatment of the Mosaic law appears to be influenced by New Testament texts, questions surrounding their direct or indirect dependence on the New Testament are complex and lie beyond the scope of this study.

7. My discussion relies more heavily on the *Dialogue* than on Justin's apologies, primarily because he repeatedly discusses the Mosaic law in this text. As Philippe Bobichon, *Justin*

logue (*Dial.* 1–9), Trypho the Jew challenges Justin to be circumcised, observe the Sabbath, and perform all the written law. Trypho argues that these observances represent the legitimate path to salvation (*Dial.* 8.3-4), and puzzles over why Christians do not visibly demonstrate their piety toward God by keeping Jewish law (*Dial.* 10.1-2). In the section of the *Dialogue* that follows (chapters 11–47), Justin provides a lengthy explanation of how Christ and his followers fulfill the will of God apart from observance of "ritual" or "ceremonial" customs of the Mosaic law.[8] Thus, in the course of discussing the Jewish scriptures with Trypho the Jew, Justin attempts to show how faith in Christ replaces Jewish observance of Mosaic law. Notwithstanding this seemingly straightforward contrast between Jewish customs and Christian faith, as we will see, Justin in fact affirms certain portions of the Mosaic code and draws on these injunctions to highlight the piety and righteous actions of Christians. In the process, he depicts the behavior of Christians as conforming to moral obligations of the Mosaic code and as alternative visible markers of covenant faithfulness.[9]

Justin begins his response to Trypho by describing the inauguration of a new form of covenant faithfulness. Whereas Trypho concludes that Justin has spurned God's covenant and commands (*Dial.* 10.3), Justin explains how Christ himself became an everlasting and final law, a definitive covenant, more binding than the law promulgated on Horeb (*Dial.* 11.2). Rather than signaling the need to change from observance of Mosaic precepts to mere belief in

Martyr: Dialogue avec Tryphon: édition critique, traduction, commentaire (2 vols.; Paradosis 47; Fribourg: Academic, 2003), 1:126-27, observes, the *Dialogue* is, in essence, an exegetical exposition of the law and the prophets that takes a dialogical format.

8. Although Justin does not use the terms "ritual" and "ceremonial" to describe Jewish observance of the Mosaic law, he certainly distinguishes between different types of Mosaic law, and concludes that some have enduring value whereas others, such as Sabbath-keeping, circumcision, performance of sacrifices, and food laws, do not (see, e.g., *Dial.* 40–45). For further discussion of Justin's divisions of Mosaic law (bipartite vs. tripartite), see Theodore G. Stylianopoulos, *Justin Martyr and the Mosaic Law* (SBLDS 20; Missoula: Scholars, 1975), 45-76; cf. Oskar Skarsaune, *The Proof from Prophecy: A Study in Justin Martyr's Proof-Text Tradition: Text-Type, Provenance, Theological Profile* (NovTSup 56; Leiden: Brill, 1987), 323-24.

9. Although Justin frequently highlights the righteous behavior of Christians, he also refers to the salvific work of the cross, albeit in a more limited way (see, especially, *Dial.* 95–96). For differing views on the presence of atonement theology in the works of Justin, see Hastings Rashdall, *The Idea of Atonement in Christian Theology: Being the Bampton Lectures for 1915* (London: Macmillan, 1919), 195-206, who argues for an absence of "any definite theory of vicarious punishment or substitution" in the writings of Justin, and Peter W. Ensor, "Justin Martyr and Penal Substitutionary Atonement," *EvQ* 83, no. 3 (2011): 217-32, who concludes that Justin clearly articulates a theology of atonement, especially in *Dial.* 95–96.

Christ, however, Justin links the role of Christ, as the promised "new covenant," with the transformed practices of Christians:

> But, our hope is not through Moses or through the Law, otherwise our customs would be the same as yours. . . . The law promulgated at Horeb is already obsolete, and was intended for you Jews only, whereas the law of which I speak is simply for all men. . . . An everlasting and final law, Christ himself, and a trustworthy covenant has been given to us, after which there shall be no law or commandment or precept. . . . If, therefore, God predicted that he would make a new covenant [Jer. 31:31-32], and this for a light to the nations [Isa. 51:4-5], and we see and are convinced that, through the name of the crucified Jesus Christ, men have turned to God, leaving behind them idolatry and other sinful practices, and have kept the faith and have practiced piety even unto death, then everyone can clearly see from these deeds and the accompanying powerful miracles that he is indeed the new law, the new covenant, and the expectation of those who, from every nation, have awaited the blessings of God. (*Dial.* 11.1-4)[10]

Here Justin clearly affirms the need for all people to turn to Christ, rather than to the Mosaic law, to find favor with God, but he lays stress on the visible practices of those who turn to God through Christ. For Justin, these actions demonstrate the efficacy of Christ's role as promulgator of a new covenant, and confirm that the God who gave the law on Horeb and instituted this new covenant are one and the same (see *Dial.* 11.1; 23.1).[11] Justin then explains how Christ, the "new lawgiver," issues commands and precepts that lead to righteous behavior (*Dial.* 14.1-7; cf. 122.1–123.9).

Elsewhere Justin reiterates this theme by describing the preaching of the apostles as the fulfillment of Micah 4:1-7 (cf. Isa. 2:2-4). In both *1 Apol.* 39.1-2 and *Dial.* 110.2-3, Justin explains how Christians have proclaimed the law to the nations:

10. All quotations from the *Dialogue* are from Thomas P. Halton, *St. Justin Martyr: Dialogue with Trypho* (ed. Michael Slusser; Washington, D.C.: Catholic University of America Press, 2003).

11. As many have noted, this latter part of Justin's argument refutes Marcionites and possibly other groups who claimed that the Creator God of Israel and the Father of Jesus are different entities. See Stylianopoulos, *Mosaic Law,* 27-28; Hans von Campenhausen, *The Formation of the Christian Bible* (trans. John Austen Baker; London: A&C Black, 1972), 94-97.

> For we Christians, who have gained knowledge of the true worship of God from the law and from the word which went forth from Jerusalem by way of the apostles of Jesus, have run for protection to the God of Jacob and the God of Israel. And we who delighted in war . . . and in every other kind of iniquity have in every part of the world converted our weapons of war into implements of peace — our swords into ploughshares, our spears into farmers' tools — and we cultivate piety, justice, brotherly charity, faith, and hope. (*Dial.* 110.2-3; cf. *1 Apol.* 39.1-2)

The proclamation of "the law," argues Justin, leads to the cultivation of acts of piety and justice. Whether he intends "law" and "word" in this passage to refer to an exposition of the Mosaic law, to the message of Christ, or to both, he clearly argues that the preaching of the apostles produces a visible transformation in ethical conduct.[12]

Justin argues in a similar vein when he outlines the difference between physical and spiritual circumcision. Again, in these contexts he does not contrast "faith" with "works" but instead juxtaposes two different types of practices. In *Dial.* 23, Justin asserts that righteousness cannot be attained through physical circumcision (23.4) but, rather, "is determined by their acts of justice and piety" (δίκαια καὶ ἐνάρετα; 23.5). Subsequently, in *Dial.* 24.1-2, he describes Christ as "another covenant" and "another law," who "circumcises with knives of stone . . . in order that they [Christ-believers] may become a righteous nation, a faithful, truthful, and peace-loving people" (ἵνα γένηται ἔθνος δίκαιον, λαὸς φυλάσσων πίστιν, ἀντιλαμβανόμενος ἀληθείας καὶ φυλάσσων εἰρήνην). The circumcision administered by Christ stands in antithetical relationship to physical circumcision: the former produces the covenant faithfulness that the latter could not. Later in the *Dialogue,* Justin outlines how Christ administers a "true circumcision by which we are circumcised from error and wickedness through our Lord Jesus Christ" (διὰ . . .Ἰησοῦ Χριστοῦ ἡμῶν; *Dial.* 41.4; 113.6-7) and, in *Dial.* 114.4, he specifies that this circumcision occurs "by means of sharp stones" (διὰ λίθων ἀκροτόμων), that is, "by the words which were proclaimed by the apostles" (διὰ τῶν λόγων τῶν διὰ τῶν ἀποστόλων [κηρυχθέντων]). Justin in this way presents the teaching of the apostles as a

12. The ensuing references to the "law of the Lord" (*1 Apol.* 40.8; cf. Psalm 1), and to divine retribution for those who fail to live in accordance with the virtue described by the Jewish prophets (*1 Apol.* 43.1-7), suggests that Justin may have ethical parts of the Mosaic law in view in *1 Apol.* 39.1-2.

second intermediary agent, which helps to perform the spiritual circumcision needed to initiate true covenant fidelity.

Although Justin clearly presents Christ as the new law, and depicts "the law promulgated at Horeb" as obsolete (*Dial.* 11.2), he nevertheless embraces certain parts of the Mosaic law as expressions of God's eternal will for humans. To do so, he distinguishes between different functions of the Mosaic law: "some precepts were given for the worship of God and the practice of virtue, whereas other commandments and customs were arranged either in respect to the mystery of Christ [or] the hardness of your people's hearts" (*Dial.* 44.2). On the one hand, Justin depicts the so-called ritual requirements of the Mosaic law as predictions about Christ, or more negatively as signs that mark Jews off for punishment or as concessions to prevent them from committing idolatry (*Dial.* 16.2-3; 19.6; 21.1; 23.3; 27.2-5; 28.4; 44.2; 46.5). On the other hand, Justin presents moral, or ethical, requirements of the Mosaic law as a positive guide for righteous conduct (*Dial.* 44.2; 47.2; 93.2).[13] For example, Justin argues that those who obeyed the Mosaic law before Christ would attain salvation because they performed the parts of the Mosaic code "that in themselves are good, holy, and just" (*Dial.* 45.3-4; cf. 28.4). Moreover, Justin claims that the new covenant and law (i.e., Christ) enables Christians to distinguish between precepts of the Mosaic code that are "eternal and fit for every nationality" and those issued only for Jews (*Dial.* 67.10).

In what sense does Christ help his followers to distinguish between different parts of the Mosaic code? Theodore Stylianopoulos maintains that Justin sees Christ as the "hermeneutical principle" who "grants the spiritual gift of interpretation." For Stylianopoulos, this means that Justin regards Christ as the "source of revelation for their understanding of Scripture."[14] Justin undoubtedly regards divine enablement by Christ as vital for the proper interpretation of the Jewish scriptures (e.g., *Dial.* 7.3; 30.1; 58.1; 78.10-11; 92.1; 100.2; 119.1), but he also depicts the teachings of Jesus as an essential guide for discerning their true import. For example, in the course of arguing that God wants "each succeeding generation of humanity always to perform the same acts of righteousness" (*Dial.* 23.1), Justin attributes his ability to distinguish between "acts

13. Although Stylianopoulos, *Mosaic Law*, 45-76, concludes that Justin uses νόμος in an exclusively negative sense to refer to ritual demands of the Mosaic law, evidence from the *Dialogue* suggests that Justin also uses νόμος to express positive statements about the Mosaic law. As discussed above, Justin argues that those who conducted themselves "according to the law of Moses" (κατά τὸν νόμον τὸν Μωϋσέως) before the time of Christ will be saved because they did what was "good, holy, and just" (*Dial.* 45.3).

14. Stylianopoulos, *Mosaic Law*, 73-74.

of piety and justice" and other requirements of the Mosaic code (*Dial.* 23.3-5) to the "heavenly doctrine,"[15] which he received from "that old man" (*Dial.* 23.3). This statement recalls Justin's conversion: he listened to a mysterious "old man" explain the true significance of the Jewish scriptures, and his spirit was ignited with "affection for the prophets and for those who are friends of Christ" (*Dial.* 7–8). The phrase "friends of Christ" (*Dial.* 8.1) probably refers to the teachings of the apostles[16] since Justin further explains that he never wants to "fall away from the Savior's words" (*Dial.* 8.2). Taken together, the passages from *Dial.* 7–8 and 23 illustrate how the teachings of Jesus, together with special revelatory insight, enable Christians to recognize and obey the enduring parts of the Mosaic code (cf. *Dial.* 93.2).[17]

Justin and Mosaic Law as Universal Law

Like many of his contemporaries, Justin draws on Greek philosophical traditions to present the beliefs and practices of Christians as the highest expression of Greco-Roman cultural values. As Whitmarsh elaborates, "Greeks had defined their particular place in the world through claims to a superior culture," and Hellenistic identity was largely constituted through the spread of Greek *paideia*.[18] Accordingly, different groups attempted to demonstrate their cultural primacy by appealing to Greek traditions. For example, Romans appropriated Greek *paideia* and claimed to be the legitimate heirs of this earlier

15. Justin also regards this illumination as divine enablement to understand other aspects of the Jewish scriptures. For example, in *1 Apol.* 49.5, he describes how the apostles went out from Jerusalem after Christ taught them and "handed over the prophecies" to them (cf. *Dial.* 53.5; 76.6-7).

16. Graham N. Stanton, *Jesus and Gospel* (Cambridge: Cambridge University Press, 2004), 97, suggests that "friends of Christ" refers to the apostles and, by implication, their writings. J. C. M. van Winden, *An Early Christian Philosopher: Justin Martyr's Dialogue with Trypho, Chapters One to Nine* (Philosophia Patrum 1; Leiden: Brill, 1971), 118-19, instead argues that the phrase refers to Christians of Justin's own time, especially martyrs.

17. In *Dial.* 93.2, Justin also shows the connection between the Mosaic law and the words of Christ by explaining how Jesus taught that "all justice and piety" could be summed up in the Mosaic commands to love God and neighbor (Deut. 6:5; Lev. 19:18; cf. Matt. 22:34-40; Mark 12:28-31; Luke 10:25-28).

18. Tim Whitmarsh, *The Second Sophistic* (New Surveys in the Classics 35; Cambridge: Cambridge University Press, 2005), 13; cf. Whitmarsh's *Greek Literature and the Roman Empire: The Politics of Imitation* (Oxford: Oxford University Press, 2001), 20-31.

Hellenistic form of education.[19] Similarly, early Jewish apologists portrayed different Jewish groups as philosophical schools and the law of Moses as a superior source of Greek *paideia*.[20] Likewise, Justin presents the teaching of Christians as an exemplary form of Hellenistic education and, in the process, depicts the Christian understanding of the Mosaic law as a definitive source of philosophical truth.

In the *Apologies*, Justin associates Christian ethical practices with the study of philosophy, in part, because of the belief that philosophical education led to moral formation. In the ancient world, the adoption of the *paideia* of a particular philosophical school involved the pursuit of virtue and the abandonment of vice, a process that took place through understanding and imitating the divine.[21] Justin ostensibly addresses the emperor and his sons as philosophers and pleads with them to judge the case of Christians reasonably, in a manner that is in keeping with their exemplary piety, philosophy, and justice (εὐσεβεῖς . . . φιλοσόφους . . . δικαιοσύνης; *1 Apol.* 2.1-2; cf. 3.1-2; 12.4-5; *2 Apol.* 2.16). This forms part of his attempt to address charges of impiety and injustice (ἀσέβειαν καὶ ἀδικίαν) against Christians (*1 Apol.* 4.7-8; cf. 23.3; *2 Apol.* 3.2; cf. *Dial.* 10.1), but his description also implies that Christians cultivate virtue (ἀρετή) and practice justice (δικαιοπράσσω); that is, they engage in a pursuit of true philosophy, which leads to moral transformation (*1 Apol.* 12.2-5; *2 Apol.* 2.13). He explains that God approves of those who imitate his inherent virtues, namely, temperance, justice, love of man (σωφροσύνην καὶ δικαιοσύνην καὶ φιλανθρωπίαν), and any other virtues that are proper to God (*1 Apol.* 10.1).[22]

19. Buell, *New Race,* 152-53.

20. For example, Philo of Alexandria (e.g., *Mos.* 1.18-29; 2.8-11, 45-65, 216; cf. *Spec.* 1.56-59; 4.133-35; *Contempl.* 25-28, 67, 69, 89); Josephus (e.g., *A.J.* 1.18-24; 13.171-73; 15.371; 18.12-20; *C. Ap.* 2.135-36, 148, 182).

21. Luke Timothy Johnson, *Among the Gentiles: Greco-Roman Religion and Christianity* (New Haven: Yale University Press, 2009), 46-47, 64-78; cf. Frances Young, "Introduction: The Literary Culture of the Earliest Christianity," in *The Cambridge History of Early Christian Literature* (ed. Andrew Louth, Frances Young, and Lewis Ayres; Cambridge: Cambridge University Press, 2004), 7-8; Abraham J. Malherbe, "Apologetic and Philosophy in the Second Century," *ResQ* 7, nos. 1-2 (1963): 30-31.

22. As Louis H. Feldman, *Jew and Gentile in the Ancient World* (Princeton: Princeton University Press, 1993), 210-32, and others have noted, the attributes of virtue (ἀρετή), piety (εὐσέβεια), and justice (δικαιοσύνη) were highly valued within Greco-Roman society (see, e.g., Polybius 6.7.5-8; 48.3; 56.1-5; Sallust, *Bell. Cat.* 11–13; Livy 1 pref.10-12; Cicero, *Rep.* 1.27-28; Plutarch, *Cat. Maj.* 1.3-4; 2.1, 3). For further discussion, see Lieu, "God-Fearers," 483-501; cf. John W. Martens, *One God, One Law: Philo of Alexandria on the Mosaic and Greco-Roman Law* (Studies in Philo of Alexandria 2; Leiden: Brill, 2003), 56-65.

Throughout the *Apologies,* Justin argues that Christians should not be punished as criminals, in part, because their virtuous lifestyle parallels that of Greek philosophers (*1 Apol.* 7.3; 20.1–22.6; 26.6). At the same time, however, he seeks to demonstrate the antiquity of Moses and the prophets over Greek writings. This approach corresponds to the common Middle Platonist belief that philosophy was at its peak during the primordial period and that the primary aim of the philosopher was to rediscover this ancient wisdom.[23] Justin thus defends Christians, but also asserts the superiority of their knowledge over that of Greeks (e.g., *1 Apol.* 23.1-2; 44.8; 54.1–55.8; 56.1-4; 57.1; 58.1-3; 62.1; 64.1); above all other groups, Christians exemplify piety and justice because they study the purest and oldest source of philosophy — Moses and the prophets.

In the *Dialogue,* Justin explains how Christians cultivate piety and justice because they use the Jewish scriptures as their source of study. In the prologue to this work, he outlines how contemporary philosophers failed to arrive at truth because they lost the original essence of philosophy (*Dial.* 2.1-2). Moses and other Jewish prophets provide the only reliable knowledge of God, he argues, because their writings are more ancient than other sources and because they received their information through divine inspiration (*Dial.* 7.1-2). Justin depicts the Jewish scriptures as a source that "a philosopher ought to know" (*Dial.* 7.2) and explains how his discovery of the true interpretation of the Jewish scriptures led him to become a philosopher (*Dial.* 8.2). This leads to his conclusion that the Christian study of the Jewish scriptures recovers the ancient, primordial philosophy that the splintered and degenerate philosophies of his contemporaries had lost. Consequently, the superior knowledge of Christians leads them to repent from injustice and to practice piety, justice, and other virtues (*Dial.* 11.2-4; 110.1-3). His claim to privileged knowledge of Moses and the prophets differentiates Christians from Jews (e.g., *1 Apol.* 39.1-4; *Dial.* 11.1-3; 12.1-2; 24.1-2; 110.1-3; 113.6-7; 114.4-5; 122.3-5), but it also demonstrates how those who embrace Christ become paragons of piety, justice, and philanthropy (εὐσεβεῖς καὶ δίκαιοι καὶ φιλάνθρωποι; *Dial.* 136.2), virtues highly cherished within the Greco-Roman world.[24]

23. As Arthur J. Droge, *Homer or Moses?: Early Christian Interpretations of the History of Culture* (HUT 26; Tübingen: Mohr Siebeck, 1989), 90-91, notes, this view was held by Aristotle and Posidonius and, in the second century CE, by Middle Platonists such as Atticus and Numenius.

24. For further discussion of virtue and piety, see Sarah Broadie, "Rational Theology," in *The Cambridge Companion to Early Greek Philosophy* (ed. A. A. Long; Cambridge: Cambridge University Press, 1999), 205-24; Judith Lieu, *Image and Reality: The Jews in the World of the Christians in the Second Century* (London: T&T Clark, 1996), 187.

As part of his description of the superior knowledge and practices of Christians, Justin utilizes, but adapts, Greek concepts of universal law. To do so, Justin follows a line of argumentation similar to that of the Jewish apologist Philo of Alexandria. Whereas Middle Platonists distinguish between a universal unwritten law of nature and the written law codes of particular nations, Philo transforms this distinction by arguing that Mosaic law serves as a written copy of an otherwise unwritten natural law.[25] Like Philo, Justin presents Mosaic law as a written copy of unwritten natural law but, unlike Philo, he maintains that only certain parts of the Mosaic law function as a universal moral guide.[26] Besides depicting Christ as an eternal and final law, and indicating that those who follow him repent from injustice and practice piety (*Dial.* 11.2-4; 34.1; 43.1; 122.5), Justin argues that Christians observe the parts of the Mosaic code that are "eternal and fit for every nationality" (*Dial.* 67.10; cf. 93.1-2). For Justin, only particular parts of the Mosaic law function as a type of universal, or natural, law code. Accordingly, those who follow these specific requirements of the Mosaic law "are universally, naturally, and eternally pleasing to God" (*Dial.* 45.3-4) and "observe lasting precepts of justice" (*Dial.* 28.4). Justin thus argues for the universal relevance of the Mosaic law, as compared with the written law codes of other nations, even as he also differentiates the Christian observance of Mosaic law from the Torah obedience of Jews.[27]

25. The concept of an unwritten law and natural justice stretches as far back as the fifth century BCE (e.g., Plato, Sophocles), but the Stoics were the first to develop the idea of a universal law. Cicero provides an especially clear description of this law of nature and develops the notion more fully than his predecessors (e.g., *Rep.* 3.33; *Leg.* 1.18-19). The idea of a universal law, or law of nature, derives from a fusion of Stoic traditions and an eclectic form of Platonic philosophy. Notably, this concept is changed by Philo, who associates it with a written Mosaic legislation. The association of natural law with a written code would have seemed alien to early Hellenistic philosophers who contrasted the two (e.g., Cicero, *Off.* 3.69). See also Hindy Najman, "The Law of Nature and the Authority of Mosaic Law," *SPhilo* 11 (1999): 55-73; Richard A. Horsley, "The Law of Nature in Philo and Cicero," *HTR* 71, nos. 1-2 (1978): 35-59; Martens, *One God, One Law,* 1-30; see also John Martens's essay in this volume.

26. In *Dial.* 46.2-7, Justin claims that Jews regard their observance of Mosaic law as keeping "eternal precepts," but he argues that their actions contribute nothing to justice or piety. Justin also explains how Sabbath-keeping does not correspond to the law of nature because the natural elements do not rest on the Sabbath day (*Dial.* 23.3) and God does not stop controlling the movement of the universe on the Sabbath (*Dial.* 29.3).

27. Stylianopoulos, *Mosaic Law,* 11, recognizes that Greek philosophical suppositions underlie Justin's description of a universal or eternal law but maintains that Jewish-Christian issues dominate this theme in the *Dialogue*. Von Campenhausen, *Christian Bible,* 96-98, asserts that Justin addresses concerns related to Jews and Greek philosophical culture but also

Other Second-Century Apologists

Perhaps in imitation of Justin, a number of other second-century apologists present the Christian study of the Jewish scriptures as a superior form of *paideia*.[28] Among these figures, only two appeal to the Mosaic law in their defense of Christians. First, the *Apology* of Aristides, in both its Greek and Syriac versions,[29] illustrates the superiority of the practices of Christians on the basis of their observance of Mosaic law. After describing in considerable detail the insufficiency of the knowledge, philosophies, and worship of other groups, Aristides refers to the knowledge of Jews as "nearer to the truth than all the peoples."[30] He ultimately argues, however, that Christians "are nearer to the truth and to exact knowledge" because of their understanding of God and proper observance of his commands (Greek — chapters 15–16; Syriac — chapters 15–17).[31] As part of his illustration of the exemplary behavior of Christians, Aristides cites injunctions from the Decalogue (Exod. 20:1-17; Deut. 5:6-21), and draws on passages from Exodus and Deuteronomy to highlight their special care for widows, orphans, and aliens (e.g., Exod. 22:22-24; Deut. 14:29; 16:11, 14).

---

concludes that Justin provides a description of the "eternal" law in order to rescue the Jewish scriptures from Marcion and so-called Gnostics.

28. See, for example, Athenagoras's *Embassy on Behalf of Christians* (e.g., 7.1-3; 9.1-2) and Tatian's *Oration to the Greeks* (e.g., 31.1; 32.1; 33.2; 35.1; 42.1). For further discussion of Justin as the inventor of the genre of Christian apology in its classical form, see Parvis, "Apologetic Tradition," 115-27.

29. The apology of Aristides is extant in Greek and Syriac, and in some Armenian fragments. For discussion of the similarities and differences between these two recensions, see Lieu, *Image and Reality*, 165; Richard A. Norris Jr., "The Apologists," in *The Cambridge History of Early Christian Literature* (ed. Andrew Louth, Frances Young, and Lewis Ayres; Cambridge: Cambridge University Press, 2004), 36-44; Robert M. Grant, *Greek Apologists of the Second Century* (Philadelphia: Westminster, 1988), 38-39.

30. Both the Greek and Syriac texts indicate that barbarians, Greeks, and Egyptians have erred because they serve created things instead of the Creator. As a result they do not perceive the true God and act wickedly (chapters 3–12). The Syriac version argues that Jews are much nearer to the truth than other peoples because they recognize and worship one God, the almighty Creator, and imitate him through their philanthropy. The Greek version more harshly indicts Jews for worshiping the idols of other nations, and killing the prophets and the "son of God."

31. The phrase "the commandment and law of Christians" occurs only in the Syriac version but the Greek text uses similar language. This emphasis on the law and manner of life of Christians leads Grant, *Greek Apologists*, 38, to conclude that Aristides presents Christianity as a new law.

Rather than identifying these requirements of the Mosaic law as Jewish teaching, Aristides circumscribes them as Christian precepts. The Syriac version weaves parts of the Decalogue seamlessly together with other Jewish and Christian traditions, and describes people who follow this teaching as those "who observe scrupulously the commandments of their Messiah."[32] The text further appropriates the Mosaic law for Christians by referring to both Mosaic and Christian ethical demands as "their [Christians'] sayings and precepts," and by arguing that Christians naturally obey these injunctions because they have them "engraved on their minds." Similarly, the Greek version describes ethical injunctions from the Mosaic law as "the commands of the Lord Jesus Christ Himself" and explicitly attributes this knowledge to the reception of the preaching of the apostles: "He had twelve disciples, who after His ascension to heaven went forth into . . . the whole world . . . proclaiming the doctrine of the truth. . . . [T]hey who still observe the righteousness enjoined by their preaching are called Christians" (chapter 15). Both recensions of Aristides draw on the Mosaic code to illustrate the exemplary practices of Christians, and fully appropriate it as Christian teaching. Aristides in this way differentiates the knowledge and practices of Christians from Jewish observance of ritual requirements of the Mosaic law (chapter 14), but — at the same time — demonstrates the superiority of the conduct of Christians over that of other groups within the Greco-Roman world.

Theophilus, a second-century bishop from Syrian Antioch, similarly attempts to show the superiority of the knowledge and conduct of Christians, in part, with reference to the Mosaic law. In his three-volume work, *Ad Autolycum,* Theophilus contrasts Hellenistic writings with the Jewish scriptures, and argues that Greek poets and philosophers plagiarized the predictions of the Jewish scriptures "in order to make their own teaching seem trustworthy" (*Autol.* 1.14; cf. 2.12, 37). In a manner similar to that of Justin and Aristides, he claims that Christians have a proper understanding of the teachings of Moses and other prophets because they have been instructed by the same Spirit (*Autol.* 2.30, 33; cf. 2.22). Theophilus thus concludes that the Jewish scriptures, together with the inspiration of the Spirit, provide forms of legislation and

32. Both the Greek and Syriac versions refer to the following parts of the Decalogue: prohibitions of adultery, idolatry, bearing false witness, denying a deposit, coveting, and the commandment to honor one's parents. Both also emphasize the care of widows, orphans, and aliens, and mingle these ethical values from the Jewish scriptures with ethics that appear to be drawn from other Jewish and Christian traditions (e.g., goodwill toward enemies, compassion on the poor, proper burial of the dead, and care for prisoners).

history that are "not only more ancient but also more true than all historians and poets" (*Autol.* 2.30; cf. 2.9-10, 33; 3.1, 16-17, 26, 29).[33]

In book 3 of the *Ad Autolycum,* Theophilus attempts to defend Christians against charges of promiscuity and cannibalism by more pointedly showing how their piety and morality correspond to the ancient teachings of the Mosaic law. After explaining that Greek literature advocates lawless behavior, Theophilus outlines the moral conduct of Christians. To do so, he draws on the Decalogue and other passages from Exodus (20:3-5, 13-17;[34] cf. 23:6-8, 9) to demonstrate that God teaches Christians "to practice justice and piety and beneficence" (δικαιοπραγεῖν καὶ εὐσεβεῖν καὶ καλοποιεῖν; *Autol.* 3.9-10; cf. 2.35).[35] Theophilus expands on these citations by appealing to prophetic texts, and arguing that the prophets and the Gospels reiterate "the justice of which the law spoke"; that is, they urge people to devote themselves to righteous practices prescribed in the Mosaic law (*Autol.* 3.11-14). In so doing, he presents both the Gospels and the prophets as Spirit-inspired continuations of Mosaic legislation; these texts remind people of the content of Mosaic law, and so call them to repentance (*Autol.* 3.11).[36]

In the course of explaining the significance of the Mosaic code, Theophilus also attempts to demonstrate its universal significance. He describes the Mosaic covenant as a "divine law," which God himself legislated for the benefit of "all the world" (*Autol.* 3.9), and maintains that the Jewish prophets were sent to "teach and remind people of the content of the law" so that both Israel and "the human race" would turn away from their sins (*Autol.* 3.10; cf. 2.14, 34-35).

33. In the final section of book 3 of *Ad Autolycum,* Theophilus also provides a chronological argument that aims to demonstrate the antiquity of the Jewish scriptures as compared with other sources (*Autol.* 3.16-30). He concludes that this chronology shows the antiquity of the prophets and the divine nature of the Christian message (3.29). The chronology appears to rely on material from Josephus's *Against Apion* (cf. *Autol.* 3.20-25 with *C. Ap.* 1.93-154). For an evaluation of the parallels between the two works, see Michael E. Hardwick, *Josephus as an Historical Source in Patristic Literature through Eusebius* (BJS 128; Atlanta: Scholars, 1989), 12-14.

34. Theophilus omits the third and fourth commandments from the Decalogue (taking God's name in vain and keeping the Sabbath).

35. The use of this terminology suggests that compliance with the Mosaic law leads to the embodiment of Greek virtues.

36. In addition to demonstrating the continuity between the Mosaic law, the prophets, and the Gospels, Theophilus argues that "the gospel voice provides a stricter teaching about purity" (3.11-13). Theophilus shows the continuity between the Jewish scriptures and the New Testament primarily by weaving citations from Matthew 5–6 with Old Testament citations in *Autol.* 3.13-14; note also citations from Rom. 13:1-3, 7-8 and 1 Tim. 2:1-2 in *Autol.* 3.14. For further discussion, see Rick Rogers, *Theophilus of Antioch: The Life and Thought of a Second-Century Bishop* (Lanham: Lexington, 2000), 130-31.

Consequently, he argues that humans who recognize and obey the true intention of the law and prophets, that is, Christians, become heirs to the writings of Moses and the prophets, and receive the eternal benefits promised to those who follow their divine commands (*Autol.* 1.14; 2.27, 30, 33).[37] Like Justin, then, Theophilus claims that Christians possess a privileged understanding of universal truth through their inspired interpretation of the Mosaic code.[38]

Virtually all early Christian apologists argue that the knowledge and practices of Christians are superior to those of other groups, but Justin, Aristides, and Theophilus show particular interest in presenting the Mosaic law as a key source of guidance for Christian piety and ethical practices. By further arguing that Christians possess a divinely inspired knowledge of the Jewish scriptures, these authors claim that their group alone understands the true import of the Mosaic legislation. For both Theophilus and Justin, this also amounts to the possession of universal truth, which God wants the entire human race to follow.

Conclusion

Justin provides a multifaceted depiction of the relationship between the Mosaic law and the practices of Christians. In the *Dialogue,* he draws a sharp contrast between the Mosaic code and Christ, the new covenant, in order to show how the latter eclipses the former. Nevertheless, Justin also distinguishes between different parts of the Mosaic code, and concludes that God has always required humanity to comply with its prescribed acts of piety and justice. According to Justin, Christ has made it possible for his followers to perform such visible righteous actions, in part, because he has enabled them to identify the parts of the Mosaic law that have enduring value. Justin in this way outlines a clear distinction between Christians and non-Christ-believing Jews, but the difference, for Justin, does not amount to a contrast between a belief-based religion (Christianity) and a praxis-based religion (Judaism). Rather, the covenant fidelity of Christians, which is mediated through Christ and leads to the cultivation of just and pious actions, represents the only adequate means of being faithful to the divine will.

37. Rogers, *Theophilus,* 120-44.

38. Theophilus refers to Moses as "our prophet" (*Autol.* 3.18), describes the Jewish scriptures as "the books which belong to us," "our scriptures," or "our sacred writings" (*Autol.* 2.30; 3.1, 26), and refers to the patriarchs as "our forefathers" (*Autol.* 3.20), but also acknowledges that Jews hold a special place as heirs of the promises of the Jewish scriptures (see, e.g., *Autol.* 3.9-11).

This emphasis on the moral conduct of Christians also serves Justin's aim of gaining recognition for the Christian community within its wider Greco-Roman context. When describing the exemplary virtue of Christians, Justin, like Aristides and Theophilus, presents the Mosaic law as a source of philosophy that rivals textual sources for Hellenistic education. In the process, he depicts the Christian understanding of the Mosaic law as a definitive source of philosophical truth, and the practices of Christians as an exemplary embodiment of virtue. For Justin, then, the ethical behavior of Christians, which is grounded in a revelation of Christ and an understanding of the true import of the Mosaic law, serves as an essential identity marker for their community vis-à-vis non-Jews, even as it also marks out a covenant faithfulness superior to that of the Jewish people.

The Law, God, and the Logos: Clement and the Alexandrian Tradition

Peter Widdicombe

Most readers of Clement agree that he had a positive view of the law, a more positive view than many in the early Christian tradition. He never disparages the literal level of the law and he does not read it exclusively as a prefiguration of Christ, even though he widely employs allegorical readings in its interpretation.[1] In the one instance where he quotes Matthew 5:17, "I did not come to destroy but to fulfil the law (νόμον)," he remarks that "the design of the Law is to divert us from extravagances and all forms of disorderly conduct; its object is to draw us from unrighteousness to righteousness"; he goes on to explain that its "fulfilment does not mean that it was defective."[2] This attitude to the law fundamentally reflects his doctrine of the transcendence of God and the role of the Logos as the intermediary between God and creation. Clement does not write systematically about the relation between the law and his doc-

1. Annewies van den Hoek, *Clement of Alexandria and His Use of Philo in the* Stromateis: *An Early Christian Reshaping of a Jewish Model* (Supplements to Vigiliae Christianae 3; Leiden: Brill, 1988), 228. Although Clement was familiar with Jewish writings, especially those of Philo, it is questionable whether he had much contact with Jews and Jewish practice. For an analysis of the principal arguments, see James Carleton Paget, "Clement of Alexandria and the Jews," in his *Jews, Christians and Jewish Christians in Antiquity* (WUNT I 251; Tübingen: Mohr Siebeck, 2010), 91-102. A discussion of Clement's allegorical reading lies outside the scope of the present study. See David Dawson, *Allegorical Readers and Cultural Revision in Ancient Alexandria* (Berkeley: University of California Press, 1992), 183-234, for a thorough treatment of the subject.

2. *Strom.* 3.46.1. Otto Stählin, *Clemens Alexandrinus* (4 vols.; GCS 12, 15, 17, 39; Leipzig: J. C. Hinrichs, 1905-36). All subsequent references to Clement's works are to this edition.

This essay was written in appreciation for the friendship and the scholarship of Steve Westerholm, a model of both.

trine of God, indeed, he could hardly be said to write systematically about his doctrine of God; nevertheless, there are patterns in his writings that demonstrate a consistency in the way in which he thinks about how both the law and the Logos make known the unknowable God. The law had its origin in the Logos: the Logos "gave the Law by the mouth of prophets, enjoining and teaching what things are to be done and what is obscure."[3] Its content was an expression of the rationality of the Logos. Accordingly, the law acted as a bridge between God and humankind and was integral to the preparing of humankind for salvation. The law is that which is in accordance with "right reason"; it is powerful, able to make the unjust just and to bring about impassibility. Its teachings concerning the virtues and the curbing of the passions, which for Clement were critical to coming to the contemplation of God, were continuous with the teachings of the Logos. But for all of that, the relation of the law to the Logos was also what limited it, for however worthy the law was, it was not the Logos himself and the Logos had been made present to humankind in the incarnation. This plays out in a particularly telling way for Clement in the contrast he perceived between Moses and the Logos. However exceptional Moses was in his knowledge of God, so exceptional that he could be identified as a theologian and Gnostic, he was only the one through whom the law had been given and not the one by whom it had been given. Although Clement never suggests that the law has been abrogated by the coming of Christ — it never ceases to be in accordance with "right reason" and when read properly continues to be a guide to it — it is put into the shade by the light of the "right reason," a "right reason," close to the Father in a way Moses could never be.

The Unknowable God

Clement shared the Middle Platonism of many of his Christian predecessors.[4] Like that of Middle Platonism, Clement's doctrine of God was characterized by an emphasis on the utter transcendence of God, an emphasis Clement thought wholly in harmony with the biblical account.[5] In a formulation typical of the negative theology of Middle Platonism, Clement contends that we cannot

3. *Strom.* 2.21.5.

4. The classic study of Middle Platonism is John M. Dillon, *The Middle Platonists: A Study of Platonism, 80 B.C. to A.D. 220* (London: Duckworth, 1977).

5. For Clement's relation to Middle Platonism, see Henny Fiska Hägg, *Clement of Alexandria and the Beginnings of Christian Apophaticism* (OECS; Oxford: Oxford University Press, 2006).

know what God is but only what he is not. While he frequently refers to God with the phrase, "He who is" or "being itself" (ὁ ὤν), from the Septuagint of Exodus 3:14, God for him is above both time and space, invisible, immutable, and impassible, this last an attribute that is central to Clement's thinking about the law. Language does not apply to God. Ineffability (ἄρρητος) is the alpha privative most commonly used by Clement to refer to the divine nature[6] and is of particular importance for our study, for while the Father is inexpressible, the Logos is expressible. As Clement explains in *Strom.* 5.65.2, the "God of the universe who is above all speech, conception and thought, can never be the object of writing, being ineffable, as he is, in his own power." Clement maintains that in the providential dispensation of the Logos, both Moses and Plato gave voice to the notion of divine ineffability, Plato having learned it from Moses.[7] Quoting two of the classic apophatic passages from Plato in conjunction with Exodus 20:21, Clement declares:

> "Now to find the Father and Maker of this universe is difficult, and having found him it is impossible to declare him to all" (*Timaeus* 28c). "For this is not possible to put into words like other subjects of study" (*Letter* VII 341c), says Plato, the lover of truth. For he had heard exceptionally well that the all-wise[8] Moses, in ascending the mountain for holy contemplation, to the summit of intelligible realities, of necessity commands all of the people not to go up with him. And when Scripture says, "Moses entered into the thick darkness where God was" (Exod. 20:21), this shows to those who are capable of understanding that God is invisible and ineffable. (*Strom.* 5.78.1-3)

Clement, of course, was fully aware that unless we are prepared to give up talking about the divine altogether, we must use words to refer to God. However, when we do, when we use such titles for God as "the One or the Good, or Mind, or Being, or Being Itself, or Father, or God, or Creator, or Lord," we

6. See Hägg, *Clement of Alexandria,* 159, for a list of the alpha privatives Clement most often ascribes to God.

7. The idea that Plato had been dependent on Moses was commonplace among early Christian writers, and Clement claims that it was held by the Greeks themselves. He cites in support the famous question of Numenius, the second-century Middle Platonist, "What is Plato but Moses speaking Greek?" (*Strom.* 1.150.4). Clement, however, worked out the supposed connection between the two in greater detail than most, and, as we will see, the idea was important for his thinking about divine providence and the law.

8. One of Clement's favorite titles for Moses.

"do not do so properly," but failing anything better, we use them "as props for the mind."[9]

This transcendent God, inexpressible by "human power," is knowable, however, but knowable only by God's own choosing. This he does, Clement assures us, by his "power."[10] In *Strom.* 2.5.4-5, Clement explains that while God is "remote in essence," inasmuch as "the generated" cannot approach the "ingenerate," God is "very near in power, by which he holds all things in his embrace." God's power, Clement goes on to remark, "is always present, taking hold of us through the power of contemplation, beneficence, and instruction." This power Clement identifies as the Logos.

The Logos

Patently, the idea of the Logos was critical in such a doctrine of God as Clement's. The Logos functioned as the intermediary between the unknowable and inexpressible Father and humankind. The term "Logos" is Clement's favorite word for the Son. He repeatedly plays on the word-reason signification of the word λόγος. The Logos, as Clement conceived the act of creation, provided the rational structure of both the universe and the human being, the latter having been made in the image of the Logos. It is the Logos who draws humankind back to reason through the law and the incarnation.

Drawing heavily on biblical texts, especially 1 Corinthians 1:24 and elsewhere where Paul links wisdom with power, Clement identifies the divine power with the Logos,[11] an identification that he claims Moses also had made. This Clement makes clear in a passage in *Strom.* 5.71.3-5 that epitomizes much of Clement's thinking about the unknowable God and the role of the Logos in making that God known.

> If then, removing all attributes from the bodies and from the so-called incorporeals, we hurl ours toward the greatness of Christ, and from there we advance in holiness toward the abyss (ἀχανές), we would somehow make an approach in our understanding of the almighty, getting to know not what he is, but what he is not. . . . The first cause is not in a place, but

9. *Strom.* 5.82.1.

10. *Strom.* 5.71.5.

11. On Clement's understanding of divine power, see David T. Runia, "Clement of Alexandria and the Philonic Doctrine of the Divine Power(s)," *VC* 58, no. 3 (2004): 256-76.

> transcends both place and time, and also name and conception. For this reason, Moses says "reveal yourself to me" (Exod. 33:13), hinting most plainly that God cannot be taught or spoken by human beings, but is knowable only through the power that proceeds from him. For the quest is formless and unseen, but the grace of the knowledge comes from God through the Son. (*Strom.* 5.71.3-5)

The knowledge of God, then, is a grace, which as we will see below, may be an allusion to John 1:17. It is a knowledge only made known by an expression of divine power and that power is the Son. There is one further thing to note before we leave this quotation — the identification of the goal of our "advance in Christ" as the "abyss." This, as we also will see, may well be an allusion to John 1:18.

At the beginning of book 7 of the *Stromateis,* Clement explains that what enables the Logos to reveal the transcendent Father is the intermediate position of the Son. However exalted he may be, the Logos lies within the realm of being. The Son is among the "intelligibles" and thus from him

> we learn about the transcendent cause, the Father of all, the most ancient and beneficent of all, no longer transmitted by speech but paid the homage of reverence in adoring silence and holy amazement, and supremely venerated; declared by the Lord, as far as those, who learned, were capable of understanding, and apprehended by those whom the Lord has chosen for knowledge.[12]

Accordingly, Clement can remark of the Son that while God is "not demonstrable, is not the object of knowledge," the Son is, by virtue of his nature, for the Son "is wisdom, knowledge, truth, and everything related to these, and thus he can be demonstrated and described."[13] In sum, the Son, as the divine reason, is able to make the truth about God known to humankind; he lies within the domain of language and by implication is the one who is capable of putting into words the one who in himself cannot be conveyed by language.

As the divine reason, the Logos exercises providential care over both creation and humankind, an affirmation that is of critical importance for Clement's conception of the law. The Son "orders all things according to the will of the Father and holds the helm of the universe in the best way,"[14] he, "the

12. *Strom.* 7.2.2-3.
13. *Strom.* 4.156.1.
14. *Strom.* 7.5.3-5.

paternal Logos, having received the holy government from the one who did the subjecting."[15] Clement is famous for having argued that the Logos exercises this providential care in three covenants. The second covenant was with the Greeks, the content of which was derived from the first, which was the covenant with the Jews, and the third is with the church.[16] Accordingly, Clement can claim that the providential willingness of the Son is evident in the "prophetic scriptures," in the giving of philosophy to the Greeks, and in the Lord's assuming flesh capable of suffering.[17] The law was central to the second covenant.

The Law

In order to understand Clement's high view of the law,[18] it is helpful to look first at his view of law in general. It too is entirely positive. Clement writes extensively in his various works about what he regards as the importance of law in bringing order to the political and social spheres, and to the sphere of the individual. All law, as indeed all truth, has its origin ultimately with the Logos, whether the laws be Greek, Jewish, or Christian. In one of his longest and pithiest discussions of law, in the first book of the *Stromateis,* Clement provides his readers with a concise definition of what he understands law to be.[19] We must bear in mind, however, that it often is unclear in any given passage whether he has in mind law generically understood, or the Mosaic law, or both, so interwoven are the two in his thinking. Having begun the chapter by observing that Plato had been aided in his formulation of laws by the "books of Moses,"[20] he then proceeds to draw on various of Plato's works, including the *Laws,* the *Statesman,* and the *Epinomis,* to demonstrate that Plato believed that the statesman was one who led "an active and just life, combined with contemplation."[21] Clement concludes the chapter by explaining what he thinks law is essentially: "Law is the opinion which is good and that which is good is

15. *Strom.* 7.5.3-4.

16. See, for instance, *Strom.* 6.41.4-7.

17. *Strom.* 7.2.6.1-4.

18. Van den Hoek, *Clement of Alexandria,* 69-115, makes helpful comments about Clement's understanding of the law in comparison with Philo's.

19. The discussion runs from 165.1 to 166.5.

20. *Strom.* 1.165.1. In *Protr.* 70.1, Clement remarks that Plato was indebted to the "Hebrews" for the laws and ideas about God that were consistent with the truth.

21. *Strom.* 1.165.2.

that which is true, and that which is true is that which finds that which is and attains it. 'He who is sent me' (Exod. 3:14), says Moses. And some, undoubtedly speaking about good opinion, have called law right reason (λόγον ὀρθόν), which enjoins what is to be done and forbids what is not to be done."[22] Although Clement does not acknowledge its provenance here, the phrase "right reason" is a reference to the Stoic concept of law.[23] Cicero had written in *Rep.* 33.3 that "[t]rue law is right reason in agreement with nature";[24] and elsewhere, in *Strom.* 2.101.2,[25] Clement observes that the Stoics believe that the fitting end of man is to live in accordance with nature, they having inappropriately substituted the word "nature" for the word "God."[26] We should also note that while he does not mention the Logos in the passage, he might well have intended the references to "reason" and "truth" to call the Logos to mind. In *Paed.* 1.101.1-2, in the context of a discussion of the control of the passions, he makes it clear that the "right reason" of the philosophers, by whom the context suggests he means the Stoics, is the Logos himself.

Here, in our quotation from the first book of the *Stromateis,* Clement assimilates the Stoic concept of law to his doctrine of God. We are to understand that, in ascending order, "law" accords with the "good," the "good" with the "true," and the "true" with "that which is," but — and this is the significance of Clement's seemingly abrupt introduction of Exodus 3:14 into the discussion — "that which is" is identical with "He who is," which, as we observed above, is a title Clement uses frequently of God. Properly understood, the reality with which law is in harmony, then, is not the order of nature but the very being of God. It is not clear with the reference from Exodus whether Clement has switched from the topic of law in general to that of the Mosaic law, which presumably he had had in mind all along in any case, but in the section that immediately follows, as he takes up the question of the role of Moses in the giving of it, he does specifically discuss the law.

22. *Strom.* 1.166.4-5.

23. Clement refers to the law as "right reason" again in *Strom.* 2.19.2, and in 19.3 quotes a fragment that he attributes to Speusippus in which the phrase occurs. On the relation between the phrase as it appears in the fragment and its occurrence in Stoicism, see Leonardo Tarán, *Speusippus of Athens: A Critical Study with a Collection of the Related Texts and Commentary* (PhA 39; Leiden: Brill, 1981), 240-41.

24. *On the Republic, On the Laws* (trans. Clinton Walker Keyes; LCL 213; Cambridge: Harvard University Press, 1928).

25. He refers to this Stoic belief again in *Strom.* 5.95.1.

26. In *Strom.* 1.181.4, he quotes Pindar's statement that law is king, but claims that the statement actually refers to God.

In the course of his various accounts of the goodness of the law (and perhaps law in general), Clement feels constrained to defend it against the charge, seemingly brought by both the Greeks and the Marcionites, that inasmuch as fear, a passion, the very thing it is intended to control, is inherent to the nature of the law, the law cannot be called good. Clement's rejection of the charge is twofold. On the one hand, he argues that there is a distinction to be made in the nature of fear — there is good fear and there is bad fear; and on the other, he argues that justice and the good are not to be seen as mutually exclusive but as complementary. One of his most sustained apologies for the law occurs in the opening book of the *Paedagogus*. In *Paed.* 1.30.3, he quotes Galatians 3:23-25, "Now before faith came, we were imprisoned and guarded under the Law until faith would be revealed. Therefore, the Law was our disciplinarian until Christ came, so that we might be justified by faith. But now that faith has come, we are no longer subject to a disciplinarian," and then goes on to observe that the law "was accompanied by fear."[27] But "the fear of the Lord," as Clement repeatedly observes, "is the beginning of wisdom" (Prov. 1:7). Therefore, we can conclude that "the knowledge of the Law is the beginning of wisdom; and a man is not wise without the Law."[28] Fear, in fact, is "a device for saving us."[29] The reason that fear goes hand in hand with the law is that the law concerns justice, and punishment is integral to justice. The threat of punishment is accompanied by fear, but fear promotes discipline and thus impassibility. The fear that proceeds from the law is "not irrational but truly conforms to the Logos." It is a "cautious fear,"[30] which induces the absence of fear.[31] In the *Paedagogus,* Clement cites verse after verse from the Old and New Testaments, and statements from Plato, to demonstrate that both the Logos and the philosophers thought that punishment and correction promote the effecting of the good.

Clement is so certain of the value of fear that he is prepared to attribute its use to Christ himself. Christ, as an educator who wields authority, employs a rod, the evidence for which Clement finds in the words of Isaiah 11:1, "a rod out of the root of Jesse"; Psalm 2:9, with its reference to the ruling with a "rod of iron"; Psalm 22:4 LXX, the comforting "rod and staff;" and elsewhere in the Psalms.[32] Should anyone "deny that the Lord is good because of the rod and

27. *Paed.* 1.31.1.
28. *Strom.* 2.33.3.
29. *Paed.* 1.81.3.
30. *Strom.* 2.32.4.
31. *Strom.* 2.39.1-3.
32. *Paed.* 1.61.1-3.

threats and the fear he resorts to" one must recognize that he is "completely good and blameless, for out of the excess of his love for humankind, he himself has experienced the sufferings that are common to every man by his nature."[33] As Clement explains of Christ, "the material he educates us in is fear of God, for this fear instructs us in the service of God, educates to the knowledge of truth, and guides by a path leading straight to heaven."[34]

This defense of the law reflects Clement's concern to ensure that there be no Marcionite distinction made between a just Creator God and the good Father. As he makes clear in the *Paedagogus* and elsewhere, God is to be perceived as one and as both good and just. In a passage of particular importance for our purposes, Clement joins justice and goodness within the Son, a conjunction that then, according to Clement, is to be seen in the law and the incarnation. But he also introduces another element into his argument, that is, the idea of love. In *Paed.* 1.71.1-3, after having cited a collage of scriptural verses to make his case for the oneness of God, he goes on to root the justice of God in the relationship of love between the Father and Son. The argument turns on his definition of justice as that which describes "equality of degree." Alluding to John 17:21-23, which he had used to help establish the oneness of God, Clement explains that as the Son is in the Father, who alone is good, the Father can also be described as just "because of their relation of love, one for the other, since justice is the term to describe equality of degree." Later in the discussion, Clement explains that the "nature of his [God's] love is the origin of his justice, making his sun to shine and sending down his own Son. The Son was the first to proclaim the good justice which is from heaven." But even in this context, Clement takes care to include the law. "Afterwards," he remarks, "justice came down among men, both in the Scriptures and in the body, in the Word and in the Law, constraining men to salutary repentance, for it was good."[35] Quoting Proverbs 3:13 and 16 in *Strom.* 1.173.5, "Blessed is the man that hath found wisdom, and the mortal who has seen understanding, for out of its mouth proceed righteousness and it bears law and mercy on its tongue," Clement grounds the harmony of goodness and justice in the preexistent Logos. The "mouth" referred to is Wisdom's mouth, which shows that "both the Law and the Gospel are one energy of one Lord, who is 'the power and wisdom of God'

33. *Paed.* 1.62.1.

34. *Paed.* 1.53.3. See Piotr Ashwin-Siejkowski, *Clement of Alexandria: A Project of Christian Perfection* (London: T&T Clark, 2008), 68-78, for a detailed discussion of the role of fear in Clement's thought.

35. *Paed.* 1.88.2-3.

(1 Cor. 1:24) and the fear which the Law engenders is merciful in orienting us to salvation."[36]

But for all his desire to bring the law and the Logos together and to celebrate the worthiness of both, the law for Clement had its limitations. While fear might well have been used by the Logos and justice may well be rooted in the divine love, Clement appears unprepared to attribute love directly to the law, something he certainly is prepared to do with respect to the Logos. The "old covenant," Clement opines in *Paed.* 1.59.1, "guided the people through fear" and in that dispensation, "the Logos was an angel." By contrast, in the "new," the "Logos has become flesh, fear has been turned into love," and "the mystic messenger of old has been born, Jesus." Although Clement does not spell this out, the implication is that in the first case the Logos acts through an intermediary, and in the second, the Logos appears in the flesh and it is this that effects the transition from fear to love.

Moses and the Logos

One of the contexts in which the difference between the law and the Logos emerges most clearly is in the contrast Clement makes between Moses and the Logos, a contrast that for him is especially evident in John 1:17 and 18. It is a contrast that closely reflects his doctrine of God. As one would expect, Moses occupies an exceptionally prominent place in Clement's thinking about the law. Moses is "a theologian, a prophet," and "an interpreter of sacred laws."[37] He is, simply, the preeminent giver of law, outclassing the law-dispensing philosophers of the Greeks; indeed, all the virtues to be found in the Greek laws, the very basis of Greek morality, had been delineated by Moses in the scriptures.[38] This preeminence Clement appears to base on the fact that Moses is the one to whom God announced himself as "He who is," for he begins his account of Moses immediately following the passage in which he gives his definition of law and its reference to "He who is" with this statement: "From which it follows that the Law was rightly said to have

36. *Strom.* 1.174.1-3. On Clement's response to Marcionism, see Eric Francis Osborn, *Clement of Alexandria* (Cambridge: Cambridge University Press, 2005), 48, 138-40; and his earlier work, *The Philosophy of Clement of Alexandria* (Cambridge: Cambridge University Press, 1957), 57-59.

37. *Strom.* 1.150.4.

38. *Strom.* 2.78.1-3. In the passage, Clement lists the cardinal virtues, courage, temperance, prudence, and justice, supplemented by endurance, patience, propriety, continence, and piety.

been given by Moses . . . and we may call it with accuracy the divine law inasmuch as it was given by God through Moses."[39] Indeed, Moses, being "governed by the good Logos," was a "living law" (νόμος ἔμψυχος).[40] His standing is sufficiently high that Clement includes Moses among the Gnostics, the status for which Christians are to strive, inasmuch as the Gnostic is the one who, having mastered the passions, is able to contemplate God.[41] As we have already seen, Clement's Moses had a profound understanding of the transcendent nature of God, and in *Strom.* 5.74.4, Clement describes Moses as a Gnostic in the context of arguing that he knew that God could not be circumscribed and thus that he had prohibited the setting up of images in the temple. Later in the work, having identified righteousness as one of the principal characteristics of the Gnostic,[42] Clement explains that Moses' glorified face (Exod. 34:29) reflected his righteousness of soul, a glorification Clement attributes to Moses' "uninterrupted intercourse with God."[43] Moses certainly then for Clement had a remarkably close relation with the inexpressible transcendent God, a relation that made him the appropriate vehicle for the communication of the law.

But however intimate Moses was with God, the Logos was all the more. This for Clement is made patent by John 1:17 and 18. As is the case with his treatment of scriptural passages generally, Clement never engages in a sustained analysis of the two verses, but he frequently either quotes them or alludes to them in various contexts, and what he has to say about them can be seen to form a coherent whole. At the heart of his interpretation lies his understanding of the meaning of the words "in the bosom of the Father" in John 1:18. According to Clement, the word "bosom" (κόλπος) in itself attests to the utter transcendence of God. As he explains in *Strom.* 5.81.3, John intended to indicate by "bosom" the "invisibility and ineffableness" of the divine nature. Because of this, some "have called it the depth (βυθόν) inasmuch as it contains and embosoms (ἐγκολπισάμενον) all things, inaccessible and boundless."[44] ("Depth" here may recall the "abyss" [ἀχανές] of *Strom.* 5.71.3, referred to above, into which the soul ascends in the greatness

39. *Strom.* 1.167.1.

40. *Strom.* 1.167.3.

41. For Clement's portrayal of Moses in the context of an analysis of his understanding of how one becomes a Gnostic, see Ashwin-Siejkowski, *Clement of Alexandria,* 152-87.

42. *Strom.* 6.102.4.

43. *Strom.* 6.103.5-6.

44. *Strom.* 5.81.3. On Clement's interpretation of "bosom of God," see Andrew C. Itter, *Esoteric Teaching in the* Stromateis *of Clement of Alexandria* (Leiden: Brill, 2009), 169-71.

of Christ.)[45] But the fact that the Son is "in" the bosom of the Father also shows, as Clement contends in *Exc.* 8.1, that the "Logos is God in God, unchangeable,[46] . . . continuous, undivided, one God." However exactly Clement intended this to be understood, it is clear that he believed that the Son has access to this inaccessible depth (and perhaps in some measure participates in it).

In one of his most detailed discussions of John 1:17, in *Quis dives salvetur,* Clement argues that there is a fundamental difference between Moses and the Logos on the basis of the latter's ability to grant eternal life, and once again this is a reflection of the Logos's closeness to the Father. After having quoted Mark 10:17-31 in full,[47] Clement claims that it was appropriate that Jesus be asked what one must do to inherit eternal life because, as "the life," he is able to grant eternal life, he having received it from God "who is the good and first and only dispenser of eternal life."[48] God is uniquely the dispenser of this life inasmuch as God is "the one who really is (τοῦ ὄντως ὄντος)," Clement here once again echoing Exodus 3:14.[49] In order to understand the greatness of the Son, a greatness that is next to the Father's, and the newness of his grace, we need only look to John 1:17, which Clement reads in conjunction with an allusion to Hebrews 3:5-6. He explains that when we read the verse, we must bear in mind that the "gifts given through a faithful slave (δούλου) are not equal to those bestowed by a genuine son (ὑπὸ τοῦ υἱοῦ γνησίου)." Clement, however, heightens the contrast between Moses and Christ by substituting δοῦλος for θεράπων in the description of Moses from Hebrews 3:5, and by inserting γνήσιος into 3:6 to describe Christ's sonship.[50] Clement then goes on simply to ask rhetorically what need there would have been for the "coming of the saviour," if the law of Moses had been able to confer eternal life.[51]

In a similar passage in *Paed.* 1.60.1-2, Clement bases his argument about the superiority of the Logos in part on an analysis of the prepositions and verbs of John 1:17, which he reads this time in conjunction with John 1:3. Having first observed that the law is the old grace (χάρις ἐστὶν παλαιά), the word "grace"

45. See the comment of Alain Le Boulluec, *Clément d'Alexandrie, Les Stromates: Stromate V. Texte. Commentaire* (SC 279; Paris: Éditions du Cerf, 1981), 263.

46. Following the reading of Mark J. Edwards, "Clement of Alexandria and His Doctrine of the Logos," *VC* 54, no. 2 (2000): 171-75.

47. *Quis div.* 4.4-10.

48. *Quis div.* 6.4.

49. *Quis div.* 7.2-3.

50. *Quis div.* 8.1.

51. *Quis div.* 8.2.

here perhaps a play on its use in 1:17, he points out that the law was not given "by" Moses but rather "by" (ὑπό) the Logos "through" (διά) Moses, who this time is described as "his servant" (θεράποντος), which, as Clement goes on to explain, "is why it was temporary." By contrast, "eternal (ἀΐδιος) grace and truth," Clement here inserting the word "eternal" into the verse,[52] "came into being through Jesus Christ." The fact that the verse actually uses "through" of Christ in relation to grace and truth does not disconcert Clement. While the law is "only given," "the truth, being the grace (χάρις) of the Father, is the eternal work of the Logos (ἔργον ἐστὶ τοῦ λόγου αἰώνιον), and thus is no longer said to be given, but rather 'came into being through Jesus,' 'without whom nothing came into being' (John 1:3)." Although he does not spell out the logic of his argument, Clement seemingly assumes that he can use the word "eternal" to describe grace and truth because truth is a grace of the Father and consequently can be identified as an eternal work of the Son. By bringing in John 1:3 to support his interpretation, Clement is able to link both the law and the truth with the Logos's role as creator. The very existence of the law, then, is attributable to the Logos.

It is the Logos's relation to the transcendent God in contrast to Moses' that accounts for what Clement views as the Logos's superiority as an interpreter of the law. This too Clement bases on John 1:18. The true legislator not only "announces what is good and noble," which is what Moses did, "but knows it. And the Law of this one who possesses knowledge is the saving command; or better, the Law is a command of knowledge. For the Logos is 'the power and wisdom of God' (1 Cor. 1:24)," the point perhaps being that the one who possesses knowledge actually is knowledge, there being no distinction. "Moreover, the interpreter of the laws is the same one by whom the law was given; he is the first interpreter of the divine commands, who makes known the bosom of the Father, the only-begotten Son."[53] In short, the Logos could both give the law and interpret it definitively because he was the one who definitively makes the unknowable God knowable.

The exceptional importance that Clement ascribes to the Son's being in the bosom of the Father and declaring him can be seen in his conjoining the image with the idea of the divine love. In an extraordinary passage in *Quis dives salvetur*, he enjoins us to

52. Something that to my knowledge he does not do elsewhere. On Clement's text of the Gospel of John, see Carl P. Cosaert, *The Text of the Gospels in Clement of Alexandria* (New Testament in the Greek Fathers 9; Atlanta: Society of Biblical Literature, 2008). See pp. 187-88 for a list of the occurrences of John 1:17 and 18.

53. *Strom.* 1.169.2-4.

> [b]ehold the mysteries of love, and then you will have a vision of the bosom of the Father, whom the only-begotten God alone declared. God in his very self is love, and out of love for us he allowed himself to be apprehended. In his ineffability he is Father, but in his sympathy for us he became mother. By his loving, the Father became feminine, and the great sign of this is the one he begot of himself, and the fruit that is born by love is love. For this also he came down. For this he clothed himself with man.[54]

We cannot here engage in an analysis of this most intriguing of statements, but we can see that it attests Clement's strength of feeling about the centrality of love to the nature of the transcendent God and to the Father-Son relation.[55] It is love that prompted God to make himself apprehendable; it is this love that prompted him to beget and then to send the Son.

Finally, it is the Father's bosom, where "eternal life is to be found," the bosom "to which," Clement declares at the end of *Quis dives salvetur,* "the Saviour himself leads the saved, he holding forth shadowless, unceasing light."[56] Moses the law-giving Gnostic, the one who entered into the dark cloud on Mount Sinai and had uninterrupted intercourse with "He who is," ultimately was not in the bosom of the Father, did not know the Father's depths, and could not lead the saved to the bosom. That was true only of the Logos, the eternal wisdom and power of God, the progenitor of the law, its definitive interpreter, and the one who embodied in the incarnation the eternal "right reason" that informed it.

Conclusion

Clement held a high view of the law, but it was a law whose essence lay in its testimony to the virtues, not in its particularity as an expression of Judaism. The virtues were those common to Greek philosophy, and if in the law they were to be seen in a more pure and effective way, they, like the Greek copy, ultimately had their source in the Logos. Clement's successors in the Alexandrian tradition increasingly saw the law as a secondary matter, as the idea of the Son as Logos came increasingly to be focused in the Father-Son relation

54. *Quis div.* 37.1-3.

55. I will be addressing the topic of Clement's understanding of the fatherhood of God in a subsequent essay.

56. *Quis div.* 42.16.

and as the revelation of the knowledge of God came increasingly to be focused in the incarnation. Ultimately for Cyril, the last of the great Alexandrian theologians of the patristic period, writing in light of the acceptance of the Creed of Nicea and its statement that the Son was of one being with the Father, the Logos incarnate was simply the presence in space and time of God, and it was there in the incarnation that the truth was fully and finally to be found.[57] The theology of the Logos, which had its beginnings in Alexandria with Clement and which accounted for his championing of the law, in the end led, perhaps ironically, to the law's receding into the background as a guide to the truth for Alexandrian Christianity.

57. For a detailed treatment of Cyril's view of Moses and the law, see John A. McGuckin, "Moses and the 'Mystery of Christ' in St. Cyril of Alexandria's Exegesis," *Coptic Church Review* 21, nos. 1-2 (2000): 24-32, 98-114.

Canonical Paul and the Law

Stephen Westerholm

More years ago than I care to compute, I met a woman on a train in Sweden whom I vaguely recognized as a fellow doctoral student at Lund University, she in Old Testament, I in New. Within a few sentences of our initial greeting, we were speaking on our one subject of commonality. I indicated that I was writing on the different approaches of Jesus and the Pharisees to certain legal issues. She appeared taken aback, though whether by the audacity or the folly of my imagining such a topic fit for a doctoral dissertation, I was not quite sure. She was writing on nautical terms in the book of Ezekiel.

God bless her[1] and other philologists (and textual critics), on whose work every biblical scholar is dependent; my own research and writing, however, have largely been devoted to major New Testament themes, none more central than Torah. My doctoral dissertation finished,[2] I followed my supervisor's advice and moved on to other parts of the New Testament, though retaining an interest in the interpretation of the law.[3] Returning to Canada, I learned that the Canadian Society of Biblical Studies had launched a "*torah/nomos* seminar"; I contributed a series of literature reviews.[4] In *Israel's Law and the*

1. I am not sure that I ever knew her name, but a check of the Old Testament series of Coniectanea Biblica turns up the following: Eva Strömberg Krantz, *Des Schiffes Weg mitten im Meer: Beiträge zur Erforschung der nautischen Terminologie des Alten Testaments* (ConBOT 19; Lund: Gleerup, 1982).

2. *Jesus and Scribal Authority* (ConBNT 10; Lund: Gleerup, 1978).

3. "The Law and the 'Just Man' (1 Tim 1,3-11)," *ST* 36 (1982): 79-95; "Letter and Spirit: The Foundation of Pauline *Ethics*," *NTS* 30, no. 2 (1984): 229-48; "On Fulfilling the Whole Law (Gal 5.14)," *SEÅ* 51-52 (1986-87): 229-37.

4. These were later published in Peter Richardson et al., *Law in Religious Communities in the Roman Period: The Debate over* Torah *and* Nomos *in Post-Biblical Judaism and Early*

Church's Faith: Paul and His Recent Interpreters,[5] I combined literature reviews (Part One) with my own discussion of issues related to Paul and the law (Part Two). *Perspectives Old and New on Paul: The "Lutheran" Paul and His Critics*[6] represents an updated and much expanded version of this work.

Paul and the Law

My views on the topic have not won universal assent (in commentaries on Acts, this is referred to as litotes), but I cannot argue for them here. The focus of this essay — on Luther's and Calvin's premodern interpretations of Paul and the law, the differences between which continue to divide modern interpreters — nonetheless requires as background at least the following summary of what I take to be Paul's own understanding of the subject.[7]

1. Human beings find themselves in an ordered world not of their making, and bound to acknowledge their Creator (Rom. 1:21) and conform to the wise ordering of his creation.[8] Life and divine favor are promised to those who do so.

2. The "moral" demands of the Mosaic law articulate the appropriate human response to life in God's creation,[9] though that law includes as well ordinances binding only on Jews, the observance of which marked them off from other nations as God's people (see 1 Cor. 9:20-21). The Mosaic law rightly promises life and divine favor to those who keep its commands (Rom. 10:5; Gal. 3:12); in

Christianity (SCJ 4; Waterloo: Wilfrid Laurier University Press, 1991), 19-91. My article "*Torah, Nomos,* and Law: A Question of 'Meaning,'" *SR* 15, no. 3 (1986): 327-36, was also written for the CSBS seminar.

5. Grand Rapids: Eerdmans, 1988.

6. Grand Rapids: Eerdmans, 2004.

7. Given that the focus of this essay is on classical interpretations of Paul's understanding of the law, I must beg readers' indulgence when, in the discussion of Paul, I frequently refer them to my earlier work and to the scholarly literature cited therein. In the first seven points listed here, I repeat the summary found in chapter 19 of *Perspectives;* references are also given below to articles where I have developed the points in question more fully.

8. Human beings are thus to live "according to nature" (see Rom. 1:26-27), which here means according to the wisdom with which God ordered his creation. In Romans 1, Paul shows how a refusal to acknowledge the Creator is followed by a refusal to conform to the wise ordering of creation.

9. Note that doing what, for Jew and Gentile alike, is "good" in Romans 2:7, 10 is the equivalent of "doing the law" in 2:13. That (what we refer to as) the "moral" commandments are in view is clear from 2:17-27, where various "moral" commandments are cited, and where circumcision is discussed as though it were not a part of the law itself.

the case of Gentiles, who were not given the Mosaic law, compliance with its moral demands is nonetheless expected since these requirements have been "written on their hearts" (Rom. 2:13-15).[10]

3. Adamic humanity does not, and cannot, submit to God's law (Rom. 8:7-8). As a result, the law cannot in fact serve as the path to righteousness and life in God's favor (Rom. 3:20, 28; Gal. 2:16, 21; 3:10-12, 21; cf. Rom. 4:13-15; 8:3).

4. The giving of the law nonetheless served to highlight, at the same time as it exacerbated, human rebellion against God and bondage to sin (Rom. 3:20; 5:13, 20; 7:7-13).

5. The righteousness of God revealed in Jesus Christ is operative apart from law, through faith in Christ. Believers thus enjoy the status of being righteous before God that they could not attain under the terms spelled out by the law (Rom. 3:20-28; 5:1; Gal. 2:16).

6. Believers in Christ also enjoy new life in the Spirit (Rom. 8:9-17; 2 Cor. 3:6; Gal. 5:16, 25). Paradoxically, a life no longer "under law" but led by the Spirit and marked by the Spirit's fruit is one that no law can condemn (Gal. 5:18, 22-23). Indeed, the love shown by such a life in effect "fulfills" the law: it constitutes the good at which the law aimed but was too "weak" (Rom. 8:3) to bring about (Gal. 5:14; cf. Rom. 8:4; 13:8-10).[11]

7. Properly speaking, those "under law" are the Jewish people, to whom the law was given (Rom. 9:4; cf. 3:19; 1 Cor. 9:20-21), including the earthly Jesus himself (Gal. 4:4). The phrase no longer applies, however, to those Jews who, by participating (through baptism) in the death of Christ, have "died" to the law; they have been "redeemed" and "set free" from the law (Rom. 6:14-15; 7:1-6; Gal. 2:19; 4:5). Until the divinely appointed time, the law served as their "pedagogue" ("custodian" [RSV], "disciplinarian" [NRSV], "guardian" [ESV, NIV]); now that Christ has come, they are no longer under its supervision (Gal. 3:23-26). At least in the first place, these texts must refer to Jewish believers.

That said, at various points in Paul's letters, it is extraordinarily difficult (and perhaps misspent energy to attempt) to limit to Jews what the apostle says about the law and the bondage to sin that it demonstrates. Such texts include several to which I have just alluded. Paul writes to "brothers [and sisters]" in Rome who have "died" to the law, been "set free from the law," so that now they "serve [God] in the new way, that of the Spirit, not in the old way, defined by

10. These first two points are developed further in my articles "The Righteousness of the Law and the Righteousness of Faith in Romans," *Int* 58 (2004): 253-64; "St. Paul and Knowledge of the Natural Law," *Journal of Law, Philosophy and Culture* 3, no. 1 (2009): 433-44.

11. See my article "On Fulfilling the Whole Law (Gal 5.14)" (note 3, above).

the law's written code" (Rom. 7:1-6; cf. 6:14-15). All of this must certainly apply to Jewish believers, who, as those once "under law," were clearly in a position to "die" to its hegemony; but the Roman church to which Paul was writing had a significant if not dominant Gentile component as well (see 1:5-6; 11:13). That he abruptly limits his comments in Romans 7 to readers who were Jews is not self-evident. To the Galatians (3:13), Paul writes, "Christ redeemed us from the curse of the law." Again, read most naturally, the first-person plural pronoun embraces both Paul and his Galatian (Gentile) readers (see also 3:23-26; 4:3-7). And perhaps, in the end, it is not too difficult to imagine why Paul would have spoken to Jewish and Gentile believers alike in these terms. He certainly believed the gospel offers salvation to all, inasmuch as all have failed to do "the good" that God requires (Rom. 2:6-12; 3:9-30). That "good," required of all, is spelled out in (the moral commandments of) the law of Moses, so that Jews (who possess the law in written form) are able to instruct Gentiles (who do not) of their mutual responsibility (Rom. 2:17-24). Is it not natural for Paul, then, to broaden (consciously or unconsciously) the category of those "under law" to include Gentiles since they, too, are expected to do the "good" that it articulates? And if so, they, too, can be said to have been "redeemed" from the law, to have "died" to its rule, and the like.

8. Strictly speaking, to be "under law" is to be subject to the conditions of the Mosaic covenant: those "under law" are obligated to keep its commandments and promised life in God's favor if they do so (Rom. 10:5; Gal. 3:12, citing Lev. 18:5), but threatened with the divine wrath and curse if they disobey (Rom. 4:15; Gal. 3:10, 13). That believers — Jewish and Gentile alike — are not "under law" means that believers — Jewish and Gentile alike — are no longer bound to observe its commandments as such, nor are they threatened by its sanctions.[12]

9. Though Paul's claim that believers are not "under law" means (in part) that they are not obligated to observe its commandments as such, several means were nonetheless open to him to derive moral guidance from Torah. Some of these are based on the ambiguity of the term (in Greek, νόμος), which he uses most frequently of the Mosaic law code, but occasionally of the Pentateuch itself, or even the divine scriptures as a whole[13] — the scriptures that, after all, were "written for our instruction" (Rom. 15:4; 1 Cor. 10:11). Paul

12. See my article "Letter and Spirit" (note 3, above). That Paul did not think Jewish believers were bound by the law (though those with "weak" consciences were free to observe it) is maintained in my essay "The Judaism Paul Left Behind Him," in *The Making of Christianity: Conflicts, Contacts, and Constructions: Essays in Honor of Bengt Holmberg* (ed. Magnus Zetterholm and Samuel Byrskog; Winona Lake: Eisenbrauns, 2012), 353-70.

13. See *Perspectives,* 298-300.

does not hesitate to draw on the stories of the Pentateuch for admonition and direction (e.g., 1 Cor. 10:1-12; 11:7-12). He cites Abraham as the model "father of those who believe" (Rom. 4:1-25; cf. Gal. 3:6-9, 29). As for the laws themselves, the proposal (adopted later by many theologians) that believers remain subject to the "moral" but not the "ritual" (or "ceremonial") and "judicial" commandments of the law does not appear to have crossed Paul's mind; for Paul, the law is the law, and one cannot be bound by some parts but not others (see Gal. 5:3). Yet, although believers are free from the law as such, they are nonetheless expected to do what is "good" (see Rom. 12:9; 13:3; 16:19), and (as we have seen) the moral demands of the law are a faithful articulation of the good God requires (see Rom. 13:8-10). Furthermore, inasmuch as the law was divinely given, it surely remains a powerful indicator of the divine mind and thus a potential source of principles for guiding Christian behavior. Thus, it is still possible, even for one who believes that the laws of Moses (as such) no longer apply to believers, to draw on those laws in instructing believers.

Instances where Paul himself does so, however, are rare (see 1 Cor. 9:8-10; perhaps 14:34; note also, from the disputed epistles, Eph. 6:2-3), and do not include even cases (like the discussion of immorality in 1 Corinthians 6, and of idolatry in 1 Corinthians 8–10) where unambiguous commands from Torah were ready to hand. No doubt his conviction that believers are not "under law" made him wary of confusing the issue by drawing on provisions of Torah to define Christian behavior; he preferred to establish, on specifically Christian grounds, principles for living even where these coincided precisely with Torah's demands (e.g., 1 Cor. 6:12-20; 8–10; 1 Thess. 4:3-8)!

Paul and Luther

The overlap between the above summary of Paul's understanding of the law and Luther's views on the subject is remarkable, whether one attributes it to Luther's adroitness as a reader of Paul or to my stubborn insistence on reading the apostle through a Lutheran lens. Though personally rather partial to the former explanation, I must limit myself here to a few comments on the reformer[14] and his relation to the apostle.

Within every human being, Luther believes, God has implanted an aware-

14. See *Perspectives,* 27-39, where fuller documentation is given. References here are to the volume and page number in Jaroslav Pelikan and Helmut T. Lehmann, eds., *Luther's Works* (55 vols.; St. Louis: Concordia, 1955-86).

ness that we are to do to others what we want done to ourselves; Luther labels this universal awareness the "law of nature" (27:53). The Mosaic law code, on the other hand, was given specifically to the Jews and incumbent on them alone (35:164-68). Yet some of its provisions serve to spell out the content of the "law of nature" that binds all human beings. In such cases (Luther has, of course, the Decalogue primarily in mind), what the Mosaic law commands must be observed by all human beings, not because the law of Moses commands it, but because that law (in part) articulates what God requires of all (35:164, 168). Thus far, I believe, Luther fairly restates what was said about Paul in the first and second points listed above.

More distinctively, Luther uses the term "law" for all that God requires of human beings in any part of scripture, including the demands of Jesus in the Gospels and the admonitions of the New Testament epistles (35:162, 236-37; of course, Paul, too, speaks exceptionally of the "law of Christ" [Gal. 6:2; cf. 1 Cor. 9:21]); and he insists that "law," in this sense and wherever it is found, must be rigorously distinguished from the "gospel," with its promise of grace to those who believe.[15] The gospel is necessary (and here Luther's emphasis is certainly Pauline) because resistance to God's will is so rooted in human nature that no one lives as God requires; thus no one is righteous, and no one obtains God's favor, by keeping the law. For Luther, then, the law's primary function is to bring to our awareness the demands of God we have not met and the consequent peril of divine judgment. When the sinner, so terrified, turns for help to the gospel, the law has served its "proper" purpose (26:148, 310).

Though this "proper" use of the law goes beyond anything that is explicit in Paul's letters, its roots are surely Pauline. The apostle himself speaks of a "knowledge of sin" that comes from the law, and in Romans 3:19-20, he claims that the result of what the law says to those subject to its demands is that "every mouth" is "stopped" and "the whole world" shown to be culpable before God

15. An explicit distinction between "law" and "gospel" is not found in Paul's writings; but Paul regularly draws a contrast between the law and faith (Rom. 3:21-22, 28; 4:13-16; Gal. 3:12, 23-25), and between the righteousness based on the law and that based on faith (the contrast is unambiguous in Phil. 3:9 [cf. Rom. 9:30-31], and provides by far the most natural reading of Rom. 10:5-13; Gal. 3:11-12 as well [see my *Perspectives,* 327 nn. 93 and 94]). Moreover, while insisting that the righteousness based on the law requires obedience to its commands (Rom. 2:13; 10:5; Gal. 3:12), Paul also insists on the gratuity of the righteousness based on faith (Rom. 3:22-24; 4:4-5; 5:16-17; necessarily, since here it is the "ungodly" who are "found righteous" [Rom. 4:5; cf. 5:6-9]). See further my article "Paul and the Law in Romans 9-11," in *Paul and the Mosaic Law* (ed. James D. G. Dunn; WUNT I 89; Tübingen: Mohr Siebeck, 1996), 215-37. Essentially, then, the distinction Luther draws between law and gospel seems true to Paul, even though the terminology is Luther's own.

(see also Rom. 7:7, 13); moreover, the dilemma thus portrayed leads naturally to a summary of the gospel (Rom. 3:21-26). We have seen that Paul himself appears, in places, to have broadened the category of those "under law" to include all of unredeemed humanity, inasmuch as the moral demands of God articulated in the law are incumbent on all. It is precisely the failure of human beings to be righteous in the ordinary sense of the word (i.e., by doing what they ought, as outlined in the law) that called for the "revelation" of a different kind of righteousness (i.e., that based on faith).[16] Is Paul likely to have proclaimed the solution without mentioning the crisis that required it? Can he have offered a gospel of "salvation" (Rom. 1:16; 2 Cor. 6:2; 1 Thess. 5:9) without mentioning the dilemma from which it provides deliverance? To be sure, Paul is not likely to have spoken of "the law" when, in his mission, he initially encountered non-Jews. It is nonetheless clear that he proclaimed to the non-Jews in Thessalonica (and elsewhere) the peril they faced at the impending divine judgment — patently because they had failed to meet divine obligations — so that they must turn for rescue to the gospel.[17] Is it not, then, both inevitable in principle and apparent from the epistles that Paul's proclamation of the gospel was accompanied by that of (what Luther calls) the law?

Furthermore, Luther, like Paul (on rare occasions), sees believers as free to take direction from commands of Moses that do not bind them. On the one hand, Luther insists that the laws of Moses (all the laws of Moses), as such, have never bound any but the Jews to whom they were given. On the other hand, "we should look to [Moses] for examples of outstanding laws and moral precepts" (27:15). Even the political laws serve to remind us that believers are to obey the laws of the land in which they live (26:448). In the ceremonial laws of Moses, we see that life on earth cannot proceed without some ceremonies and rituals; hence, the church rightly has its own "festivals, prescribed times, prescribed places, etc.," so that "all things [may] be done decently and in order (1 Cor. 14:40)" (26:448).

And what of the law's moral demands? Here it must be remembered that Luther uses the term "law" not simply for the Mosaic code, but for God's demands wherever they occur in scripture, and that he sharply distinguishes "law" in this sense from "gospel." Moreover, Luther insists (based on his reading of Romans 7 and Galatians 5) that the life of believers is marked through-

16. See my article "The Righteousness of the Law and the Righteousness of Faith in Romans" (note 10, above).

17. See my *Justification Reconsidered: Rethinking a Pauline Theme* (Grand Rapids: Eerdmans, 2013), 1-22; also *Perspectives*, 354 n. 10.

out by a struggle with the sinful "flesh": they are, and remain throughout their earthly lives, both "sinners" (inasmuch as sin remains a daily reality) and "righteous" (in God's eyes, because of Christ). It follows that, throughout their earthly lives, they retain a need for the knowledge, the discipline, and the warnings that come from the law. Indeed, Luther finds in the Decalogue a summary of God's will for human beings, and demonstrates the point in profound expositions of its commandments.[18] There is in every believer's life a time for law as well as a time for grace (26:341). But when the conscience of the believer is troubled by the ongoing struggle with sin, then grace, not law, must prevail. Here the believing bride must return to the bridal chamber with the divine Groom; law, with its demands and threats, must not be allowed to intrude (26:120).

Calvin and Canonical Paul[19]

While students of Paul will differ in their assessments of Luther as a reader of the apostle, it is perfectly clear that Luther's understanding of scripture in general, and of what scripture more specifically says about law, is based on his reading of Paul. Consider, for example, Luther's understanding of Christ's moral teaching, of God's law as extolled (for example) in Psalm 19, and of the epistle of James. The moral teachings of Christ himself are categorized as law and contrasted with the gospel, a distinction Luther derived from Paul (see 26:10-11, 150). All the glories ascribed to the law in Psalm 19 are retained, but they are attributed to "the word" ("the word 'law' is used for God's Word, as is common and customary in Holy Scripture" [12:142, on Ps. 19:7]).[20] If James differs from Paul, the solution is straightforward: James must be wrong (35:395-96).[21] Generally speaking, one does not find, before the rise of historical-critical approaches to scripture, discussions specifically of Paul's understand-

18. See *Treatise on Good Works* (44:21-114); *The Large Catechism of Martin Luther* (Philadelphia: Fortress, 1959), 9-55.

19. By "canonical Paul," I mean the letters of Paul when read with the conviction that their message coheres with that of scripture as a whole. What Paul writes can thus be used to illuminate other parts of scripture, and other parts of scripture can be drawn on to illuminate Paul.

20. On "the word" in Luther, see Jaroslav Pelikan, *Luther the Expositor: Introduction to the Reformer's Exegetical Writings* (St. Louis: Concordia, 1959), 48-70.

21. For this and other reasons, Luther did not believe the epistle of James should be included among the "genuine sacred books"; he was not, however, inclined to impose this view on others (35:395-97).

ing of the law, or that of any other single author of scripture; after all, where the primary author of scripture throughout is taken to be the Holy Spirit, it follows that anything said within its compass forms part of a coherent whole. This remains Luther's way of thinking as well: he believes that he is simply clarifying what scripture says about the law. The terms in which he does so, however, are clearly defined by his reading of Paul.

But if Luther reads (and defines!) the canon of scripture in Pauline terms, we may say that John Calvin, by way of contrast, reads Paul from a canonical perspective. In the remainder of this essay, I hope to illustrate the latter point in relation to the law.[22]

As we have seen, Luther characteristically contrasts law and gospel, in a usage that (I have argued) is essentially faithful to Paul, though (among other things) it requires him to read what is said of "the law" in the Psalms as referring to God's "word." Calvin reverses the order. He finds ways (as we will see) to deal with the Pauline passages, but allows the term "law" in the Psalms to stand, and (in a non-Pauline way) makes of "law" the all-encompassing term for God's dealings with humankind. In this, (for Calvin) its proper sense, "law" is not contrasted with "gospel," but embraces it: "David, in praising [the law], as he here does [Psalm 19], speaks of the whole doctrine of the law, which includes also the gospel, and, therefore, under the law he comprehends Christ" (*Com. Ps.* 19:8; cf. *Com. Isa.*, preface).[23]

The point, for Calvin, is that since the divine plan for humankind has remained constant throughout the ages, there can be no contrast between the Mosaic law (rightly understood) and the gospel, nor should one speak of different covenants: the "eternal and inviolable covenant" God made with Abraham governs God's relations with his people in all ages.[24] The salvation

22. References to Calvin's commentaries on Old Testament books are taken from *Calvin's Commentaries* (45 vols.; Edinburgh: Calvin Translation Society, 1844-56; repr. in 23 vols.; Grand Rapids: Baker, 2009); for those to commentaries on books from the New Testament, see *Calvin's New Testament Commentaries* (ed. David W. Torrance and Thomas F. Torrance; Grand Rapids: Eerdmans, 1959-72); for Calvin's *Institutes,* see *Institutes of the Christian Religion* (ed. John T. McNeill; trans. Ford Lewis Battles; 2 vols.; Philadelphia: Westminster, 1960).

23. For "law" as the entire "doctrine" of scripture (including, specifically, the gospel), see also *Com. Isa.* 2:3; *Com. Jer.* 31:34.

24. The penchant of Calvin (and of a host of interpreters in his wake) to speak of, and give fundamental importance to, a single divine "covenant" again lacks a basis in Paul's writings: there the term occurs but rarely, and when it does, a contrast between a "new" covenant and an "old" is generally implied if not explicit (see 1 Cor. 11:25; 2 Cor. 3:6, 14; Gal. 4:24; and note the "covenants" [plural] of Rom. 9:4; also Eph. 2:12). Calvin's general point can, of course, stand: God (as Paul, too, understood God) had a single plan for redemption in mind from all

enjoyed by Christians today represents the fulfillment of the promise given to Abraham that blessing would come through his "seed" (*Com. Exod.* 19:1; *Com. Jer.* 31:31).[25] For Calvin, it was no new covenant that was enacted at Mount Sinai, but a renewal of the covenant given to Abraham.[26] In this renewed form of the covenant, salvation in Christ found a place in the way various ceremonial laws foreshadowed his redemptive work.[27] If scripture nonetheless speaks of an "old" covenant and a "new," it refers to differences in form,[28] not substance, between God's dealings with his church before and after the coming of Christ (*Com. Jer.* 31:31; cf. *Inst.* 2.10.1; 2.11.1). It should also, of course, be said that the grace of the gospel was not fully revealed until the coming of Christ (*Com. John* 1:17): with the arrival of the reality to which Old Testament figures and types had pointed, God could now speak "openly" rather than "under a veil," as he had done through Moses (*Com. Jer.* 31:31; cf. 31:33). But that which is fulfilled and openly spoken of in the New Testament remains in substance the same as that which was foreshadowed and obscurely presented in the Old; only the form has changed.

> The ancient ceremonies . . . were like the rough outlines which are the foreshadowings of the living picture. Before they put on the true colours with paint artists usually draw an outline in pencil of the representation which they intend. . . . The apostle has established this difference between the Law and the Gospel, that the former has foreshadowed in elementary and sketchy outline what today has been expressed in living and graphically printed colour. . . . It is to be noticed that the things which were shown to [the Old Testament fathers] from a distance are the same as those which are now set before our eyes. Both are shown the same Christ,

eternity. My observation here is simply that Calvin's language marks a clear departure from Paul — though I would add that precision in Pauline interpretation even today is not helped by using Pauline terms in non-Pauline ways. See *Perspectives,* 286-96.

25. Here, to be sure, Galatians 3 and Romans 4 provide the basis for Calvin's claim.

26. Note, again, by way of contrast, how Paul treats the law given to Moses as different in its very essence from the promise given to Abraham, though he finds a place for both in God's purposes (Gal. 3:17-21; Rom. 4:13-16).

27. "The gospel did not so supplant the entire law as to bring forward a different way of salvation. Rather, it confirmed and satisfied whatever the law had promised, and gave substance to the shadows" (*Inst.* 2.9.4).

28. Though God desires only the spiritual worship spoken of in the New Testament, he accommodated himself to human weakness in enjoining the external rites of Israel's worship as a kind of "preparatory training" for children (*Com. Isa.* 1:13; *Com. John* 4:23; *Inst.* 2.7.1).

the same justice, sanctification, and salvation. Only in the manner of the painting is there difference. (*Com. Heb.* 10:1)

But what has happened, we may well want to ask Calvin, to the law element of "law"? And does not Paul declare that the Mosaic law has been done away, and that believers have "died" to its statutes (Rom. 7:4-6; Gal. 2:19; 3:19-25)? Surely here there is a substantial difference between what we must nonetheless take to be an old covenant and a new? Calvin solves the problems by suggesting that "law" is used in different ways, and by distinguishing between the use and the abuse of God's eternal law.

Calvin sees the Mosaic law as consisting essentially of two parts: "a promise of salvation and eternal life, and a rule for a godly and holy living" (*Com. Hos.*, argument).[29] The essence of the latter is found in the Decalogue: "Nothing can be wanted as the rule of a good and upright life beyond the Ten Commandments" (*Mosaic Harmony*, preface).[30] In the Ten Commandments, the difference between good and evil is set forth. That difference remains, whether or not human beings respect it; the content of "a good and upright life" is not subject to change. In fact, of course, human beings do not obey God's moral law, and the law condemns them: that is why Paul can speak of the "ministry" of the law *tout court* as one of condemnation and death (2 Cor. 3:7, 9). This effect of the law, however, is "accidental" to its nature, determined by human response to its demands rather than by the nature of those demands themselves (*Com. Acts* 7:38). Like Luther, Calvin sees a divine purpose in the way the disobeyed law makes evident human corruption and liability to judgment, thus driving sinful human beings to seek grace in the Savior (*Com. John* 16:10; *Inst.* 2.5.6-8). But for Calvin, the same law whose service Paul calls a ministry of death is said by David (in Psalm 19) to be "sweeter than honey and more to be desired than gold. . . . It cheers hearts, converts to the Lord and quickens." Paul, he concludes, is speaking of the law's effect on sinners; David, of how the same law affects those born again by God's Spirit (*Com. 1 John* 5:3). Thus, taking (we may say) his cue from David, Calvin sees the moral law of the Ten Commandments as still applying to believers: in the "perfection to which it exhorts us, the law points out the goal toward which throughout life we are to strive" (*Inst.* 2.7.13). It is only from the law's condemnation and curse that

29. Calvin goes on to add that the law has a third part, allowing a separate category for the "threatenings and reproofs" that are designed to restore transgressors to the fear of God (*Com. Hos.*, argument; cf. *Com. Isa.*, preface).

30. *Mosaic Harmony* refers to Calvin's commentary on Exodus through Deuteronomy (*Commentary on the Last Four Books of Moses, Arranged in the Form of a Harmony*).

believers are delivered. And even these aspects of the law are not simply done away; rather, believers are freed from their effects because Christ has borne them (*Inst.* 2.7.15).

Nor will Calvin allow that the ceremonial parts of the law have been eliminated. They were commanded, and meant to be observed, not for their own sake — on their own, they are "vain and trifling" — but for the sake of the Christ to whom they pointed (*Mosaic Harmony,* preface). And, to be sure, they need no longer be observed now that their educational and foreshadowing work has been accomplished. But it is only the observance that has ended; what the ceremonial commandments of the law signified remains and is of lasting importance. "So Christ's coming did not take anything away, even from the ceremonies. . . . One does not do away with ceremonies, when their reality is kept, and their shadow omitted" (*Com. Matt.* 5:17-18; cf. *Inst.* 2.7.16).[31] In this way, the law — including both its moral and its ceremonial provisions — is seen to be eternal; the gospel is seen to be contained in the law; and Christ is seen as the law's "goal" or fulfillment (see Rom. 10:4).

But does not Paul often distinguish the law, its commands and condemnation, from Christ, the gospel, and the grace of salvation? Calvin (of course) grants the point since, for Calvin, too, what Paul says on the subject must find a place in a proper understanding of the law even if (as I am arguing) it is not allowed to shape that understanding. Calvin insists that in these Pauline texts, "law" is being used to mean something less than "law," properly speaking.[32] When contrasted with the gospel, what the law shares with the gospel — the work and grace of Christ, foreshadowed in its ceremonies — is left out of the picture, so that only what is distinctive of the law remains: its demands and the threats of judgment for transgressors (*Com. Rom.* 10:5; *Com. 2 Cor.* 3:7).[33] Paul, Calvin suggests, found it important to speak in this way in responding to

31. Thus when scripture says that statutes concerning the tabernacle's candlestick and lamps are to be observed "forever," the point is that they were to be observed until the day when the reality was revealed of which they were a type (*Com. Exod.* 27:20-21).

32. C. E. B. Cranfield, in the spirit of Calvin but with his own distinctive twist, claimed that Paul used νόμος to mean "legalism" (he cannot have meant the Mosaic law as such) when he contrasted it with the gospel. For references and discussion, see *Perspectives,* 201-8, 330-35.

33. "Without Christ there is in the law nothing but inexorable rigour, which adjudges all mankind to the wrath and curse of God. And farther, without Christ, there remains within us a rebelliousness of the flesh, which kindles in our hearts a hatred of God and of his law, and from this proceed the distressing bondage and awful terror of which the Apostle speaks. . . . The design of Paul is to show what the law can do for us, taken by itself; that is to say, what it can do for us when, without the promise of grace, it strictly and rigorously exacts from us the duty which we owe to God" (*Com. Ps.* 19:8).

people who misused the law and wished to make observance of its ceremonial demands binding even on believers (*Mosaic Harmony,* "Use of the Law"). But the "bare" law of which he speaks in these contexts is not the law in its fullness; it is the law apart from Christ (*Com. Gal.* 4:24) — and apart from Christ, the law is like a dead body without a soul (*Com. John* 9:28). "If you separate the Law from Christ nothing remains in it save empty shapes" (*Com. John* 1:17; cf. *Com. 2 Cor.* 3:17). "Without Christ the whole ministry of Moses vanishes" (*Com. John* 5:46).

This is surely an impressive attempt at formulating a biblical theology of law; by no means do I intend to disparage its merits when I point out that, though what Paul says about the law finds a place in Calvin's scheme, the scheme itself is not readily derived from Paul's writings. Here "law" is made the all-encompassing designation for God's eternal plan, not the temporary institution of which Paul speaks (added 430 years after the divine promise to Abraham and in force only until the latter found its fulfillment in the coming of the promised "seed" [Gal. 3:17-19; cf. 3:23-25; 4:1-5; also 2 Cor. 3:11, 14]). Paul nowhere speaks of the demands of the law as though, taken by themselves, they represent the law deprived of its essence (the "bare" law).[34] On the contrary, the essence of the law for Paul lies precisely in its commandments and the attendant promise of life for those who obey them (Rom. 10:5; Gal. 3:12, citing Lev. 18:5). Because the essence of the law lies in commandments that require doing but are not done, Paul concludes that "righteousness" cannot come through the law but must come through faith (Rom. 3:19-22; Gal. 2:16; 3:10-13, 19-22). By Calvin's scheme, righteousness, in effect, does come through the law, once it is rightly understood.[35]

34. To be sure, a Pauline basis for speaking of the law apart from Christ as deprived of its essence (and thus a "bare" law) can be found if one interprets the ambiguous Romans 10:4 to say that Christ is the "goal" rather than the "end" of the law. Even here, however, "end" appears the more natural reading (see *Perspectives,* 300, 329-30, 399); and texts like Romans 10:5 and Galatians 3:12 speak straightforwardly enough of what Paul sees as the essence of the law. Romans 8:3-4 portrays the work of God's Son, not as the essence of the law when it is rightly understood, but as the remedy for the law's essential weakness (see also Gal. 3:2-5). In 1 Corinthians 15:56, Paul introduces (quite gratuitously in this context) what he takes to be axiomatic about the law ("the power of sin is the law"); the term is here hardly equivalent to the whole counsel of God. It is, moreover, characteristic of Paul (as we have seen) to contrast faith with the law.

35. Very much in the spirit of Calvin, though so curious an exegetical maneuver that not even he entertained it, is the interpretation (advanced initially by Gerhard Friedrich and Eduard Lohse) of "law of faith" in Romans 3:27 as referring to the Mosaic law and indicating

Conclusion

Consideration of Paul's understanding of the law is characteristic of historical-critical scholarship. In earlier periods, it was assumed that what Paul says on the subject forms but a part of the Holy Spirit's teaching; for the (coherent) whole, one must read Pauline texts together with other relevant texts in scripture. Both Luther and Calvin did so. But Luther read "other relevant texts in scripture" in the light of his understanding of Paul (an understanding that, to my mind, is essentially faithful to the apostle); Calvin found a place for Pauline texts in his understanding of law, but read them in the light of his understanding of "other relevant texts in scripture."

Tell it not in Gath, but it seems to me that this brief study highlights a weakness in premodern readings of the Bible to which historical-critical scholarship provides a needed corrective. Let it be said at once that it works both ways. I am myself among those convinced that modern students of the Bible have much to learn from premodern interpretations: for one thing (though much else could be said), inasmuch as our forebears wrestled to find coherence in the biblical text, they offer their own corrective to the contemporary penchant to settle too readily (if not complacently) in a judgment of diversity or contradiction not only between the writings of different biblical authors, but even within different verses in the same text. The point here, however, is that the delight of (some) modern scholars in facile findings of diversity represents but one extreme of the pendulum. At the other extreme, ironically enough, we find that the very reverence for scripture shown by our forebears, combined with a conviction of its coherence, led not infrequently to facile harmonizations and dubious attempts at systematization that no less obviously distort the texts.

It is, to be sure, natural to human beings — in the language of another day, it would even be called their "glory" — to want to bring order to the world of their experience; to reduce the incomprehensible to comprehension; to find, within their paradigms of thought, a place for phenomena that appear contradictory. And biblical scholarship is eminently a human undertaking. When modern scholars find diversity within the writings of scripture, they are in fact fitting texts within preferred contemporary paradigms of thought no less than the premoderns did when they found coherence; the latter observation, however, is the issue for the moment. I have already pointed out how Calvin, in search of a way of speaking about law that can apply to all the biblical texts,

---

that, properly understood, that law calls for faith, not works (refuted, to my mind, decisively by Räisänen; for references, see *Perspectives*, 322-25).

failed to do justice to the radical nature of much that Paul says on the subject. Luther, for his part, captured important Pauline emphases in his distinction between law and gospel; and it should be remembered (it is often forgotten) that Luther saw a continuing place for "law" even in the life of the believer. Nonetheless, it seems clear (to me at least) that when the term "law" — in Luther's sense, and as opposed to "gospel" — is applied to the ethical teaching of Jesus and the exhortations in the epistles, the force of these texts has been blunted. Can a firm distinction between "law" and "gospel" really serve as the key to understanding the Gospel of Matthew? Or the book of Deuteronomy? Or the Psalms?

What, then, is the student of scripture to do in cases such as this, where interpreters even of the stature of Luther and Calvin seem incapable of convincingly reconciling different biblical texts?

1. Many will be content to see disunity in such cases. Indeed, as suggested above, the fashion of our day is to celebrate the Bible's diversity, particularly inasmuch as it appears sufficient to refute earlier understandings of scripture and approaches to biblical interpretation.

2. Those disinclined to follow the fashion of the day, or whose conviction that scripture is the word of God carries with it the corollary that, appearances notwithstanding, its writings are coherent, will continue the search for unity. It is not difficult (for example) to show that much that distinguishes Luther's view of the law in scripture from that of Calvin pertains to terminology rather than to substance.[36] In principle, there can be nothing inappropriate in searching for coherence even in cases where earlier attempts have proven inadequate. After all, cheap claims of disunity discredit biblical scholarship no less than cheap harmonizations.

3. Where the search for coherence brings no convincing results, the believer need feel no shame in admitting as much: to acknowledge one's limitations is not to compromise the faith! Our interpretations may be faulty. Or perhaps the error lies in our (human) assumptions about what kind of unity the word of God ought to display: believers' expectations of what God's word ought to look like have certainly proven unfounded in the past.[37] In any case, given

36. Though (as we have seen) Luther and Calvin differ widely in their understanding of the term "law" (there is, indeed, much overlap between what Calvin means by "law" and what Luther means by God's "word"), they agree (i) that the laws of Moses serve to show the inherent sinfulness of humankind and the need of the sinner for the grace of the gospel; (ii) that the Decalogue sums up the will of God for all human beings; (iii) that the ceremonial laws of Moses foreshadowed the work of Christ and are no longer to be observed by his followers.

37. Much grief would have been spared had, for example, Galileo's opponents recognized

that believers readily acknowledge that the Creator's ways and thoughts are far beyond their own, they need not hesitate to concede that parts of God's word defy their comprehension.

4. Prepared though believers ought to be to acknowledge that "the secret things belong to the LORD our God," they will also want to search out fully all that has been "revealed" (Deut. 29:29). In my view (as argued above), Luther failed in his attempt to identify the single hermeneutical key to all of scripture, and Calvin failed in his attempt to organize all that scripture says about "law" into a single comprehensive scheme. I do not, however, think their attempts misguided. Given that the ultimate authority on which formulations of Christian doctrine must be based is the Bible, and given that the preservation and transmission of Christian faith require such formulations, it is essential that those so gifted within communities of faith wrestle with the biblical texts in attempting to arrive at a coherent understanding of the truth they convey.

The reminder remains nonetheless in order: however divine the subject matter, systematic theology, like biblical scholarship, is eminently a human undertaking. That it be undertaken is essential to the health of Christian communities. That its proposals be carefully measured against the biblical texts is equally essential. That its most persuasive results amount to no more than "raid[s] on the inarticulate with shabby equipment" is inevitable.

---

that possibility at the outset. Galileo appropriately cited Augustine in noting that discredit is brought on scripture and the Christian faith when zealots, claiming the Bible in support, argue for positions others know to be false ("Letter to the Grand Duchess Christina [1615]," in *Discoveries and Opinions of Galileo* [trans. Stillman Drake; Garden City: Doubleday, 1957], 206-9).

Bibliography

Abramovitz, Hayim Yitshak. *Va-hai bahem: pikuah nefesh ba-halakhah: leket mekorot meforashim me-rishone ha-tanaim ve-ʾad aharone ha-poskim.* Jerusalem: Orot, 1957. [in Hebrew]

Adamson, James B. *James: The Man and His Message.* Grand Rapids: Eerdmans, 1989.

Alexander, Philip S. "Jesus and the Golden Rule." Pages 363-88 in *Hillel and Jesus: Comparative Studies of Two Major Religious Leaders.* Edited by James H. Charlesworth and Loren L. Johns. Minneapolis: Fortress, 1997.

———. "Jewish Law in the Time of Jesus: Towards a Clarification of the Problem." Pages 44-58 in *Law and Religion: Essays on the Place of the Law in Israel and Early Christianity.* Edited by Barnabas Lindars. Cambridge: James Clarke, 1988.

Allison, Dale C. *A Critical and Exegetical Commentary on the Epistle of James.* ICC. New York: Bloomsbury T&T Clark, 2013.

———. *Studies in Matthew: Interpretation Past and Present.* Grand Rapids: Baker Academic, 2005.

Ashwin-Siejkowski, Piotr. *Clement of Alexandria: A Project of Christian Perfection.* London: T&T Clark, 2008.

Attridge, Harold W. *The Interpretation of Biblical History in the* Antiquitates Judaicae *of Flavius Josephus.* HDR 7. Missoula: Scholars, 1976.

Badenas, Robert. *Christ the End of the Law: Romans 10.4 in Pauline Perspective.* JSNTSup 10. Sheffield: JSOT, 1985.

Baer, David A., and Robert P. Gordon. "חסד." Pages 211-18 in vol. 2 of *New International Dictionary of Old Testament Theology and Exegesis.* Edited by Willem A. VanGemeren. 5 vols. Grand Rapids: Zondervan, 1997.

Banks, Robert J. *Jesus and the Law in the Synoptic Tradition.* SNTSMS 28. Cambridge: Cambridge University Press, 1975.

Barclay, John M. G. "'Do We Undermine the Law?' A Study of Romans 14.1–15.6." Pages 287-308 in *Paul and the Mosaic Law.* Edited by James D. G. Dunn. WUNT I 89. Tübingen: Mohr Siebeck, 1996.

———. *Flavius Josephus: Translation and Commentary,* vol. 10, *Against Apion*. Leiden: Brill, 2007.

———. "Paul and Philo on Circumcision: Romans 2:25-29 in Social and Cultural Context." Pages 61-79 in *Pauline Churches and Diaspora Jews*. WUNT I 275. Tübingen: Mohr Siebeck, 2011.

Barr, James. *The Semantics of Biblical Language*. London: Oxford University Press, 1961.

Barrett, C. K. *The First Epistle to the Corinthians*. HNTC. New York: Harper & Row, 1954.

Barton, John. *Oracles of God: Perceptions of Ancient Prophecy in Israel after the Exile*. London: Darton, Longman and Todd, 1986. Repr., New York: Oxford University Press, 1988.

Bauckham, Richard. "James, 1 and 2 Peter, Jude." Pages 303-15 in *It Is Written: Scripture Citing Scripture: Essays in Honour of Barnabas Lindars, SSF*. Edited by D. A. Carson and H. G. M. Williamson. Cambridge: Cambridge University Press, 1988.

———. *James: Wisdom of James, Disciple of Jesus the Sage*. New Testament Readings. London: Routledge, 1999.

———. "James and the Gentiles (Acts 15.13-21)." Pages 154-84 in *History, Literature and Society in the Book of Acts*. Edited by Ben Witherington III. Cambridge: Cambridge University Press, 1996.

Beker, J. Christiaan. *Paul the Apostle: The Triumph of God in Life and Thought*. Philadelphia: Fortress, 1980.

Bell, Richard H. *Provoked to Jealousy: The Origin and Purpose of the Jealousy Motif in Romans 9–11*. WUNT II 63. Tübingen: Mohr Siebeck, 1994.

Berg, Shane. "Sin's Corruption of the Knowledge of God and the Law in Romans 1–8." Pages 119-38 in *The Unrelenting God: Essays on God's Action in Scripture in Honor of Beverly Roberts Gaventa*. Edited by David J. Downs and Matthew L. Skinner. Grand Rapids: Eerdmans, 2013.

Bernier, Jonathan. Aposynagōgos *and the Historical Jesus in John: Rethinking the Historicity of the Johannine Expulsion Passages*. Biblical Interpretation Series 122. Leiden: Brill, 2013.

Betz, Hans Dieter. *Der Apostel Paulus und die sokratische Tradition: Eine exegetische Untersuchung zu seiner Apologie 2 Korinther, 10–13*. BHT 45. Tübingen: Mohr Siebeck, 1972.

Binder, Donald D. *Into the Temple Courts: The Place of the Synagogues in the Second Temple Period*. Atlanta: Society of Biblical Literature, 1999.

———. "The Mystery of the Magdala Stone." Pages 17-48 in *City Set on a Hill: Essays in Honor of James F. Strange*. Edited by Daniel Warner and Donald D. Binder. Mountain Home, Ark.: BorderStone, 2014.

———. "The Synagogue and the Gentiles." Pages 109-25 in *Attitudes to Gentiles in Ancient Judaism and Early Christianity*. Edited by David C. Sim and James S. McLaren. LNTS 499. London: Bloomsbury T&T Clark, 2013.

Blenkinsopp, Joseph. *Sage, Priest, Prophet: Religious and Intellectual Leadership in Ancient Israel*. Louisville: Westminster John Knox, 1995.

Blomberg, Craig L. "The Law in Luke-Acts." *JSNT* 22 (1984): 53-80.

Bobichon, Philippe. *Justin Martyr: Dialogue avec Tryphon: édition critique, traduction, commentaire*. 2 vols. Paradosis 47. Fribourg: Academic, 2003.

Bockmuehl, Markus. *Jewish Law in Gentile Churches: Halakhah and the Beginning of Christian Public Ethics*. Edinburgh: T&T Clark, 2000.

Borgen, Peder. *The Gospel of John: More Light from Philo, Paul and Archaeology: The Scriptures, Tradition, Exposition, Settings, Meaning*. NovTSup 154. Leiden: Brill, 2014.

Bovon, François. "The Law in Luke-Acts." Pages 59-73 in *Studies in Early Christianity*. Grand Rapids: Baker Academic, 2005.

Boyarin, Daniel. *Border Lines: The Partition of Judaeo-Christianity*. Philadelphia: University of Philadelphia Press, 2004.

Broadie, Sarah. "Rational Theology." Pages 205-24 in *The Cambridge Companion to Early Greek Philosophy*. Edited by A. A. Long. Cambridge: Cambridge University Press, 1999.

Brown, Alexandra R. *The Cross and Human Transformation: Paul's Apocalyptic Word in 1 Corinthians*. Minneapolis: Fortress, 1995.

Brown, Raymond E. *The Gospel according to John: A New Translation with Introduction and Commentary*. 2 vols. AB 29. Garden City: Doubleday, 1966-70.

Bruce, F. F. *The Book of the Acts*. Rev. ed. NICNT. Grand Rapids: Eerdmans, 1988.

Brueggemann, Walter. *Theology of the Old Testament*. Minneapolis: Fortress, 1997.

Bryan, Christopher. "A Further Look at Acts 16:1-3." *JBL* 107, no. 2 (1988): 292-94.

Buell, Denise Kimber. *Why This New Race: Ethnic Reasoning in Early Christianity*. New York: Columbia University Press, 2005.

Bultmann, Rudolf. "The Significance of the Old Testament for the Christian Faith." Pages 8-35 in *The Old Testament and Christian Faith: A Theological Discussion*. Edited by Bernhard W. Anderson. New York: Harper & Row, 1963.

———. *Theologie des Neuen Testaments*. Tübingen: Mohr Siebeck, 1953.

Burridge, Richard A. *Imitating Jesus: An Inclusive Approach to New Testament Ethics*. Grand Rapids: Eerdmans, 2007.

Calvin, John. *Calvin's Commentaries*. 45 vols. Edinburgh: Calvin Translation Society, 1844-56.

———. *Calvin's New Testament Commentaries*. Edited by David W. Torrance and Thomas F. Torrance. Grand Rapids: Eerdmans, 1959-72.

———. *Institutes of the Christian Religion*. Edited by John T. McNeill. Translated by Ford Lewis Battles. 2 vols. Philadelphia: Westminster, 1960.

Campbell, Douglas A. "Galatians 5.11: Evidence of an Early Law-Observant Mission by Paul?" *NTS* 57, no. 3 (2011): 325-47.

Campenhausen, Hans von. *The Formation of the Christian Bible*. Translated by John Austen Baker. London: A&C Black, 1972.

Caragounis, Chrys C. *The Development of Greek and the New Testament: Morphology, Syntax, Phonology, and Textual Transmission*. Grand Rapids: Baker Academic, 2006.

Carras, George P. "Philo's *Hypothetica*, Josephus' *Contra Apionem* and the Question of

Sources." Pages 431-50 in *Society of Biblical Literature Seminar Papers 1990*. Edited by David J. Lull. Atlanta: Scholars, 1990.

Carson, D. A. "James." Pages 997-1013 in *Commentary on the New Testament Use of the Old Testament*. Edited by G. K. Beale and D. A. Carson. Grand Rapids: Baker Academic, 2007.

Chancey, Mark A. *The Myth of a Gentile Galilee*. SNTSMS 118. Cambridge: Cambridge University Press, 2002.

Chilton, Bruce. *Rabbi Jesus: An Intimate Biography*. New York: Image, 2000.

Chrysostom, John. *Chrysostom: Homilies on the Gospel of Saint Matthew*. Edited by Philip Schaff. NPNF 10. Peabody: Hendrickson, 1994.

Cicero, Marcus Tullius. *De officiis*. Translated by Walter Miller. LCL 30. Cambridge: Harvard University Press, 1913.

———. *On the Republic, On the Laws*. Translated by Clinton Walker Keyes. LCL 213. Cambridge: Harvard University Press, 1928.

Cohen, Shaye J. D. *The Beginnings of Jewishness: Boundaries, Varieties, Uncertainties*. Berkeley: University of California Press, 1999.

Conzelmann, Hans. *1 Corinthians*. Hermeneia. Philadelphia: Fortress, 1975.

———. *The Theology of St. Luke*. New York: Harper & Row, 1961.

Cosaert, Carl P. *The Text of the Gospels in Clement of Alexandria*. New Testament in the Greek Fathers 9. Atlanta: Society of Biblical Literature, 2008.

Cranfield, C. E. B. *A Critical and Exegetical Commentary on the Epistle to the Romans*. 2 vols. ICC. Edinburgh: T&T Clark, 1975-79.

Crossley, James G. *The Date of Mark's Gospel: Insight from the Law in Earliest Christianity*. JSNTSup 266. London: T&T Clark, 2004.

Culpepper, R. Alan. *The Gospel and Letters of John*. Nashville: Abingdon, 1998.

Dahl, Nils Alstrup. "'A People for His Name' (Acts XV. 14)." *NTS* 4 (1957): 319-27.

Davids, Peter H. "James and Jesus." Pages 63-84 in *The Jesus Tradition outside the Gospels*. Edited by David Wenham. Gospel Perspectives 5. Sheffield: JSOT, 1985.

Davies, W. D., and Dale C. Allison. *A Critical and Exegetical Commentary on the Gospel according to Saint Matthew*. 3 vols. ICC. Edinburgh: T&T Clark, 1988-97.

Davis, Ellen F. *Proverbs, Ecclesiastes, and the Song of Songs*. Westminster Bible Companion. Louisville: Westminster John Knox, 2000.

Dawson, David. *Allegorical Readers and Cultural Revision in Ancient Alexandria*. Berkeley: University of California Press, 1992.

Dearman, J. Andrew. *The Book of Hosea*. NICOT. Grand Rapids: Eerdmans, 2010.

De Boer, Martinus C. *The Defeat of Death: Apocalyptic Eschatology in 1 Corinthians 15 and Romans 5*. JSNTSup 22. Sheffield: Sheffield Academic, 1988.

Deines, Roland. *Jüdische Steingefäße und pharisäische Frömmigkeit. Ein archäologisch-historischer Beitrag zum Verständnis von Johannes 2,6 und der jüdischen Reinheitshalacha zur Zeit Jesu*. WUNT II 52. Tübingen: Mohr Siebeck, 1993.

Dillon, John M. *The Middle Platonists: A Study of Platonism, 80 B.C. to A.D. 220*. London: Duckworth, 1977.

Dodd, C. H. *The Parables of the Kingdom*. New York: Charles Scribner's Sons, 1961.

Doering, Lutz. "Sabbath Laws in the New Testament Gospels." Pages 207-53 in *The New Testament and Rabbinic Literature*. Edited by Reimund Bieringer, Florention Garcia Martinez, Didier Pollefeyt, and Peter J. Tomson. JSJSup 136. Leiden: Brill, 2010.

———. *Schabbat: Sabbathalacha und -praxis im antiken Judentum und Urchristentum*. TSAJ 78. Tübingen: Mohr Siebeck, 1999.

Donahue, John R., and Daniel J. Harrington. *The Gospel of Mark*. SP 2. Collegeville: Liturgical, 2002.

Donaldson, Terence L. "'Gentile Christianity' as a Category in the Study of Christian Origins." *HTR* 106, no. 4 (2013): 433-58.

———. *Judaism and the Gentiles: Jewish Patterns of Universalism (to 135 CE)*. Waco: Baylor University Press, 2007.

———. *Paul and the Gentiles: Remapping the Apostle's Convictional World*. Minneapolis: Fortress, 1997.

Downing, Gerald F. "Law and Custom: Luke-Acts and Late Hellenism." Pages 148-58 in *Law and Religion: Essays on the Place of the Law in Israel and Early Christianity*. Edited by Barnabas Lindars. Cambridge: James Clarke, 1988.

Droge, Arthur J. *Homer or Moses?: Early Christian Interpretations of the History of Culture*. HUT 26. Tübingen: Mohr Siebeck, 1989.

Dunn, James D. G. *Romans*. 2 vols. WBC. Waco: Word, 1988.

Dupont, Jacques. *Gnosis. La connaissance religieuse dans les Épîtres de Saint Paul*. Paris: Gabalda, 1949.

Ebeling, Gerhard. "Existenz zwischen Gott und Gott: ein Beitrag zur Frage nach der Existenz Gottes." *ZTK* 62, no. 1 (1965): 86-113.

Edwards, Mark J. "Clement of Alexandria and His Doctrine of the Logos." *VC* 54, no. 2 (2000): 159-77.

Ensor, Peter W. "Justin Martyr and Penal Substitutionary Atonement." *EvQ* 83, no. 3 (2011): 217-32.

Esler, Philip Francis. *Community and Gospel in Luke-Acts: The Social and Political Motivations of Lucan Theology*. SNTSMS 57. Cambridge: Cambridge University Press, 1987.

Esler, Philip Francis, and Ronald A. Piper. *Lazarus, Mary and Martha: Social-Scientific Approaches to the Gospel of John*. Minneapolis: Fortress, 2006.

Estes, Douglas F. "Wisdom and Biblical Theology." Pages 853-58 in *Dictionary of the Old Testament: Wisdom, Poetry and Writings*. Edited by Peter Enns and Tremper Longman III. Downers Grove: IVP Academic, 2008.

Fee, Gordon D. *The First Epistle to the Corinthians*. NICNT. Grand Rapids: Eerdmans, 1987.

Feldman, Louis H. *Jew and Gentile in the Ancient World*. Princeton: Princeton University Press, 1993.

Fishbane, Michael. *Biblical Interpretation in Ancient Israel*. Oxford: Clarendon, 1985.

Fletcher-Louis, Crispin H. T. "The Destruction of the Temple and the Relativization of the Old Covenant: Mark 13:31 and Matthew 5:18." Pages 145-69 in *"The Reader Must Understand": Eschatology in Bible and Theology*. Edited by Kent E. Brower and Mark W. Elliott. Leicester: Apollos, 1997.

Foster, Paul. *Community, Law, and Mission in Matthew's Gospel*. WUNT II 177. Tübingen: Mohr Siebeck, 2004.

France, Richard T. *The Gospel of Mark: A Commentary on the Greek Text*. NIGTC. Grand Rapids: Eerdmans, 2002.

———. *The Gospel of Matthew*. NICNT. Grand Rapids: Eerdmans, 2007.

Galilei, Galileo. *Discoveries and Opinions of Galileo*. Translated by Stillman Drake. Garden City: Doubleday, 1957.

Gaston, Lloyd. *Paul and the Torah*. Vancouver: University of British Columbia Press, 1987.

Gaventa, Beverly Roberts. *The Acts of the Apostles*. ANTC. Nashville: Abingdon, 2003.

———. "The Character of God's Faithfulness: A Response to N. T. Wright." *Journal for the Study of Paul and His Letters* 4, no. 1 (2014): 71-80.

———. "On the Calling-Into-Being of Israel: Romans 9:6-29." Pages 255-69 in *Between Gospel and Election: Explorations in the Interpretation of Romans 9–11*. Edited by Florian Wilk and J. Ross Wagner with the assistance of Frank Schleritt. WUNT I 257. Tübingen: Mohr Siebeck, 2010.

Gillihan, Yonder Moynihan. *Civic Ideology, Organization, and Law in the Rule Scrolls: A Comparative Study of the Covenanters' Sect and Contemporary Voluntary Associations in Political Context*. STDJ 97. Leiden: Brill, 2012.

Glueck, Nelson. *Hesed in the Bible*. Cincinnati: Hebrew Union College Press, 1967.

Goodenough, Erwin Ramsdell. *By Light, Light: The Mystic Gospel of Hellenistic Judaism*. New Haven: Yale University Press, 1935.

Goulder, M. D. "ΣΟΦΙΑ in 1 Corinthians." *NTS* 37, no. 4 (1991): 516-34.

Grant, Robert M. *Greek Apologists of the Second Century*. Philadelphia: Westminster, 1988.

———. "The Wisdom of the Corinthians." Pages 51-55 in *The Joy of Study: Papers on New Testament and Related Subjects Presented to Honor Frederick Clifton Grant*. Edited by Sherman E. Johnson. New York: Macmillan, 1951.

Gundry, Robert H. *The Use of the Old Testament in St. Matthew's Gospel with Special Reference to the Messianic Hope*. NovTSup 18. Leiden: Brill, 1967.

Haenchen, Ernst. *The Acts of the Apostles: A Commentary*. Hermeneia. Philadelphia: Westminster, 1971.

Hägg, Henny Fiska. *Clement of Alexandria and the Beginnings of Christian Apophaticism*. OECS. Oxford: Oxford University Press, 2006.

Hagner, Donald A. *Matthew 1–13*. WBC 33A. Dallas: Word, 1993.

Halpern-Amaru, Betsy. "Land Theology in Josephus' *Jewish Antiquities*." *JQR* 71, no. 4 (1981): 201-29.

Halton, Thomas P. *St. Justin Martyr: Dialogue with Trypho*. Edited by Michael Slusser. Washington, D.C.: Catholic University of America Press, 2003.

Hardwick, Michael E. *Josephus as an Historical Source in Patristic Literature through Eusebius*. BJS 128. Atlanta: Scholars, 1989.

Harland, Philip A. *Associations, Synagogues, and Congregations: Claiming a Place in Ancient Mediterranean Society*. Minneapolis: Fortress, 2003.

Harnack, Adolf von. "Das Alte Testament in den Paulinischen Briefen und in den Paulinischen Gemeinden." *SPAW* (1928): 124-41.

Hartin, Patrick J. *James and the Q Sayings of Jesus*. JSNTSup 47. Sheffield: JSOT, 1991.

———. "James and the Q Sermon on the Mount/Plain." Pages 440-57 in *Society of Biblical Literature 1989 Seminar Papers*. Edited by David J. Lull. Atlanta: Scholars, 1989.

Hay, David M. "Philo of Alexandria." Pages 357-79 in *Justification and Variegated Nomism*, vol. 1, *The Complexities of Second Temple Judaism*. Edited by D. A. Carson, Peter T. O'Brien, and Mark A. Seifrid. WUNT II 140. Tübingen: Mohr Siebeck, 2001.

Hays, Richard B. "Apocalyptic *Poiēsis* in Galatians: Paternity, Passion, and Participation." Pages 200-219 in *Galatians and Christian Theology: Justification, the Gospel, and Ethics in Paul's Letter*. Edited by Mark W. Elliott, Scott J. Hafemann, N. T. Wright, and John Frederick. Grand Rapids: Baker Academic, 2014.

———. *The Conversion of the Imagination: Paul as Interpreter of Israel's Scripture*. Grand Rapids: Eerdmans, 2005.

———. "The Conversion of the Imagination: Scripture and Eschatology in 1 Corinthians." *NTS* 45, no. 3 (1999): 391-412.

———. *Echoes of Scripture in the Letters of Paul*. New Haven: Yale University Press, 1989.

———. *First Corinthians*. Interpretation. Louisville: John Knox, 1997.

———. *The Moral Vision of the New Testament: Community, Cross, New Creation: A Contemporary Introduction to New Testament Ethics*. New York: HarperCollins, 1996.

———. "The Role of Scripture in Paul's Ethics." Pages 30-47 in *Theology and Ethics in Paul and His Interpreters: Essays in Honor of Victor Paul Furnish*. Edited by Eugene H. Lovering and Jerry L. Sumney. Nashville: Abingdon, 1996.

Hill, David. "On the Use and Meaning of Hosea Vi. 6 in Matthew's Gospel." *NTS* 24, no. 1 (1977): 107-19.

Hoek, Annewies van den. *Clement of Alexandria and His Use of Philo in the* Stromateis: *An Early Christian Reshaping of a Jewish Model*. Supplements to Vigiliae Christianae 3. Leiden: Brill, 1988.

Hollander, John. *The Figure of Echo: A Mode of Allusion in Milton and After*. Berkeley: University of California Press, 1981.

Holtz, Traugott. "Zum Selbstverständnis des Apostels Paulus." *TLZ* 91, no. 5 (1966): 321-30.

Hooker, Morna D. "'Beyond the Things Which Are Written': An Examination of 1 Cor. IV.6." *NTS* 10, no. 1 (1963): 127-32.

Hopkins, Keith. *A World Full of Gods: The Strange Triumph of Christianity*. New York: Free Press, 1999.

Horbury, William. "Extirpation and Excommunication." *VT* 35, no. 1 (1985): 13-38.

Horsley, Richard A. *1 Corinthians*. ANTC. Nashville: Abingdon, 1998.

———. "How Can Some of You Say That There Is No Resurrection of the Dead? Spiritual Elitism in Corinth." *NovT* 20, no. 3 (1978): 203-31.

———. "The Law of Nature in Philo and Cicero." *HTR* 71, nos. 1-2 (1978): 35-59.

Hübner, Hans. *Biblische Theologie des Neuen Testaments*. Vol. 2. Göttingen: Vandenhoeck & Ruprecht, 1993.

Inowlocki, Sabrina. "'Neither Adding nor Omitting Anything': Josephus' Promise Not to Modify the Scriptures in Greek and Latin Context." *JJS* 56, no. 1 (2005): 48-65.

Itter, Andrew C. *Esoteric Teaching in the* Stromateis *of Clement of Alexandria*. Leiden: Brill, 2009.

Jervell, Jacob. "The Church of Jews and Godfearers." Pages 11-20 in *Luke-Acts and the Jewish People: Eight Critical Perspectives*. Edited by Joseph B. Tyson. Minneapolis: Augsburg, 1988.

———. *Luke and the People of God: A New Look at Luke-Acts*. Minneapolis: Augsburg, 1972.

Johansson, Daniel. "*Kyrios* in the Gospel of Mark." *JSNT* 33, no. 1 (2010): 101-24.

Johnson, Luke Timothy. *Among the Gentiles: Greco-Roman Religion and Christianity*. New Haven: Yale University Press, 2009.

———. *Brother of Jesus, Friend of God: Studies in the Letter of James*. Grand Rapids: Eerdmans, 2004.

———. *The Letter of James: A New Translation with Introduction and Commentary*. AB 37A. New York: Doubleday, 1995.

———. *The Literary Function of Possessions in Luke-Acts*. SBLDS 39. Missoula: Scholars, 1977.

Josephus, Flavius. *Josephus*. Translated by H. St J. Thackeray, Ralph Marcus, Allen Wikgren, and Louis H. Feldman. 10 vols. LCL. Cambridge: Harvard University Press, 1926-65.

Kanagaraj, Jey J. "The Implied Ethics of the Fourth Gospel: A Reinterpretation of the Decalogue." *TynBul* 52, no. 1 (2001): 33-60.

Karakolis, Christos. "Semeia Conveying Ethics in the Gospel according to John." Pages 192-212 in *Rethinking the Ethics of John: "Implicit Ethics" in the Johannine Writings*. Edited by Jan G. van der Watt and Ruben Zimmermann. WUNT I 291. Tübingen: Mohr Siebeck, 2012.

Käsemann, Ernst. *Commentary on Romans*. London: SCM, 1980.

———. "Gottesgerechtigkeit bei Paulus." Pages 181-93 in *Exegetische Versuche und Besinnungen*. Vol. 2. Göttingen: Vandenhoeck & Ruprecht, 1964.

———. "On the Subject of Primitive Christian Apocalyptic." Pages 108-37 in *New Testament Questions of Today*. Philadelphia: Fortress, 1969.

———. "Zum Thema der urchristlichen Apokalyptik." Pages 104-31 in *Exegetische Versuche und Besinnungen*. Vol. 2. Göttingen: Vandenhoeck & Ruprecht, 1964.

Keener, Craig S. *The Gospel of John: A Commentary*. 2 vols. Peabody: Hendrickson, 2003.

Keith, Chris. *Jesus against the Scribal Elite: The Origins of the Conflict*. Grand Rapids: Baker Academic, 2014.

Klawans, Jonathan. *Impurity and Sin in Ancient Judaism*. Oxford: Oxford University Press, 2000.

———. *Josephus and the Theologies of Ancient Judaism*. Oxford: Oxford University Press, 2012.

———. "Notions of Gentile Impurity in Ancient Judaism." *AJS Review* 20, no. 2 (1995): 285-312.

Klinghardt, Matthias. *Gesetz und Volk Gottes: das lukanische Verständnis des Gesetzes nach Herkunft, Funktion und seinem Ort in der Geschichte des Urchristentums*. WUNT II 32. Tübingen: Mohr Siebeck, 1988.

Kloppenborg, John S. "Disaffiliation in Associations and the Ἀποσυνάγωγος of John." *HvTSt* 67, no. 1 (2011).

———. "The Emulation of the Jesus Tradition in the Letter of James." Pages 121-50 in *Reading James with New Eyes: Methodological Reassessments of the Letter of James*. Edited by John S. Kloppenborg and Robert L. Webb. LNTS 342. London: T&T Clark, 2007.

———. "The Reception of the Jesus Tradition in James." Pages 91-139 in *The Catholic Epistles and the Tradition*. Edited by Jacques Schlosser. BETL 176. Leuven: Peeters, 2004.

Koch, Dietrich-Alex. *Die Schrift als Zeuge des Evangeliums: Untersuchungen zur Verwendung und zum Verständnis der Schrift bei Paulus*. BHT 69. Tübingen: Mohr Siebeck, 1986.

Konradt, Matthias. *Gericht und Gemeinde: Eine Studie zur Bedeutung und Funktion von Gerichtsaussagen im Rahmen der paulinischen Ekklesiologie und Ethik im 1 Thess und 1 Kor*. BZNW 117. Berlin: De Gruyter, 2003.

———. *Israel, Church, and the Gentiles in the Gospel of Matthew*. BMSEC. Waco: Baylor University Press, 2014.

Korner, Ralph. "Before 'Church': Political, Ethno-Religious and Theological Implications of the Collective Designation of Pauline Christ-Followers as *Ekklēsiai*." Ph.D. diss., McMaster University, 2014.

Kuck, David W. *Judgment and Community Conflict: Paul's Use of Apocalyptic Judgment Language in 1 Corinthians 3:5–4:5*. NovTSup 66. Leiden: Brill, 1992.

Kugel, James L. "Some Unanticipated Consequences of the Sinai Revelation: A Religion of Laws." Pages 1-14 in *The Significance of Sinai: Traditions About Sinai and Divine Revelation in Judaism and Christianity*. Edited by George J. Brooke, Hindy Najman, and Loren T. Stuckenbruck. Themes in Biblical Narrative 12. Leiden: Brill, 2008.

Labahn, Michael. "'It's Only Love' — Is That All? Limits and Potentials of Johannine 'Ethic' — A Critical Evaluation of Research." Pages 3-43 in *Rethinking the Ethics of John: "Implicit Ethics" in the Johannine Writings*. Edited by Jan G. van der Watt and Ruben Zimmermann. WUNT I 291. Tübingen: Mohr Siebeck, 2012.

Lake, Kirsopp. "The Apostolic Council of Jerusalem." Pages 195-212 in vol. 5 of *The Beginnings of Christianity Part I: The Acts of the Apostles*. Edited by Henry J. Cadbury and Kirsopp Lake. 5 vols. London: Macmillan, 1933.

Le Boulluec, Alain. *Clément d'Alexandrie, Les Stromates: Stromate V. Texte. Commentaire.* SC 279. Paris: Éditions du Cerf, 1981.

Levine, Lee I. *The Ancient Synagogue: The First Thousand Years.* New Haven: Yale University Press, 2005.

———. *Visual Judaism in Late Antiquity: Historical Contexts of Jewish Art.* New Haven: Yale University Press, 2012.

Lieu, Judith. *Image and Reality: The Jews in the World of the Christians in the Second Century.* London: T&T Clark, 1996.

———. "The Race of the God-Fearers." *JTS* 46, no. 2 (1995): 483-501.

Lim, Timothy H. "Not in Persuasive Words of Wisdom, but in the Demonstration of the Spirit and Power." *NovT* 29, no. 2 (1987): 137-49.

Lindars, Barnabas, ed. *Law and Religion: Essays on the Place of the Law in Israel and Early Christianity.* Cambridge: James Clarke, 1988.

Lindemann, Andreas. "Die Schrift als Tradition: Beobachtungen zu den biblischen Zitaten im Ersten Korintherbrief." Pages 199-225 in *Schrift und Tradition: Festschrift für Josef Ernst zum 70. Geburtstag.* Edited by Knut Backhaus and Franz Georg Untergassmair. Paderborn: Ferdinand Schöningh, 1996.

Litfin, A. Duane. *St. Paul's Theology of Proclamation: 1 Corinthians 1–4 and Greco-Roman Rhetoric.* SNTSMS 79. Cambridge: Cambridge University Press, 1994.

Livesey, Nina E. "Theological Identity Making: Justin's Use of Circumcision to Create Jews and Christians." *JECS* 18, no. 1 (2010): 51-79.

Loader, William. "Jesus and the Law." Pages 2745-72 in vol. 3 of *Handbook for the Study of the Historical Jesus.* Edited by Tom Holmén and Stanley E. Porter. 4 vols. Leiden: Brill, 2011.

———. *Jesus' Attitude towards the Law: A Study of the Gospels.* Grand Rapids: Eerdmans, 2002.

———. "The Law and Ethics in John's Gospel." Pages 143-58 in *Rethinking the Ethics of John: "Implicit Ethics" in the Johannine Writings.* Edited by Jan G. van der Watt and Ruben Zimmermann. WUNT I 291. Tübingen: Mohr Siebeck, 2012.

Longenecker, Bruce W. *Remember the Poor: Paul, Poverty, and the Greco-Roman World.* Grand Rapids: Eerdmans, 2010.

Luther, Martin. *The Large Catechism of Martin Luther.* Philadelphia: Fortress, 1959.

———. *The Sermon on the Mount and the Magnificat.* Edited by Jaroslav Pelikan. Luther's Works. St. Louis: Concordia, 1956.

Luz, Ulrich. *Das Evangelium nach Matthäus.* 4 vols. EKKNT. Zürich: Benziger, 1985-2002.

———. *Matthew 1–7: A Continental Commentary.* Minneapolis: Fortress, 1989.

Lyall, Sarah. "Who Is a Jew? Court Ruling in Britain Raises Question." *The New York Times*, November 8, 2009.

Magen, Yitzhak. *The Stone Vessel Industry in the Second Temple Period: Excavations at Hizma and the Jerusalem Temple Mount.* Jerusalem: Israel Exploration Society, 2002.

Malherbe, Abraham J. "Apologetic and Philosophy in the Second Century." *ResQ* 7, nos. 1-2 (1963): 19-32.

———. *Paul and the Popular Philosophers*. Minneapolis: Fortress, 1989.

Malina, Bruce J., and Richard L. Rohrbaugh. *Social-Science Commentary on the Gospel of John*. Minneapolis: Fortress, 1998.

Marcus, Joel. *Mark 1–8: A New Translation with Introduction and Commentary*. AB 27. New Haven: Yale University Press, 2000.

———. *Mark 8–16: A New Translation with Introduction and Commentary*. AB 27A. New Haven: Yale University Press, 2009.

Marguerat, Daniel. "Paul and the Torah in the Acts of the Apostles." Pages 98-117 in *Torah in the New Testament: Papers Delivered at the Manchester-Lausanne Seminar of June 2008*. Edited by Michael Tait and Peter Oakes. LNTS 401. Edinburgh: T&T Clark, 2009.

Marshall, Peter. *Enmity in Corinth: Social Conventions in Paul's Relations with the Corinthians*. WUNT II 23. Tübingen: Mohr Siebeck, 1987.

Martens, John W. "'Do Not Sexually Abuse Children': The Language of Early Christian Sexual Ethics." Pages 227-54 in *Children in Late Ancient Christianity*. Edited by Cornelia B. Horn and Robert R. Phenix. STAC 58. Tübingen: Mohr Siebeck, 2009.

———. *One God, One Law: Philo of Alexandria on the Mosaic and Greco-Roman Law*. Studies in Philo of Alexandria 2. Leiden: Brill, 2003.

Martyn, J. Louis. "Apocalyptic Theology in Galatians." Pages 97-105 in *Galatians: A New Translation with Introduction and Commentary*. AB 33A. New York: Doubleday, 1997.

———. "Epistemology at the Turn of the Ages." Pages 89-110 in *Theological Issues in the Letters of Paul*. Nashville: Abingdon, 1997.

———. *Galatians: A New Translation with Introduction and Commentary*. AB 33A. New York: Doubleday, 1997.

———. "*Nomos* Plus Genitive Noun in Paul: The History of God's Law." Pages 575-87 in *Early Christianity and Classical Culture: Comparative Studies in Honor of Abraham J. Malherbe*. Edited by John T. Fitzgerald, Thomas H. Olbricht, and L. Michael White. NovTSup 110. Leiden: Brill, 2003.

———. *Theological Issues in the Letters of Paul*. Nashville: Abingdon, 1997.

Mason, Steve. *Flavius Josephus on the Pharisees: A Composition-Critical Study*. StPB 39. Leiden: Brill, 1991.

Mays, James Luther. *Hosea: A Commentary*. OTL. Philadelphia: Westminster, 1969.

McGuckin, John A. "Moses and the 'Mystery of Christ' in St. Cyril of Alexandria's Exegesis." *Coptic Church Review* 21, nos. 1-2 (2000): 24-32, 98-114.

McKnight, Scot. "James' Secret: Wisdom in James in the Mode of Receptive Reverence." Pages 201-16 in *Preaching Character: Reclaiming Wisdom's Paradigmatic Imagination for Transformation*. Edited by Dave Bland and David Fleer. Abilene: Abilene Christian University Press, 2010.

———. *The Letter of James*. NICNT. Grand Rapids: Eerdmans, 2011.

McNeile, Alan Hugh. *The Gospel according to St. Matthew*. London: Macmillan, 1915.

Meeks, Wayne A. "'And Rose Up to Play': Midrash and Paraenesis in 1 Corinthians 10:1-22." *JSNT*, no. 16 (1982): 64-78.

———. "The Ethics of the Gospel of John." Pages 317-26 in *Exploring the Gospel of John: In Honor of D. Moody Smith*. Edited by R. Alan Culpepper and C. Clifton Black. Louisville: Westminster John Knox, 1996.

———. "Man from Heaven in Johannine Sectarianism." *JBL* 91, no. 1 (1972): 44-72.

———. *The Moral World of the First Christians*. Philadelphia: Westminster, 1986.

Meier, John P. *Law and History in Matthew's Gospel: A Redactional Study of Mt. 5:17-48*. Rome: Biblical Institute, 1976.

———. *Law and Love*. A Marginal Jew: Rethinking the Historical Jesus 4. New Haven: Yale University Press, 2009.

Meissner, Stefan. *Die Heimholung des Ketzers: Studien zur jüdischen Auseinandersetzung mit Paulus*. WUNT II 87. Tübingen: Mohr Siebeck, 1996.

Mendelson, Alan. *Philo's Jewish Identity*. Atlanta: Scholars, 1988.

Mettinger, Tryggve N. D. *No Graven Image? Israelite Aniconism in Its Ancient Near Eastern Context*. ConBOT 42. Stockholm: Almqvist & Wiksell International, 1995.

Meyer, Paul W. "The Worm at the Core of the Apple: Exegetical Reflections on Romans 7." Pages 57-77 in *The Word in This World: Essays in New Testament Exegesis and Theology*. Louisville: Westminster John Knox, 2004.

Miller, David M. "Seeing the Glory, Hearing the Son: The Function of the Wilderness Theophany Narratives in Luke 9:28-36." *CBQ* 72, no. 3 (2010): 498-517.

Mitchell, Margaret M. *Paul and the Rhetoric of Reconciliation: An Exegetical Investigation of the Language and Composition of 1 Corinthians*. HUT 28. Tübingen: Mohr Siebeck, 1991.

Moloney, Francis J. *Love in the Gospel of John: An Exegetical, Theological, and Literary Study*. Grand Rapids: Baker Academic, 2013.

Montefiore, Claude G. *Judaism and St. Paul: Two Essays*. London: Max Goschen, 1914.

Moo, Douglas J. "Jesus and the Authority of the Mosaic Law." *JSNT* 20 (1984): 3-49.

———. *The Letter of James*. PNTC. Grand Rapids: Eerdmans, 2000.

Morris, Leon. *Testaments of Love: A Study of Love in the Bible*. Grand Rapids: Eerdmans, 1981.

Moyise, Steve. *Evoking Scripture: Seeing the Old Testament in the New*. London: T&T Clark, 2008.

Mynott, Adam. "Row Rages Over Defining Who Is a Jew." *BBC News Middle East*, July 20, 2010.

Myre, André. "Les caractéristiques de la loi mosaïque selon Philon d'Alexandrie." *ScEs* 27, no. 1 (1975): 35-69.

Najman, Hindy. "The Law of Nature and the Authority of Mosaic Law." *SPhilo* 11 (1999): 55-73.

———. *Seconding Sinai: The Development of Mosaic Discourse in Second Temple Judaism*. JSJSup 77. Leiden: Brill, 2003.

Nanos, Mark D., and Magnus Zetterholm, eds. *Paul within Judaism: Restoring the First-Century Context to the Apostle*. Minneapolis: Fortress, 2015.

Nissen, Johannes. "Community and Ethics in the Gospel of John." Pages 194-212 in *New Readings in John: Literary and Theological Perspectives. Essays from the Scandinavian Conference on the Fourth Gospel in Århus 1997*. Edited by Johannes Nissen and Sigfred Pedersen. JSNTSup 182. Sheffield: Sheffield Academic, 1999.

Nolland, John. "A Fresh Look at Acts 15:10." *NTS* 27, no. 1 (1980): 105-15.

———. *The Gospel of Matthew: A Commentary on the Greek Text*. NIGTC. Grand Rapids: Eerdmans, 2005.

Norris, Richard A., Jr. "The Apologists." Pages 36-44 in *The Cambridge History of Early Christian Literature*. Edited by Andrew Louth, Frances Young, and Lewis Ayres. Cambridge: Cambridge University Press, 2004.

O'Day, Gail R. "Jeremiah 9:22-23 and 1 Corinthians 1:26-31: A Study in Intertextuality." *JBL* 109, no. 2 (1990): 259-67.

Oegema, Gerbern S. *Für Israel und die Völker: Studien zum alttestamentlich-jüdischen Hintergrund der paulinischen Theologie*. NovTSup 95. Leiden: Brill, 1999.

Oliver, Isaac W. *Torah Praxis after 70 CE: Reading Matthew and Luke-Acts as Jewish Texts*. WUNT II 355. Tübingen: Mohr Siebeck, 2013.

Osborn, Eric Francis. *Clement of Alexandria*. Cambridge: Cambridge University Press, 2005.

———. *The Philosophy of Clement of Alexandria*. Cambridge: Cambridge University Press, 1957.

Paget, James Carleton. "Clement of Alexandria and the Jews." Pages 91-102 in *Jews, Christians and Jewish Christians in Antiquity*. WUNT I 251. Tübingen: Mohr Siebeck, 2010.

Parvis, Sara. "Justin Martyr and the Apologetic Tradition." Pages 115-27 in *Justin Martyr and His Worlds*. Edited by Sara Parvis and Paul Foster. Minneapolis: Fortress, 2007.

Pearson, Birger A. *The Pneumatikos-Psychikos Terminology in 1 Corinthians: A Study in the Theology of the Corinthian Opponents of Paul and Its Relation to Gnosticism*. SBLDS 12. Missoula: Scholars, 1973.

Pelikan, Jaroslav. *Luther the Expositor: Introduction to the Reformer's Exegetical Writings*. St. Louis: Concordia, 1959.

Pelikan, Jaroslav, and Helmut T. Lehmann, eds. *Luther's Works*. 55 vols. St. Louis: Concordia, 1955-86.

Perdue, Leo G. *Wisdom Literature: A Theological History*. Louisville: Westminster John Knox, 2007.

Philo. *Philo*. Translated by Francis Henry Colson, George Herbert Whitaker, and Ralph Marcus. 12 vols. LCL. Cambridge: Harvard University Press, 1929-62.

Pogoloff, Stephen M. *Logos and Sophia: The Rhetorical Situation of 1 Corinthians*. SBLDS 134. Atlanta: Scholars, 1992.

Popkes, Wiard. "James and Scripture: An Exercise in Intertextuality." *NTS* 45, no. 2 (1999): 213-29.

Porter, Virgil V., Jr. "The Sermon on the Mount in the Book of James." *BSac* 162, nos. 647-48 (2005): 344-60, 470-82.

Rabens, Volker. "Johannine Perspectives on Ethical Enabling in the Context of Stoic and Philonic Ethics." Pages 114-39 in *Rethinking the Ethics of John: "Implicit Ethics" in the Johannine Writings*. Edited by Jan G. van der Watt and Ruben Zimmermann. WUNT I 291. Tübingen: Mohr Siebeck, 2012.

Rajak, Tessa. *Josephus: The Historian and His Society*. London: Duckworth, 1983.

Rashdall, Hastings. *The Idea of Atonement in Christian Theology: Being the Bampton Lectures for 1915*. London: Macmillan, 1919.

Reinhartz, Adele. *Befriending The Beloved Disciple: A Jewish Reading of the Gospel of John*. New York: Continuum, 2001.

———. "The Gospel according to John." Pages 152-96 in *The Jewish Annotated New Testament*. Edited by Amy-Jill Levine and Marc Z. Brettler. Oxford: Oxford University Press, 2011.

———. "Great Expectations: A Reader-Oriented Approach to Johannine Christology and Eschatology." *Literature and Theology* 3, no. 1 (1989): 61-76.

———. "Jesus as Prophet: Predictive Prolepses in the Fourth Gospel." *JSNT* 36 (1989): 3-16.

———. "The Meaning of *Nomos* in Philo's *Exposition of the Law*." *SR* 15, no. 3 (1986): 337-46.

———. *The Word in the World: The Cosmological Tale in the Fourth Gospel*. SBLMS 45. Atlanta: Scholars, 1992.

Richardson, Peter, Stephen Westerholm, Albert I. Baumgarten, and Cecilia Wassen. *Law in Religious Communities in the Roman Period: The Debate over* Torah *and* Nomos *in Post-Biblical Judaism and Early Christianity*. SCJ 4. Waterloo: Wilfrid Laurier University Press, 1991.

Robinson, James M., and Helmut Koester. *Trajectories through Early Christianity*. Philadelphia: Fortress, 1971.

Rodgers, Zuleika. "Josephus' '*Theokratia*' and Mosaic Discourse: The Actualization of the Revelation at Sinai." Pages 129-48 in *The Significance of Sinai: Traditions About Sinai and Divine Revelation in Judaism and Christianity*. Edited by George J. Brooke, Hindy Najman, and Loren T. Stuckenbruck. Themes in Biblical Narrative 12. Leiden: Brill, 2008.

Rogers, Rick. *Theophilus of Antioch: The Life and Thought of a Second-Century Bishop*. Lanham: Lexington, 2000.

Rosner, Brian S. *Paul, Scripture and Ethics: A Study of 1 Corinthians 5–7*. AGJU 22. Leiden: Brill, 1994.

———. *Paul and the Law: Keeping the Commandments of God*. NSBT 31. Downers Grove: IVP Academic, 2013.

Runesson, Anders. "Building Matthean Communities: The Politics of Textualization."

Pages 379-408 in *Mark and Matthew I: Comparative Readings: Understanding the Earliest Gospels in Their First Century Settings*. Edited by Eve-Marie Becker and Anders Runesson. WUNT I 271. Tübingen: Mohr Siebeck, 2011.

———. *The Origins of the Synagogue: A Socio-Historical Study*. ConBNT 37. Stockholm: Almqvist & Wiksell International, 2001.

———. "Purity, Holiness, and the Kingdom of Heaven in Matthew's Narrative World." Pages 144-80 in *Purity, Holiness, and Identity in Judaism and Christianity: Essays in Memory of Susan Haber*. Edited by Carl S. Ehrlich, Anders Runesson, and Eileen M. Schuller. WUNT I 305. Tübingen: Mohr Siebeck, 2013.

———. "Rethinking Early Jewish-Christian Relations: Matthean Community History as Pharisaic Intragroup Conflict." *JBL* 127, no. 1 (2008): 95-132.

Runesson, Anders, Donald D. Binder, and Birger Olsson. *The Ancient Synagogue from Its Origins to 200 C.E.: A Source Book*. Leiden: Brill, 2008.

Runia, David T. "Clement of Alexandria and the Philonic Doctrine of the Divine Power(s)." *VC* 58, no. 3 (2004): 256-76.

Salo, Kalervo. *Luke's Treatment of the Law: A Redaction-Critical Investigation*. Helsinki: Suomalainen Tiedeakatemia, 1991.

Sandelin, Karl-Gustav. "Does Paul Argue against Sacramentalism and Over-Confidence in 1 Cor 10.1-14?" Pages 165-82 in *The New Testament and Hellenistic Judaism*. Edited by Peder Borgen and Søren Giversen. Aarhus: Aarhus University Press, 1995.

Sanders, E. P. "Common Judaism Explored." Pages 11-23 in *Common Judaism: Explorations in Second-Temple Judaism*. Edited by Wayne O. McCready and Adele Reinhartz. Minneapolis: Fortress, 2008.

———. *Judaism: Practice and Belief: 63 BCE–66 CE*. Philadelphia: Trinity Press International, 1992.

———. *Paul, the Law, and the Jewish People*. Minneapolis: Fortress, 1983.

———. *Paul and Palestinian Judaism: A Comparison of Patterns of Religion*. Philadelphia: Fortress, 1977.

Sariola, Heikki. *Markus und das Gesetz: Eine redaktionskritische Untersuchung*. Helsinki: Suomalainen Tiedeakatemia, 1990.

Schrage, Wolfgang. *Der erste Brief an die Korinther*. EKKNT 7/1-2. Neukirchen-Vluyn: Neukirchener, 1991, 1995.

Schwartz, Seth. *Imperialism and Jewish Society, 200 B.C.E. to 640 C.E.* Princeton: Princeton University Press, 2001.

Schweitzer, Albert. *Die Mystik des Apostels Paulus*. Tübingen: Mohr Siebeck, 1930.

Schweizer, Eduard. *The Good News according to Matthew*. Atlanta: John Knox, 1975.

Scott, James M. "Covenant." Pages 491-94 in *The Eerdmans Dictionary of Early Judaism*. Edited by John J. Collins and Daniel C. Harlow. Grand Rapids: Eerdmans, 2010.

Segal, Alan F. *Paul the Convert: The Apostolate and Apostasy of Saul the Pharisee*. New Haven: Yale University Press, 1990.

Seifrid, Mark A. "Jesus and the Law in Acts." *JSNT* 30 (1987): 39-57.

Sellin, Gerhard. *Der Streit um die Auferstehung der Toten: eine religionsgeschichtliche und exegetische Untersuchung von 1 Korinther 15*. FRLANT 138. Göttingen: Vandenhoeck & Ruprecht, 1986.

Shepherd, Massey H. "The Epistle of James and the Gospel of Matthew." *JBL* 75, no. 1 (1956): 40-51.

Sim, David C. *The Gospel of Matthew and Christian Judaism: The History and Social Setting of the Matthean Community*. Edinburgh: T&T Clark, 1998.

Skarsaune, Oskar. *The Proof from Prophecy: A Study in Justin Martyr's Proof-Text Tradition: Text-Type, Provenance, Theological Profile*. NovTSup 56. Leiden: Brill, 1987.

Smith, D. Moody. *John*. ANTC. Nashville: Abingdon, 1999.

Snodgrass, Klyne R. "Matthew and the Law." Pages 99-127 in *Treasures New and Old: Contributions to Matthean Studies*. Edited by David R. Bauer and Mark Allan Powell. Atlanta: Scholars, 1996.

Soden, Hans von. "Sakrament und Ethik bei Paulus." Pages 239-75 in *Urchristentum und Geschichte: Gesammelte Aufsätze und Vorträge*. Vol. 1. Tübingen: Mohr Siebeck, 1951.

Soulen, R. Kendall. "Supersessionism." Pages 413-14 in *A Dictionary of Jewish-Christian Relations*. Edited by Edward Kessler and Neil Wenborn. Cambridge: Cambridge University Press, 2005.

Spicq, Ceslas. *Theological Lexicon of the New Testament*. Translated by James D. Ernest. 3 vols. Peabody: Hendrickson, 1994.

Spilsbury, Paul. "God and Israel in Josephus: A Patron-Client Relationship." Pages 172-91 in *Understanding Josephus: Seven Perspectives*. Edited by Steve Mason. JSPSup 32. Sheffield: Sheffield Academic, 1998.

———. "Josephus." Pages 241-60 in *Justification and Variegated Nomism*, vol. 1, *The Complexities of Second Temple Judaism*. Edited by D. A. Carson, Peter T. O'Brien, and Mark A. Seifrid. WUNT II 140. Tübingen: Mohr Siebeck, 2001.

Sprinkle, Preston M. *Law and Life: The Interpretation of Leviticus 18:5 in Early Judaism and in Paul*. WUNT II 241. Tübingen: Mohr Siebeck, 2008.

Sproston North, Wendy E. *The Lazarus Story within the Johannine Tradition*. JSNTSup 212. Sheffield: Sheffield Academic, 2001.

Stählin, Otto. *Clemens Alexandrinus*. 4 vols. GCS 12, 15, 17, 39. Leipzig: J. C. Hinrichs, 1905-36.

Stanley, Christopher D. *Paul and the Language of Scripture: Citation Technique in the Pauline Epistles and Contemporary Literature*. SNTSMS 69. Cambridge: Cambridge University Press, 1992.

Stanton, Graham N. *Jesus and Gospel*. Cambridge: Cambridge University Press, 2004.

Stowers, Stanley K. *A Rereading of Romans: Justice, Jews and Gentiles*. New Haven: Yale University Press, 1994.

Strange, James F. "Archaeology and Ancient Synagogues up to about 200 CE." Pages 37-62 in *The Ancient Synagogue from Its Origins until 200 C.E.* Edited by Birger Olsson and Magnus Zetterholm. ConBNT 39. Stockholm: Almqvist & Wiksell International, 2003.

Strange, W. A. *The Problem of the Text of Acts*. SNTSMS 71. Cambridge: Cambridge University Press, 1992.

Strömberg Krantz, Eva. *Des Schiffes Weg mitten im Meer: Beiträge zur Erforschung der nautischen Terminologie des Alten Testaments*. ConBOT 19. Lund: Gleerup, 1982.

Stylianopoulos, Theodore G. *Justin Martyr and the Mosaic Law*. SBLDS 20. Missoula: Scholars, 1975.

Tait, Michael, and Peter Oakes, eds. *The Torah in the New Testament: Papers Delivered at the Manchester-Lausanne Seminar of June 2008*. LNTS 401. London: T&T Clark, 2009.

Tannehill, Robert C. *The Narrative Unity of Luke-Acts: A Literary Interpretation*, vol. 2, *The Acts of the Apostles*. Philadelphia: Fortress, 1990.

Tarán, Leonardo. *Speusippus of Athens: A Critical Study with a Collection of the Related Texts and Commentary*. PhA 39. Leiden: Brill, 1981.

Thiessen, Matthew. *Contesting Conversion: Genealogy, Circumcision, and Identity in Ancient Judaism and Christianity*. Oxford: Oxford University Press, 2011.

Thiselton, Anthony C. "Realized Eschatology at Corinth." *NTS* 24, no. 4 (1978): 510-26.

Thompson, James W. *Moral Formation according to Paul: The Context and Coherence of Pauline Ethics*. Grand Rapids: Baker Academic, 2011.

Thompson, Richard P. "'Say It Ain't So, Paul!': The Accusations against Paul in Acts 21 in Light of His Ministry in Acts 16–20." *BR* 45 (2000): 34-50.

Tobin, Thomas H. *Paul's Rhetoric in Its Contexts: The Argument of Romans*. Peabody: Hendrickson, 2004.

Tomson, Peter J. *Paul and the Jewish Law: Halakha in the Letters of the Apostle to the Gentiles*. CRINT 3/1. Assen: Van Gorcum, 1990.

Troiani, Lucio. "The ΠΟΛΙΤΕΙΑ of Israel in the Graeco-Roman Age." Pages 11-22 in *Josephus and the History of the Greco-Roman World: Essays in Memory of Morton Smith*. Edited by Fausto Parente and Joseph Sievers. Leiden: Brill, 1994.

Tuckett, C. M. "The Corinthians Who Say 'There Is No Resurrection of the Dead' (1 Cor 15,12)." Pages 247-75 in *The Corinthian Correspondence*. Edited by Reimund Bieringer. BETL 125. Louvain: Leuven University Press, 1996.

Vermes, Geza. "A Summary of the Law by Flavius Josephus." *NovT* 24, no. 4 (1982): 289-303.

Wachob, Wesley Hiram. "The Epistle of James and the Book of Psalms: A Socio-Rhetorical Perspective of Intertexture, Culture, and Ideology in Religious Discourse." Pages 264-80 in *Fabrics of Discourse: Essays in Honor of Vernon K. Robbins*. Harrisburg: Trinity Press International, 2003.

———. *The Voice of Jesus in the Social Rhetoric of James*. SNTSMS 106. Cambridge: Cambridge University Press, 2000.

Wagner, J. Ross. *Heralds of the Good News: Isaiah and Paul "in Concert" in the Letter to the Romans*. NovTSup 101. Leiden: Brill, 2002.

———. "'Not beyond the Things Which Are Written': A Call to Boast Only in the Lord (1 Cor 4.6)." *NTS* 44, no. 2 (1998): 279-87.

Wallace, Daniel B. *Greek Grammar beyond the Basics: An Exegetical Syntax of the New Testament*. Grand Rapids: Zondervan, 1996.

Wassen, Cecilia. "Do You Have to Be Pure in a Metaphorical Temple? Sanctuary Metaphors and Construction of Sacred Space in the Dead Sea Scrolls and Paul's Letters." Pages 55-86 in *Purity, Holiness, and Identity in Judaism and Christianity: Essays in Memory of Susan Haber*. Edited by Carl S. Ehrlich, Anders Runesson, and Eileen M. Schuller. WUNT I 305. Tübingen: Mohr Siebeck, 2013.

———. "What Do Angels Have against the Blind and the Deaf? Rules of Exclusion in the Dead Sea Scrolls." Pages 115-29 in *Common Judaism: Explorations in Second-Temple Judaism*. Edited by Wayne O. McCready and Adele Reinhartz. Minneapolis: Fortress, 2008.

Watson, Francis. *Paul and the Hermeneutics of Faith*. London: T&T Clark, 2004.

Watt, Jan G. van der. "Ethics through the Power of Language: Some Explorations in the Gospel according to John." Pages 139-67 in *Moral Language in the New Testament: The Interrelatedness of Language and Ethics in Early Christian Writings*. Edited by Ruben Zimmermann and Jan G. van der Watt in cooperation with Suzanne Luther. WUNT II 296. Tübingen: Mohr Siebeck, 2010.

———. "Radical Social Redefinition and Radical Love: Ethics and Ethos in the Gospel according to John." Pages 107-33 in *Identity, Ethics, and Ethos in the New Testament*. Edited by Jan G. van der Watt. BZNW 141. Berlin: De Gruyter, 2006.

Watts, Rikk E. "Mark." Pages 111-249 in *Commentary on the New Testament Use of the Old Testament*. Edited by G. K. Beale and D. A. Carson. Grand Rapids: Baker Academic, 2007.

Wedderburn, Alexander J. M. *Baptism and Resurrection: Studies in Pauline Theology against Its Graeco-Roman Background*. WUNT 44. Tübingen: Mohr Siebeck, 1987.

Weiss, Johannes. *Der erste Korintherbrief*. MeyerK. Göttingen: Vandenhoeck & Ruprecht, 1925.

Wendel, Susan J. *Scriptural Interpretation and Community Self-Definition in Luke-Acts and the Writings of Justin Martyr*. NovTSup 139. Leiden: Brill, 2011.

Wendland, Heinz-Dietrich. *Die Briefe an die Korinther*. NTD 7. Göttingen: Vandenhoeck & Ruprecht, 1954.

Wenham, Gordon J. *Psalms as Torah: Reading Biblical Song Ethically*. Grand Rapids: Baker Academic, 2012.

Westerholm, Stephen. "Is Nothing Sacred? Holiness in the Writings of Paul." Pages 87-99 in *Purity, Holiness, and Identity in Judaism and Christianity: Essays in Memory of Susan Haber*. Edited by Carl S. Ehrlich, Anders Runesson, and Eileen M. Schuller. WUNT I 305. Tübingen: Mohr Siebeck, 2013.

———. *Israel's Law and the Church's Faith: Paul and His Recent Interpreters*. Grand Rapids: Eerdmans, 1988.

———. *Jesus and Scribal Authority*. ConBNT 10. Lund: Gleerup, 1978.

———. "The Judaism Paul Left Behind Him." Pages 353-70 in *The Making of Christianity:*

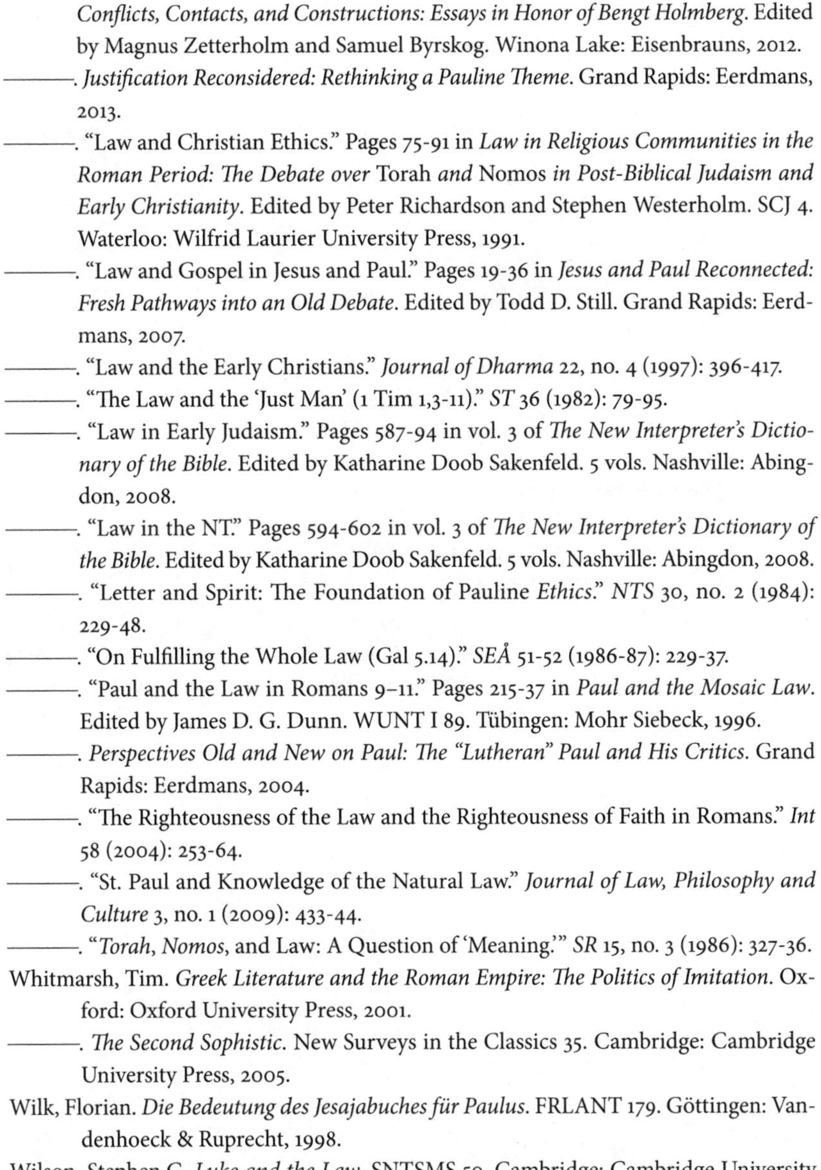

Conflicts, Contacts, and Constructions: Essays in Honor of Bengt Holmberg. Edited by Magnus Zetterholm and Samuel Byrskog. Winona Lake: Eisenbrauns, 2012.

———. *Justification Reconsidered: Rethinking a Pauline Theme*. Grand Rapids: Eerdmans, 2013.

———. "Law and Christian Ethics." Pages 75-91 in *Law in Religious Communities in the Roman Period: The Debate over* Torah *and* Nomos *in Post-Biblical Judaism and Early Christianity*. Edited by Peter Richardson and Stephen Westerholm. SCJ 4. Waterloo: Wilfrid Laurier University Press, 1991.

———. "Law and Gospel in Jesus and Paul." Pages 19-36 in *Jesus and Paul Reconnected: Fresh Pathways into an Old Debate*. Edited by Todd D. Still. Grand Rapids: Eerdmans, 2007.

———. "Law and the Early Christians." *Journal of Dharma* 22, no. 4 (1997): 396-417.

———. "The Law and the 'Just Man' (1 Tim 1,3-11)." *ST* 36 (1982): 79-95.

———. "Law in Early Judaism." Pages 587-94 in vol. 3 of *The New Interpreter's Dictionary of the Bible*. Edited by Katharine Doob Sakenfeld. 5 vols. Nashville: Abingdon, 2008.

———. "Law in the NT." Pages 594-602 in vol. 3 of *The New Interpreter's Dictionary of the Bible*. Edited by Katharine Doob Sakenfeld. 5 vols. Nashville: Abingdon, 2008.

———. "Letter and Spirit: The Foundation of Pauline *Ethics*." *NTS* 30, no. 2 (1984): 229-48.

———. "On Fulfilling the Whole Law (Gal 5.14)." *SEÅ* 51-52 (1986-87): 229-37.

———. "Paul and the Law in Romans 9–11." Pages 215-37 in *Paul and the Mosaic Law*. Edited by James D. G. Dunn. WUNT I 89. Tübingen: Mohr Siebeck, 1996.

———. *Perspectives Old and New on Paul: The "Lutheran" Paul and His Critics*. Grand Rapids: Eerdmans, 2004.

———. "The Righteousness of the Law and the Righteousness of Faith in Romans." *Int* 58 (2004): 253-64.

———. "St. Paul and Knowledge of the Natural Law." *Journal of Law, Philosophy and Culture* 3, no. 1 (2009): 433-44.

———. "*Torah, Nomos*, and Law: A Question of 'Meaning.'" *SR* 15, no. 3 (1986): 327-36.

Whitmarsh, Tim. *Greek Literature and the Roman Empire: The Politics of Imitation*. Oxford: Oxford University Press, 2001.

———. *The Second Sophistic*. New Surveys in the Classics 35. Cambridge: Cambridge University Press, 2005.

Wilk, Florian. *Die Bedeutung des Jesajabuches für Paulus*. FRLANT 179. Göttingen: Vandenhoeck & Ruprecht, 1998.

Wilson, Stephen G. *Luke and the Law*. SNTSMS 50. Cambridge: Cambridge University Press, 1983.

Winden, J. C. M. van. *An Early Christian Philosopher: Justin Martyr's Dialogue with Trypho, Chapters One to Nine*. Philosophia Patrum 1. Leiden: Brill, 1971.

Winter, Bruce W. *Philo and Paul among the Sophists*. SNTSMS 79. Cambridge: Cambridge University Press, 1997.

Witherington, Ben W., III. *Conflict and Community in Corinth: A Socio-Rhetorical Commentary on 1 and 2 Corinthians*. Grand Rapids: Eerdmans, 1995.

Wolff, Hans Walter. *Hosea: A Commentary on the Book of the Prophet Hosea*. Hermeneia. Philadelphia: Fortress, 1974.

Young, Frances. "Introduction: The Literary Culture of the Earliest Christianity." Pages 5-10 in *The Cambridge History of Early Christian Literature*. Edited by Andrew Louth, Frances Young, and Lewis Ayres. Cambridge: Cambridge University Press, 2004.

Zimmermann, Ruben. "The 'Implicit Ethics' of New Testament Writings: A Draft on a New Methodology for Analysing New Testament Ethics." *Neot* 43, no. 2 (2009): 399-423.

———. "Is There Ethics in the Gospel of John? Challenging an Outdated Consensus." Pages 44-80 in *Rethinking the Ethics of John: "Implicit Ethics" in the Johannine Writings*. Edited by Jan G. van der Watt and Ruben Zimmermann. WUNT I 291. Tübingen: Mohr Siebeck, 2012.

———. "The Narrative Hermeneutics of John 11: Learning with Lazarus How to Understand Death, Life, and Resurrection." Pages 75-101 in *The Resurrection of Jesus in the Gospel of John*. Edited by Craig R. Koester and Reimund Bieringer. WUNT I 222. Tübingen: Mohr Siebeck, 2008.

Zissu, Boaz, and David Amit. "Common Judaism, Common Purity, and the Second Temple Period Judean *Miqwa'ot* (Ritual Immersion Baths)." Pages 47-62 in *Common Judaism: Explorations in Second-Temple Judaism*. Edited by Wayne O. McCready and Adele Reinhartz. Minneapolis: Fortress, 2008.

Author Index

Subject Index

Scripture and Other Ancient Literature Index